Essential COM

idl
.rc
.cpp

The DevelopMentor Series
Don Box, Editor

Addison-Wesley has joined forces with DevelopMentor, a premiere developer resources company, to produce a series of technical books written by developers for developers. DevelopMentor boasts a prestigious technical staff that includes some of the world's best-known computer science professionals.

*"Works in **The DevelopMentor Series** will be practical and informative sources on the tools and techniques for applying component-based technologies to real-world, large-scale distributed systems."*
—Don Box

Titles in the Series:

Essential COM
Don Box
0-201-63446-5

Essential XML
Beyond Markup
Don Box, Aaron Skonnard, and John Lam
0-201-70914-7

Programming Windows Security
Keith Brown
0-201-60442-6

Advanced Visual Basic 6
Power Techniques for Everyday Programs
Matthew Curland
0-201-70712-8

Transactional COM+
Building Scalable Applications
Tim Ewald
0-201-61594-0

ASP Internals
Jon Flanders
0-201-61618-1

Essential IDL
Interface Design for COM
Martin Gudgin
0-201-61595-9

Debugging Windows Programs
Strategies, Tools, and Techniques for Visual C++ Programmers
Everett N. McKay and Mike Woodring
0-201-70238-X

Watch for future titles in The DevelopMentor Series.

Essential COM

Don Box

ADDISON–WESLEY

Boston • San Francisco • New York • Toronto • Montreal
London • Munich • Paris • Madrid
Capetown • Sydney • Tokyo • Singapore • Mexico City

Many of the designations used by manufacturers and sellers to distinguish their products are claimed as trademarks. Where those designations appear in this book, and we were aware of a trademark claim, the designations have been printed in initial capital letters or in all capitals.

The author and publisher have taken care in the preparation of this book, but make no expressed or implied warranty of any kind and assume no responsibility for errors or omissions. No liability is assumed for incidental or consequential damages in connection with or arising out of the use of the information or programs contained herein.

The publisher offers discounts on this book when ordered in quantity for special sales. For more information, please contact:

Pearson Education Corporate Sales Division
One Lake Street
Upper Saddle River, NJ 07458
(800) 382-3419
corpsales@pearsontechgroup.com

Visit AW on the Web: www.awl.com/cseng/

Library of Congress Cataloging-in-Publication Data
Box, Don, 1962–
    Essential COM / Don Box.
        p.   cm.
    Includes bibliographical references and index.
    ISBN 0-201-63446-5 (alk. paper)
    1. Object-oriented programming (Computer science)   2. C++
(Computer program language)   I. Title.
OA76.64.8693 1998
005.1—dc21   97-45836
                                                                        CIP

ISBN 0-201-63446-5
Text printed on recycled paper
7 8 9 10 11—MA—0403020100
7th printing, November 2000

To Judith S.,
who helped me master the one
thing more daunting than COM
and made this book possible,
and Barbara, who stayed long
enough to see how it all
turned out.

Contents

Foreword

As I sat down to write this foreword I was struck with several thoughts:

- Will Don's picture be on the back cover, and if so, how long will his hair be?
- Will the readers of the book realize that Don has personalized license plates that read "IUNKNWN"?
- What the heck does one write in a foreword to a book?

I had two ideas about what to write here. The first was to say some things about the design of COM that I've wanted to write down for a long time. The second idea was to flatter Don Box as much as he has flattered me by asking me to write the foreword to his book. In the end I decided to do both.

What *is* COM? Why was it invented? Don succinctly answers these questions in Chapter 1. The introductory section ends with ". . . this chapter presents an architecture for component reuse that allows dynamic and efficient composition of systems from independently developed binary components." The rest of the chapter steps you through the thought process that filled the minds of the designers of COM from 1988 to 1993, when COM was first released.

I think there are several elements of COM's design that have contributed to its long success. First and foremost is pragmatism followed by simplicity, which results in flexibility or malleability.

Pragmatism

COM addresses software design in a very pragmatic way. Instead of providing a solution based on an almost religious academic dogma of object-oriented programming, COM's design takes into account both human nature and capitalism. The best, most *commercially* proven aspects of classical object orientation were identified by the design team and coupled with what had been learned in attempting to achieve reuse in previous software projects both inside and outside Microsoft.

Most classic OO texts describe a system or language as object oriented if it supports encapsulation (information hiding), polymorphism, and inheritance. Inheritance is often emphasized as the primary vehicle for reuse. The COM designers disagree with this emphasis. They felt that this is an overly simplistic view and that there are actually two kinds of inheritance. Implementation inheritance assumes that actual implementation (behavior) is inherited. Interface inheritance assumes that only the specification of behavior is inherited. It is the latter form of inheritance that enables polymorphism. This type of inheritance is fully supported by COM. Implementation inheritance, on the other hand, is simply one mechanism for reusing an existing implementation. However, if reuse is the ultimate goal, then implementation inheritance is simply a means to an end but not an end unto itself.

It has been widely accepted in both research and commercial software development circles that implementation inheritance is a useful and powerful tool but also one that can lead to undue coupling between a base class and a derived class. Because implementation inheritance often causes details of a base class' implementation to "leak," violating the encapsulation of the class, COM's designers felt that the use of implementation inheritance should be restricted to programming *within* components. While COM does not support implementation inheritance *across* components, it does support it within components. COM also fully supports interface inheritance (in fact, it relies on it).

The COM designers deemphasized inheritance per se in favor of what inheritance is often thought to achieve, that is, reuse. The fundamental concept used to model reuse in COM is encapsulation, not inheritance. Instead, COM uses inheritance to model type relationships between objects that share similar functionality. By building COM's reuse model on encapsulation, the designers were encouraging a form of *black-box* reuse suitable for the anticipated component marketplace. The idea is that clients should treat objects as opaque components with respect to what is inside them and how they are implemented. The COM designers believed the architecture should be designed to enforce this idea. Why would anyone design a system with a different model for reuse? Good question. The fact is, however, that the world is full of "object-oriented" systems that do not enforce black-box encapsulation and even make it difficult to achieve it. C++ is a classic example of this. In the first chapter of this book, Don illustrates very clearly what I mean by this.

The following equations illustrate the differences between object-oriented programming and component-oriented programming.

Object-Oriented Programming = Polymorphism + (Some) Late Binding + (Some) Encapsulation + Inheritance

Component-Oriented Programming = Polymorphism + (Really) Late Binding + (Real, Enforced) Encapsulation + Interface Inheritance + Binary Reuse

In any case, for me, the whole debate is kind of amusing. The OO purists who live on comp.object and comp.object.corba get completely bent out of shape while pointing their fingers at COM saying "but it's not *really* object oriented." You can argue against this in two ways:

1. "It is too! It's just that *your* definition of OO is wrong."

2. "*So what!?!* COM is a phenomenal commercial success and has allowed thousands of independent software developers to build insanely great software that interpolates and integrates. And they're making money. Lots of it.[1] The software components they write are getting purchased, used, and reused. Isn't *that* really the point of any technology? Besides, I can always argue that *only* COM is truly component oriented.[2] So there!"

Simplicity Leads to Malleability

mal·le·a·ble (màl'ê-e-bel) *adjective*

1. Capable of being shaped or formed, as by hammering or pressure: *a malleable metal.*

2. Easily controlled or influenced; tractable.

3. Able to adjust to changing circumstances; adaptable: *the malleable mind of the pragmatist.*[3]

---

[1]A study by Giga (commissioned by Microsoft) shows that in 1997 there was a $410M market for commercial COM-based components. It is estimated that this market will grow to over $2.8B by the year 2001. These numbers do not include Microsoft products.

[2]Exercise for the reader: Name a single commercially available object system, other than COM, that provides a model for binary reuse and supports robust versioning, location transparency, and programming language independence. If you say CORBA you've been duped and don't know it.

[3]Excerpted from *The American Heritage Dictionary of the English Language, Third Edition* © 1996 by Houghton Mifflin Company. Electronic version licensed from INSO Corporation; further reproduction and distribution in accordance with the Copyright Law of the United States. All rights reserved.

The first real application of COM was as the substrate for Microsoft's second attempt at a compound document architecture, Object Linking & Embedding 2.0. If you consider the multitude of ways COM is being applied today, you will immediately recognize what I mean when I say it is malleable. Programmers are using COM to provide plug-in architectures for their applications, build large-scale transacted multitier client/server applications for running businesses, provide eye candy on Web pages, control and monitor manufacturing processes, and even track spy satellites by remotely controlling arrays of telescopes.

This malleability comes from the fact that COM's designers focused on making the core of the model as simple as it needed to be and no simpler. One illustrative aspect of this is the relative "grunginess" of COM programming to date. Developers working in C or C++ have to deal with all kinds of gunk, including GUIDs and reference counting. All kinds of complexity could have been added to COM to make it easier. But the architects instead emphasized making the model work, knowing that if they were successful, tool support would come later. This assumption has been borne out with recent releases of easy-to-use COM tools such as Visual Basic, COM support in Visual C++ 5.0, and the Active Template Library. By the time you read this, Microsoft will have announced future plans to radically simplify COM development through a common runtime that will be available to all tools: COM+.

Folklore

Any technology in as widespread use as COM begins to have some folklore. Just for fun, here are some items you may not have known. Some of them are even true.

- There were many, many more people from groups all over Microsoft who contributed significantly to the design of COM, but the principal architects of COM were Bob Atkinson, Tony Williams, and Craig Wittenberg. All three are still at Microsoft working on really neat stuff.

- Bob, Tony, and Craig were part of a cross-group team chartered with delivering the core technology that would allow Bill Gates' vision of IAYF (Information at Your Fingertips) to become reality.[4] While these three had a clear vision of the future power of COM, they were burdened with actually shipping something that used it: OLE 2.0. This helps explain why it took so long to get the COM documentation into shape. Sorry.

- The first implementation of COM shipped in a release form as part of OLE 2.0 in May 1993.

---

[4]You may recall Bill's 1990 Comdex speech on IAYF.

- The root interface (it wasn't called IUnknown at the time) had a GetClassID method. The fact that it was moved to IPersist illustrates the principle of keeping the COM model as simple as possible.

- At one point, IUnknown didn't have an AddRef method. It became clear that not allowing people to duplicate interface pointers was too limiting.

- The "Unknown" in "IUnknown" came about as a result of a December 1988 internal Microsoft paper by Tony Williams titled *Object Architecture: Dealing with the Unknown—or—Type Safety in a Dynamically Extensible Class Library.*

- The decision to use RPC as the interprocess remoting mechanism was made in the first two months of 1991. A memo by Bob Atkinson titled *IAYF Requirements for RPC* documents the requirements placed on the RPC team by what was then called the "IAYF team." This team was responsible for building the substrate that would enable Bill Gates' vision of "Information at Your Fingertips." This substrate was COM (although it was not called that yet).

- Monikers are more powerful than you think.

- It is Mark Ryland's fault that some people call COM the "Common Object Model." He deeply regrets it and apologizes profusely.

- "MEOW" doesn't really stand for the Microsoft Extensible Object Wire representation. Rick just made it up.

- Windows NT 3.5 included the first release of 32-bit COM and OLE. Someone accidentally left a "#pragma optimization off" in one of the root header files. Oops.

If there is a book (in English) about COM, DCOM, OLE, or ActiveX, I have read it, and you'll most likely find my name in the credits as a technical reviewer. I have also written many articles about these technologies myself and I was the primary editor for the COM Specification. I've given untold hundreds of presentations on COM to both technical and nontechnical audiences. It should be obvious that I have spent a great deal of time and energy trying to figure out the best way to explain COM.

It appears that all of my hard work was wasted because after reading the final draft of this book it is clear to me that nobody explains COM better than Don Box.

I hope you enjoy the ride as much as I have.

Charlie Kindel
COM guy, Microsoft Corporation
September 1997

Foreword

Sometimes there are so many good things to say about one book, it's worth saying twice. That's one reason why Don's book has two forewords—it's that good.

If you are building systems for Windows 95 or NT, you can't escape COM. Visual Studio—and especially Visual Basic—hide some of the complexities of COM, but if you a) really want to understand what's happening behind the scenes and/or b) exploit the power of COM, then Don's book is for you.

What I especially like about this book is the way that Don organizes his coverage of COM, such that you are first exposed to the issues of building distributed and concurrent systems, and then you are carefully and completely shown how COM addresses those issues. Even if you know nothing about COM when you start this book, you'll be guided through a clear and simple conceptual model for COM that will leave you with an understanding of the problems and the forces that give COM the structure and behavior that it has. If you are an experienced COM developer, then you'll especially appreciate Don's discussion on various idioms for using COM to solve common problems.

COM is the most widely-used object model for developing distributed and concurrent systems. This book will help you use COM to deploy such systems successfully.

Grady Booch

Preface

My work is done. I can finally rest, knowing that I have finally put into writing what many have termed the *rich oral history of COM*. This book reflects the evolution of my own understanding of this rogue technology that Microsoft was kind enough to reveal to the programming world in 1993. Although I did not attend the original OLE Professional Developer's Conference, I still feel as if I have been doing COM forever. After almost four years of working with COM, I can barely remember the pre-COM era of computing. I can, however, vividly remember my own painful trek across the COM landscape in early 1994.

It took me roughly six months before I felt I understood anything about COM. During this initial six-month period of working with COM, I could successfully write COM programs and almost explain why they worked. However, I had no organic understanding of why the COM programming model was the way it was. Fortunately, one day (August 8, 1994, roughly six months after buying the book *Inside OLE2*), I had an intense epiphany and at once COM seemed obvious to me. This by no means meant that I understood every COM interface and API function, but rather that I understood the primary motivating factors behind COM. From this, it became clear how to apply the programming model to everyday programming problems. Many other developers have related similar experiences to me. As I write this preface three Augusts after the fact, developers still must go through this six-month waiting period prior to becoming productive members of COM society. I would like to think that this book might shorten that time period, but I make no promises.

As this book emphasizes, COM is more a programming discipline than a technology. To this end, I have attempted not to bludgeon the reader with detailed descriptions of each parameter to each method from each interface. Rather, I have tried to distill the essence of what COM is really about, leaving the SDK documentation to fill in the gaps left behind by each chapter. Wherever possible, I have attempted to address the underlying tensions that motivate a particular aspect of COM rather than provide detailed examples of how to apply each interface and API function to a contrived example program. My own experience has shown that once the *why* is understood, the *how* follows fairly naturally. Conversely, simply knowing the *how* rarely provides adequate insight to extrapolate beyond the documentation. This insight is critical if one hopes to keep up with the programming model's continual evolution.

COM is an extremely flexible substrate for building distributed object-oriented systems. To take advantage of COM's flexibility, one must often think outside the constraints of the SDK documentation, articles, or books. My personal recommendation is to assume that anything you read (including this book) may be incorrect or woefully out of date and instead form your own personal understanding of the programming model. The surest way to understand the programming model is to focus on mastering the basic vocabulary of COM. This can be accomplished only through writing COM programs and analyzing why those programs work the way they work. Reading books, articles, and documentation can help, but ultimately, dedicating the time to contemplate the four core concepts of COM (interfaces, classes, apartments, and security) can only enhance your effectiveness as a COM developer.

To help the reader focus on these core concepts, I have tried to include as much code as possible without explicitly providing elaborate implementations for readers to simply copy into their own source code. To ensure that COM programming techniques are also presented in context, Appendix B contains one complete COM application that is an example of many of the concepts discussed throughout the book. In addition, the downloadable code for this book contains a library of COM utility code that I have found useful in my own development. Some parts of this library are discussed in the book in detail, but the entire library is included as a demonstration of how to architect de facto C++ implementations. Also note that much of the code that appears in each chapter uses the C runtime library macro assert to emphasize that certain pre- or post-conditions must be met. In production code, many of these assert statements should be replaced with somewhat more forgiving error-handling code.

One downside of published books is that they are often obsolete by the time they arrive at the local bookstore. This book is no different. In particular, the pending release of COM+ and Windows NT 5.0 will certainly render various aspects of this book incorrect or at least incomplete. I have tried to anticipate the evolution of the model imposed by the release of Windows NT 5.0; however, at the time of this writing, Windows NT 5.0 has not yet entered its public beta cycle and all information is subject to change. COM+ promises to evolve the model even further; however, it was impossible to include COM+ coverage and still deliver my manuscript this year. I highly encourage you to investigate both Windows NT 5.0 and COM+ when they become available.

One rather painful decision I had to make was how to address the various commercial libraries used to implement COM components in C++. After observing the common questions that appear on various Internet newsgroups, I elected to ignore ATL (and MFC) and instead focus on the bread-and-butter topics of COM that every developer must master irrespective of the library used. More and more developers are generating ATL spaghetti and wondering why things don't work. I firmly believe one cannot learn COM by programming in ATL or MFC. This does not mean that ATL and MFC are not useful tools for developing COM components. It simply means that they are not suited to demonstrating or learning COM programming concepts and techniques. This makes ATL inappropriate for a book focused on the COM programming model. Fortunately, most developers find that once COM is understood, the basics of ATL can be mastered in short order.

Finally, the quotations that begin each chapter are a chance for me to write whatever I felt like for a small section of the book. In an effort to keep my writing as direct as possible, I restricted my wild off-topic stories to no more than 15 lines of C++ code per chapter. Usually, the code/quotation represents the pre-COM approach to a problem or concept presented in the chapter. I leave it as an exercise for the reader to deconstruct my state of mind when writing a particular chapter based on these hints.

Acknowledgments

Writing a book is incredibly hard—at least it was for me. Two people who I know for certain suffered more than I did were my patient wife, Barbara, and my tolerant son, Max (who prefers COM to other object models despite his youth). To both of you, thanks for tolerating my absence and generally cranky disposition while I tried to write. Fortunately, my freshly instantiated daughter, Evan, was born after the bulk of this book was written and has had a fairly present and pleasant father. A related thanks goes out to all the staffers at DevelopMentor who had to cover for me when I "went dark" to crank out chapters.

A lot of my early thinking about distributed systems was formed working for Tatsuya Suda at UC Irvine in the early 1990s. Tatsuya taught me how to write, how to read, and how to deal with unruly train passengers in Tokyo. Thanks and sorry.

Thanks to my old officemate Doug Schmidt for introducing me to Stan Lippman at the C++ Report. Despite Stan's rousing rejection of my first article, I first got my name in lights thanks to you two.

Thanks to Mike Hendrickson and Alan Feuer at Addison Wesley for getting this project started. Thanks to Ben Ryan and John Wait for being patient. Thanks to Carter Shanklin for sticking with the project to the end.

Thanks to the folks at Microsoft Systems Journal who tolerated my late submissions during the production of this book. In particular, thanks to

Joanne Steinhart, Gretchen Bilson, Dave Edson, Joe Flanigen, Eric Maffei, Michael Longacre, Joshua Trupin, Laura Euler, and Joan Levinson. I promise never to be late again.

Thanks to David Chappell for writing the finest book on COM available. I heartily recommend that everyone buy a copy and read it at least twice.

Thanks to the CORBA and Java partisans and zealots who have engaged me in flame wars on various Usenet newsgroups over the years. Your constant vigilance has made my own understanding of COM infinitely better. Despite the fact that I still feel many of your arguments are specious and somewhat Martian, I respect your desire to survive.

Several people at Microsoft proper have been very helpful to me over the years and either directly or indirectly helped me write this book. Sara Williams was the first COM person from Microsoft I had ever met. Right after explaining that she didn't know Bill all that well, she introduced me to Gretchen Bilson and Eric Maffei at Microsoft Systems Journal as consolation. Sara has always been a great "Box Evangelist" within the big house and I am forever grateful. Charlie Kindel wrote the nice foreword to my book despite his heavy schedule and exceedingly regular trips to the barber. Nat Brown was the first person to show me apartments and has irrevocably polluted my vocabulary with the word "schwing." Kraig Brockschmidt explained to me that one particular aspect of COM that looks incredibly elegant was actually a grotesque last-minute hack. Dave Reed introduced me to Viper and listens to my clams each time I visit Redmond. Pat Helland spent the entire week of TechEd '97 twisting my brain and forcing me to reexamine most of my basic assumptions about COM. Scott Robinson, Andreas Luther, Markus Horstmann, Mary Kirtland, Rebecca Norlander, and Greg Hope have been great at keeping me out of the dark. Ted Hase helped me spread the word. Rick Hill and Alex Armanasu did a great job watching my back on the technical front. Other Microsoft people who have influenced my work through their own include Tony Williams, Bob Atkinson, Craig Wittenberg, Crispin Goswell, Paul Leach, David Kays, Jim Springfield, Christian Beaumont, Mario Goertzel, and Michael Montague.

The DCOM mail reflector has been a great source of inspiration and ideas for this book. Special thanks go to the following DCOM-listers: the infamous Mark Ryland, COM *wunderkind* Mike Nelson, Keith Brown, Tim Ewald, Chris Sells, Saji Abraham, Henk De Koning, Steve Robinson, Anton von Stratten, and Randy Puttick.

The story in this book has been greatly influenced by my teaching COM at DevelopMentor for the past several years. The story has been shaped as much by the students as it has by my fellow instructors. Although I wish I could thank every student personally (Addison Wesley has limited my preface to less than 20 pages), I can thank the current set of DevelopMentor-ites who have helped me refine my own understanding by teaching our Essential COM course and providing invaluable feedback: Ron Sumida, Fritz Onion, Scott Butler, Owen Tallman, George Shepherd, Ted Pattison, Keith Brown, Tim Ewald, and Chris Sells. Thanks guys! Thanks also to Mike Abercrombie of DevelopMentor for creating an environment where personal growth isn't stifled by commerce.

This book would have been released considerably earlier had it not been for Terry Kennedy and friends at Software AG. Terry was nice enough to invite me to help with the DCOM/UNIX effort in Germany during the sabbatical I had initially carved out to write the book. Although this book is a year late because I couldn't say no to Terry (this is my fault, not Terry's), I think that the book is infinitely better due to the time I spent working on the project. In particular, I gained many insights working with Harald Stiehl, Winnie Froehlich, Volker Denkhaus, Deitmar Gaertner, Jeff Lee, Deiter Kesler, Martin Koch, Blauer Aff, Uli Kaess, Steve Wild and the notorious Thomas Vogler.

A special thanks to the following close readers who found errors in earlier printings of this book: Ted Neff, Dan Moyer, Purush Rudrakshala, Heng de Koneng, Dave Hale, George Reilly, Steve DeLassus, Warren Young, Jeff Prosise, Richard Grimes, Barry Klawans, James Bowmer, Stephan Sas, Peter Zaborski, Christopher L. Akerley, Robert Brooks, Jonathan Pryor, Allen Chambers, Timo Kettunen, Atulx Mohidekar, Chris Hyams, Max Rubinstein, Bradey Honsinger, Sunny Thomas, Gardner von Holt, and Tony Vervilos.

Finally, thanks to Shah Jehan and the Coca-Cola Corporation for fueling this effort by respectively producing the most delicious Indian food and soft drinks available.

Don Box
Redondo Beach, CA
August 1997
http://www.develop.com/dbox

CHAPTER

1 | COM as a Better C++

```
template <class T, class Ex>
class list_t : virtual protected CPrivateAlloc {
  list<T**> m_list;
  mutable TWnd m_wnd;
  virtual ~list_t(void);
protected:
  explicit list_t(int nElems, ...);
  inline operator unsigned int *(void) const
  { return reinterpret_cast<int*>(this); }
  template <class X> void clear(X& rx) const throw(Ex);
};
```
Anonymous, 1996

C++ has been with us for some time now. The community of C++ programmers is quite large, and much is known about the traps and pitfalls of the language. From its inception, C++ has benefited from a highly literate team of developers who, while working at Bell Laboratories, not only produced the first C++ development product (CFRONT) but also published many of the seminal works on C++. Most of the C++ canon was published in the late 1980s and early 1990s. During this era, many C++ developers (including the authors of virtually every important C++ book) worked on UNIX workstations and built fairly monolithic applications using the compiler and linker technology of the day. The environment in which this generation of developers worked has understandably shaped much of the mindset of the C++ community at large.

One of the principal goals for C++ was to allow programmers to build user-defined types (UDTs) that could be reused outside their original implementation context. This principle underpins the idea of class libraries or frameworks as we know them today. Since the introduction of C++, a marketplace for C++ class libraries emerged, albeit rather slowly. One reason that this marketplace has not grown as fast as one might expect is related to the

NIH (not-invented-here) factor among C++ developers. Often the notion of reusing another developer's code seems like more effort than simply reimplementing from scratch. Sometimes this perception is due to sheer hubris on the part of the developer. Other times, the resistance to reuse is based on the mental overhead required to understand someone else's design and programming style. This is especially true for wrapper-style libraries, where one needs to understand not only the underlying technology being wrapped but also the additional abstractions added by the library itself.

To exacerbate the problem, many libraries are documented in a manner that assumes the user of the library will refer to the library's source code as the ultimate reference. This sort of white box reuse often results in a tremendous amount of coupling between the client application and class library, adding to the fragility of the overall code base over time. The coupling effect reduces the modularity of a class library and makes it more difficult to adapt to changes in the underlying library implementation. This encourages clients to treat the library as yet another part of the project's source code base and not as a modular reusable component. In fact, developers have actually been known to modify commercial class library sources to fit their own needs, producing a "private build" that is better suited to the programmer's application but no longer really the original library.

Reuse has always been one of the classic motivations for object orientation. Despite this fact, writing C++ classes that are *easily* reused is fairly difficult. Beyond the design-time and development-time obstacles to reuse that are part of the C++ culture, there are also a fair number of runtime obstacles that make the C++ object model a less than ideal substrate for building reusable software components. Many of these obstacles stem from the compilation and linkage model assumed by C++. This chapter will look at the technical challenges to treating C++ classes as reusable components. Each challenge will be addressed by presenting programming techniques based on currently available off-the-shelf technology. Through disciplined application of these techniques, this chapter presents an architecture for component reuse that allows dynamic and efficient composition of systems from independently developed binary components.

Software Distribution and C++

To understand the problems related to using C++ as a component substrate, it helps to examine how C++ libraries were distributed in the late 1980s. Consider a library vendor who has developed an algorithm that can perform substring searches on $O(1)$ time (*i.e.,* the search time will be constant and not proportional to the length of the target string). This is a nontrivial task, admittedly. To make the algorithm as simple to use as possible, the vendor would create a string class based on the algorithm that would represent fast text strings in any client program. To do this, the vendor would prepare a header file that contains a class definition:

```
// faststring.h /////////////////////////////
class FastString {
  char *m_psz;
public:
  FastString(const char *psz);
  ~FastString(void);
  int Length(void) const; // returns # of characters
  int Find(const char *psz) const; // returns offset
};
```

With the class definition in place, the vendor would implement the member functions in a separate source file:

```
// faststring.cpp /////////////////////////////////
#include "faststring.h"
#include <string.h>
FastString::FastString(const char *psz)
: m_psz(new char[strlen(psz) + 1]) {
  strcpy(m_psz, psz);
}

FastString::~FastString(void) {
  delete[] m_psz;
}

int FastString::Length(void) const {
  return strlen(m_psz);
}

int FastString::Find(const char *psz) const {
  // O(1) lookup code deleted for clarity[1]
}
```

---

[1] At the time of this writing, the author did not have a working implementation of this algorithm suitable for publication. The details of such an implementation are left as an exercise for the reader.

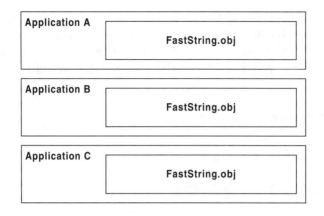

Figure 1.1 Three FastString Clients

Traditionally, C++ libraries have been distributed in source code form. The users of a library would be expected to add the implementation source files to their make system and recompile the library sources locally using their C++ compiler. Assuming that the library adhered to a commonly supported subset of the C++ programming language, this was a perfectly workable approach. The net effect of this procedure was that the executable code of the library would be bundled as part of the overall client application.

Assume that for the FastString class just shown, the generated machine code for the four methods occupied 16MB worth of space in the target executable image (remember, to perform $O(1)$ search, a lot of code might be needed given the standard time versus space trade-off that binds most algorithms). As shown in Figure 1.1, if three applications use the FastString library, each of the three executables will contain the 16MB worth of code. This means that if an end-user installs all three client applications, the FastString implementation occupies 48MB worth of disk space. Worse yet, if the end-user runs the three client applications simultaneously, the FastString code occupies 48MB worth of virtual memory, as the operating system cannot detect the duplicate code that is present in each executable image.

One additional problem with this scenario is that once the library vendor finds a defect in the FastString class, there is no way to field-replace the implementation. Once the FastString code is linked into the client application, one can no longer simply replace the FastString code directly at the end-user's machine. Instead, the library vendor must broadcast source code updates to the developer of each client application and hope that they will rebuild their applications to take advantage of the repairs that were made. Clearly, the modularity of the FastString component is lost once the client runs the linker and produces the final executable.

Dynamic Linking and C++

One technique for solving the problems just stated is to package the FastString class as a Dynamic Link Library (DLL). This can be done in a variety of ways. The simplest technique is to use a class-level compiler directive to force all of the methods of FastString to be exported from the DLL. The Microsoft C++ compiler provides the __declspec(dllexport) keyword for just this purpose:

```
class __declspec(dllexport) FastString {
  char *m_psz;
public:
  FastString(const char *psz);
  ~FastString(void);
  int Length(void) const; // returns # of characters
  int Find(const char *psz) const; // returns offset
};
```

When this technique is used, all of the methods of FastString will be added to the exports list of the FastString DLL, allowing runtime resolution of each method name to its address in memory. In addition, the linker will produce an import library that exposes the symbols for FastString's methods. Instead of containing the actual code, the import library simply contains references to the file name of the DLL and the names of the exported symbols. When the client links against the import library, stubs are added to the executable that inform the loader at runtime to load the FastString DLL dynamically and resolve any imported symbols to their corresponding locations in memory. This resolution happens transparently when the client program is started by the operating system.

Figure 1.2 illustrates the runtime model of FastString when exposed from a DLL. Note that the import library is fairly small (roughly twice the combined size of exported symbol text). When the class is exported from a DLL, the FastString machine code needs to exist only once on the user's hard disk. When multiple clients access the code for the library, the operating system's loader is smart enough to share the physical memory pages containing FastString's read-only executable code between all client programs. In addition, if the library vendor finds a defect in the source code, it is theoretically possible to ship a new DLL to the end-user, repairing the defective implementation for all client applications *en masse*. Clearly, moving the FastString library into a DLL is an important step toward turning the original C++ class into a field-replaceable and efficient reusable component.

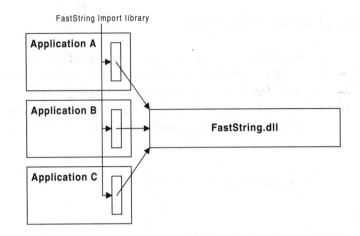

Figure 1.2 FastString as a DLL

C++ and Portability

Once the decision is made to distribute a C++ class as a DLL, one is faced with one of the fundamental weaknesses of C++, that is, lack of standardization at the binary level. Although the ISO/ANSI C++ Draft Working Paper attempts to codify which programs will compile and what the semantic effects of running them will be, it makes no attempt to standardize the binary runtime model of C++. The first time this problem will become evident is when a client tries to link against the FastString DLL's import library from a C++ development environment other than the one used to build the FastString DLL.

To allow operator and function overloading, C++ compilers typically mangle the symbolic name of each entry point to allow many uses of the same name (either with different argument types or in different scopes) without breaking existing C-based linkers. This technique is often referred to as *name mangling*. Despite the fact that the C++ Annotated Reference Manual (ARM) documented the encoding scheme used by CFRONT, many compiler vendors have elected to invent their own proprietary mangling scheme. Because the FastString import library and DLL export symbols using the mangling scheme of the compiler that built the DLL (*e.g.,* GNU C++), clients that are compiled using a different compiler (*e.g.,* Borland C++) will not be able to link successfully with the import library. The classic technique of using extern "C" to disable symbolic mangling would not help in this case, as the DLL is exporting member functions, not global functions.

One technique that could alleviate this problem is to play tricks on the client's linker by using a Module Definition File (commonly known as a DEF file). One feature of DEF files is that they allow exported symbols to be aliased to different imported symbols. Given enough time and information about each compiler's mangling scheme, the library vendor can produce a custom import library for each compiler. While tedious, this allows any compiler to gain link-level compatibility with the DLL, provided the library vendor has anticipated its use ahead of time and has provided a proper DEF file.

Once one overcomes the issues related to linking, one now has to deal with the far more problematic area of incompatibilities related to the generated code. For all but the simplest language constructs, compiler vendors often elect to implement language features in proprietary ways that render objects "untouchable" by code generated by any other compiler. Exceptions are a classic example of such a language feature. A C++ exception thrown from a function compiled with the Microsoft compiler cannot be caught reliably by a client program compiled with the Watcom compiler. This is because the DWP does not mandate what a language feature must look like at runtime, so it is perfectly legal for each compiler vendor to implement a language feature in a unique and innovative manner. For building a stand-alone single-binary executable, this is a nonissue, as all of the code will be compiled and linked using a common development environment. For building multibinary component-based executables this is a tremendous issue, as each component could conceivably be built using a different compiler and linker. The lack of a C++ binary standard limits what language features can be used across DLL boundaries. This means that simply exporting C++ member functions from DLLs is not enough to create a vendor-independent component substrate.

Encapsulation and C++

Assuming that one could overcome the compiler and linker issues outlined in the previous section, the next obstacle to building binary components in C++ is related to encapsulation. Consider what would happen if an organization that was using FastString in an application managed to accomplish the unaccomplishable: finishing development and testing two months prior to a product's ship date. Assume that during this two-month period, some of the more skeptical developers decide to test FastString's $O(1)$ search algorithm by running a profiler on their application. Much to their surprise, FastString::Find would in fact execute extremely quickly irrespective of the presented string length. The Length operation, however, would not fare as well. FastString::Length uses the C runtime library strlen routine, which performs a linear search through the string's data looking for a null terminator. This is an $O(n)$ algorithm that runs slower as the string data gets larger.

Given the fact that the client application may call the Length operation many times, the library vendor will probably be contacted by the once-skeptical developer and asked to increase the speed of Length to operate in constant time as well. There is one catch. The developer has completed development and may not be willing to change one line of source code to take advantage of the newly enhanced Length method. Also, several other vendors may already have shipped products based on the current version of FastString, so the library vendor is morally bound not to break these applications along the way.

At this point, one simply needs to look at the class definition for FastString and decide what can change and what must remain constant in order to keep the installed base happy. Fortunately, FastString was designed with encapsulation in mind, and all of its data members are private. This should afford a great deal of flexibility, as no client programs can write code that directly accesses FastString data members. Provided that no changes are made to the four public members of the class, no changes will be required in any client application. Armed with this belief, the library vendor sets off to implement version 2.0 of FastString.

The obvious enhancement is to cache the length of the string in the constructor and return the cached length in a new version of the Length method. As the string cannot be modified after construction, there is no need to worry about recalculating the length multiple times. In fact, the length is already calculated once in the constructor to allocate the buffer, so only a handful of additional machine instructions will be needed. Here is the modified class definition:

```
// faststring.h version 2.0
class __declspec(dllexport) FastString {
  const int m_cch; // count of characters
  char *m_psz;
public:
  FastString(const char *psz);
  ~FastString(void);
  int Length(void) const; // returns # of characters
  int Find(const char *psz) const; // returns offset
};
```

Note that the only modification is the addition of a *private* data member. To initialize this member properly, the constructor would need to be modified as follows:

```
FastString::FastString(const char *psz)
  : m_cch(strlen(psz)), m_psz(new char[m_cch + 1]) {
```

```
    strcpy(m_psz, psz);
}
```

Given this cached length, the `Length` method now becomes trivial:

```
int FastString::Length(void) const {
    return m_cch; // return cached length
}
```

With these three modifications in place, the library vendor can now rebuild the `FastString` DLL and the corresponding test harness that fully exercises every aspect of the `FastString` class. The vendor would be pleasantly surprised that the principle of encapsulation payed off and that no source-level modifications were required in the test harness. Once the new DLL has been verified to work properly, the library vendor ships version 2.0 of `FastString` to the client, confident that all work is finished.

When the clients who contracted the changes receive the updated `FastString`, they integrate the new class definition and DLL into their source code control system and fire off a build to test the new and improved `FastString`. Like the library vendor, they too are pleasantly surprised, as no source code modifications are required to take advantage of the new version of `Length`. Encouraged by this experience, the development team convinces management to add the new DLL to the final "golden master" CD that is about to go to press. In a rare occurrence, management caves in to the wishes of the enthusiastic developers and adds the new DLL to the final product. Like most installation programs, the setup script for the client's product is designed to silently overwrite any older versions of the `FastString` DLL that may be present on the end-user's machine. This seems innocent enough, as the modifications did not affect the public interface of the class, so the silent machine-wide upgrading to `FastString` version 2.0 should only enhance any existing client applications that had been previously installed.

Imagine the following scenario: End-users finally receive their copies of the client's highly anticipated product. Each end-user immediately drops everything and installs the new application on their machine to try it out. After the thrill of being able to perform extremely fast text searches wears off, the end-user goes back to his or her normal life and launches a previously installed application that also happens to use the `FastString` DLL. For the first few minutes all is well. Then, suddenly, a dialog appears indicating that an exception has occurred and that all of the end user's work has been lost. The end-user tries to launch the application again and this time gets the exception dialog almost immediately. The end-user, accustomed to using modern commercial

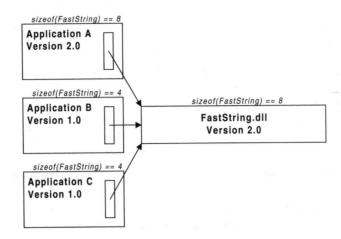

Figure 1.3   C++ and Encapsulation

software, reinstalls the operating system and all applications, but even this does not keep the exception from reoccurring. What happened?

What happened was that the library vendor was lulled into believing that C++ supported encapsulation. Whereas C++ does support *syntactic* encapsulation via its private and protected keywords, the C++ draft standard has no notion of *binary* encapsulation. This is because the compilation model of C++ requires the client's compiler to have access to all information regarding object layout in order to instantiate an instance of a class or to make nonvirtual method calls. This includes information about the size and order of the object's private and protected data members. Consider the scenario shown in Figure 1.3. Version 1.0 of `FastString` required four bytes per instance (assuming `sizeof(char *) == 4`). Clients written to version 1.0 of the class definition allocate four bytes of memory to pass to the class's constructor. Version 2.0 of the constructor, destructor, and methods (which are the versions present in the DLL on the end-user's machine) all assume that the client has allocated eight bytes per instance (assuming `sizeof(int) == 4`) and have no reservations about writing to all eight bytes. Unfortunately, in version 1.0 clients, the second four bytes of the object really belong to someone else and writing a pointer to a text string at this location is considered rude, as the exception dialog indicates.

One common solution to the versioning problem is to rename the DLL each time a new version is produced. This is the strategy taken by the Microsoft Foundation Classes (MFC). When the version number is encoded into the DLL's file name (*e.g.,* `FastString10.DLL`, `FastString20.DLL`), clients always load the version of the DLL that they were built against, irrespective of what other versions may be present on the system. Unfortunately, over time, the number of versioned DLLs present on the end-user's system could conceivably exceed the number of actual client applications due to poor software configuration practices. Simply examining the system directory of any computer that has been in use for more than six months would reinforce this.

Ultimately, this versioning problem is rooted in the compilation model of C++, which was not designed to support independent binary components. By requiring client knowledge of object layout, C++ introduces a tight binary coupling between the client and object executables. Normally, binary coupling works to C++'s favor, as it allows compilers to produce extremely efficient code. Unfortunately, this tight binary coupling prevents class implementations from being replaced without client recompilation. Because of this coupling and the compiler and linker incompatibilities mentioned in the previous section, simply exporting C++ class definitions from DLLs does *not* provide a reasonable binary component architecture.

Separating Interface from Implementation

The concept of encapsulation is based on separating what an object looks like (its interface) from how it actually works (its implementation). The problem with C++ is that this principle does not apply at a binary level, as a C++ class is both interface and implementation simultaneously. This weakness can be addressed by modeling the two abstractions as two distinct entities and C++ classes. By defining one C++ class to represent the interface to a data type and another C++ class as the data type's actual implementation, the object implementor can theoretically modify the implementation class's details while holding the interface class constant. All that is needed is a way to associate the interface with its implementation without revealing any implementation details to the client.

The interface class should describe only what the implementor wants the client to think the underlying data type looks like. Since the interface should not betray any implementation details, the C++ interface class should not contain any of the data members that will be used in the implementation of the object. Instead, the interface class should contain only method declarations for each public operation of the object. The C++ implementation class will contain the actual data members required to implement the object's functionality. One simple approach would be to use a handle class as the interface. The handle class would simply contain an opaque pointer whose type would never be fully defined in the client's scope. The following class definition demonstrates this technique:

```
// faststringitf.h
class __declspec(dllexport) FastStringItf {
  class FastString; // introduce name of impl. class
  FastString *m_pThis; // opaque pointer
                        // (size remains constant)
public:
  FastStringItf(const char *psz);
  ~FastStringItf(void);
  int Length(void) const; // returns # of characters
  int Find(const char *psz) const; // returns offset
};
```

Note that the binary layout of this interface class does not change as data members are added to or removed from the implementation class, FastString. Also, the use of forward declaration means that the class definition for FastString is not needed for this header file to compile. This effectively hides all details of FastString's implementation from the client's compiler. When using this technique, the machine code for the interface methods becomes the only entry point into the object's DLL and their binary signatures will never change. The implementations of the interface class's methods simply forward the method calls on to the actual implementation class:

```
// faststringitf.cpp/// (part of DLL, not client) //
#include "faststring.h"
#include "faststringitf.h"
FastStringItf::FastStringItf(const char *psz)
: m_pThis(new FastString(psz)) {
  assert(m_pThis != 0);
}

FastStringItf::~FastStringItf(void) {
  delete m_pThis;
}

int FastStringItf::Length(void) const {
  return m_pThis->Length();
}

int FastStringItf::Find(const char *psz) const {
  return m_pThis->Find(psz);
}
```

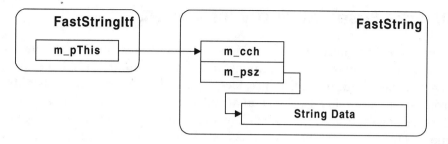

Figure 1.4 Handle Classes as Interfaces

These forwarding methods would be compiled as part of the FastString DLL, so as the layout of the C++ implementation class FastString changes, the call to the new operator in FastStringItf's constructor will be recompiled simultaneously, ensuring that enough memory is always allocated. Again, the client never includes the class definition of the C++ *implementation* class FastString. This affords the FastString implementor the flexibility to evolve the implementation over time without breaking existing clients.

Figure 1.4 shows the runtime model of using handle classes to separate interface from implementation. Note that the level of indirection introduced by the interface class imposes a binary firewall between the client and the object implementation. This binary firewall is a very precise contract describing how the client can communicate with the implementation. All client-object communications take place through the interface class, which imposes a very simple binary protocol for entering the domain of the object's implementation. This protocol does not rely on any details of the C++ implementation class.

Although the approach of using handle classes has its merits and certainly brings us closer to being able to safely expose a class from a DLL, it also has its weaknesses. Note that the interface class needs to forward each method call to the implementation class explicitly. For a simple class like FastString with only two public operations, a constructor and a destructor, this is not a burden. For a large class library with hundreds or thousands of methods, writing these forwarding routines would become quite tedious and potentially error prone. Also, for performance-critical domains, the cost of making two function calls for each method (one call to the interface, one nested call to the implementation) is less than ideal. Finally, the handle class technique does not completely address the problems of compiler/linker compatibility, which ultimately must be solved if we are to have a truly usable substrate for reusable components.

Abstract Bases as Binary Interfaces

It turns out that applying the technique of separation of interface from implementation can solve C++'s compiler/linker compatibility problems as well; however, the definition of the interface class must take a somewhat different form. As noted previously, the compatibility problems stem from various compilers having different ideas of (1) how to represent language features at runtime and (2) how symbolic names will be represented at link time. If one were to devise a technique for hiding compiler/linker implementation details behind some sort of binary interface, this would make a C++-based DLL usable by a much larger audience.

Ensuring that the binary firewall imposed by the C++ interface class uses no compiler-variant language features can solve the problem of compiler/linker dependence. To accomplish this independence, one must first identify the aspects of the language that have uniform implementations across compilers. Certainly, the runtime representation of composite types such as C-style structs can be held invariant across compilers. This is a basic assumption that any C-based system-call interface must make, and it is sometimes achieved by using conditionally compiled type definitions, pragmas, or other compiler directives. The second assumption that can be made is that all compilers can be coerced to pass function parameters in the same order (right to left, left to right) and that stack cleanup can be done in a uniform manner. Like struct compatibility, this is also a solved problem that often requires conditionally compiled compiler directives to enforce a uniform stack discipline. The WINAPI/WINBASEAPI macros from the Win32 API are an example of this technique. Each function exposed from the system DLLs is defined with these macros:

```
WINBASEAPI void WINAPI Sleep(DWORD dwMsecs);
```

Each compiler vendor defines these preprocessor symbols to produce compliant stack frames. Although in a production environment one would want to use a similar technique for all method definitions, the code fragments in this chapter do not use this technique for the sake of exposition.

The third assumption of compiler invariance is the most critical assumption of all, as it enables the definition of a binary interface: All C++ compilers on a given platform implement the virtual function call mechanism equivalently. In fact, this assumption of uniformity needs to apply only to classes that have no data members and at most one base class that also has no data members. This assumption implies that for the following simple class definition:

```
class calculator {
public:
  virtual void add1(short x);
  virtual void add2(short x, short y);
};
```

all compilers on a given platform must produce equivalent machine code sequences for the following client code fragment:

```
extern calculator *pcalc;
pcalc->add1(1);
pcalc->add2(1, 2);
```

Although the generated machine code does not need to be *identical* for all compilers, it needs to be *equivalent*. This means that each compiler must make the same assumptions about how an object of such a class will be represented in memory and how its virtual functions are dynamically invoked at runtime.

It turns out that this is not the tremendous leap of faith that it may seem to be. The runtime implementation of virtual functions in C++ takes the form of vptrs and vtbls in virtually all production compilers. This technique is based on the compiler silently generating a static array of function pointers for each class that contains virtual functions. This array is called the virtual function table (or vtbl) and contains one function pointer for each virtual function defined in the class or its base class. Each instance of the class contains a single invisible data member called the virtual function pointer (or vptr) that is automatically initialized by the constructor to point to the class's vtbl. When a client calls a virtual function, the compiler generates the code to dereference the vptr, index into the vtbl, and call through the function pointer found at the designated location. This is how polymorphism and dynamic call dispatching are implemented in C++. Figure 1.5 shows the runtime representation of the vptr/vtbl layout for the class calculator shown above.

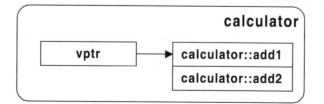

Figure 1.5 vptr/vtbl Layout

Virtually every production-quality C++ compiler currently in use uses the basic concepts of vptrs and vtbls. There are two basic techniques for laying out vtbls: the CFRONT technique and the adjustor thunk technique. Each of these two techniques has its own way of dealing with the subtleties of multiple inheritance. Fortunately, on any given platform, one technique tends to dominate (Win32 compilers use adjustor thunks, Solaris compilers use CFRONT-style vtbls). Fortunately, neither vtbl format affects the C++ source code that one must write but rather is an artifact of the generated code. Consult Stan Lippman's most excellent *Inside the C++ Object Model* for a great discussion of both techniques.

Based on the assumptions made so far, it is now possible to solve the problem of compiler dependence. Assuming that all compilers on a given platform implement the virtual function call mechanism in the same manner, the C++ interface class can be defined to expose the public operations of the data type as virtual functions, confident that all compilers will generate equivalent machine code for client-side method invocations. This assumption of uniformity requires that no interface class can have data members and no interface class can derive directly from more than one other interface class. Because there are no data members in the interface class, one cannot implement these methods in any sensible manner.

To reinforce this, it is useful to define the interface members as pure virtual functions, indicating that the interface class defines only the potential to call the methods, not their actual implementations:

```
// ifaststring.h //////////
class IFastString {
public:
  virtual int Length(void) const = 0;
  virtual int Find(const char *psz) const = 0;
};
```

Defining the methods as pure virtual also informs the compiler that no implementation of these methods is required from the interface class. When the compiler generates the vtbl for the interface class, the entry for each pure virtual function will either be null or point to a C runtime routine (_purecall under Microsoft C++) that fires an assertion when called. Had the method definition not been declared as pure virtual, the compiler would have attempted to populate the corresponding vtbl entry with the interface class's method implementation, which of course does not exist. This would result in a link error.

The interface class just defined is an abstract base class. The corresponding C++ implementation class must derive from the interface class and override each of the pure virtual functions with meaningful implementations. This inheritance relationship will result in objects that have an object layout that is a binary superset of the layout of the interface class (which ultimately is just a vptr/vtbl). This is because the "is-a" relationship between derived and base class applies at the binary level in C++ just as it applies at the modeling level in object-oriented design:

```
class FastString : public IFastString {
  const int m_cch; // count of characters
  char *m_psz;
public:
  FastString(const char *psz);
  ~FastString(void);
  int Length(void) const; // returns # of characters
  int Find(const char *psz) const; // returns offset
};
```

Because FastString derives from IFastString, the binary layout of FastString objects must be a superset of the binary layout of IFastString. This means that FastString objects will contain a vptr that points to an IFastString-compatible vtbl. Since FastString is a concrete instantiable data type, its vtbl will contain pointers to actual implementations of the Length and Find methods. This relationship is illustrated in Figure 1.6.

Even though the public operations of the data type have been hoisted to become pure virtual functions in an interface class, the client cannot instantiate FastString objects without having the class definition of the implementation class. Revealing the implementation class definition to the client would bypass the binary encapsulation of the interface, which would defeat the purpose of using an interface class. One reasonable technique for allowing clients to instantiate FastString objects would be to export a global function from the

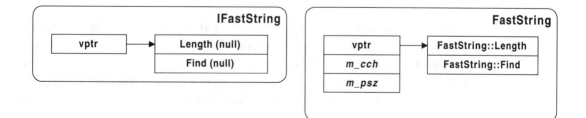

Figure 1.6 Interface/Implementation Classes in Binary

DLL that would call the new operator on behalf of the client. Provided that this routine is exported using extern "C", it would still be accessible from any C++ compiler.

```
// ifaststring.h ///////////
class IFastString {
public:
   virtual int Length(void) const = 0;
   virtual int Find(const char *psz) const = 0;
};

extern "C"
IFastString *CreateFastString(const char *psz);

// faststring.cpp (part of DLL) ///////////
IFastString *CreateFastString (const char *psz) {
   return new FastString(psz);
}
```

As was the case in the handle class approach, the new operator is called exclusively from within the confines of the FastString DLL, which means that the size and layout of the object will be established using the same compiler that compiles all of the implementation's methods.

The last remaining barrier to overcome is related to object destruction. The following client code will compile, but the results are unexpected:

```
int f(void) {
   IFastString *pfs = CreateFastString("Deface me");
   int n = pfs->Find("ace me");
   delete pfs;
   return n;
}
```

The unexpected behavior stems from the fact that the destructor for the interface class is not virtual. This means that the call to the delete operator will not dynamically find the most derived destructor and recursively destroy the object from the outermost type to the base type. Because the FastString destructor is never called, the preceding example leaks the buffer memory used to hold the string "Deface me".

One obvious solution to this problem is to make the destructor virtual in the interface class. Unfortunately, this pollutes the compiler independence of the interface class, as the position of the virtual destructor in the vtbl can vary from compiler to compiler. One workable solution to this problem is to add an explicit Delete method to the interface as another pure virtual function and have the derived class delete itself in its implementation of this method. This results in the correct destructor being executed. The updated version of the interface header file looks like this:

```
// ifaststring.h ///////////
class IFastString {
public:
  virtual void Delete(void) = 0;
  virtual int Length(void) const = 0;
  virtual int Find(const char *psz) const = 0;
};
extern "C"
IFastString *CreateFastString (const char *psz);
```

which implies the corresponding implementation class definition:

```
// faststring.h //////////////////////////////////
#include "ifaststring.h"
class FastString : public IFastString {
  const int m_cch; // count of characters
  char *m_psz;
public:
  FastString(const char *psz);
  ~FastString(void);
  void Delete(void); // deletes this instance
  int Length(void) const; // returns # of characters
  int Find(const char *psz) const; // returns offset
};
// faststring.cpp //////////////////////////////////
#include <string.h>
#include "faststring.h"
IFastString* CreateFastString (const char *psz) {
  return new FastString(psz);
}

FastString::FastString(const char *psz)
: m_cch(strlen(psz)), m_psz(new char[m_cch + 1]) {
  strcpy(m_psz, psz);
}
```

```
    void FastString::Delete(void) {
      delete this;
    }
    FastString::~FastString(void) {
      delete[] m_psz;
    }

    int FastString::Length(void) const {
      return m_cch;
    }

    int FastString::Find(const char *psz) const {
      // O(1) lookup code deleted for clarity
    }
```

Figure 1.7 shows the runtime layout of FastString.

To use the FastString data type, clients simply need to include the interface definition file and call CreateFastString to begin working:

```
    #include "ifaststring.h"

    int f(void) {
      int n = -1;
      IFastString *pfs = CreateFastString("Hi Bob!");
      if (pfs) {
        n = pfs->Find("ob");
        pfs->Delete();
      }
      return n;
    }
```

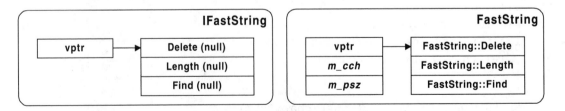

Figure 1.7 FastString Using Abstract Bases as Interfaces

Note that all but one of the entry points into the FastString DLL are virtual functions. The virtual functions of the interface class are always called indirectly via a function pointer stored in a vtbl, without requiring the client to link against their symbolic names at development time. This means that the interface methods are immune to symbolic mangling differences between compilers. The only entry point that is explicitly linked against by name is CreateFastString, the global function that bootstraps the client into the world of FastString. Note, however, that this function was exported using extern "C", which suppresses symbolic mangling. This implies that all C++ compilers expect the import library and DLL to export the same symbol. The net result of using this technique is that one can safely expose a class from a DLL using one C++ environment and access the class from any other C++ development environment. This capability is critical for building a vendor-neutral substrate for reusable components.

Runtime Polymorphism

Deploying class implementations using abstract base classes as interfaces opens up a new world of possibilities in terms of what can happen at runtime. Note that the FastString DLL exports only one symbol, CreateFastString. This makes it fairly trivial for the client to load the DLL dynamically on demand using LoadLibrary and resolve that one entry point using GetProcAddress:

```
IFastString *CallCreateFastString(const char *psz) {
  static IFastString * (*pfn)(const char *) = 0;
  if (!pfn) { // init ptr 1st time through
    const TCHAR szDll[] = __TEXT("FastString.DLL");
    const char  szFn[] = "CreateFastString";
    HINSTANCE h = LoadLibrary(szDll);
    if (h)
      *(FARPROC*)&pfn = GetProcAddress(h, szFn);
  }
  return pfn ? pfn(psz) : 0;
}
```

This technique has several possible applications. One motivation for using the technique is to avoid having operating system (OS)–generated errors when the client program is run on a machine that does not have the object implementation installed. Applications that use optional system components such as WinSock or MAPI use a similar technique to allow an application to run on minimally configured machines. Because the client never needs to link against the DLL's import library, the client has no load dependences on the DLL and can execute on machines that do not have the DLL installed. Another motivation for using this technique might be lazy initialization of the process's address space. Again, because the DLL is not automatically loaded at process initialization time, if the object implementation is never actually used, the DLL is never loaded. Other benefits of using this technique include faster start-up in the client and conservation of address space for long-lived processes that may never actually use the DLL.

Perhaps one of the most interesting applications of this technique is to allow the client to select dynamically between various implementations of the same interface. Given the publicly available definition of the IFastString interface, nothing is stopping FastString's original implementor or other third-party implementors from deriving additional implementation classes from the same interface. Like the original implementation class FastString, these new implementations will have layouts that are binary compatible with the original interface class. To access these "plug-compatible" implementations, all the client must do is specify the correct filename for the desired implementation's DLL.

To understand how this technique could be applied, assume that the original implementation of IFastString performed searches in left-to-right order. This behavior is perfect for languages that parse from left to right (*e.g.,* English, French, German). For languages that parse from right to left, a second implementation of IFastString that performs searches using right-to-left order would be more appropriate. This alternative implementation could be built as a second DLL with a distinguished name (*e.g.,* FastStringRL.DLL). Assuming both DLLs are installed on an end-user's machine, the client can dynamically select the desired implementation of IFastString simply by loading the appropriate DLL at runtime:

```
IFastString *
CallCreateFastString(const char *psz,
                     bool bLeftToRight = true) {
  static IFastString * (*pfnlr)(const char *) = 0;
  static IFastString * (*pfnrl)(const char *) = 0;

  IFastString *(**ppfn)(const char *) = &pfnlr;
  const TCHAR *pszDll = __TEXT("FastString.DLL");

  if (!bLeftToRight) {
    pszDll = __TEXT("FastStringRL.DLL");
```

```
      ppfn = &pfnrl;
    }

    if (!(*ppfn)) { // init ptr 1st time through
      const char  szFn[] = "CreateFastString";
      HINSTANCE h = LoadLibrary(pszDll);
      if (h)
        *(FARPROC*)ppfn = GetProcAddress(h, szFn);
    }
    return (*ppfn) ? (*ppfn)(psz) : 0;
}
```

When the client calls the function with no second parameter

```
pfs = CallCreateFastString("Hi Bob!");
n = pfs->Find("ob");
```

the original `FastString` DLL is loaded and the search is performed from left
to right. If the client indicates that the string is in a spoken language that
parses from right to left

```
pfs = CallCreateFastString("Hi Bob!", false);
n = pfs->Find("ob");
```

the alternative version of the DLL (`FastStringRL.DLL`) is loaded and the
search will be performed starting at the rightmost position of the string. The
key observation is that callers of `CallCreateFastString` do not care which
DLL is used to implement the object's methods. All that matters is that a
pointer to an `IFastString`-compatible vptr is returned by the function and
that the vptr provides useful and semantically correct functionality. This form
of runtime polymorphism is extremely useful for building a dynamically composed system from binary components.

Object Extensibility

The techniques presented so far allow clients to select and load binary components dynamically that can evolve their implementation layout over time
without requiring client recompilation. This by itself is extremely useful for
building dynamically composable systems. However, one aspect of the object
that cannot evolve over time is its interface. This is because the client compiles

against the precise signature of the interface class, and any changes to the interface definition require that the client recompile to take advantage of the change. Worse yet, changing the interface definition completely violates the encapsulation of the object (its public interface has changed) and would break all existing clients. Even the most innocuous change, such as changing the semantics of a method while holding its signature constant, renders the installed client base useless. This implies that interfaces are immutable binary and semantic contracts that must never change. This immutability is required to have a stable, predictable runtime environment.

Despite the immutability of interfaces, it is often necessary to expose additional functionality that may not have been anticipated when an interface was initially designed. It is tempting to take advantage of the knowledge of vtbl layout and simply append new methods to the end of an existing interface definition. Consider the initial version of IFastString:

```
class IFastString {
public:
  virtual void Delete(void) = 0;
  virtual int Length(void) = 0;
  virtual int Find(const char *psz) = 0;
};
```

Simply modifying the interface class to have additional virtual function declarations *after the existing method declarations* would result in a binary vtbl format that is a superset of the original version, as any new vtbl entries would appear after those that correspond to the original methods. Object implementations that compile against the new interface definition would have any additional method entries *appended* to the original vtbl layout:

```
class IFastString {
public:
// faux version 1.0
  virtual void Delete(void) = 0;
  virtual int Length(void) = 0;
  virtual int Find(const char *psz) = 0;
// faux version 2.0
  virtual int FindN(const char *psz, int n) = 0;
};
```

This solution almost works. Clients compiled against the original version of the interface are blissfully ignorant of any vtbl entries beyond the first three. When older clients get newer objects that have the vtbl entry for FindN, they continue to work properly. The problem arises when new clients that expect IFastString to have four methods happen to use older objects that do not implement this method. When the client calls the FindN method on an object compiled against the original interface definition, the results are very well defined. The program crashes.

The problem with this technique is that it breaks the encapsulation of the object by modifying the public interface. Just as changing the public interface to a C++ class can cause compile-time errors when the client code is rebuilt, changing the binary interface definition will cause runtime errors when the client code is reexecuted. This implies that interfaces must be immutable and cannot change once published. The solution to this problem is to allow an implementation class to expose more than one interface. This can be achieved either by designing an interface to derive from another related interface or by allowing an implementation class to inherit from several unrelated interface classes. In either case, the client could use C++'s Runtime Type Identification (RTTI) feature to interrogate the object at runtime to ensure that the requested functionality is indeed supported by the object currently in use.

Consider the simple case of an interface extending another interface. To add a FindN operation to IFastString that allows finding the nth occurrence of a substring, one would derive a second interface from IFastString and add the new method definition there:

```
class IFastString2 : public IFastString {
public:
// real version 2.0
   virtual int FindN(const char *psz, int n) = 0;
};
```

Clients can interrogate the object reliably at runtime to discover whether or not the object is IFastString2 compatible by using C++'s dynamic_cast operator:

```
int Find10thBob(IFastString *pfs) {
   IFastString2 *pfs2=dynamic_cast<IFastString2*>(pfs);
   if (pfs2) // the object derives from IFastString2
     return pfs2->FindN("Bob", 10);
   else { // object doesn't derive from IFastString2
     error("Cannot find 10th occurrence of Bob");
     return -1;
   }
}
```

If the object derives from the extended interface, then the `dynamic_cast` operator returns a pointer to the `IFastString2`-compliant aspect of the object and the client can call the object's extended method. If the object does not derive from the extended interface, then the `dynamic_cast` operator will return a null pointer and the client can either choose another implementation technique, log an error message, or just silently continue without the extended operation. This capability of client-defined graceful degradation is critical for building robust dynamic systems that can provide extended functionality over time.

A more interesting scenario arises when new orthogonal functionality needs to be exposed from the object. Consider what it would take to add persistence to the `FastString` implementation class. Although one could conceivably add Load and Save methods to an extended version of `IFastString`, it is likely that other types of objects that are not `IFastString` compatible can also be persistent. Simply creating a new interface that extends `IFastString`:

```
class IPersistentObject : public IFastString {
public:
  virtual bool Load(const char *pszFileName) = 0;
  virtual bool Save(const char *pszFileName) = 0;
};
```

requires all persistent objects to support the Length and Find operations as well. For some very small subset of objects, this might make sense. However, to make the `IPersistentObject` interface as generic as possible, it should really be its own interface and not derive from `IFastString`:

```
class IPersistentObject {
public:
  virtual void Delete(void) = 0;
  virtual bool Load(const char *pszFileName) = 0;
  virtual bool Save(const char *pszFileName) = 0;
};
```

This does not prohibit the `FastString` implementation from becoming persistent; it simply means that the persistent version of `FastString` must implement both the `IFastString` *and* `IPersistentObject` interfaces:

```
class FastString : public IFastString,
                   public IPersistentObject {
```

```
  int    m_cch; // count of characters
  char *m_psz;
public:
  FastString(const char *psz);
  ~FastString(void);
// Common methods
  void Delete(void); // deletes this instance
// IFastString methods
  int Length(void) const; // returns # of characters
  int Find(const char *psz) const; // returns offset
// IPersistentObject methods
  bool Load(const char *pszFileName);
  bool Save(const char *pszFileName);
};
```

To save a FastString to disk, clients can simply use RTTI to bind a pointer to the IPersistentObject interface that is exposed by the object:

```
bool SaveString(IFastString *pfs, const char *pszFN){
  bool bResult = false;
  IPersistentObject *ppo =
            dynamic_cast<IPersistentObject*>(pfs);
  if (ppo)
    bResult = ppo->Save(pszFN);
  return bResult;
}
```

This technique works because the compiler has enough knowledge about the layout and type hierarchy of the implementation class to examine an object at runtime to determine whether it in fact derives from IPersistentObject. Therein lies the problem.

RTTI is a very compiler-dependent feature. Again, the DWP mandates the syntax and semantics for RTTI, but each compiler vendor's implementation of RTTI is unique and proprietary. This effectively destroys the compiler independence that has been achieved by using abstract base classes as interfaces. This is unacceptable for a vendor-neutral component architecture. One very tractable solution to the problem is to leverage the semantics of dynamic_cast without using the actual compiler-dependent language feature. Exposing a well-known method explicitly from each interface that will perform the semantic equivalent of dynamic_cast can achieve the desired effect without requiring all entities to use the same C++ compiler:

```
class IPersistentObject {
public:
  virtual void *Dynamic_Cast(const char *pszType) =0;
  virtual void Delete(void) = 0;
  virtual bool Load(const char *pszFileName) = 0;
  virtual bool Save(const char *pszFileName) = 0;
};

class IFastString {
public:
  virtual void *Dynamic_Cast(const char *pszType) =0;
  virtual void Delete(void) = 0;
  virtual int Length(void) = 0;
  virtual int Find(const char *psz) = 0;
};
```

As all interfaces need to expose this method in addition to the Delete method
already present, it makes a great deal of sense to hoist the common subset of
methods to a base interface that all subsequent interfaces could then derive
from:

```
class IExtensibleObject {
public:
  virtual void *Dynamic_Cast(const char* pszType) =0;
  virtual void Delete(void) = 0;
};

class IPersistentObject : public IExtensibleObject {
public:
  virtual bool Load(const char *pszFileName) = 0;
  virtual bool Save(const char *pszFileName) = 0;
};

class IFastString : public IExtensibleObject {
public:
  virtual int Length(void) = 0;
  virtual int Find(const char *psz) = 0;
};
```

With this type hierarchy in place, the client is able to query an object dynamically for a given interface using a compiler-independent construct:

```
bool SaveString(IFastString *pfs, const char *pszFN){
   bool bResult = false;
   IPersistentObject *ppo = (IPersistentObject*)
               pfs->Dynamic_Cast("IPersistentObject");
   if (ppo)
     bResult = ppo->Save(pszFN);
   return bResult;
}
```

Assuming the client usage just shown, the required semantics and mechanism for type discovery are in place, but each implementation class must implement this functionality by hand:

```
class FastString : public IFastString,
                   public IPersistentObject {
   int    m_cch; // count of characters
   char *m_psz;
public:
   FastString(const char *psz);
   ~FastString(void);
// IExtensibleObject methods
   void *Dynamic_Cast(const char *pszType);
   void Delete(void); // deletes this instance
// IFastString methods
   int Length(void) const; // returns # of characters
   int Find(const char *psz) const; // returns offset
// IPersistentObject methods
   bool Load(const char *pszFileName);
   bool Save(const char *pszFileName);
};
```

The implementation of Dynamic_Cast needs to simulate the effects of RTTI by navigating the type hierarchy of the object. Figure 1.8 illustrates the type hierarchy for the FastString class just shown. Because the implementation class derives from each interface that it exposes, FastString's implementation of Dynamic_Cast can simply use explicit static casts to limit the scope of the this pointer based on the subtype requested by the client:

```
void *FastString::Dynamic_Cast(const char *pszType) {
   if (strcmp(pszType, "IFastString") == 0)
```

Type Hierarchy

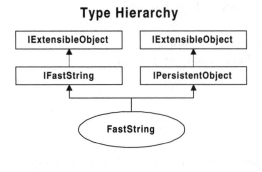

Binary Layout

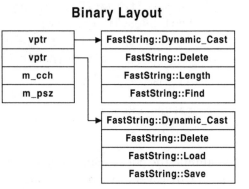

Figure 1.8   FastString Type Hierarchy

```
      return static_cast<IFastString*>(this);
   else if (strcmp(pszType, "IPersistentObject") == 0)
      return static_cast<IPersistentObject*>(this);
   else if (strcmp(pszType, "IExtensibleObject") == 0)
      return static_cast<IFastString*>(this);
   else
      return 0; // request for unsupported interface
}
```

Because the object derives from the type used in the cast, the compiled versions of the cast statements simply add a fixed offset to the object's this pointer to find the beginning of the base class's layout.

Note that when asked for the common base interface IExtensibleObject, the implementation statically casts itself to IFastString. This is because the intuitive version of the statement

```
return static_cast<IExtensibleObject*>(this);
```

is ambiguous because IFastString and IPersistentObject both derive from IExtensibleObject. If IExtensibleObject was a virtual base class of both IFastString and IPersistentObject, then this cast would not be ambiguous and the statement would compile. However, introducing virtual base classes adds needless runtime complexity to the resultant object and also introduces compiler dependences. This is because virtual bases are yet another C++ language feature that has several proprietary implementations.

Resource Management

One remaining problem with supporting multiple interfaces from a single object becomes clear when examining the client usage pattern of the Dynamic_Cast method. Consider the following client code:

```
void f(void) {
  IFastString *pfs = 0;
  IPersistentObject *ppo = 0;
  pfs = CreateFastString("Feed BOB");
  if (pfs) {
    ppo = (IPersistentObject *)
              pfs->Dynamic_Cast("IPersistentObject");
    if (!ppo)
      pfs->Delete();
    else {
      ppo->Save("C:\\autoexec.bat");
      ppo->Delete();
    }
  }
}
```

Although the object was initially bound via its IFastString interface, the client code is calling the Delete method through the IPersistentObject interface. Given the behavior of multiple inheritance in C++, this is not an issue, as all of the class's IExtensibleObject-derived vtbls will point to the single implementation of the Delete method. However, the client now has to keep track of which pointers are associated with which objects and call Delete only once per object. For the simple code just shown, this is not a tremendous burden. In more complex client code, managing these relationships becomes quite complex and error prone. One way to simplify the client's task is to push the responsibility for managing the lifetime of the object down to the implementation. After all, allowing the client to delete an object explicitly betrays yet another implementation detail: the fact that the object is allocated on the heap.

One simple solution to this problem is to have each object maintain a reference count that is incremented when an interface pointer is duplicated and decremented when an interface pointer is destroyed. This means changing the definition of IExtensibleObject from:

```
class IExtensibleObject {
public:
  virtual void *Dynamic_Cast(const char* pszType) =0;
  virtual void Delete(void) = 0;
};
```

to

```
class IExtensibleObject {
public:
  virtual void *Dynamic_Cast(const char* pszType) =0;
  virtual void DuplicatePointer(void) = 0;
  virtual void DestroyPointer(void) = 0;
};
```

With these methods in place, all users of IExtensibleObject must now adhere to the following two mandates: (1) When an interface pointer is duplicated, a call to DuplicatePointer is required. (2) When an interface pointer is no longer in use, a call to DestroyPointer is required.

These methods could be implemented in each object simply by noting the number of live pointers and destroying the object when no outstanding pointers remain:

```
class FastString : public IFastString,
                   public IPersistentObject {
  int    m_cPtrs; // count of outstanding ptrs
    :      :
public:
// initialize pointer count to zero
  FastString(const char *psz) : m_cPtrs(0) {}
  void DuplicatePointer(void) {
// note duplication of pointer
    ++m_cPtrs;
  }
  void DestroyPointer(void) {
// destroy object when last pointer destroyed
    if (--m_cPtrs == 0)
      delete this;
  }
    :
    :
};
```

This extremely boilerplate code could easily be put into a base class or C preprocessor macro for all implementations to use.

To support these methods, all code that manipulates or manages interface pointers must adhere to the two simple rules of DuplicatePointer/ DestroyPointer. For the implementation of FastString, this means modifying two functions. The CreateFastString function takes the initial pointer that is returned by the C++ new operator and duplicates it onto the stack to return to the client. This implies that a call to DuplicatePointer is required:

```
IFastString* CreateFastString(const char *psz) {
  IFastString *pfsResult = new FastString(psz);
  if (pfsResult)
    pfsResult->DuplicatePointer();
  return pfsResult;
}
```

The other location where the implementation duplicates a pointer is in the Dynamic_Cast method:

```
void *FastString::Dynamic_Cast(const char *pszType) {
  void *pvResult = 0;
  if (strcmp(pszType, "IFastString") == 0)
    pvResult = static_cast<IFastString*>(this);
  else if (strcmp(pszType, "IPersistentObject") == 0)
    pvResult = static_cast<IPersistentObject*>(this);
  else if (strcmp(pszType, "IExtensibleObject") == 0)
    pvResult = static_cast<IFastString*>(this);
  else
    return 0; // request for unsupported interface
// pvResult now contains a duplicated pointer, so
// we must call DuplicatePointer prior to returning
  ((IExtensibleObject*)pvResult)->DuplicatePointer();
  return pvResult;
}
```

With these two modifications in place, the corresponding client code now becomes much more uniform and unambiguous:

```
void f(void) {
  IFastString *pfs = 0;
  IPersistentObject *ppo = 0;
```

```
            pfs = CreateFastString("Feed BOB");
            if (pfs) {
              ppo = (IPersistentObject *)
                          pfs->Dynamic_Cast("IPersistentObject");
              if (ppo) {
                ppo->Save("C:\\autoexec.bat");
                ppo->DestroyPointer();
              }
              pfs->DestroyPointer();
            }
          }
```

Because each pointer is now treated as an autonomous entity with respect to lifetime, the client does not need to be concerned with which pointer refers to which object. Instead, the client simply follows the two simple rules and allows the object to manage its own lifetime. If desired, the idiom of calling DuplicatePointer and DestroyPointer could easily be hidden behind a C++ smart pointer.

Using this reference counting scheme allows an object to expose multiple interfaces in an extremely uniform manner. The capability to expose multiple interfaces from a single implementation class allows a data type to participate in a variety of contexts. For example, a new persistence subsystem could define its own custom interface for telling objects to load and save themselves to some customized storage medium. The FastString class could add support for this functionality simply by deriving from the subsystem's persistence interface. Adding this support does not in any way affect the installed base of clients that may be using the prior persistence interface to save and load a string to disk. Having a mechanism for runtime interface negotiation can act as a cornerstone for building a dynamic system from components that can evolve over time.

Where Are We?

This chapter started with a simple C++ class and examined the issues related to exposing the class as a reusable binary component. The first step was to deploy the class as a Dynamic Link Library (DLL) to decouple the physical package of the class from the packaging of its clients. We then used the notion of interfaces and implementations to encapsulate the implementation details of the data type behind a binary firewall, allowing the object's layout to evolve without requiring client recompilation. When using the abstract base class approach to define interfaces, this firewall took the form of a vptr and vtbl. We then examined techniques for dynamically selecting different polymorphic implementations of a given interface at runtime using LoadLibrary and GetProcAddress. Finally, we used an RTTI-like construct for dynamically interrogating an object to discover whether it in fact implements a desired interface. This construct gave us a technique for extending existing versions of an interface as well as exposing multiple unrelated interfaces from a single object.

In short, we have just engineered the Component Object Model.

CHAPTER

2 | Interfaces

```
void *pv = malloc(sizeof(int));
int *pi = (int*)pv;
(*pi)++;
free(pv);
```
Anonymous, 1982

The previous chapter presented a series of C++ programming techniques that enable the development of reusable binary components that can evolve over time. In spirit, these techniques are identical to those used by COM. The slight differences between the techniques from the previous chapter and those used by COM are mostly details and are almost always imposed for a reason. Conceptually, however, the previous chapter told the story of COM, which is first and foremost that of separation of interface from implementation.

Interfaces and Implementations Revisited

The motivation for separating interface from implementation was to hide from the client all details about an object's inner workings. This fundamental principle provided a level of indirection that allowed the number (or order) of data members to change in an implementation class without requiring the client to recompile. This principle also allowed clients to discover extended functionality via runtime interrogation of an object. Finally, this principle allowed a DLL to decouple itself from the particular C++ compiler used by the client.

Although this last aspect is useful, it does not go far enough in providing a universal substrate for binary components. The important observation is that while clients can use any C++ compiler they choose, ultimately they must use a C++ compiler. The techniques described in the previous chapter provide compiler independence. Ultimately, language independence is what is needed to create a truly universal substrate for binary components. To achieve language independence, the principle of separation of interface from implementation must be applied one more time.

Consider the interface definitions that were used in the previous chapter. Each interface definition took the form of a C++ abstract base class definition in a C++ header file. The fact that the interface definition resides in a file that is parsable from only one language betrays one remaining implementation detail of the object: the language used to produce it. Ultimately, the object should be accessible from any language, not just the language chosen by the object implementor. By providing only a C++-compatible interface definition, the object implementor is forcing the component's target audience also to work in C++.

Although C++ is an extremely useful programming language, there are many programming domains for which other languages are better suited to the task at hand. Just as link compatibility problems could be solved by providing module definition files for every possible compiler, one could also conceivably translate the C++ version of the interface definition into every possible programming language. Since the binary signature of an interface is just a simple vptr/vtbl, this could be done for a large class of languages.

Producing these alternative language mappings for all known interfaces would require a tremendous amount of labor and, ultimately, it would be impossible to keep up with the torrent of programming languages the software industry manages to invent every decade. Ideally, one would just write a tool that parsed C++ class definitions into some abstract intermediate state. From this intermediate state, this tool could then produce language mappings for any programming language that has a supporting back-end generator. As additional languages become important, new back-end generators could be added once and all previously defined interfaces would instantly become usable in an entirely new context.

Unfortunately, the C++ programming language is fraught with ambiguities that make it less than ideal for mapping to all possible languages. Many of these ambiguities are related to the loose relationship between pointers, memory, and arrays that are nonissues when both the caller and the callee are compiled in C or C++ but have no natural mapping to many languages without additional qualification. To decouple the interface definition from the language used by any particular implementation, one must separate the language used for defining *interfaces* from the language used for defining *implementations*. If all parties agree on a single language for defining interfaces, it is possible to define the interface once and derive new implementation language–specific mappings as they are needed. COM provides such a language that takes the basic well-known syntax of C and adds the ability to disambiguate precisely any C language features that are subject to interpretation in other languages. This language is called the Interface Definition Language or IDL.

IDL

COM IDL is based on the Open Software Foundation Distributed Computing Environment Remote Procedure Call (OSF DCE RPC) IDL. DCE IDL allows remote procedure calls to be described in a language-neutral manner that also enables an IDL compiler to generate networking code that transparently remotes the described operations over a variety of network transports. COM IDL simply adds a few COM-specific extensions to DCE IDL to support the object-oriented nature of COM (*e.g.,* inheritance, polymorphism). Not coincidentally, when COM objects are accessed across execution context[1] or machine boundaries, all client-object communications use MS-RPC (an implementation of DCE RPC that is part of Windows NT and Windows 95) as the underlying transport.

The Win32 SDK includes an IDL compiler called MIDL.EXE that parses COM IDL files and generates several artifacts. As shown in Figure 2.1, MIDL generates C/C++-compatible header files that contain the abstract base class definitions that correspond to the interfaces that are defined in the original

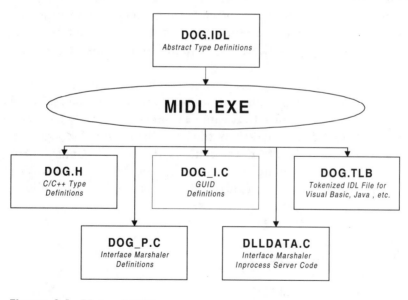

Figure 2.1 Using MIDL

---

[1] The term *execution context* is used by the COM specification to describe what has since been renamed an *apartment*. An apartment is neither a thread nor a process; however, it shares common attributes with both. Apartments are fully described in Chapter 5.

IDL file. These header files also contain C-compatible structure-based definitions that allow C programs to access or implement the IDL-described interfaces. The fact that MIDL automatically generates the C/C++ header file implies that no COM interfaces should be defined manually in C++. Having a single point of definition avoids having multiple incompatible versions of an interface definition that can fall out of sync over time. MIDL also generates source code that allows the interface to be used across thread, process, and host boundaries. This code will be discussed in Chapter 5. Finally, MIDL can also generate a binary file that allows other COM-aware environments to produce language mappings for the interfaces defined in the original IDL file. This binary file is called a type library and contains tokenized IDL in an efficiently parsed form. Type libraries are typically distributed as part of the implementation's executable and allow languages such as Visual Basic, Java, or Object Pascal to use the interfaces that are exposed by the implementation.

To understand IDL, one needs to look at an interface from two perspectives: the logical and the physical. Discussions of an interface's methods and the operations they perform focus on the logical aspect of an interface. Discussions of memory, stack frames, network packets, or other runtime phenomena usually refer to the physical aspect of an interface. Some physical aspects of an interface are directly derivable from a logical description (*e.g.,* vtbl ordering, order of parameters on the stack). Other physical aspects (*e.g.,* array boundaries, network representations of complex data types) require additional qualification.

IDL allows interface designers to work mainly in the logical realm using C-style syntax. However, IDL also allows interface designers to precisely specify any aspects of an interface that cannot be derived directly from its C-style logical description using annotations that are formally called attributes. IDL attributes are distinguished from the primary IDL text stream by surrounding the comma-delimited attribute list with brackets. Attributes always precede the definition of the subject of the attribute. For example, in the following IDL fragment:

```
[
    v1_enum, helpstring("This is a color!")
]
enum COLOR { RED, GREEN, BLUE };
```

the v1_enum attribute applies to the enumeration definition COLOR. This particular attribute informs the IDL compiler that the network representation for COLOR should be 32 bits, not 16 bits, which is the default. The helpstring attribute also applies to COLOR and injects the string "This is a color!" into the generated type library as documentation for the enumeration. If one ignores the attributes in an IDL file, the syntax is simply that of C. IDL supports structures, unions, arrays, enumerations, and typedefs with a syntax identical to that of their C counterparts.

When defining COM methods in IDL, one needs to indicate explicitly whether the caller or the callee will be writing or reading each method parameter. This is accomplished using the parameter attributes [in] and [out]:

```
void Method1([in] long arg1,
             [out] long *parg2,
             [in, out] long *parg3);
```

For this IDL fragment, the caller is expected to pass a value to the object in arg1 and in the location referred to by parg3. Upon completion, the object is expected to pass values back to the caller through the locations referred to by parg2 and parg3. This means that for the following caller sequence:

```
long arg2 = 20, arg3 = 30;
p->Method1(10, &arg2, &arg3);
```

the object cannot count on receiving the actual value of 20 via parg2. If the object is running in the same execution context as the caller and both parties are implemented in C++, then *parg2 will in fact contain the value of 20 on method entry. However, if the object is accessed from a different execution context or one party is implemented in a language that optimizes away the initialization of the out-only parameter, then the caller's initialization will be lost.

Methods and Results

Method results are one aspect of COM where the logical and physical worlds diverge. Virtually all COM methods physically return an error number of type HRESULT. The use of a uniform result type allows COM's remoting architecture to overload the result of a method and also indicate communications errors simply by reserving a range of values for RPC errors. HRESULTs are 32-bit integers that provide information to the caller's runtime environment about what type of error may have occurred (*e.g.*, network errors, server failures). For many COM-compatible implementation languages (*e.g.*, Visual Basic, Java), these HRESULTs are intercepted by a supporting runtime or virtual machine and mapped to programmatic exceptions.

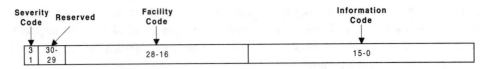

Figure 2.2 HRESULTs

As shown in Figure 2.2, HRESULTs are partitioned into three bit-fields: the severity bit, the facility code, and the information code. The severity bit indicates whether the operation succeeded or not, the facility code indicates what technology the HRESULT corresponds to, and the information code is the precise result within the specified technology and severity. The SDK headers define two macros that simplify coding with HRESULTs:

```
#define SUCCEEDED(hr) (long(hr) >= 0)
#define FAILED(hr) (long(hr) < 0)
```

These two macros take advantage of the fact that the severity bit is also the sign bit when treating an HRESULT as a signed integer.

The SDK headers contain the definitions of all standard HRESULTs. These HRESULTs have symbolic names that correspond to the three components of an HRESULT using the following format:

```
<facility>_<severity>_<information>
```

For example, the HRESULT STG_S_CONVERTED indicates that the facility code is FACILITY_STORAGE (which means that this result is related to Structured Storage or Persistence); the severity bit is SEVERITY_SUCCESS (which means that the call was able to perform the operation successfully) and that, in this case, the operation converted the underlying file to support structured storage. HRESULTs that are universal and are not tied to a particular technology use FACILITY_NULL and their symbolic name does not contain the facility code prefix. Some common FACILITY_NULL HRESULTs are

```
S_OK - successful normal operation
S_FALSE - used to return logical false successfully
E_FAIL - generic failure
E_NOTIMPL - method not implemented
E_UNEXPECTED - method called at incorrect time
```

FACILITY_ITF is used by interface-specific HRESULTs and is also the only legal facility code for user-defined HRESULTs. FACILITY_ITF values need only be unique in the context of a particular interface. The standard headers define the MAKE_HRESULT macro for composing user-defined HRESULTs from the three required fields:

```
const HRESULT CALC_E_IAMHOSED =
                MAKE_HRESULT(SEVERITY_ERROR,
                          FACILITY_ITF, 0x200 + 15);
```

The convention for user-defined HRESULTs is to select information code values above 0x200 to avoid reusing values already used by system HRESULTs. Although not crucial, this avoids overloading values that already have meaning for standard interfaces. For example, most HRESULTs have text-based human-readable descriptions that can be resolved at runtime using the FormatMessage API function. By selecting HRESULTs that do not collide with system-defined values, there is no chance that an erroneous error message may be found.

To allow methods to return a logical result that is not related to the method's physical HRESULT, COM IDL supports the retval parameter attribute. The retval attribute indicates that the associated physical method parameter is actually the logical result of the operation and, in environments that support this, the parameter should be mapped as the result of the operation. Given the following IDL method definition:

```
HRESULT Method2([in] short arg1,
                [out, retval] short *parg2);
```

the Java mapping looks like this:

```
public short Method2(short arg1);
```

whereas Visual Basic maps the method definition as follows:

```
Function Method2(arg1 as Integer) As Integer
```

Because C++ uses no supporting runtime to access COM interfaces, the Microsoft C++ mapping of this method looks like this:

```
virtual HRESULT __stdcall Method2(short arg1,
                                  short *parg2) = 0;
```

This means that the following C++ client code:

```
short sum = 10;
short s;
HRESULT hr = pItf->Method2(20, &s);
if (FAILED(hr))
  throw hr;
sum += s;
```

is roughly equivalent to the following Java code:

```
short sum = 10;
short s = itf.Method2(20);
sum += s;
```

If the HRESULT returned by the method indicates an abnormal result, the Java Virtual Machine will map the HRESULT to a Java exception. The C++ code fragment needs to manually inspect the HRESULT returned by the method and handle the abnormal result accordingly.

Interfaces and IDL

Method definitions in IDL are simply annotated C function prototypes. Interface definitions in IDL require an extension to C, as C has no intrinsic support for the concept. The IDL interface keyword is used to begin the definition of an interface. The interface definition has four components: the interface name, the base interface name, the interface body, and the interface attributes. The interface body is simply a collection of method definitions and supporting type definition statements:

```
[ attribute1, attribute2, ...]
interface IThisInterface : IBaseInterface {
    typedef1;
    typedef2;
       :
    method1;
    method2;
       :
}
```

Every COM interface must have two IDL attributes. The `[object]` attribute is required to indicate that the interface definition is a COM interface and not a DCE-style interface. The second nonoptional attribute indicates the physical name of the interface (in the preceding IDL fragment, `IThisInterface` is the logical name of the interface).

To understand why COM interfaces require a physical name that is distinct from the logical name of the interface, consider the following situation. Two developers independently decide to develop an interface that models a hand-held calculator. The two interface definitions would probably be similar given the common problem domain, but in all likelihood the actual order of method definitions and perhaps the method signatures would be somewhat different. However, both developers would probably choose the same logical name, `ICalculator`.

On a particular end-user's machine, it is possible that a client program implemented against the interface definition from the first developer might run against an object created by the second developer. Because the two interfaces share a common logical name, if the client were to interrogate the object for `ICalculator` support simply using the string `"ICalculator"`, the object would satisfy the request by returning a non-null interface pointer. However, the client's notion of what `ICalculator` looks like is in conflict with what the object believes `ICalculator` to be, and the resultant pointer is incompatible with what the client is expecting. The two interfaces are completely different despite the fact that they share a common logical name.

To eliminate the name collision, all COM interfaces are assigned a unique binary name at design time that is the physical name of the interface. These physical names are called Globally Unique Identifiers or GUIDs (rhymes with *squids*[2]). GUIDs are used throughout COM to name static entities, such as interfaces or implementations. GUIDs are 128-bit extremely large numbers that are guaranteed to be unique in both time and space. COM GUIDs are based on the Universally Unique Identifiers (UUIDs) used in DCE RPC. When used to name COM interfaces, GUIDs are often called Interface IDs or IIDs. Implementations in COM are also named using GUIDs, and in this context, GUIDs are referred to as Class IDs or CLSIDs. When represented textually, GUIDs are always displayed in the following canonical form:

```
BDA4A270-A1BA-11d0-8C2C-0080C73925BA
```

---

[2] The exact pronunciation of GUID is a subject of heated debate among COM developers. Although the COM Specification states that GUID rhymes with *fluid*, not *squid*, the author believes that the COM Specification is simply incorrect, citing the word *languid* as setting the precedent.

These 32 hexadecimal digits represent the 128-bit value of the GUID. Naming interfaces and implementations using GUIDs is important for avoiding name collisions across multiple components.

To create a new GUID, COM exposes an API function that uses a decentralized uniqueness algorithm to produce a new 128-bit value that will never again occur in nature:

```
HRESULT CoCreateGuid(GUID *pguid);
```

The algorithm used by CoCreateGuid uses the local machine's network interface address, wall clock time, and a pair of persistent counters to compensate for clock resolution and abnormal system clock changes (*e.g.,* daylight savings time, manual time adjustment of system clock). If the current machine does not have a network interface, a statistically unique value is synthesized and CoCreateGuid returns a distinguished HRESULT indicating that the value is only statistically unique globally but is truly unique when used only on the local machine. Although calling CoCreateGuid directly is occasionally useful, most developers call it indirectly using the GUIDGEN.EXE SDK tool. Figure 2.3 shows GUIDGEN in action. GUIDGEN calls CoCreateGuid and for-

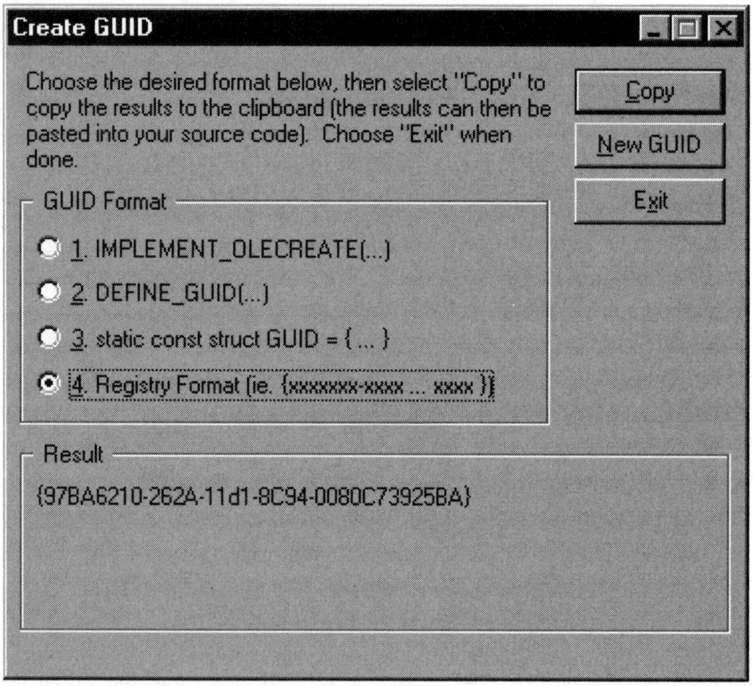

Figure 2.3 GUIDGEN

mats the resultant GUID into one of four formats suitable for inclusion in IDL or C++ source code. When working in IDL, the fourth format (the canonical text form) is what is needed.

To associate the physical name of the interface with its definition in IDL, the second nonoptional interface attribute, [uuid], is used. The [uuid] attribute accepts one parameter, the canonical textual form of the GUID:

```
[object, uuid(BDA4A270-A1BA-11d0-8C2C-0080C73925BA)]
interface ICalculator : IBaseInterface {
  HRESULT Clear(void);
  HRESULT Add([in] long n);
  HRESULT Sum([out, retval] long *pn);
}
```

When programming against the physical name of an interface in C or C++, the IID of a given interface is simply the interface's logical name prepended with the IID_ prefix. For example, the interface ICalculator would have an IID that could be manipulated programmatically using the IDL-generated constant IID_ICalculator. C++ namespaces can be used to deal with symbolic name collisions between interfaces.

Because few C++ compilers can support 128-bit integers, COM defines a C structure to represent the 128-bit value of a GUID and provides aliases for the types IID and CLSID using typedefs:

```
typedef struct _GUID {
  DWORD Data1;
  WORD Data2;
  WORD Data3;
  BYTE Data4[ 8 ];
} GUID;
typedef GUID IID; typedef GUID CLSID;
```

The internal structure of a GUID is irrelevant to most programmers, as the only meaningful operation that can be performed on GUIDs is equivalence testing. To allow GUID values to be passed efficiently as function arguments, COM also provides constant reference aliases for each GUID type:

```
#define REFGUID const GUID&
#define REFIID const IID&
#define REFCLSID const CLSID&
```

To allow comparison of GUID values, COM provides equivalence functions and overloads operator == and operator != for constant GUID references:

```
inline BOOL IsEqualGUID(REFGUID r1, REFGUID r2)
{ return !memcmp(&r1, &r2, sizeof(GUID)); }
#define IsEqualIID(r1, r2) IsEqualGUID((r1), (r2))
#define IsEqualCLSID(r1, r2) IsEqualGUID((r1), (r2))
inline BOOL operator == (REFGUID r1, REFGUID r2)
{ return !memcmp(&r1, &r2, sizeof(GUID)); }
inline BOOL operator != (REFGUID r1, REFGUID r2)
{ return !(r1 == r2); }
```

The actual SDK headers contain conditionally compiled C-compatible versions of the typedefs, macros, and inline functions shown above.

Given that the runtime representations of interface names are GUIDs and not strings, this means that the Dynamic_Cast method described in the previous chapter needs to be revisited. In fact, the entire IExtensibleObject interface needs to be reexamined and converted to its COM-compatible analogue: IUnknown.

IUnknown

The COM interface IUnknown serves the same purpose as the IExtensibleObject interface defined in the previous chapter. The following is the final version of IExtensibleObject that appeared at the end of the chapter:

```
class IExtensibleObject {
public:
  virtual void *Dynamic_Cast(const char* pszType) = 0;
  virtual void DuplicatePointer(void) = 0;
  virtual void DestroyPointer(void) = 0;
}
```

The Dynamic_Cast method was used for runtime type discovery and was analogous to C++'s dynamic_cast operator. The DuplicatePointer method was used to notify the object that an interface pointer had been duplicated. The DestroyPointer method was used to notify the object that an interface pointer had been destroyed and any resources it held could be released. The following is the C++ definition of IUnknown:

```
extern "C" const IID IID_IUnknown;

interface IUnknown {
  virtual HRESULT STDMETHODCALLTYPE
         QueryInterface(REFIID riid, void **ppv) = 0;
  virtual ULONG STDMETHODCALLTYPE AddRef(void) = 0;
  virtual ULONG STDMETHODCALLTYPE Release(void) = 0;
};
```

The SDK header files alias the symbol interface to the C++ struct key-word using the C preprocessor. Because COM interfaces are defined as structs instead of classes, the public keyword is not needed to make the interface methods publicly visible. The STDMETHODCALLTYPE macro is required to produce COM-compliant stack frames for the target platform. Under the Microsoft C++ compiler, this macro expands to __stdcall when targeting Win32 platforms.

IUnknown is functionally equivalent to IExtensibleObject. The QueryInterface method is used for runtime type discovery and is analogous to C++'s dynamic_cast operator. The AddRef method is used to notify the object that an interface pointer has been duplicated. The Release method is used to notify the object that an interface pointer has been destroyed and any resources the object held on behalf of the client can be released. The primary distinction between IUnknown and the interface defined in the previous chapter is that IUnknown uses GUIDs, not strings, to identify interface types at runtime.

The IDL definition of IUnknown can be found in the file unknwn.idl from the SDK include directory:

```
// unknwn.idl - system IDL file

[
  local,
  object,
  uuid(00000000-0000-0000-C000-000000000046)
]
interface IUnknown {
  HRESULT QueryInterface([in] REFIID riid,
                         [out] void **ppv);
  ULONG AddRef(void);
  ULONG Release(void);
}
```

The [local] attribute suppresses the generation of networking code for this interface. This attribute is necessary to relax COM's requirement that all remotable methods must return HRESULTs. As discussed in later chapters, IUnknown is treated specially when dealing with remote objects. Note that the actual IDL interface definitions found in the SDK headers will vary slightly from the definitions found in this text. The actual definitions often contain additional attributes to optimize the generated networking code that are not relevant to the discussion at hand. When in doubt, consult the latest version of the SDK header files for the complete definition.

IUnknown is the root of all COM interfaces. IUnknown is the only COM interface that does not derive from another COM interface. Every other legal COM interface must derive from IUnknown directly or from one other legal COM interface, which itself must derive either from IUnknown directly or from one other legal COM interface. This means that at the binary level all COM interfaces are pointers to vtbls that begin with the three entries QueryInterface, AddRef, and Release. Any interface-specific methods will have vtbl entries that appear after these common three entries.

To derive from an interface in IDL, either define the base interface in the same IDL file or use the import directive to make the external IDL definition of the base interface visible in the current scope:

```
// calculator.idl

[object, uuid(BDA4A270-A1BA-11d0-8C2C-0080C73925BA)]
interface ICalculator : IUnknown {
  import "unknwn.idl"; // bring in def. of IUnknown
  HRESULT Clear(void);
  HRESULT Add([in] long n);
  HRESULT Sum([out, retval] long *pn);
}
```

The import statement can either appear inside the interface definition as shown here or may precede the interface definition at global scope. In either case, the import statement is idempotent and a single IDL file can be imported many times without harm. Because the generated C/C++ header file will need to have the C/C++ versions of the imported IDL file in order to perform the derivation, the import statement in the IDL file will be translated into a #include statement in the generated C/C++ header:

```
// calculator.h - generated by MIDL

// bring in def. of IUnknown
#include "unknwn.h"
```

```
extern "C" const IID IID_ICalculator;
interface ICalculator : public IUnknown {
  virtual HRESULT STDMETHODCALLTYPE Clear(void) = 0;
  virtual HRESULT STDMETHODCALLTYPE Add(long n) = 0;
  virtual HRESULT STDMETHODCALLTYPE Sum(long *pn) =0;
}
```

The MIDL compiler will also generate a C source file that contains the actual definitions of any GUIDs contained in the source IDL file:

```
// calculator_i.c - generated by MIDL
const IID IID_ICalculator =
  { 0xBDA4A270, 0xA1BA, 0x11d0,  { 0x8C, 0x2C,
                0x00, 0x80, 0xC7, 0x39, 0x25, 0xBA } };
```

Every project that will use this interface must either add `calculator_i.c` to its makefile or include `calculator_i.c` in one C or C++ source file using the C preprocessor. If this is not done, then the symbol `IID_ICalculator` will not have storage allocated for its 128-bit value and the project will not link due to unresolved external symbols.

COM imposes no limitations on the depth of an interface hierarchy, provided that the terminal base interface is IUnknown. The following IDL is completely legal and reasonable COM:

```
import "unknwn.idl";

[object, uuid(DF12E151-A29A-11d0-8C2D-0080C73925BA)]
interface IAnimal : IUnknown {
  HRESULT Eat(void);
}

[object, uuid(DF12E152-A29A-11d0-8C2D-0080C73925BA)]
interface ICat : IAnimal {
  HRESULT IgnoreMaster(void);
}

[object, uuid(DF12E153-A29A-11d0-8C2D-0080C73925BA)]
interface IDog : IAnimal {
  HRESULT Bark(void);
}

[object, uuid(DF12E154-A29A-11d0-8C2D-0080C73925BA)]
interface IPug : IDog {
```

```
        HRESULT Snore(void);
    }


    [object, uuid(DF12E155-A29A-11d0-8C2D-0080C73925BA)]
    interface IOldPug : IPug {
      HRESULT SnoreLoudly(void);
    }
```

COM does impose one limitation on interface inheritance: COM interfaces cannot derive directly from more than one interface. The following is not legal in COM:

```
    [object, uuid(DF12E156-A29A-11d0-8C2D-0080C73925BA)]
    interface ICatDog : ICat, IDog { // illegal, multiple bases
      HRESULT Meowbark(void);
    }
```

COM prohibits multiple interface inheritance for a variety of reasons. One reason is that the binary representation of the resultant C++ abstract base class would not be compiler invariant. This would render COM useless as a vendor-neutral binary standard. Another reason stems from the close relationship between COM and DCE RPC. By limiting interface inheritance to one base interface, the mapping between COM interfaces and DCE RPC interface vectors is fairly straightforward. Ultimately, the lack of support for multiple base interfaces is not a limitation, as any implementation can elect to expose as many interfaces as it desires. This means that a COM-based Cat/Dog is still possible at the *implementation* level:

```
    class CatDog : public ICat, public IDog {
      // ...
    };
```

A client that wants to treat an object as a Cat/Dog simply uses QueryInterface to bind both types of pointers to the object. If one of the QueryInterface calls fails, then the object in question is not a Cat/Dog and the client can cope with this as it chooses. Because implementations can expose multiple interfaces, there is little loss of semantic or type information in prohibiting interfaces from having more than one base inheritance.

COM supports a notation technique that expresses which interfaces are available from an object. This technique adheres to the COM philosophy of separation of interface from implementation and does not betray any implementation details of the object other than the list of interfaces it exposes.

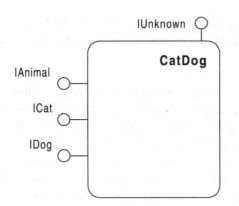

Figure 2.4 COM Standard Notation

Figure 2.4 shows the standard notation for the CatDog class. Note that the only inference one can make from this diagram is that, barring catastrophic failure, CatDog objects will expose the four interfaces ICat, IDog, IAnimal, and IUnknown.

Resource Management and IUnknown

As was the case with DuplicatePointer and DestroyPointer from the previous chapter, IUnknown's AddRef and Release methods have a very simple protocol that all interface pointer users must adhere to. These rules free the client from managing the lifetime of an object when multiple interface pointers may or may not point to the same object. Clients need only follow the simple AddRef/Release rules uniformly for every interface pointer that they encounter and the object will manage its own lifetime.

The Component Object Model Specification contains very precise definitions of the reference counting rules of COM. Understanding the motivation behind these definitions is critical for mastering COM programming in C++. COM's reference counting rules can be distilled down to the following three simple axioms:

1. When a non-null interface pointer is copied from one memory location to another, AddRef should be called to notify the object of the additional reference.

2. Release must be called prior to overwriting a memory location that contains a non-null interface pointer to notify the object that the reference is being destroyed.

3. Redundant calls to AddRef and Release can be optimized away if there is special knowledge about the relationship between two or more memory locations.

The special knowledge axiom exists primarily to allow otherwise confusing situations to map to sane and sensible coding idioms (*e.g.,* temporary call stacks and compiler-generated enregistering of a variable do not need to be reference counted). One could spend months finding special relationships between explicit interface pointer variables in a program and optimize away redundant AddRef and Release calls, but to do so would be folly. The benefits of removing these redundant calls are fairly insignificant, as even in the worst case in which an object is accessed remotely over 8,500 miles of 14.4kbs transmission medium, these redundant calls never leave the caller's thread and rarely require more than a handful of instructions to complete.

Based on the three simple axioms regarding reference counting and interface pointers stated previously, it helps to map these onto actual programming guidelines to determine when and when not to call AddRef and Release. The following are some common situations that require calls to the AddRef method:

A1. When writing a non-null interface pointer to a local variable.

A2. When a callee writes a non-null interface pointer to an [out] or [in, out] parameter of a method or function.

A3. When a callee returns a non-null interface pointer as the physical result of a function.

A4. When writing a non-null interface pointer to a data member of an object.

The common situations that require calls to the Release method include

R1. Prior to overwriting a non-null local variable or data member.

R2. Prior to leaving the scope of a non-null local variable.

R3. When callee overwrites an [in, out] parameter of a method or function whose initial value is non-null. Note that [out] parameters are assumed to be null on input and must never be released by the callee.

R4. Prior to overwriting a non-null data member of an object.

R5. Prior to leaving the destructor of an object that has a non-null interface pointer as a data member.

One common situation in which the special knowledge rule applies arises when passing interface pointers to functions as [in] parameters:

S1. When a caller passes a non-null interface pointer to a function or method through an [in] parameter, no call to AddRef or Release is required, as the lifetime of the temporary variable on the call stack is a proper subset of the lifetime of the expression used to initialize the formal argument.

These ten guidelines capture situations that occur over and over again in COM programming and are well worth remembering.

To make the rules of COM reference counting concrete, assume that there is a global function that returns an interface pointer to an object:

```
void GetObject([out] IUnknown **ppUnk);
```

and that there is another global function that performs some useful work on an object:

```
void UseObject([in] IUnknown *pUnk);
```

The following code uses these routines to manipulate some objects and return an interface pointer to its caller. The guideline that applies is shown in comments at each applicable statement:

```
void GetAndUse(/* [out] */ IUnknown ** ppUnkOut) {
  IUnknown *pUnk1 = 0, *pUnk2 = 0;
  *ppUnkOut = 0;                                      // R3

// get pointers to one (or two) objects
  GetObject(&pUnk1);                                  // A2
  GetObject(&pUnk2);                                  // A2

// set pUnk2 to point to first object
  if (pUnk2)  pUnk2->Release();                       // R1
  if (pUnk2 = pUnk1) pUnk2->AddRef();                 // A1

// pass pUnk2 to some other function
  UseObject(pUnk2);                                   // S1

// return pUnk2 to caller using ppUnkOut parameter
  if (*ppUnkOut = pUnk2)  (*ppUnkOut)->AddRef();      // A2

// falling out of scope so clean up
  if (pUnk1) pUnk1->Release();                        // R2
```

```
    if (pUnk2) pUnk2->Release();                        // R2
}
```

It is important to note that the A2 guideline applies twice in the preceding code, but from two different perspectives. When calling GetObject, the code acts as the caller and GetObject's implementation is the callee. This means that the implementation of GetObject is responsible for calling AddRef through the [out] parameter. When overwriting the memory referred to by ppUnkOut, the code acts as callee and correctly calls AddRef through the interface pointer prior to returning control to the caller.

There are some subtleties regarding AddRef and Release that bear discussion. Both AddRef and Release are prototyped to return a 32-bit unsigned integer. This integer reflects the total number of outstanding references *after* performing the AddRef or Release operation. However, for a variety of reasons related to multithreading, remote access, and multiprocessor architectures, this value is not guaranteed to be an accurate representation of the total number of outstanding interface pointers and the client should ignore it except for diagnostic purposes during debugging.

The only result that has any meaning is when Release returns zero. A zero result from Release does reliably indicate that the object is no longer valid in any way. However, the converse cannot be implied. That is, when Release returns nonzero, one cannot assume that the object is still valid. In fact, once Release has been called on an interface pointer the same number of times that AddRef has been called on the same pointer, the interface pointer is invalid and no longer guaranteed to point to a valid object. Although it is possible that the object is still valid due to other outstanding pointers, this is simply an accident and will likely change at the most embarrassing moment. One strategy for ensuring that interface pointers are not used once released is to set them to null immediately after calling the Release method:

```
inline void SafeRelease(IUnknown * &rpUnk) {
  if (rpUnk) {
    rpUnk->Release();
    rpUnk = 0; // rpUnk passed by reference
  }
}
```

When this technique is used, any use of the interface pointer after its release will trigger an access violation immediately. This error could then be reproduced reliably and, one hopes, caught during development.

One additional subtlety related to AddRef and Release arises on exiting a block of code. The GetAndUse function shown previously had only one exit point. This meant that the statements that released the interface pointers at the end of the function would always execute prior to completion of the function. If the function somehow exits prior to reaching these statements because either an explicit return statement or, more problematically, an unhandled C++ exception, these final statements are bypassed and any resources held by the unreleased interface pointers are leaked for the duration of the client's program. This implies that COM interface pointers should be treated with care, especially when used in environments known to use C++ exceptions. This is no different from any other system resource one comes in contact with, such as semaphores or dynamically allocated memory. Later in this chapter a COM smart pointer is discussed which ensures that Release is called in all situations.

Type Coercion and IUnknown

The previous chapter described the motivations for needing runtime type discovery in a dynamically composed system. The C++ language provides a reasonable mechanism for dynamic type discovery through its dynamic_cast operator. Although this language feature has a proprietary implementation for each compiler, the previous chapter was able to leverage the concept by adding an explicit method to each interface that performs the semantic equivalent of dynamic_cast. COM's IUnknown interface also has such a method and it is called QueryInterface. The following is the IDL description of QueryInterface:

```
HRESULT QueryInterface([in] REFIID riid,
                       [out] void **ppv);
```

The first parameter (riid) is the physical name of the interface being requested. The second parameter (ppv) points to an interface pointer variable that on successful completion will contain the requested interface pointer.

In response to a QueryInterface request, if the object does not support the requested interface type, it must return E_NOINTERFACE after setting *ppv to null. If the object does support the requested interface, it must overwrite *ppv with a pointer of the requested type and return the HRESULT S_OK. Because ppv is an [out] parameter, the implementation of QueryInterface must AddRef the resultant pointer prior to returning control to the caller (see guideline A2 from earlier in this chapter). This AddRef call must be matched by a Release call from the client. The following shows runtime type discovery using C++'s dynamic_cast operator based on the Dog/Cat type hierarchy described earlier in this chapter:

```
void TryToSnoreAndIgnore(/* [in] */ IUnknown *pUnk) {
  IPug *pPug = 0;
  pPug = dynamic_cast<IPug*>(pUnk);
  if (pPug) // the object is Pug-compatible
    pPug->Snore();

  ICat *pCat = 0;
  pCat = dynamic_cast<ICat*>(pUnk);
  if (pCat) // the object is Cat-compatible
    pCat->IgnoreMaster();
}
```

If the object presented to this function is both ICat and IPug compatible, then both functionalities are exploited. If the object is not in fact ICat or IPug compatible, then this particular function simply ignores the missing aspect(s) of the object. The following is the semantically equivalent version using QueryInterface:

```
void TryToSnoreAndIgnore(/* [in] */ IUnknown *pUnk) {
  HRESULT hr;
  IPug *pPug = 0;
  hr = pUnk->QueryInterface(IID_IPug, (void**)&pPug);
  if (SUCCEEDED(hr)) {// the object is Pug-compatible
    pPug->Snore();
    pPug->Release(); // R2
  }

  ICat *pCat = 0;
  hr = pUnk->QueryInterface(IID_ICat, (void**)&pCat);
  if (SUCCEEDED(hr)) {// the object is Cat-compatible
    pCat->IgnoreMaster();
    pCat->Release(); // R2
  }
}
```

Although there are obvious syntactic differences, the only significant difference between the two code fragments is that the QueryInterface-based version adheres to COM's reference counting rules.

There are some subtleties regarding QueryInterface and its usage. QueryInterface can only return pointers to the same COM object. Chapter 4 is dedicated to explaining every nuance of this statement. However, it is worth noting up front that the client must not treat AddRef and Release as operations on an *object*. Instead, they must be treated as operations on an *interface pointer*. That means that the following code is illegal:

```
void BadCOMCode(/*[in]*/ IUnknown *pUnk) {
  ICat *pCat = 0;  IPug *pPug = 0;
  HRESULT hr;
  hr = pUnk->QueryInterface(IID_ICat, (void**)&pCat);
  if (FAILED(hr)) goto cleanup;
  hr = pUnk->QueryInterface(IID_IPug, (void**)&pPug);
  if (FAILED(hr)) goto cleanup;
  pPug->Bark(); pCat->IgnoreMaster();
cleanup:
  if (pCat) pUnk->Release(); // pCat got AddRefed in QI
  if (pPug) pUnk->Release(); // pDog got AddRefed in QI
}
```

Despite the fact that pCat, pPug, and pUnk all point to the same object, it is illegal for the client to counterbalance the AddRefs that occurred on pPug and pCat when QueryInterface was called with calls to Release through pUnk. The correct form of this code is

```
cleanup:
  if (pCat) pCat->Release(); // use AddRefed ptr
  if (pPug) pPug->Release(); // use AddRefed ptr
```

Here, Release is called through exactly the same *interface pointer* that received the AddRef (which happened implicitly when the pointer was returned from QueryInterface). This requirement affords the developer a great deal of flexibility when implementing an object. For example, an object may elect to perform per-interface reference counting to allow aggressive reclamation of resources that are used only by a particular interface on an object.

One additional subtlety related to QueryInterface concerns its second parameter, which is of type void **. It is very ironic that QueryInterface, the underpinning of the COM type system, has a fairly type-unsafe prototype in C++:

```
HRESULT __stdcall QueryInterface(REFIID riid,
                                 void** ppv);
```

As previously described, clients call QueryInterface providing the object with a pointer to an interface pointer as the second parameter together with an IID that identifies the type of interface pointer that is expected:

```
IPug *pPug = 0;
hr = punk->QueryInterface(IID_IPug, (void**)&pPug);
```

Unfortunately, the following looks equally correct to the C++ compiler:

```
IPug *pPug = 0;
hr = punk->QueryInterface(IID_ICat, (void**)&pPug);
```

This more subtle variation also compiles correctly:

```
IPug *pPug = 0;
hr = punk->QueryInterface(IID_IPug, (void**)pPug);
```

Given that the rules of inheritance do not apply to pointers, this alternative definition of QueryInterface does not alleviate the problem:

```
HRESULT QueryInterface(REFIID riid, IUnknown** ppv);
```

as implicit upcasting applies only to instances and pointers to instances, not pointers to pointers to instances:

```
IDerived **ppd;
IBase **ppb = ppd; // illegal
```

This same limitation applies to references to pointers as well. The following alternative definition is arguably more convenient for clients to use:

```
HRESULT QueryInterface(const IID& riid, void* ppv);
```

as it allows clients to forgo the cast. Unfortunately, this solution does not reduce the number of errors (both of the preceding errors are still possible) and, by eliminating the need for a cast, removes a visual indicator that C++ type safety might be in jeopardy. Given the desired semantics of QueryInterface, the argument types Microsoft chose are reasonable, if not type safe or elegant. The simplest way to avoid QueryInterface-related errors is to always be certain that the IID matches the type of the interface pointer that is passed as the second parameter to QueryInterface. In effect, the first parameter to

`QueryInterface` describes the "shape" of the second parameter's pointer type. This relationship can be enforced at compile time through the use of the following C preprocessor macro:

```
#define IID_PPV_ARG(Type, Expr) IID_##Type, \
    reinterpret_cast<void**>(static_cast<Type **>(Expr))
```

Given this macro,[3] the compiler will ensure that the expression used in the following call to `QueryInterface` is of the correct type and that the appropriate level of indirection is in use:

```
IPug *pPug = 0;
hr = punk->QueryInterface(IID_PPV_ARG(IPug, &pPug));
```

This macro closes the hole introduced by the `void **` parameter without imposing any runtime costs.

Implementing IUnknown

Given the client-side usage patterns that have been described, implementing the methods of `IUnknown` is fairly straightforward. Assume the Dog/Cat type hierarchy previously described. To define a C++ class that implements the `IPug` and `ICat` interfaces, one simply needs to add the most derived versions of each interface to the list of base classes:

```
class PugCat : public IPug, public ICat
```

When using derivation, the C++ compiler ensures that the binary layout of the derived class will be compatible with each base class. For the `PugCat` class, this means that all `PugCat` objects will contain a vptr that points to an `IPug`-compatible vtbl. `PugCat` objects will also contain a vptr that points to a second `ICat`-compatible vtbl. Figure 2.5 illustrates how interfaces as base classes relate to object layout.

Because all member functions in COM interface definitions are pure virtual, the derived class must provide an implementation of every method that is present in any of its interfaces. Methods that are common to two or more interfaces (*e.g.,* `QueryInterface`, `AddRef`, etc.) need to be implemented only once,

---

[3] Which was highly inspired by a discussion between the author and Tye McQueen during a COM seminar.

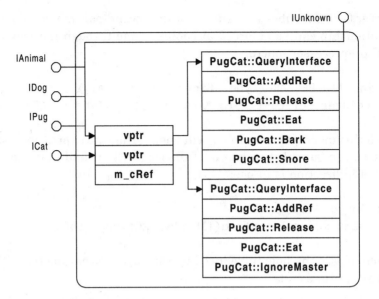

Figure 2.5 PugCat

as the compiler and linker will initialize each vtbl to point to the single method implementation. This is a natural side effect of using multiple inheritance in C++.

The following is a class definition that produces objects that support the IPug and ICat interfaces:

```
class PugCat : public IPug, public ICat {
  LONG m_cRef;
protected:
  virtual ~PugCat(void);
public:
  PugCat(void);
// IUnknown methods
  STDMETHODIMP QueryInterface(REFIID riid,
                              void **ppv);
  STDMETHODIMP_(ULONG) AddRef(void);
  STDMETHODIMP_(ULONG) Release(void);
// IAnimal methods
  STDMETHODIMP Eat(void);
// IDog methods
  STDMETHODIMP Bark(void);
```

```
// IPug methods
  STDMETHODIMP Snore(void);
// ICat methods
  STDMETHODIMP IgnoreMaster(void);
};
```

Note that the class must implement every method that is defined in each interface it derives from as well as those defined in any implied base interfaces (*e.g.,* IDog, IAnimal). The use of the macros STDMETHODIMP and STDMETHODIMP_ is required to produce COM-compliant stack frames. When targeting Win32 platforms using the Microsoft C++ compiler, the SDK headers define these two macros as follows:

```
#define STDMETHODIMP  HRESULT __stdcall
#define STDMETHODIMP_(type) type __stdcall
```

The SDK header files also define the macros STDMETHOD and STDMETHOD_, which can be used when defining interfaces without the IDL compiler. These two macros are not needed in mainstream COM programming.

Implementing AddRef and Release is extremely straightforward. The m_cRef data member keeps track of how many outstanding interface pointers are held on the object. The constructor of the class initializes the reference count to a well-known state:

```
PugCat::PugCat(void)
  : m_cRef(0) // initialize reference count to zero
{
}
```

The class's implementation of AddRef notes that the caller has duplicated an interface pointer by incrementing the reference count. The updated reference count is returned for diagnostic purposes:

```
STDMETHODIMP_(ULONG) AddRef(void) {
  return ++m_cRef;
}
```

The implementation of Release notes the destruction of an interface pointer by simply decrementing the reference count and taking the appropriate action when the reference count reaches zero. For heap-based objects, this means calling the delete operator to destroy the object:

```
STDMETHODIMP_(ULONG) Release(void) {
  LONG res = --m_cRef;
  if (res == 0)
    delete this;
  return res;
}
```

The use of a temporary variable to cache the updated reference count is necessary, as it is illegal to refer to an object's data members after the object has been destroyed.

Notice that the implementations of AddRef and Release that have been shown use the native C++ increment and decrement operators. For a naïve implementation, this is completely reasonable, as COM will not allow more than one thread to access an object unless the object implementor explicitly enables multithreaded access (why and how an implementor would do this are described in detail in Chapter 5). For objects that will be accessed in a multithreaded environment, the Win32 InterlockedIncrement and InterlockedDecrement routines should be used to adjust the reference count atomically:

```
STDMETHODIMP_(ULONG) AddRef(void) {
  return InterlockedIncrement(&m_cRef);
}
STDMETHODIMP_(ULONG) Release(void) {
  LONG res = InterlockedDecrement(&m_cRef);
  if (res == 0)
    delete this;
  return res;
}
```

This code is slightly less efficient than the versions using the native C++ operators. In general, however, it is a reasonable practice to always use the slightly less efficient InterlockedIncrement/InterlockedDecrement versions, as they are known to be safe in all contexts and relieve the developer from maintaining two versions of essentially the same code.

The implementations of AddRef and Release that have been shown assume that the object will only be allocated on the heap using the C++ new operator. The class definition made the destructor a protected operation to ensure that no instances of the class could be defined in any other way. However, it is sometimes desirable to have objects that are not allocated on the heap. For these objects, calling delete in their final Release invocation would be disastrous. Because the only reason the object kept a reference count in the first place was to call delete this, it is legal to optimize away the reference count for non-heap-based objects:

```
STDMETHODIMP_(ULONG) GlobalVar::AddRef(void) {
  return 2;  // any non-zero value is legal
}

STDMETHODIMP_(ULONG) GlobalVar::Release(void) {
  return 1; // any non-zero value is legal
}
```

This implementation takes advantage of the fact that the results of AddRef and Release are only advisory and do not have to be accurate.

With the implementation of AddRef and Release in place, the only remaining IUnknown method to implement is QueryInterface. Implementations of QueryInterface must traverse the type hierarchy of the object and use static typecasts to return the correct pointer type for all supported interfaces. For the class definition of PugCat shown previously, the following is a correct implementation of QueryInterface:

```
STDMETHODIMP PugCat::QueryInterface(REFIID riid,
                                    void **ppv) {
  assert(ppv != 0); // or return E_POINTER in production
  if (riid == IID_IPug)
    *ppv = static_cast<IPug*>(this);
  else if (riid == IID_IDog)
    *ppv = static_cast<IDog*>(this);
  else if (riid == IID_IAnimal) // cat or pug?
    *ppv = static_cast<IDog*>(this);
  else if (riid == IID_IUnknown) // cat or pug?
    *ppv = static_cast<IDog*>(this);
  else if (riid == IID_ICat)
    *ppv = static_cast<ICat*>(this);
  else { // unsupported interface
    *ppv = 0;
    return E_NOINTERFACE;
  }
// if we reach this point, *ppv is non-null
// and must be AddRef'ed (guideline A2)
  reinterpret_cast<IUnknown*>(*ppv)->AddRef();
  return S_OK;
}
```

The use of static_cast is recommended over using traditional C-style casts:

```
*ppv = (IPug*)this;
```

as the static_cast version will cause a compile-time error if the attempted cast does not correspond to an actual base class.

Note that in the QueryInterface implementation shown here, when a request is made for an interface that is supported by more than one base interface (*e.g.,* IUnknown, IAnimal), the type-cast must explicitly select a more precise base class. For the class PugCat, the following innocent-looking code will not compile:

```
if (riid == IID_IUnknown)
  *ppv = static_cast<IUnknown*>(this);
```

As was shown in the case of FastString and IExtensibleObject from the previous chapter, this code will not compile because the cast is ambiguous and could be satisfied by using more than one base class. Instead, the implementation needs to select a more precise type to use in the cast:

```
if (riid == IID_IUnknown)
  *ppv = static_cast<IDog*>(this);
```

or

```
if (riid == IID_IUnknown)
  *ppv = static_cast<ICat*>(this);
```

Either of these two code fragments is legal for the implementation of PugCat. The former version is preferred, as many compilers produce slightly more efficient code when the leftmost base class is used.[4]

Using COM Interface Pointers

C++ programmers must use the methods of IUnknown explicitly because the C++ language mapping of COM does not provide a runtime layer between the client's code and the object's code. To this end, IUnknown is simply a set of promises that all COM programmers make to one another. In general, this

---

[4] The entries in the vtbl for the leftmost base class do not require an adjustor thunk to adjust the this pointer prior to entering the method implementation. This applies only to compilers that use adjustor thunks and place the leftmost base at the top of the object layout. The Microsoft C++ compiler fits this description.

works to the C++ programmer's advantage, as C++ can produce code that is potentially more performant than languages that require a runtime layer to deal with COM.

Unlike C++ programmers, Visual Basic and Java programmers never see QueryInterface, AddRef, or Release. For these two languages, the details of IUnknown are hidden deep below each language's supporting virtual machine. In Java, QueryInterface simply maps to a type-cast:

```java
public void TryToSnoreAndIgnore(Object obj) {
  IPug pug;
  try {
    pug = (IPug)obj; // VM calls QueryInterface
    pug.Snore();
  } catch (Throwable ex) {
    // ignore method or QI failures
  }
  ICat cat;
  try {
    cat = (ICat)obj; // VM calls QueryInterface
    cat.IgnoreMaster();
  } catch (Throwable ex) {
    // ignore method or QI failures
  }
}
```

Visual Basic does not require clients to type-cast. Instead, when an interface pointer is assigned to a type-incompatible variable, the Visual Basic VM silently calls QueryInterface on behalf of the client:

```vb
Sub TryToSnoreAndIgnore(obj as Object)
  On Error Resume Next ' ignore errors
  Dim pug as IPug
  Set pug = obj ' VM calls QueryInterface
  If Not (pug is Nothing) Then
    pug.Snore
  End if
  Dim cat as ICat
  Set cat = obj ' VM calls QueryInterface
  If Not (cat is Nothing) Then
    cat.IgnoreMaster
  End if
End Sub
```

Both the Visual Basic and Java virtual machines will raise distinguished exceptions when QueryInterface fails. In both environments, the virtual machine automatically maps the language's concept of variable liveness to explicit calls to AddRef and Release, freeing the client programmer from this detail as well.

One technique that can potentially simplify using COM interface pointers from C++ is to hide them behind a smart pointer class, eliminating the need to make raw IUnknown calls. Ideally, a COM smart interface pointer would

1. Correctly handle AddRef/Release calls during assignment.

2. Auto-release the interface in a destructor, reducing the potential for resource leaks and improving exception safety.

3. Leverage the C++ type system to simplify calls to QueryInterface.

4. Transparently replace raw interface pointers in legacy code *without compromising program correctness*.

This last clause turns out to be a tremendously hard problem to solve. The Internet is littered with COM smart pointers that support transparent replacement of raw pointers but introduce as many potential errors as they claim to eliminate. In fact, Visual C++ 5.0 ships with three such pointers (one for MFC, one for ATL, one for its Direct-to-COM support) that are very easy to use both correctly and incorrectly. Two articles that document many of the potential hazards of using smart pointers appeared in the September 1995 and February 1996 issues of *C++ Report*.[5] The source code that accompanies this book contains a COM smart pointer, developed as a product of writing these two articles. It attempts to address the common errors that occur in both raw and smart COM pointers. This smart pointer class, SmartInterface, takes two template parameters: the C++ type of the interface and a pointer to the corresponding IID. All access to IUnknown methods is hidden through overloaded operators:

```
#include "smartif.h"

void TryToSnoreAndIgnore(/* [in] */ IUnknown *pUnk) {
// copy constructor calls QueryInterface
   SmartInterface<IPug, &IID_IPug> pPug = pUnk;
```

---

[5] These *C++ Report* articles are available at http://www.develop.com/dbox/cxx/InterfacePtr.htm and http://www.develop.com/dbox/cxx/SmartPtr.htm.

```
   if (pPug) // typecast operator returns null-ness
     pPug->Snore(); // operator-> returns safe raw ptr

// copy constructor calls QueryInterface
   SmartInterface<ICat, &IID_ICat> pCat = pUnk;
   if (pCat) // typecast operator returns null-ness
     pCat->IgnoreMaster();
// operator-> returns safe raw ptr
// destructors release held pointers on leaving scope
}
```

Smart pointers seem very attractive at first glance but can be very dangerous as they lull the programmer into a dream-like state in which nothing COM-related seems to matter. Smart pointers do solve real problems, especially in the face of exceptions; however, when used carelessly, smart pointers can introduce as many defects as they prevent. For example, many smart pointers allow any interface method to be accessed via the smart pointer's operator ->. Unfortunately, this allows clients to call Release via the arrow operator without notifying the underlying smart pointer that its automatic Release call in its destructor is now redundant and not allowed.

Optimizing QueryInterface

The de facto implementation of QueryInterface shown earlier in this chapter is fairly straightforward and easily maintained by anyone who has a basic understanding of COM and C++. However, many production environments and frameworks favor a data-driven implementation to achieve greater extensibility and better performance due to code size reduction. Such implementations assume that each COM-compliant class provides a table that maps each supported IID onto some aspect of the object using fixed offsets or some other technique. In essence, the implementation of QueryInterface shown earlier in this chapter builds a table based on the compiled machine code for each sequential if statement and the fixed offsets are calculated using the static_cast operator (static_cast simply adds the offset of the base class to find the type-compatible vptr).

To implement a table-driven QueryInterface, one first needs to define what the table will contain. At a minimum, each table entry will need to contain a pointer to an IID and some additional state that allows the implementation to find the object's vptr for the requested interface. For maximum flexibility, storing a function pointer at each table entry would support the addition of new techniques for finding interfaces beyond the normal offset calculation used when simply casting to a base class. The source code that accompanies this book includes a header file, inttable.h, that defines interface table entries as follows:

```
// inttable.h  (book-specific header file) ///////

// typedef for extensibility function
typedef HRESULT (*INTERFACE_FINDER)
(void *pThis, DWORD dwData, REFIID riid, void **ppv);

// pseudo-function to indicate entry is just offset
#define ENTRY_IS_OFFSET INTERFACE_FINDER(-1)

// basic table layout
typedef struct _INTERFACE_ENTRY
{
    const IID * pIID;            // the IID to match
    INTERFACE_FINDER pfnFinder;  // finder function
    DWORD         dwData;        // offset/aux data
} INTERFACE_ENTRY;
```

The header file also contains the following macros for composing interface tables inside a class definition:

```
// inttable.h  (book-specific header file) ///////

#define BASE_OFFSET(ClassName, BaseName) \
(DWORD(static_cast<BaseName*>(reinterpret_cast\
<ClassName*>(0x10000000))) - 0x10000000)
#define BEGIN_INTERFACE_TABLE(ClassName) \
typedef ClassName _ITCls;\
const INTERFACE_ENTRY *GetInterfaceTable(void) {\
    static const INTERFACE_ENTRY table[] = {\

#define IMPLEMENTS_INTERFACE(Itf) \
{&IID_##Itf,ENTRY_IS_OFFSET,BASE_OFFSET(_ITCls,Itf)},

#define IMPLEMENTS_INTERFACE_AS(req, Itf) \
{&IID_##req,ENTRY_IS_OFFSET,BASE_OFFSET(_ITCls,Itf)},
```

```
#define END_INTERFACE_TABLE() \
        { 0, 0, 0 } }; return table; }
```

All that is required is a routine that can parse an interface table in response to a QueryInterface request. The file inttable.cpp contains such a
function:

```cpp
// inttable.cpp   (book-specific source file) ///////

HRESULT InterfaceTableQueryInterface(void *pThis,
                const INTERFACE_ENTRY *pTable,
                REFIID riid, void **ppv) {
  if (InlineIsEqualGUID(riid, IID_IUnknown)) {
    // first entry must be an offset
    *ppv = (char*)pThis + pTable->dwData;
    ((IUnknown*)(*ppv))->AddRef();   // A2
    return S_OK;
  }
  else {
    HRESULT hr = E_NOINTERFACE;
    while (pTable->pfnFinder) { // null fn ptr == EOT
      if (!pTable->pIID || InlineIsEqualGUID(riid,
                                    *pTable->pIID)) {
        if (pTable->pfnFinder == ENTRY_IS_OFFSET) {
          *ppv = (char*)pThis + pTable->dwData;
          ((IUnknown*)(*ppv))->AddRef(); // A2
          hr = S_OK;
          break;
        }
        else {
          hr = pTable->pfnFinder(pThis,
                        pTable->dwData, riid, ppv);
          if (hr == S_OK)   break;
        }
      }
      pTable++;
    }
    if (hr != S_OK) *ppv = 0;
    return hr;
  }
}
```

When given a pointer to the object being queried, InterfaceTable-QueryInterface walks through a table looking for a table entry that matches the requested IID and either adds the corresponding offset or calls the corresponding function, whichever is appropriate. The preceding code uses an optimized version of IsEqualGUID that produces somewhat larger code but results in an overall speedup of roughly 20 to 30 percent over the de facto non-table-driven implementation. Since the code for InterfaceTableQueryInterface will appear only once in the target executable, this is a very worthwhile trade-off.

It is very simple to automate COM support for any C++ class based on this table-driven approach simply by using the C preprocessor. The following excerpt from impunk.h defines QueryInterface, AddRef, and Release for an object that uses interface tables and is allocated on the heap:

```
// impunk.h (book-specific header file) ////////

// AUTO_LONG is just a long that constructs to zero
struct AUTO_LONG {
    LONG value;
    AUTO_LONG(void) : value(0) {}
};
#define IMPLEMENT_UNKNOWN(ClassName) \
AUTO_LONG m_cRef;\
STDMETHODIMP QueryInterface(REFIID riid,void **ppv){\
    return InterfaceTableQueryInterface(this,\
                    GetInterfaceTable(), riid, ppv);\
}\
STDMETHODIMP_(ULONG) AddRef(void) { \
    return InterlockedIncrement(&m_cRef.value); \
}\
STDMETHODIMP_(ULONG) Release(void) {\
    ULONG res = InterlockedDecrement(&m_cRef.value);\
    if (res == 0) \
        delete this;\
    return res;\
}\
```

The actual header file contains additional macros to support non-heap-based objects as well.

To implement the PugCat example from earlier in this chapter, one simply needs to remove the current implementations of QueryInterface, AddRef, and Release and insert the appropriate macros:

```
class PugCat : public IPug, public ICat {
protected:
  virtual ~PugCat(void);
public:
  PugCat(void);
// IUnknown methods
  IMPLEMENT_UNKNOWN(PugCat)
  BEGIN_INTERFACE_TABLE(PugCat)
    IMPLEMENTS_INTERFACE(IPug)
    IMPLEMENTS_INTERFACE(IDog)
    IMPLEMENTS_INTERFACE_AS(IAnimal,IDog)
    IMPLEMENTS_INTERFACE(ICat)
  END_INTERFACE_TABLE()
// IAnimal methods
  STDMETHODIMP Eat(void);
// IDog methods
  STDMETHODIMP Bark(void);
// IPug methods
  STDMETHODIMP Snore(void);
// ICat methods
  STDMETHODIMP IgnoreMaster(void);
};
```

When these preprocessor macros are used, no additional code is required
to support IUnknown. All that remains to be done is to implement the actual
interface methods that make this class unique.

Data Types

All COM interfaces must be defined in IDL. IDL allows fairly complex data
types to be described in a language- and platform-neutral manner. Figure 2.6
shows the base types that are supported by IDL and their mappings onto the
C, Java, and Visual Basic languages. The integral and floating point types are
fairly self-explanatory. The first "interesting" data types one encounters in
COM programming are characters and strings.

All characters in COM are represented using the OLECHAR data type.
Under Windows NT, Windows 95, Win32s, and Solaris, OLECHAR is simply a
typedef to the C data type wchar_t. Consult the local documentation for the
specifics regarding other platforms. Win32 platforms use the wchar_t data

Language	IDL	Microsoft C++	Visual Basic	Microsoft Java
Base Types	boolean	unsigned char	unsupported	char
	byte	unsigned char	unsupported	char
	small	char	unsupported	char
	short	short	Integer	short
	long	long	Long	int
	hyper	__int64	unsupported	long
	float	float	Single	float
	double	double	Double	double
	char	unsigned char	unsupported	char
	wchar_t	wchar_t	Integer	short
	enum	enum	Enum	int
	Interface Pointer	Interface Pointer	Interface Ref.	Interface Ref.
Extended Types	VARIANT	VARIANT	Variant	ms.com.Variant
	BSTR	BSTR	String	java.lang.String
	VARIANT_BOOL	short [-1/0]	Boolean [True/False]	boolean [true/false]

Figure 2.6 COM Base Types

type to represent 16-bit Unicode characters.[6] Because pointer types in IDL are assumed to point to single instances, not arrays, IDL introduces the [string] attribute to indicate that a pointer points to a null-terminated array of characters:

```
HRESULT Method([in, string] const OLECHAR *pwsz);
```

To allow OLECHAR-compliant string and character literals to be defined, COM provides the OLESTR macro that prepends the L to a string or character constant, informing the compiler that the constant is of type wchar_t. For example, the following is the correct way to initialize an OLECHAR pointer using a string literal:

```
const OLECHAR *pwsz = OLESTR("Hello");
```

---

[6] The OLECHAR type was chosen in favor of the common TCHAR data type used by the Win32 API to alleviate the need to support two versions of each interface (CHAR and WCHAR). By supporting only one character type, object developers are decoupled from the state of the UNICODE preprocessor symbol used by their clients.

Under Win32 or Solaris, this is equivalent to

```
const wchar_t *pwsz = L"Hello";
```

The former is preferred, as it will reliably compile under all platforms.

Because it is often necessary to copy wchar_t-based strings to normal char-based buffers, the C runtime library provides two conversion routines:

```
size_t mbstowcs(wchar_t *pwsz, const char *psz, int cch);
size_t wcstombs(char *psz, const wchar_t *pwsz, int cch);
```

These two routines work similarly to the strncpy C runtime routine, except that these routines widen or narrow the string as part of the copy operation. The following code demonstrates how an OLECHAR-based method parameter can be copied to a char-based data member:

```
class BigDog : public ILabrador {
  char m_szName[1024];
public:
  STDMETHODIMP SetName(/*[in,string]*/ const OLECHAR *pwsz){
    HRESULT hr = S_OK;
    size_t cb = wcstombs(m_szName, pwsz, 1024);
// check for buffer overflow or bad conversion
    if (cb == sizeof(m_szName) || cb == (size_t)-1) {
      m_szName[0] = 0;
      hr = E_INVALIDARG;
    }
    return hr;
  }
};
```

The preceding code is fairly simple, although the programmer does need to be aware that two distinct character types are in use. A somewhat more complex (and common) case is conversion between OLECHAR and the Win32 TCHAR data type. As TCHAR is conditionally compiled to either char or wchar_t, the method implementation would need to properly deal with both scenarios:

```
class BigDog : public ILabrador {
  TCHAR m_szName[1024]; // note TCHAR-based string
public:
  STDMETHODIMP SetName(/*[in,string]*/ const OLECHAR *pwsz){
```

```
        HRESULT hr = S_OK;
#ifdef UNICODE
// Unicode build (TCHAR == wchar_t)
        wcsncpy(m_szName, pwsz, 1024);
// check for buffer overflow
        if (m_szName[1023] != 0) {
          m_szName[0] = 0;
          hr = E_INVALIDARG;
        }
#else
// Non-Unicode build (TCHAR == char)
        size_t cb = wcstombs(m_szName, pwsz, 1024);
// check for buffer overflow or bad conversion
        if (cb == sizeof(m_szName) || cb == (size_t)-1) {
          m_szName[0] = 0;
          hr = E_INVALIDARG;
        }
#endif
      return hr;
   }
};
```

Obviously, handling OLECHAR-to-TCHAR conversions is much more complex. Unfortunately, it is the most common scenario in Win32-based COM programming.

One approach to simplifying text conversion is to leverage the C++ type system and use function overloading to select the correct string routine based on parameter types. The header file ustring.h that accompanies this book contains a family of string library routines that parallel the standard C library routines found in string.h. For example, the strncpy function has four corresponding routines based on either parameter being of either of the two possible character types (wchar_t or char):

```
// from ustring.h (book-specific header) //////
inline bool ustrncpy(char *p1, const wchar_t *p2, size_t c){
    size_t cb = wcstombs(p1, p2, c);
    return cb != c && cb != (size_t)-1;
}
inline bool ustrncpy(wchar_t *p1,const wchar_t*p2,size_t c){
    wcsncpy(p1, p2, c);
    return p1[c - 1] == 0;
}
```

```
inline bool ustrncpy(char *p1, const char *p2, size_t c) {
    strncpy(p1, p2, c);
    return p1[c - 1] == 0;
}
inline bool ustrncpy(wchar_t *p1, const char *p2, size_t c){
    size_t cch = mbstowcs(p1, p2, c);
    return cch != c && cch != (size_t)-1;
}
```

Note that for any combination of character types, a corresponding overload of ustrncpy can be found and that the result indicates whether or not
the complete string was copied or converted. As these routines are declared
as inline, their use incurs no performance penalty. With these routines in
place, the preceding code fragment is considerably simpler and requires no
conditional compilation:

```
class BigDog : public ILabrador {
  TCHAR m_szName[1024]; // note TCHAR-based string
public:
  STDMETHODIMP SetName(/*[in,string]*/ const OLECHAR *pwsz){
    HRESULT hr = S_OK;
// use book-specific overloaded ustrncpy to copy or convert
    if (!ustrncpy(m_szName, pwsz, 1024)) {
      m_szName[0] = 0;
      hr = E_INVALIDARG;
    }
    return hr;
  }
};
```

Corresponding overloads for strlen, strcpy, and strcat are also included in
the ustring.h header file.

For copying strings from one buffer to another as shown, the solution proposed on the basis of overloaded library routines yields the best performance,
smallest code, and least programmer overhead. However, one common scenario arises when using COM and Win32 API functions together that does not
lend itself to using this technique. Consider the following code fragment,
which reads a string from an edit control and converts it to an IID:

```
HRESULT IIDFromHWND(HWND hwnd, IID& riid) {
  TCHAR szEditText[1024];
// call a TCHAR-based Win32 routine
```

```
    GetWindowText(hwnd, szEditText, 1024);
// call an OLECHAR-based COM routine
    return IIDFromString(szEditText, &riid);
}
```

Assuming that the code is compiled with the C preprocessor symbol UNICODE defined, this code works perfectly well, as both TCHAR and OLECHAR are simply aliases to wchar_t and no conversion is necessary. However, if the function is compiled against the non-Unicode version of the Win32 API, then TCHAR is an alias to char, and the first parameter to IIDFromString is of the incorrect type. One remedy for this problem is to rely on conditional compilation:

```
HRESULT IIDFromHWND(HWND hwnd, IID& riid) {
    TCHAR szEditText[1024];
    GetWindowText(hwnd, szEditText, 1024);
#ifdef UNICODE
    return IIDFromString(szEditText, &riid);
#else
    OLECHAR wszEditText[1024];
    ustrncpy(wszEditText, szEditText, 1024);
    return IIDFromString(wszEditText, &riid);
#endif
}
```

Although this code fragment does generate optimal code, it is very tedious to use this technique every time a parameter is of the wrong character type. One technique for dealing with this problem is to use a shim class that has a constructor that accepts either type of character string as a parameter. This shim class also needs typecast operators that allow it to be used where either const char * or const wchar_t * is expected. In these cast operators, the shim class either allocates a duplicate buffer and performs the necessary conversion or simply returns the original string if no conversion was necessary. The shim class's destructor can then free any allocated buffers. The ustring.h header file contains two such shim classes: _U and _UNCC. The former is for normal use; the latter is for use with non-const-correct functions and methods[7] (such as IIDFromString). Given the availability of the two shim classes, the previous code fragment can be simplified considerably:

---

[7] _UNCC is simply a version of _U that also provides typecast operators for wchar_t * and char *. Although this extended version could be used anywhere, the author chooses to use it only when interfacing with non-const-correct interfaces to emphasize that the type system is being somewhat compromised. Alas, much of the COM API is not const-correct, so the _UNCC shim class gets lots of use.

```
HRESULT IIDFromHWND(HWND hwnd, IID& riid) {
  TCHAR szEditText[1024];
  GetWindowText(hwnd, szEditText, 1024);
// use _UNCC shim class to convert if necessary
  return IIDFromString(_UNCC(szEditText), &riid);
}
```

Note that no conditional compilation is needed. If the code is compiled against the Unicode version of Win32, then the _UNCC class will simply pass the original buffer through its typecast operator. If the code is compiled against the non-Unicode version of Win32, then the _UNCC class will allocate a buffer and convert the string to Unicode. The _UNCC's destructor then frees the buffer when the statement is completely evaluated.[8]

One additional text-related data type that must be discussed is the BSTR. The BSTR string type must be used in all interfaces that will be used from Visual Basic or Java. BSTRs are length-prefixed, null-terminated strings of OLECHARs. The length prefix indicates the number of *bytes* the string consumes (not including the terminating null) and is stored as a four-byte integer that immediately precedes the first character of the string. Figure 2.7 shows the string "Hi" as a BSTR. To allow BSTRs to be freely returned from methods without concern for memory allocation, all BSTRs are allocated from a COM-managed memory allocator. COM provides several API functions for managing BSTRs:

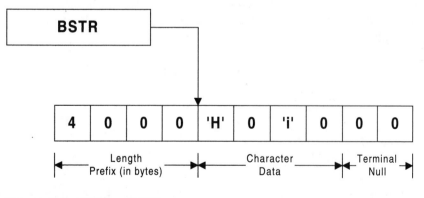

Figure 2.7 "Hi" as BSTR

---

[8] Although the author finds the string utilities in ustring.h more than adequate for managing COM-based text processing, the ATL and MFC libraries use a somewhat different approach based on alloca and macros. Consult the local documentation for more information on these techniques.

```
// from oleauto.h
// allocate and initialize a BSTR
BSTR SysAllocString(const OLECHAR *psz);
BSTR SysAllocStringLen(const OLECHAR *psz, UINT cch);

// reallocate and initialize a BSTR
INT  SysReAllocString(BSTR *pbstr, const OLECHAR *psz);
INT  SysReAllocStringLen(BSTR *pbstr, const OLECHAR * psz,
                         UINT cch);

// free a BSTR
void SysFreeString(BSTR bstr);

// peek at length-prefix as characters or bytes
UINT SysStringLen(BSTR bstr);
UINT SysStringByteLen(BSTR bstr);
```

When passing strings to a method as [in] parameters, it is the caller's responsibility to call SysAllocString prior to invoking the method and to call SysFreeString once the method has completed. Consider the following method definition:

```
HRESULT SetString([in] BSTR bstr);
```

Assuming that the caller already has an OLECHAR-compliant string, the following would be necessary to convert the string to a BSTR prior to invoking the method:

```
// convert raw OLECHAR string to a BSTR
BSTR bstr = SysAllocString(OLESTR("Hello"));
// invoke method
HRESULT hr = p->SetString(bstr);
// free BSTR
SysFreeString(bstr);
```

A shim class for dealing with BSTRs, _UBSTR, is included in the ustring.h header file:

```
// from ustring.h (book-specific header file) /////
class _UBSTR {
    BSTR m_bstr;
```

```
    public:
        _UBSTR(const char *psz)
            : m_bstr(SysAllocStringLen(0, strlen(psz))) {
            mbstowcs(m_bstr, psz, INT_MAX);
        }

        _UBSTR(const wchar_t *pwsz)
        : m_bstr(SysAllocString(pwsz)) {  }

        operator BSTR (void)  const { return m_bstr; }

        ~_UBSTR(void) { SysFreeString(m_bstr); }
    };
```

With this shim class in place, the preceding code fragment is considerably
simpler:

```
// invoke method
HRESULT hr = p->SetString(_UBSTR(OLESTR("Hello")));
```

Note that either a char- or wchar_t-based string can be used with the _UBSTR
shim class.

When passing strings from a method as an [out] parameter, it is the responsibility of the object to call SysAllocString to allocate a buffer for the resultant string. It is then the responsibility of the caller to release the buffer by
calling SysFreeString. Consider the following method definition:

```
HRESULT GetString([out, retval] BSTR *pbstr);
```

The method implementation would need to create a new BSTR to return to the
caller:

```
STDMETHODIMP MyClass::GetString(BSTR *pbstr) {
    *pbstr = SysAllocString(OLESTR("Goodbye!"));
    return S_OK;
}
```

It is then the caller's job to free the string once it has copied it to an application-
managed string buffer:

```
extern OLECHAR g_wsz[]; BSTR bstr = 0;
HRESULT hr = p->GetString(&bstr);
```

```
   if (SUCCEEDED(hr)) {
     wcscpy(g_wsz, bstr);
     SysFreeString(bstr);
   }
```

One important aspect of BSTRs has not yet been mentioned. It is legal to pass a null pointer as a BSTR to indicate an empty string. This means that the preceding code fragment is not quite correct. The call to wcscpy:

```
   wcscpy(g_wsz, bstr);
```

needs to protect itself against possible null pointers:

```
   wcscpy(g_wsz, bstr ? bstr : OLESTR(""));
```

To simplify the use of BSTRs, the ustring.h header file contains the following simple inline function:

```
   inline OLECHAR *SAFEBSTR(BSTR b){return b ? b : OLESTR("");}
```

Although allowing null pointers as BSTRs does make the datatype more efficient in terms of memory utilization, it causes code to be littered with these simple tests.

The primitive types shown in Figure 2.6 can be composed using C-style structures. IDL follows the C rules for the tag namespace, which means most IDL interface definitions either use typedef statements:

```
   typedef struct tagCOLOR {
      double red;
      double green;
      double blue;
   } COLOR;
   HRESULT SetColor([in] const COLOR *pColor);
```

or must use the struct keyword to qualify the tagname:

```
   struct COLOR {
      double red;
      double green;
      double blue;
   };
   HRESULT SetColor([in] const struct COLOR *pColor);
```

The former is the preferred form. Simple structures like the one shown can be used from both Visual Basic and Java; however, at the time of this writing, the current version of Visual Basic can only access interfaces that use structures, it cannot be used to implement interfaces that use structures as method parameters.

IDL and COM also support unions. To ensure that the actual interpretation of the union is unambiguous, IDL expects that a discriminator will be provided along with the union that indicates which union member is actually in use. The discriminator must be of an integral type and must appear at the same logical level as the union. If the union is declared outside the scope of a structure, it is considered a nonencapsulated union:

```
union NUMBER {
  [case(1)] long  i;
  [case(2)] float f;
};
```

The [case] attribute is used to match the actual union member in use to its discriminator. To associate a discriminator with the usage of a nonencapsulated union, the [switch_is] attribute must be used:

```
HRESULT Add([in, switch_is(t)] union NUMBER *pn,
            [in] short t);
```

When the union is bundled with its discriminator in a surrounding structure, the aggregate type is called an encapsulated or *discriminated* union:

```
struct UNUMBER {
  short t;
  [switch_is(t)] union VALUE {
    [case(1)] long i;
    [case(2)] float f;
  };
};
```

COM predefines one common discriminated union for use with Visual Basic. This union is called a VARIANT[9] and can hold instances or references to a subset of the base types supported by IDL. Each supported type has a corresponding discriminator value:

---

[9] Also referred to as a VARIANTARG. The term VARIANTARG refers to variants that are legal parameter types. The term VARIANT refers to variants that are legal method results. The data type VARIANTARG is simply an alias to VARIANT and the two types can be used interchangeably.

```
VT_EMPTY          nothing
VT_NULL           SQL style Null
VT_I2             short
VT_I4             long
VT_R4             float
VT_R8             double
VT_CY             CY (64-bit currency)
VT_DATE           DATE (double)
VT_BSTR           BSTR
VT_DISPATCH       IDispatch *
VT_ERROR          HRESULT
VT_BOOL           VARIANT_BOOL (True=-1, False=0)
VT_VARIANT        VARIANT *
VT_UNKNOWN        IUnknown *
VT_DECIMAL        16 byte fixed point
VT_UI1            opaque byte
```

The following two flags can be combined with these tags to indicate that the variant contains either a reference or an array of the specified type.

```
VT_ARRAY     Indicates variant contains a SAFEARRAY
VT_BYREF     Indicates variant is a reference
```

COM provides several API functions for managing VARIANTs:

```
// initialize a variant to empty
void    VariantInit(VARIANTARG * pvarg);
// release any resources held in a variant
HRESULT VariantClear(VARIANTARG * pvarg);
// deep-copy one variant to another
HRESULT VariantCopy(VARIANTARG * plhs, VARIANTARG * prhs);
// dereference and deep-copy one variant into another
HRESULT VariantCopyInd(VARIANT * plhs, VARIANTARG * prhs);
// convert a variant to a designated type
HRESULT VariantChangeType(VARIANTARG * plhs,
        VARIANTARG * prhs, USHORT wFlags, VARTYPE vtlhs);
// convert a variant to a designated type (explicit locale)
HRESULT VariantChangeTypeEx(VARIANTARG * plhs,
            VARIANTARG * prhs, LCID lcid, USHORT wFlags,
            VARTYPE vtlhs);
```

These routines greatly simplify manipulating VARIANTs.

To understand how these API routines are used, consider a method that accepts a VARIANT as an [in] parameter:

```
HRESULT UseIt([in] VARIANT var);
```

The following code fragment illustrates how to pass an integer to this method:

```
VARIANT var;
VariantInit(&var);              // initialize VARIANT
V_VT(&var) = VT_I4;             // set discriminator
V_I4(&var) = 100;               // set union
HRESULT hr = pItf->UseIt(var);  // use VARIANT
VariantClear(&var);             // free any resources in VARIANT
```

Note that this code fragment uses the standard accessor macros to access the data members of the VARIANT. The two lines

```
V_VT(&var) = VT_I4;
V_I4(&var) = 100;
```

are equivalent to the following code that accesses the raw data members:

```
var.vt = VT_I4;
var.lVal = 100;
```

The former version is preferred, as it will compile under C compilers that do not support anonymous unions.

Assuming the method shown before this, the following method implementation uses the VARIANT parameter as a string:

```
STDMETHODIMP MyClass::UseIt(/*[in]*/ VARIANT var) {
// declare and init a second VARIANT
  VARIANT var2; VariantInit(&var2);
// convert var to a BSTR and store it in var2
  HRESULT hr = VariantChangeType(&var2, &var, 0, VT_BSTR);
// use the string
  if (SUCCEEDED(hr)){
    ustrcpy(m_szSomeDataMember, SAFEBSTR(V_BSTR(&var2)));
// free any resources held by var2
  VariantClear(&var2);
  }
```

```
      return hr;
   }
```

Note that the VariantChangeType API routine handles the potentially complex conversion between whatever type of VARIANT the client passes and the desired type (in this case, BSTR).

One final data type that bears discussion is the COM interface. COM interfaces can be passed as method parameters in one of two ways. If the type of interface pointer is known at design time, the interface type can be declared statically:

```
HRESULT GetObject([out] IDog **ppDog);
```

If the type is not known at design time, the interface designer can give the user the opportunity to specify the type at runtime. To support dynamically typed interfaces, IDL supports the [iid_is] attribute:

```
HRESULT GetObject([in] REFIID riid,
                  [out, iid_is(riid)] IUnknown **ppUnk);
```

Although this form will work perfectly well, the following is preferred due to its similarity to QueryInterface:

```
HRESULT GetObject([in] REFIID riid,
                  [out, iid_is(riid)] void **ppv);
```

The [iid_is] attribute can be used with both [in] and [out] parameters of type IUnknown * or void *. To use a dynamically typed interface parameter, one simply specifies the IID of the desired type of pointer:

```
IDog *pDog = 0;
HRESULT hr = pItf->GetObject(IID_IDog, (void**)&pDog);
```

The corresponding implementation would simply use the desired object's QueryInterface method to initialize the parameter:

```
STDMETHODIMP Class::GetObject(REFIID riid, void **ppv) {
   extern IUnknown * g_pUnkTheDog;
   return g_pUnkTheDog->QueryInterface(riid, ppv);
}
```

Dynamically typed interface pointers should *always* be used in lieu of statically typed interface pointers of type IUnknown to reduce additional client-object method calls.

Attributes and Properties

It is occasionally useful to indicate that an object has certain publicly visible properties that can be either accessed and/or modified via a COM interface. COM IDL allows interface methods to be annotated to reflect that a given method either modifies or reads a named attribute of the object. Consider the following interface definition:

```
[ object, uuid(0BB3DAE1-11F4-11d1-8C84-0080C73925BA) ]
interface ICollie : IDog {
// Age is a read-only property
   [propget] HRESULT Age([out, retval] long *pVal);
// HairCount is a read/write property
   [propget] HRESULT HairCount([out, retval] long *pVal);
   [propput] HRESULT HairCount([in] long val);
// CurrentThought is a write-only property
   [propput] HRESULT CurrentThought([in] BSTR val);
}
```

The use of the [propput] and [propget] attributes informs the IDL compiler that the methods they correspond to should be mapped to property mutators or accessors in languages that explicitly support properties. In Visual Basic, this means that the members Age, HairCount, and CurrentThought can be manipulated using the same syntax as structure member access:

```
Sub UseCollie(fido as ICollie)
   fido.HairCount = fido.HairCount - (fido.Age * 1000)
   fido.CurrentThought = "I wish I had a bone"
End Sub
```

The C++ mapping of this interface simply adorns the method names with put_ or get_ to give the programmer a hint that a property is being accessed:

```
void UseCollie(ICollie *pFido) {
   long n1, n2;
   HRESULT hr = pFido->get_HairCount(&n1);
```

```
        assert(SUCCEEDED(hr));
        hr = pFido->get_Age(&n2);
        assert(SUCCEEDED(hr));
        hr = pFido->put_HairCount(n1 - (n2 * 1000));
        assert(SUCCEEDED(hr));
        BSTR bstr = SysAllocString(OLESTR("I wish I had a bone"));
        hr = pFido->put_CurrentThought(bstr);
        assert(SUCCEEDED(hr));
        SysFreeString(bstr);
    }
```

Although properties do not explicitly enable any development techniques, they are useful for providing natural mappings for languages that support them.[10]

Exceptions

COM has specific support for throwing exceptions from method implementations. Because there is no binary standard for C++ language exceptions, COM provides explicit API functions for throwing and catching COM exception objects:

```
// throw an exception
HRESULT SetErrorInfo([in] ULONG reserved, // m.b.z.
                     [in] IErrorInfo *pei);


// catch an exception
HRESULT GetErrorInfo([in] ULONG reserved, // m.b.z.
                     [out] IErrorInfo **ppei);
```

The SetErrorInfo routine is called from within a method implementation to associate an exception object with the current logical thread.[11] GetErrorInfo fetches the exception object from the current logical thread and clears the exception so that subsequent calls to GetErrorInfo will return S_FALSE, indicating that there is no pending exception. As implied by these routines, COM exception objects must support at least the IErrorInfo interface:

---

[10] Microsoft's Direct-to-COM support does allow clients to treat properties as public data members of an interface through some very twisted machinery.

[11] The COM Specification uses the term *logical thread* to refer to a chain of method calls that may transcend more than one physical OS thread.

```
[ object, uuid(1CF2B120-547D-101B-8E65-08002B2BD119) ]
interface IErrorInfo: IUnknown {
// get IID of interface that threw exception
  HRESULT GetGUID([out] GUID * pGUID);
// get class name of object that threw exception
  HRESULT GetSource([out] BSTR * pBstrSource);
// get human-readable description of exception
  HRESULT GetDescription([out] BSTR * pBstrDescription);
// get WinHelp filename of documentation of error
  HRESULT GetHelpFile([out] BSTR * pBstrHelpFile);
// get WinHelp context ID for documentation of error
  HRESULT GetHelpContext([out] DWORD * pdwHelpContext);
}
```

Custom exception objects can elect to implement additional exception-specific interfaces in addition to IErrorInfo.

COM provides a default implementation of IErrorInfo that can be instantiated using the COM API function CreateErrorInfo:

```
HRESULT CreateErrorInfo([out] ICreateErrorInfo **ppcei);
```

In addition to IErrorInfo, default exception objects expose the ICreateErrorInfo interface to allow the user to initialize the state of the new exception:

```
[ object, uuid(22F03340-547D-101B-8E65-08002B2BD119) ]
interface ICreateErrorInfo: IUnknown {
// set IID of interface that threw exception
  HRESULT SetGUID([in] REFGUID rGUID);
// set class name of object that threw exception
  HRESULT SetSource([in, string] OLECHAR* pwszSource);
// set human-readable description of exception
  HRESULT SetDescription([in, string] OLECHAR* pwszDesc);
// set WinHelp filename of documentation of error
  HRESULT SetHelpFile([in, string] OLECHAR* pwszHelpFile);
// set WinHelp context ID for documentation of error
  HRESULT SetHelpContext([in] DWORD dwHelpContext);
}
```

Note that this interface simply allows the user to populate the exception object with the five basic attributes that are accessible from the IErrorInfo interface.

The following method implementation throws a COM exception to its caller using the default exception object:

```
STDMETHODIMP PugCat::Snore(void) {
  if (this->IsAsleep( )) //ok to perform operation?
    return this->DoSnore( );   //do operation and return
//otherwise create an exception object
  ICreateErrorInfo *pcei = 0;
  HRESULT hr = CreateErrorInfo(&pcei);
  assert(SUCCEEDED(hr));
// initialize the exception object
  hr = pcei->SetGUID(IID_IPug);
  assert(SUCCEEDED(hr));
  hr = pcei->SetSource(OLESTR("PugCat"));
  assert(SUCCEEDED(hr));
  hr = pcei->SetDescription(OLESTR("I am not asleep!"));
  assert(SUCCEEDED(hr));
  hr = pcei->SetHelpFile(OLESTR("C:\\PugCat.hlp"));
  assert(SUCCEEDED(hr));
  hr = pcei->SetHelpContext(5221);
  assert(SUCCEEDED(hr));
// "throw" exception
  IErrorInfo *pei = 0;
  hr = pcei->QueryInterface(IID_IErrorInfo, (void**)&pei);
  assert(SUCCEEDED(hr));
  hr = SetErrorInfo(0, pei);
// release resources and return a SEVERITY_ERROR result
  pei->Release();
  pcei->Release();
  return PUG_E_PUGNOTASLEEP;
}
```

Note that once the exception object is passed to the SetErrorInfo routine, COM holds a reference to the exception until it is "caught" by the caller using GetErrorInfo.

The objects that throw COM exceptions must implement the ISupportErrorInfo interface to indicate which interfaces support exceptions. This interface is used by clients to determine whether or not the result of GetErrorInfo is reliable.[12] This interface is extremely simple:

---

[12] An object that implements ISupportErrorInfo advertises that it explicitly programs using COM exceptions and that no erroneous exceptions thrown by subordinate objects have been accidentally propagated.

```
[ object, uuid(DF0B3D60-548F-101B-8E65-08002B2BD119) ]
interface ISupportErrorInfo: IUnknown {
  HRESULT InterfaceSupportsErrorInfo([in]  REFIID riid);
}
```

Assuming that the PugCat class from this chapter throws exceptions from each of its supported interfaces, its implementation would be as follows:

```
STDMETHODIMP PugCat::InterfaceSupportsErrorInfo(REFIID riid)
{
  if (riid == IID_IAnimal || riid == IID_ICat ||
      riid == IID_IDog || riid ==IID_IPug)
    return S_OK;
  else
    return S_FALSE;
}
```

The following is an example of a client that handles exceptions safely using ISupportErrorInfo and GetErrorInfo:

```
void TellPugToSnore(/*[in]*/ IPug *pPug) {
// call a method
  HRESULT hr = pPug->Snore();
  if (FAILED(hr)) {
// check to see if object supports COM exceptions
    ISupportErrorInfo *psei = 0;
    HRESULT hr2 =pPug->QueryInterface( IID_ISupportErrorInfo,
                                       (void**)&psei);
    if (SUCCEEDED(hr2)) {
// check if object supports COM exceptions via IPug methods
      hr2 = psei->InterfaceSupportsErrorInfo(IID_IPug);
      if (hr2 == S_OK) {
// read exception object for this logical thread
        IErrorInfo *pei = 0;
        hr2 = GetErrorInfo(0, &pei);
        if (hr2 == S_OK) {
// scrape out source and description strings
          BSTR bstrSource = 0, bstrDesc = 0;
          hr2 = pei->GetDescription(&bstrDesc);
          assert(SUCCEEDED(hr2));
          hr2 = pei->GetSource(&bstrSource);
          assert(SUCCEEDED(hr2));
```

```
        // display error information to end-user
                MessageBoxW(0, bstrDesc ? bstrDesc : L"",
                          bstrSource ? bstrSource : L"", MB_OK);
    // free resources
                SysFreeString(bstrSource);
                SysFreeString(bstrDesc);
                pei->Release();
            }
        }
        psei->Release();
    }
  }
  if (hr2 != S_OK) // something went wrong with exception
    MessageBoxA(0, "Snore Failed", "IPug", MB_OK);
}
```

It is fairly simple to map COM exceptions to C++ exceptions where desired. Assume the following class that bundles a COM exception object and
an HRESULT into a single C++ class:

```
struct COMException {
  HRESULT m_hresult; // hresult to return
  IErrorInfo *m_pei; // exception to throw
  COMException(HRESULT hresult, REFIID riid,
              const OLECHAR *pszSource,
              const OLECHAR *pszDesc,
              const OLECHAR *pszHelpFile = 0,
              DWORD dwHelpContext = 0)    {
// create and init an error info object
    ICreateErrorInfo *pcei = 0;
    HRESULT hr = CreateErrorInfo(&pcei);
    assert(SUCCEEDED(hr));
    hr = pcei->SetGUID(riid);
    assert(SUCCEEDED(hr));
    if (pszSource)
      hr=pcei->SetSource(const_cast<OLECHAR*>(pszSource));
    assert(SUCCEEDED(hr));
    if (pszDesc)
      hr=pcei->SetDescription(const_cast<OLECHAR*>(pszDesc));
    assert(SUCCEEDED(hr));
    if (pszHelpFile)
```

```
    hr=pcei->SetHelpFile(const_cast<OLECHAR*>(pszHelpFile));
    assert(SUCCEEDED(hr));
    hr = pcei->SetHelpContext(dwHelpContext);
    assert(SUCCEEDED(hr));
// hold the HRESULT and IErrorInfo ptr as data members
    m_hresult = hresult;
    hr=pcei->QueryInterface(IID_IErrorInfo, (void**)&m_pei);
    assert(SUCCEEDED(hr));
    pcei->Release();
  }
};
```

Given the COMException C++ class just shown, the Snore method shown
previously can be modified to map arbitrary C++ exceptions to COM exceptions:

```
STDMETHODIMP PugCat::Snore(void) {
  HRESULT hrex = S_OK;
  try {
    if (this->IsAsleep())
      return this->DoSnore();
    else
      throw COMException(PUG_E_PUGNOTASLEEP, IID_IPug,
              OLESTR("PugCat"), OLESTR("I am not asleep!"));
  }
  catch (COMException& ce) {
// a C++ COMException was thrown
    HRESULT hr = SetErrorInfo(0, ce.m_pei);
    assert(SUCCEEDED(hr));
    ce.m_pei->Release();
    hrex = ce.m_hresult;
  }
  catch (...) {
// some unidentified C++ exception was thrown
    COMException ex(E_FAIL, IID_IPug, OLESTR("PugCat"),
                    OLESTR("A C++ exception was thrown"));
    HRESULT hr = SetErrorInfo(0, ex.m_pei);
    assert(SUCCEEDED(hr));
    ex.m_pei->Release();
    hrex = ex.m_hresult;
  }
```

```
        return hrex;
    }
```

Note that the method implementation is careful not to allow pure C++ exceptions to be propagated beyond the method boundary. This is an absolute requirement of COM.

Where Are We?

This chapter presented the concept of a COM interface. COM interfaces have simple binary signatures that allow any client to access an object, irrespective of the programming language used by the client or the object implementor. To facilitate multiple language support, COM interfaces are defined in IDL. These IDL interface definitions can also be used to generate communications code that allows an object to be accessed over a network.

A large part of this chapter was dedicated to IUnknown, the fundamental interface upon which all of COM is built. All COM interfaces must derive from IUnknown. By inference, all COM objects must implement IUnknown. IUnknown provides three method signatures through which the client can safely navigate the type hierarchy of an object to access extended functionality that the object exports. In this respect, QueryInterface can be thought of as the type-cast operator of COM. By the same logic, IUnknown can be thought of as the "void *" of interface pointers, as it is not very useful until it is "cast" to something more meaningful using QueryInterface.

It is worth noting that no significant system calls were made when accessing or implementing IUnknown. In this respect, IUnknown is simply a protocol or set of promises that all programs must adhere to. This allows COM objects to be very lightweight and efficient. Implementing IUnknown in C++ requires a few lines of extremely boilerplate code. To automate the implementation of IUnknown in C++, a series of preprocessor macros were presented that implemented QueryInterface in a table-driven manner. While these macros were by no means necessary, they removed most of the common boilerplate code from each class definition without adding undue complexity to the implementation.

3 | Classes

```
int cGorillas = Gorilla::GetCount();
IApe *pApe = new Gorilla();
pApe->GetYourStinkingPawsOffMeYouDamnDirtyApe();
```
Charleton Heston, 1968

The previous chapter discussed the fundamentals of COM interfaces in general and the IUnknown interface in particular. The techniques for managing interface pointers from C++ were presented, and the de facto techniques for implementing IUnknown were discussed in detail. What was not mentioned was how clients typically get an initial interface pointer to an object, or how object implementors allow their objects to be discovered by external clients. This chapter illustrates how COM object implementations integrate into the COM runtime environment to allow clients to find or create objects of a given concrete type.

Interface and Implementation Revisited

The previous chapter defined a COM interface as an abstract collection of operations that express one functionality that an object can export. COM interfaces are defined in IDL and have a logical name that indicates the functionality that they model. The following is an IDL definition of the COM interface IApe:

```
[object,uuid(753A8A7C-A7FF-11d0-8C30-0080C73925BA)]
interface IApe : IUnknown {
  import "unknwn.idl";
  HRESULT EatBanana(void);
  HRESULT SwingFromTree(void);
  [propget] HRESULT Weight([out, retval] long *plbs);
}
```

The corresponding IApe documentation would specify the rough semantics for the three operations EatBanana, SwingFromTree, and Weight. All objects that expose IApe via QueryInterface must ensure that their implementations of these methods adhere to the semantic contract of IApe. However, interface definitions almost always deliberately leave room for interpretation by object implementors. This means that clients can never be completely certain about the precise behavior of any given method, only that its behavior will follow the rough guidelines described in the interface's documentation. This controlled degree of uncertainty is a fundamental characteristic of polymorphism and is one of the foundations of object-oriented software development.

Consider the IApe interface just shown. It is possible (in fact, likely) that there will be more than one implementation of the IApe interface. Because the definition of IApe is generic to all implementations, the assumptions that clients can make about the behavior of the EatBanana method must be sufficiently vague to allow gorillas, chimpanzees, and orangutans (all of which might implement the IApe interface) each to have legal (but subtly different) interpretations of this operation. Without this flexibility, polymorphism is impossible.

COM explicitly treats interfaces, implementations, and classes as three distinct concepts. Interfaces are abstract protocols for communicating with an object. Implementations are concrete data types that support one or more interfaces by providing precise semantic interpretations of each of the interface's abstract operations. Classes are named implementations that represent concrete instantiable types and are formally known as COM classes or *coclasses*.

In the spirit of encapsulation, all that is known of a COM class is its name and potentially the list of interfaces it exposes. Like COM interfaces, COM classes are named using GUIDs, although when used to name COM classes, GUIDs are called CLSIDs. Like interface names, these class names must be well known to the client prior to using them. Because COM interfaces are semantically vague to allow polymorphism, COM does not allow clients simply to request *any available* implementation of a given interface. Instead, clients must specify the precise implementation that is desired. This reinforces the fact that COM interfaces are simply abstract communication protocols whose sole purpose is to allow clients to communicate with objects that belong to concrete, meaningful implementation classes.[1]

---

[1] Although it makes little sense to ask for "any available implementation" of a given interface, it sometimes does make sense to have semantic groupings of implementations, all of which share certain high-level traits, such as being an animal or providing a logging service. To support this type of component discovery, COM supports advertising such taxonomies through the use of *component categories*. While it is often the case that all classes that belong to a given component category will implement a shared set of interfaces, this is by no means a sufficient condition for belonging to a component category.

In addition to allowing implementations to be named by a CLSID, COM supports text-based aliases called *programmatic IDs* or *ProgIDs*. ProgIDs come in the form of *libraryname.classname.version* and, unlike CLSIDs, are unique only by convention. Clients can map between ProgIDs and CLSIDs using the COM API functions CLSIDFromProgID and ProgIDFromCLSID:

```
HRESULT CLSIDFromProgID(
            [in, string] const OLECHAR *pwszProgID,
            [out]        CLSID *pclsid);
HRESULT ProgIDFromCLSID(
            [in] REFCLSID rclsid,
            [out, string] OLECHAR **ppwszProgID);
```

To convert a ProgID to a CLSID, one simply calls CLSIDFromProgID:

```
HRESULT GetGorillaCLSID(CLSID& rclsid) {
   const OLECHAR wszProgID[] = OLESTR("Apes.Gorilla.1");
   return CLSIDFromProgID(wszProgID, &rclsid);
}
```

The COM runtime will look in its configuration database for a mapping of the ProgID Apes.Gorilla.1 onto a CLSID that corresponds to a COM implementation class.

Class Objects

A basic requirement of all COM classes is that they must have a class object. A class object is a per-class singleton that implements the instanceless functionality of the class. A class object acts as the metaclass for a given implementation, and the methods it implements fill the role of static member functions from C++. Logically, there is only one class object per class; however, given the distributed nature of COM, a given class may have one class object per host machine, per user account, or per process, depending on how the class is deployed. The first point of entry into a class's implementation is through its class object.

Class objects are very useful programming abstractions. Class objects can act as well-known objects (where their CLSID acts as the name of the object) that allow multiple clients to bind to the same object based on a given CLSID. While entire systems could be built using class objects exclusively, class objects are often used as brokers to create new instances of a class or to find existing instances based on some well-known object name. When used in these capacities, the class object will usually expose only one or two intermediary interfaces that allow clients to create or find the instances that ultimately will do the interesting work. For example, consider the interface IApe described previously. It would not violate the laws of COM for a class object to expose the IApe interface:

```
class GorillaClass : public IApe {
public:
// class objects are singletons, so don't delete
   IMPLEMENT_UNKNOWN_NO_DELETE(GorillaClass)
   BEGIN_INTERFACE_TABLE(GorillaClass)
     IMPLEMENTS_INTERFACE(IApe)
   END_INTERFACE_TABLE()
// IApe methods
   STDMETHODIMP EatBanana(void);
   STDMETHODIMP SwingFromTree(void);
   STDMETHODIMP get_Weight(long *plbs);
};
```

Given that this C++ class will act as a singleton (as do all COM class objects), there can be only one gorilla at any given instant. For some domains, singletons are all that is needed. In the case of gorillas, however, it is highly likely that clients may want to build applications that use multiple *distinct* gorillas simultaneously. To support this usage, the gorilla class object should not export the IApe interface but instead should export a new interface that allows clients to create new gorillas and/or find well-known gorillas by their name. This will require the implementor to define two C++ classes: one to implement the class object and one to implement the actual instances of the class. For the gorilla implementation, the C++ class that defines gorilla instances will implement IApe:

```
class Gorilla : public IApe {
public:
// instances are heap-based, so delete when done
   IMPLEMENT_UNKNOWN(Gorilla)
   BEGIN_INTERFACE_TABLE(Gorilla)
     IMPLEMENTS_INTERFACE(IApe)
   END_INTERFACE_TABLE()
// IApe methods
   STDMETHODIMP EatBanana(void);
```

```
    STDMETHODIMP SwingFromTree(void);
    STDMETHODIMP get_Weight(long *plbs);
};
```

A second interface will be needed to define the operations that the Gorilla class object will implement:

```
[object,uuid(753A8AAC-A7FF-11d0-8C30-0080C73925BA)]
interface IApeClass : IUnknown {
  HRESULT CreateApe([out, retval] IApe **ppApe);
  HRESULT GetApe([in] long nApeID,
                 [out, retval] IApe **ppApe);
    [opget] HRESULT AverageWeight([out, retval] long *plbs);
}
```

Given this interface definition, the class object would implement the IApeClass methods by either creating new instances of the C++ class Gorilla (in the case of CreateApe) or mapping an arbitrary object name (in this case an integer) to a particular instance (in the case of GetApe):

```
class GorillaClass : public IApeClass {
public:
    IMPLEMENT_UNKNOWN_NO_DELETE(GorillaClass)
    BEGIN_INTERFACE_TABLE(GorillaClass)
      IMPLEMENTS_INTERFACE(IApeClass)
    END_INTERFACE_TABLE()

    STDMETHODIMP CreateApe(IApe **ppApe) {
      if ((*ppApe = new Gorilla) == 0)
        return E_OUTOFMEMORY;
      (*ppApe)->AddRef();
      return S_OK;
    }

    STDMETHODIMP GetApe(long nApeID, IApe **ppApe) {
// assume that a table of well-known gorillas is
// being maintained somewhere else
      extern Gorilla *g_rgWellKnownGorillas[];
      extern int g_nMaxGorillas;
// assert that nApeID is a valid index
      *ppApe = 0;
```

```
        if (nApeID > g_nMaxGorillas || nApeID < 0)
          return E_INVALIDARG;
  // assume that the ID is simply the index into the table
        if ((*ppApe = g_rgWellKnownGorillas[nApeID]) == 0)
          return E_INVALIDARG;
        (*ppApe)->AddRef();
        return S_OK;
    }

    STDMETHODIMP get_AverageWeight(long *plbs) {
      extern Gorilla *g_rgWellKnownGorillas[];
      extern int g_nMaxGorillas;
      *plbs = 0; long lbs;
      for (int i = 0; i < g_nMaxGorillas; i++) {
        g_rgWellKnownGorillas[i]->get_Weight(&lbs);
        *plbs += lbs;
      }

      // assumes g_nMaxGorillas is non-zero
      *plbs /= g_nMaxGorillas;
      return S_OK;
    }
  };
```

Note that this code assumes that an external table of well-known gorillas is being maintained, either by the Gorilla instances themselves or by some other agent.

Activation

Clients need a mechanism for finding class objects. Because of the dynamic nature of COM, this may involve loading a DLL or starting a server process. This act of bringing an object to life is called object activation.

COM has three activation models that can be used to bring objects into memory to allow method calls to be invoked. Clients can ask COM to bind to the class object of a given class. Clients can also ask COM to create new instances of a class based on a CLSID. Finally, clients can ask COM to bring a persistent object to life based on the persistent state of the object. Of these three models, only the first model (binding to a class object) is absolutely necessary. The other two models are simply optimizations of commonly used activation idioms. Additional user-defined activation models can be implemented in terms of one (or more) of these three primitives.

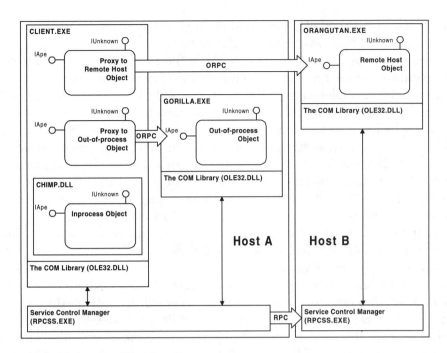

Figure 3.1 The COM Library and SCM

Each of COM's three activation models uses the services of the COM Service Control Manager or SCM.[2] The SCM is the central rendezvous point for all activation requests on a particular machine. Each host machine that supports COM has its own local SCM that forwards remote activation requests to the SCM on the remote machine, where the activation request will be treated as a local activation request. The SCM is used only to activate the object and bind the initial interface pointer. Once the object is activated, the SCM is not involved with client-object method invocation. As shown in Figure 3.1, under Windows NT the SCM is implemented in the RPCSS Service. The services of the SCM are exposed to programs as high-level moniker types[3] and as low-level API functions, all of which are implemented in what the Component Object Model Specification calls the COM library. Under Windows NT, the majority of the COM library is implemented in OLE32.DLL. For efficiency, the COM library

---

[2] Windows NT also has a subsystem known as the Service Control Manager that is used to start logon-independent processes known as Services. For the remainder of this book, the Windows NT Service Control Manager will be referred to as the NT SCM to distinguish it from the COM SCM.

[3] Monikers are locator objects that hide the details of an activation or binding algorithm. Monikers are discussed in greater detail later in this chapter.

can use local or cached state to avoid making unnecessary interprocess communication (IPC) requests to the RPCSS service.

Recall that the first principle of COM is the separation of interface from implementation. One implementation detail that is hidden from the client is where an object implementation resides. Not only is it impossible to detect generically which host machine an object is activated at, it is also impossible to detect whether a local object was activated in the client's process or in a distinct process on the local machine. This gives object implementors a great deal of flexibility in terms of deciding how and where to deploy object implementations, taking into account issues such as robustness, security, load balancing, and performance. The client does get an opportunity at activation time to indicate a preference as to where an object will be activated; however, many clients indicate that they don't care, in which case the SCM will decide based on the current configuration of the desired class.

When an object is activated in process, the DLL that implements the object's methods is loaded into the client process and all of the object's data members reside in the client's address space. This makes method invocation extremely efficient, as no process-switch is required. In addition, the client's thread can be used to execute the method code directly, provided the object's threading requirements match those of the client. If the client and the object have compatible threading requirements, then no thread-switch is required either. When method calls can execute using the client's thread, no intermediate runtime is involved after the object is activated and the method invocation cost is simply that of making a virtual function call. This makes in-process COM especially well suited for performance-sensitive applications, as method invocation is no more expensive than a normal global function call into a DLL.[4]

When an object is activated out of process (*i.e.,* in a different process on the local or remote machine), the code that implements the object's methods executes in a distinct server process and all of the object's data members reside in the server process's address space. To allow the client to communicate with the out-of-process object, COM transparently returns a proxy to the client at activation-time. As is discussed in detail in Chapter 5, this proxy runs on the client's thread and translates method invocations into RPC requests to the server's execution context, where these RPC requests are then translated back into method invocations on the actual object. This makes method invocation less efficient, as a thread-switch and process-switch are required for each access to the object. The benefits of out-of-process activation include fault isolation, distribution, and increased security. Chapter 6 will discuss out-of-process activation in detail.

---

[4] The level of indirection needed to call into an external DLL is roughly equivalent to that of calling a function through a vtbl entry.

Using the SCM

Recall that the SCM supports three activation primitives (binding to class objects, binding to class instances, binding to persistent instances from files). As shown in Figure 3.2, these primitives are layered upon one another logically.[5] The lowest-level primitive is to bind to a class object. This primitive is also the simplest to understand.

Instead of manually loading the class's code, clients use the services of the SCM via the low-level COM API function CoGetClassObject. This function asks the SCM to bind a pointer to the requested class object:

```
HRESULT CoGetClassObject(
        [in] REFCLSID rclsid,      // which class object?
        [in] DWORD dwClsCtx,       // locality?
        [in] COSERVERINFO *pcsi,   // host/security info
        [in] REFIID riid,          // which interface?
        [out, iid_is(riid)] void **ppv); // put it here!
```

The first parameter to CoGetClassObject indicates which implementation class is desired. The last parameter is a reference to the interface pointer to be bound, and the fourth parameter is simply the IID that describes the type of interface pointer referred to by the last parameter. The more interesting

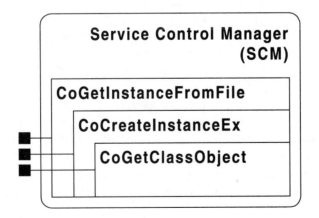

Figure 3.2 Activation Primitives

---

[5] This layering is largely conceptual, as the COM library and wire-protocol implement each primitive as a distinct code path and packet format.

parameters are the second and third parameters, which determine where the class object should be activated.

CoGetClassObject takes as its second parameter a bitmask that allows the client to indicate the desired latency and robustness characteristics of the object (*i.e.,* whether the object should run in process, out of process, or on a different host machine). The valid values for this bitmask are defined in the standard CLSCTX enumeration:

```
enum tagCLSCTX {
    CLSCTX_INPROC_SERVER    = 0x1,  // run inprocess
    CLSCTX_INPROC_HANDLER   = 0x2,  // see note⁶
    CLSCTX_LOCAL_SERVER     = 0x4,  // run out-of-process
    CLSCTX_REMOTE_SERVER    = 0x10 // run off-host
} CLSCTX;
```

These flags can be bitwise-ORed together, and when more than one requested CLSCTX is available, COM will select the most efficient type of server (which means that COM will use the least significant bit of the bitmask when possible). The SDK header files also include several shortcut macros that combine several CLSCTX flags used in many common scenarios:

```
#define CLSCTX_INPROC  (CLSCTX_INPROC_SERVER|\
                        CLSCTX_INPROC_HANDLER)
#define CLSCTX_SERVER  (CLSCTX_INPROC_SERVER|\
                        CLSCTX_LOCAL_SERVER|\
                        CLSCTX_REMOTE_SERVER)
#define CLSCTX_ALL     (CLSCTX_INPROC_SERVER|\
                        CLSCTX_INPROC_HANDLER|\
                        CLSCTX_LOCAL_SERVER|\
                        CLSCTX_REMOTE_SERVER)
```

Note that environments such as Visual Basic and Java always use CLSCTX_ALL, indicating that any available implementation will suffice. The third parameter to CoGetClassObject is a pointer to a structure that contains remoting and security information. This structure is of type

---

[6] In-process handlers are largely a holdover from OLE Documents. In-process handlers are in-process components that act as the client-side representation of an object that actually resides in a different process. Handlers are used in OLE Documents to cache renderings at the client in order to reduce IPC traffic when redrawing the screen. Although handlers make sense in the general case, they have not been widely deployed outside the context of OLE Documents. Windows NT 5.0 will provide additional facilities for implementing handlers, but the details of how this will be accomplished were sketchy at the time of this writing.

COSERVERINFO and allows clients to specify explicitly which machine to activate the object at as well as how to configure the security settings used to make the object activation request:

```
typedef struct _COSERVERINFO {
    DWORD       dwReserved1; // reserved, must be zero
    LPWSTR      pwszName;    // desired host name, or null
    COAUTHINFO *pAuthInfo;   // desired security settings
    DWORD       dwReserved2; // reserved, must be zero
} COSERVERINFO;
```

If the client does not specify a host name but uses only the CLSCTX_ REMOTE_SERVER flag, then COM will use per-CLSID configuration information to determine which machine should be used to activate the object. If the client passes an explicit host name, this host name overrides any preconfigured host names that COM may know about. If the client does not wish to pass explicit security information or a host name to CoGetClassObject, a null COSERVERINFO pointer is acceptable.

Given the availability of CoGetClassObject, the client can ask the SCM to bind an interface pointer to a class object:

```
HRESULT GetGorillaClass(IApeClass * &rpgc) {
// declare the CLSID for Gorilla as a GUID
  const CLSID CLSID_Gorilla = { 0x571F1680, 0xCC83, 0x11d0,
    { 0x8C, 0x48, 0x00, 0x80, 0xC7, 0x39, 0x25, 0xBA } };
// call CoGetClassObject directly
  return CoGetClassObject(CLSID_Gorilla, CLSCTX_ALL, 0,
                          IID_IApeClass, (void**)&rpgc);
}
```

Note that if the requested class is available as an in-process server, COM will automatically load the corresponding DLL and call a well-known exported function that returns a pointer to the desired class object. COM then returns that pointer to provide the client with direct accesses to the desired class object.[7] Once the call to CoGetClassObject is completed, the COM library and the SCM are completely out of the picture. Had the class been available only from an out-of-process or remote server, COM would instead have returned a proxy that would allow the client to access the class object remotely.

---

[7] Technically, the concurrency requirements of the class must be compatible with those of the calling thread.

Recall that the IApeClass interface is designed to allow clients to find or create instances of a given class. Consider the following example:

```
HRESULT FindAGorillaAndEatBanana(long nGorillaID) {
  IApeClass *pgc = 0;
// find the class object via CoGetClassObject
  HRESULT hr = CoGetClassObject(CLSID_Gorilla, CLSCTX_ALL,
                        0, IID_IApeClass, (void**)&pgc);
  if (SUCCEEDED(hr)) {
    IApe *pApe = 0;
// use the class object to find an existing gorilla
    hr = pgc->GetApe(nGorillaID, &pApe);
    if (SUCCEEDED(hr)) {
// tell the designated gorilla to eat a banana
      hr = pApe->EatBanana();
      pApe->Release();
    }
    pgc->Release();
  }
  return hr;
}
```

This example uses the class object for Gorilla to find a named object and inform it to eat a banana. For this example to work, some external agent must have provided the caller with the name of a well-known gorilla. If, instead, any anonymous gorilla could be used to satisfy the request, the following example would suffice:

```
HRESULT CreateAGorillaAndEatBanana(void) {
  IApeClass *pgc = 0;
// find the class object via CoGetClassObject
  HRESULT hr = CoGetClassObject(CLSID_Gorilla, CLSCTX_ALL,
                          0, IID_IApeClass, (void**)&pgc);
  if (SUCCEEDED(hr)) {
    IApe *pApe = 0;
// use the class object to create a new gorilla
    hr = pgc->CreateApe(&pApe);
    if (SUCCEEDED(hr)) {
// tell the new gorilla to eat a banana
      hr = pApe->EatBanana();
      pApe->Release();
```

```
      }
      pgc->Release();
   }
   return hr;
}
```

Note that except for the particular IApeClass method used, the two examples are the same. Because class objects can export arbitrarily complex interfaces, they can be used to model fairly sophisticated object activation, initialization, and location policies.

Classes and Servers

A COM server is a binary file that contains the method code for one or more COM classes. A server can be packaged as either a dynamic link library or a normal executable. In either case, the SCM is responsible for loading either type of server automatically.

If an activation request for an object indicates in-process activation, a DLL-based version of the server must be available to be loaded into the client's address space. If an activation request instead indicates out-of-process or off-host activation, an executable will be used to start the server process on the designated host machine (which may be the same host as the client). COM also supports hosting DLL-based servers in surrogate processes to allow out-of-process and off-host activation of legacy in-process servers. The details of how surrogates relate to out-of-process and off-host activation will be covered in Chapter 6.

To allow clients to activate objects without concern for which type of package is used or where the file is installed, COM keeps a configuration database that maps CLSIDs onto the server that implements that class. Under Windows NT 5.0 or greater, the primary location of this configuration database is the NT Directory. The NT Directory is a distributed secure database that keeps track of user accounts, host machines, and other administrative information. The NT Directory can contain information about COM classes as well. This information is stored in a part of the directory known as the COM Class Store. COM uses the Class Store to resolve CLSIDs onto implementation files (in the case of local activation requests) or remote host names (in the case of remote activation requests). When an activation request for a CLSID is made on a given machine, a local cache is first consulted. If no configuration information is available in the local cache, COM sends a request to the Class Store to ask that the implementation be made available from the local machine. This may mean simply adding some information to the local cache to redirect the request to a different host machine, or it may result in downloading a class implementation to the local machine and running an installation program. In either case, once the class is registered in the Class Store, it is available for the client's activation request, barring security constraints.

The local cache referred to in the discussion of the Class Store is formally called the Registry. The Registry is a per-machine file-based hierarchical database that COM uses to map CLSIDs onto either filenames (in the case of local activation) or remote host names (in the case of remote activation). Prior to Windows NT 5.0, the Registry was the sole location for COM configuration information. The Registry can be searched efficiently based on hierarchical *keys,* which are named by backslash-delimited strings. Each key in the Registry can have one or more *values,* which can contain strings, integral values, or binary data. The NT 4.0 implementation of COM stores most of its configuration information under the key

```
HKEY_LOCAL_MACHINE\Software\Classes
```

although most programs use the more convenient alias

```
HKEY_CLASSES_ROOT
```

The Windows NT 5.0 implementation of COM continues to use HKEY_CLASSES_ROOT for machine-wide settings but also allows per-user configuration of CLSIDs to provide greater security and flexibility. Under Windows NT 5.0, COM first consults

```
HKEY_CURRENT_USER\Software\Classes
```

prior to looking under HKEY_CLASSES_ROOT. For notational convenience, the abbreviations HKLM, HKCR, and HKCU are often used in lieu of HKEY_LOCAL_ MACHINE, HKEY_CLASSES_ROOT, and HKEY_CURRENT_USER, respectively.[8]

COM keeps machine-wide information related to CLSIDs under the registry key

```
HKCR\CLSID
```

---

[8] These abbreviations are not legal in source code or in configuration files. They simply make it possible for long key names to appear as a single nonbreaking line in documentation or other writings on COM. The reader should expand the abbreviations when spoken aloud or when typed into source code.

Under Windows NT 5.0 or greater, COM looks for per-user class information under

```
HKCU\Software\Classes\CLSID
```

Under either of these keys, a list of locally known CLSIDs will be stored, one subkey per CLSID. For example, the Gorilla class used earlier in this chapter might have a machine-wide entry at

```
[HKCR\CLSID\{571F1680-CC83-11d0-8C48-0080C73925BA}]⁹
@="Gorilla"
```

To allow local activation of Gorilla objects, the Gorilla's CLSID entry in the registry must have a subkey that indicates which file contains the executable code for the class's methods. If the server is packaged as a DLL, the following entry would be required:

```
[HKCR\CLSID\{571F1680-CC83-11d0-8C48-0080C73925BA}\InprocServer32]
@="C:\ServerOfTheApes.dll"
```

To indicate that the code is contained in an executable, the following entry would be required:

```
[HKCR\CLSID\{571F1680-CC83-11d0-8C48-0080C73925BA}\LocalServer32]
@="C:\ServerOfTheApes.exe"
```

It is legal to provide both entries and allow the client to select the locality based on latency and robustness requirements. To support the ProgIDFromCLSID function, the following subkey is needed:

```
[HKCR\CLSID\{571F1680-CC83-11d0-8C48-0080C73925BA}\ProgID]
@="Apes.Gorilla.1"
```

Conversely, to support the CLSIDFromProgID function, the following keys are needed:

```
[HKCR\Apes.Gorilla.1]
@="Gorilla"
```

---

⁹ The notation shown here uses standard REGEDIT4 syntax. The strings contained within the brackets correspond to key names. The *name=value* pairs beneath the key indicate the values stored at the indicated key. The distinguished name "@" indicates the default value of the key.

```
[HKCR\Apes.Gorilla.1\CLSID]
@="{571F1680-CC83-11d0-8C48-0080C73925BA}"
```

ProgIDs are optional but are recommended to allow environments that cannot easily cope with raw CLSIDs to make activation calls.

All well-implemented COM servers support self-registration. For an in-process server, this means that the DLL must export the well-known functions

```
STDAPI DllRegisterServer(void);
STDAPI DllUnregisterServer(void);
```

Note that STDAPI is simply a macro that indicates that the function returns an HRESULT and uses COM's standard calling convention for global functions. These routines must be explicitly exported, using either a module definition file, linker switches, or compiler directives. These routines are used by the Class Store to configure the local cache after downloading the file to the client machine. In addition to the Class Store, these well-known routines are used by various environments (e.g., Microsoft Transaction Server, ActiveX Code Download, miscellaneous setup utilities) to install or uninstall servers on host machines. The Win32 SDK includes a utility, REGSVR32.EXE, that will install or uninstall a COM in-process server using these well-known exported functions.

An in-process server's implementations of DllRegisterServer and DllUnregisterServer must make calls to the Registry to insert or delete the appropriate keys that map the server's CLSIDs and ProgIDs onto the server's file name. Although there are various techniques for implementing these routines, the most flexible and efficient technique is to create a string table that contains the appropriate keys, value names, and values and simply enumerate the entries in the table, calling either RegSetValueEx for installation or RegDeleteKey for de-installation. To implement registration based on this technique, the server could simply define an $N \times 3$ array of strings, where each row of the array would contain the strings to use as keys, value names, and values:

```
const char *g_RegTable[][3] = {
// format is { key, value name, value }
{ "CLSID\\{571F1680-CC83-11d0-8C48-0080C73925BA}",  0,
"Gorilla" },
{ "CLSID\\{571F1680-CC83-11d0-8C48-0080C73925BA}\\InprocServer32",
  0, (const char*)-1 // rogue value indicating file name
```

```
},
{ "CLSID\\{571F1680-CC83-11d0-8C48-0080C73925BA}\\ProgID",
  0, "Apes.Gorilla.1"
},
{ "Apes.Gorilla.1", 0,  "Gorilla" },
{ "Apes.Gorilla.1\\CLSID",
   0,  "{571F1680-CC83-11d0-8C48-0080C73925BA}" },
};
```

Given this table, the implementation of DllRegisterServer is fairly straightforward:

```
STDAPI DllRegisterServer(void) {
  HRESULT hr = S_OK;
// look up server's file name
  char szFileName[MAX_PATH];
  GetModuleFileNameA(g_hinstDll, szFileName, MAX_PATH);
// register entries from table
  int nEntries = sizeof(g_RegTable)/sizeof(*g_RegTable);
  for (int i = 0; SUCCEEDED(hr) && i < nEntries; i++) {
    const char *pszKeyName   = g_RegTable[i][0];
    const char *pszValueName = g_RegTable[i][1];
    const char *pszValue     = g_RegTable[i][2];
// map rogue value to module file name
    if (pszValue == (const char*)-1)
      pszValue = szFileName;
    HKEY hkey;
// create the key
    long err = RegCreateKeyA(HKEY_CLASSES_ROOT,
                            pszKeyName, &hkey);
    if (err == ERROR_SUCCESS) {
// set the value
      err = RegSetValueExA(hkey, pszValueName, 0,
                          REG_SZ, (const BYTE*)pszValue,
                          (strlen(pszValue) + 1));
      RegCloseKey(hkey);
    }
    if (err != ERROR_SUCCESS) {
// if cannot add key or value, back out and fail
      DllUnregisterServer();
      hr = SELFREG_E_CLASS;
```

```
        }
      }
      return hr;
    }
```

The corresponding `DllUnregisterServer` would look like this:

```
STDAPI DllUnregisterServer(void) {
    HRESULT hr = S_OK;
    int nEntries = sizeof(g_RegTable)/sizeof(*g_RegTable);
    for (int i = nEntries - 1; i >= 0; i--){
      const char *pszKeyName = g_RegTable[i][0];

      long err = RegDeleteKeyA(HKEY_CLASSES_ROOT, pszKeyName);
      if (err != ERROR_SUCCESS)
        hr = S_FALSE;
    }
    return hr;
}
```

Note that the implementation of `DllUnregisterServer` walks the table backward starting at the last entry. This is to overcome the limitation of `RegDeleteKey`, which allows only keys with no subkeys to be deleted. The implementation of `DllUnregisterServer` assumes that the table is arranged so that all subkeys of a key appear after the parent key's entry in the table.

Once COM maps a CLSID onto a given implementation file, some standard technique must be used to expose the server's class objects to COM. For an executable-based server, COM provides explicit API functions for associating class objects with their CLSIDs. These API functions will be discussed in detail in Chapter 6. For a DLL-based server, the DLL must export a well-known function that will be called by `CoGetClassObject` when a class object is required. This function must be exported using a module definition file and must have the following prototype:

```
HRESULT DllGetClassObject(
      [in] REFCLSID rclsid, // which class object?
      [in] REFIID riid,     // which interface?
      [out, iid_is(riid)] void **ppv); // put it here!
```

For efficiency and convenience, a given server can contain the code for more than one class. The first parameter of `DllGetClassObject` indicates which class is being requested. The second and third parameters simply allow the function to return a typed interface pointer to COM.

Consider a server that implements three classes: Gorilla, Chimp, and Orangutan. The server would probably contain six distinct C++ classes: three that model the instances of each class, three that model the class objects of each class. Given this scenario, the server's implementation of DllGetClassObject would look like this:

```
STDAPI DllGetClassObject(REFCLSID rclsid,
                         REFIID riid, void **ppv) {
// define a singleton class object for each class
   static GorillaClass s_gorillaClass;
   static OrangutanClass s_orangutanClass;
   static ChimpClass s_chimpClass;
// return interface pointers to known classes
   if (rclsid == CLSID_Gorilla)
     return s_gorillaClass.QueryInterface(riid, ppv);
   else if (rclsid == CLSID_Orangutan)
     return s_orangutanClass.QueryInterface(riid, ppv);
   else if (rclsid == CLSID_Chimp)
     return s_chimpClass.QueryInterface(riid, ppv);
// if we get to here, rclsid is a class we don't implement,
// so fail with well-known error code
   *ppv = 0;
   return CLASS_E_CLASSNOTAVAILABLE;
}
```

Note that this code does not care which interface is exposed from each class object. It simply forwards the QueryInterface request to the appropriate class object.

The following pseudocode demonstrates how the API function CoGetClassObject relates to the server's DllGetClassObject:

```
// pseudo-code from OLE32.DLL
HRESULT CoGetClassObject(REFCLSID rclsid, DWORD dwClsCtx,
              COSERVERINFO *pcsi, REFIID riid, void **ppv) {
   HRESULT hr = REGDB_E_CLASSNOTREG;
   *ppv = 0;
   if (dwClsCtx & CLSCTX_INPROC) {
// try to perform inproc activation
     HRESULT (*pfnGCO)(REFCLSID,REFIID,void**) = 0;
```

```
// look in table of already loaded servers in this process
    pfnGCO = LookupInClassTable(rclsid,dwClsCtx);
    if (pfnGCO == 0) {// not loaded yet!
// ask class store or registry for DLL name
        char szFileName[MAX_PATH];
        hr = GetFileFromClassStoreOrRegistry(rclsid,dwClsCtx, szFileName);
        if (SUCCEEDED(hr)) {
// try to load the DLL and scrape out DllGetClassObject
            HINSTANCE hInst = LoadLibrary(szFileName);
            if (hInst == 0)
                return CO_E_DLLNOTFOUND;
            pfnGCO = GetProcAddress(hInst, "DllGetClassObject");
            if (pfnGCO == 0)
                return CO_E_ERRORINDLL;
// cache DLL for later use
            InsertInClassTable(rclsid, dwClsCtx, hInst, pfnGCO);
        }
    }
// call function to get pointer to class object
        hr = (*pfnGCO)(rclsid, riid, ppv);
    }
    if ((dwClsCtx&(CLSCTX_LOCAL_SERVER|CLSCTX_REMOTE_SERVER))
        && hr == REGDB_E_CLASSNOTREG) {
// handle out-of-proc/remote request
    }
    return hr;
}
```

Note that the implementation of CoGetClassObject is the only entity that calls DllGetClassObject. To reinforce this fact, COM-aware linkers will emit a warning if the DllGetClassObject entry point is exported without using the private keyword in the corresponding module definition file:

```
// from APELIB.DEF
LIBRARY APELIB
EXPORTS
    DllGetClassObject private
```

In fact, COM-aware linkers prefer that all COM-related entry points use this keyword.

Generalizations

The previous example treated the IApeClass interface as a class-level interface that was specific to classes that expose the IApe interface from their instances. This interface allows clients to create new objects or find existing objects, but in either case, the resultant objects need to implement the IApe interface. If a new class wanted to allow clients to create or find non-IApe-compatible objects, its class object would need to implement a different interface. Because creating and finding objects are common requirements that most classes will want to support, COM defines standard interfaces for modeling object discovery and creation generically. One standard interface for object discovery is called IOleItemContainer:

```
// from oleidl.idl
[ object,uuid(0000011c-0000-0000-C000-000000000046) ]
interface IOleItemContainer : IOleContainer {

// ask for object named by pszItem
  HRESULT GetObject(
        [in] LPOLESTR pszItem,        // which object?
        [in] DWORD dwSpeedNeeded,   // deadline
        [in, unique] IBindCtx *pbc,// binding info
        [in] REFIID riid,            // which interface?
        [out, iid_is(riid)] void **ppv); // put it here!

// remaining methods deleted for clarity
}
```

Note that the GetObject method allows the client to specify the type of the resultant interface pointer. The actual class of the resultant object is context sensitive and dependent upon the particular implementation of IOleItemContainer. The following example asks the Gorilla class object to find the object named "Ursus":

```
HRESULT FindUrsus(IApe * &rpApe) {
// bind a reference to the Gorilla class object
  rpApe = 0;
  IOleItemContainer *poic = 0;
  HRESULT hr = CoGetClassObject(CLSID_Gorilla, CLSCTX_ALL,0,
                    IID_IOleItemContainer, (void**)&poic);
  if (SUCCEEDED(hr)) {
```

```
      // ask Gorilla class object for Ursus
         hr = poic->GetObject(OLESTR("Ursus"),
                              BINDSPEED_INDEFINITE, 0,
                              IID_IApe, (void**)&rpApe);
         poic->Release();
      }
      return hr;
   }
```

Although this usage is completely legal, the IOleItemContainer interface was designed to work in tandem with the Item Moniker, which is discussed later in this chapter.

COM also defines a standard interface for object creation. This interface is called IClassFactory:

```
// from unknwn.idl
[object,uuid(00000001-0000-0000-C000-000000000046)]
interface IClassFactory : IUnknown {
   HRESULT CreateInstance([in] IUnknown *pUnkOuter,
                          [in] REFIID riid,
                          [out, iid_is(riid)] void **ppv);
   HRESULT LockServer([in] BOOL bLock);
}
```

Although instances of a class could export the IClassFactory interface, this interface is usually exported by class objects only. Class objects are not required to implement IClassFactory, but, for uniformity, they often do. At the time of this writing, classes that need to integrate into the Microsoft Transaction Server environment *must* implement IClassFactory (in fact, no other class object interfaces will be recognized under MTS).

The IClassFactory interface has two methods: LockServer and CreateInstance. The LockServer method is called internally by COM during out-of-process activation requests and is discussed in detail in Chapter 6. The CreateInstance method is used to request that the class object create a new instance of the class. As was the case for IApeClass::CreateApe, the type of object that will be instantiated is determined by the class object to which the client is sending the CreateInstance request. The first CreateInstance parameter is used in COM aggregation and is discussed in Chapter 4. For the purposes of this chapter's discussion, this parameter must always be null. The second and third parameters of CreateInstance allow the method to return a dynamically typed interface pointer to the client.

Assuming that the gorilla class object exports the IClassFactory interface instead of IApeClass, clients must now use the IClassFactory::CreateInstance method to create new Gorilla instances:

```
HRESULT CreateAGorillaAndEatBanana() {
  IClassFactory *pcf = 0;
// find the class object
  HRESULT hr = CoGetClassObject(CLSID_Gorilla, CLSCTX_ALL,0,
                        IID_IClassFactory, (void**)&pcf);
  if (SUCCEEDED(hr)) {
    IApe *pApe = 0;
// use the gorilla class object to create a gorilla
    hr = pcf->CreateInstance(0, IID_IApe, (void**)&pApe);
// we're done with the class object, so release it
    pcf->Release();
    if (SUCCEEDED(hr)) {
// tell the new gorilla to eat a banana
      hr = pApe->EatBanana();
      pApe->Release();
    }
  }
  return hr;
}
```

This code is semantically identical to the version of the function that used the IApeClass interface instead of the IClassFactory interface.

To allow the previous example to work properly, the gorilla class object needs to implement IClassFactory:

```
class GorillaClass : public IClassFactory {
public:
  IMPLEMENT_UNKNOWN_NO_DELETE(GorillaClass)
  BEGIN_INTERFACE_TABLE(GorillaClass)
    IMPLEMENTS_INTERFACE(IClassFactory)
  END_INTERFACE_TABLE()

  STDMETHODIMP CreateInstance(IUnknown *pUnkOuter,
                        REFIID riid, void **ppv) {
    *ppv = 0;
    if (pUnkOuter != 0) // we don't support aggregation yet
      return CLASS_E_NOAGGREGATION;
```

```
    // create a new instance of our C++ class Gorilla
       Gorilla *p = new Gorilla;
       if (p == 0)
          return E_OUTOFMEMORY;
    // increment reference count by one
       p->AddRef();
    // store the resultant interface pointer into *ppv
       HRESULT hr = p->QueryInterface(riid, ppv);
    // decrement reference count by one, which will delete the
    // object if QI fails
       p->Release();
    // return result of Gorilla::QueryInterface
       return hr;
    }
    STDMETHODIMP LockServer(BOOL bLock);
};
```

The implementation of LockServer will be discussed later in this chapter.
Note that the implementation of CreateInstance first creates a new C++ object based on the class Gorilla and asks the object if it supports the requested interface. If the object does support the requested interface, then the
QueryInterface call will trigger a call to AddRef and the client will ultimately make the corresponding call to Release. If QueryInterface fails, then
some mechanism is needed for deleting the newly created object. The preceding example uses the standard technique of bracketing the call to
QueryInterface between an AddRef/Release pair. If the QueryInterface call
fails, then the Release call will bring the reference count to zero, triggering
the deletion of the object. If the call to QueryInterface succeeds, then the
Release call will bring the reference count to one. The remaining reference
belongs to the client, who will make the final call to Release when the object
is no longer needed.

Optimizations

One of the advantages of having a standard interface for instantiation is that
COM can provide a more efficient technique for instantiation. Consider the following code, which creates a new instance of the class Chimp:

```
HRESULT CreateChimp(/*[out]*/ IApe * &rpApe) {
    extern const CLSID CLSID_Chimp;
```

```
    rpApe = 0;
    IClassFactory *pcf = 0;
    HRESULT hr = CoGetClassObject(CLSID_Chimp, CLSCTX_ALL, 0,
                            IID_IClassFactory, (void**)&pcf);
    if (SUCCEEDED(hr)) {
        hr = pcf->CreateInstance(0, IID_IApe, (void**)&rpApe);
        pcf->Release();
    }
    return hr;
}
```

This code performs one operation: creating a Chimp object. Note that to perform one operation, three suboperations were required (CoGetClassObject, CreateInstance, Release). If the server is loaded as an in-process server, these three suboperations will not be particularly expensive. However, if the server is an out-of-process or off-host server, then each of these suboperations will require a round trip between the client and server processes. Although COM uses a very efficient IPC/RPC transport, each of these suboperations will have a nontrivial performance cost. Ideally, it would be better to ask COM to go to the server process once and, while there, use the class object to call CreateInstance on behalf of the client. If the class object is being used only to implement IClassFactory, this technique will be more efficient than the three-step technique shown earlier. COM provides an API function, CoCreateInstanceEx, that subsumes the functionality of CoGetClassObject and IClassFactory::CreateInstance to allow single round trip creation of new objects.

CoCreateInstanceEx allows the client to specify a CLSID that identifies the kind of object to instantiate. On successful completion, CoCreateInstanceEx returns one or more interface pointers that refer to a new instance of the specified class. When using CoCreateInstanceEx, the client never sees the intermediate class object that is used to instantiate the object. However, server implementors do not need to implement any additional functionality to enable clients to call CoCreateInstanceEx. From the server's perspective, all that is required is to expose its class objects as required by CoGetClassObject. The implementation of CoCreateInstanceEx will use the same techniques used by CoGetClassObject to find the corresponding class object. The primary difference is that once the class object is found, CoCreateInstanceEx takes the additional step of calling IClassFactory::CreateInstance potentially followed by one or more calls to QueryInterface *all while executing in the process of the class object.* If the activation request must be satisfied by a distinct process, this can result in considerable performance savings.

Like `CoGetClassObject`, `CoCreateInstanceEx` allows the client to specify the desired `CLSCTX` and `COSERVERINFO` parameters. In addition, `CoCreateInstanceEx` allows the client to ask for more than one interface pointer to the newly created object. It does this by allowing the client to pass an array of `MULTI_QI` structures that will be used to call `QueryInterface` on the new instance while executing in the server's process:

```
typedef struct tagMULTI_QI {
// which interface is desired?
  const IID *piid;
// null on input, will contain the pointer on output
  [iid_is(piid)] IUnknown *pItf;
// will contain the HRESULT from QueryInterface on output
  HRESULT hr;
} MULTI_QI;
```

By allowing the client to request more than one interface pointer to the new object, the client will not need to call `QueryInterface` explicitly if more than one type of interface pointer is desired. Because these `QueryInterface` calls will be made by COM on behalf of the client while running inside the process of the class object, no additional client-object round trips will be needed. Note that each of the interface pointers returned by `CoCreateInstanceEx` will point to the same object. COM does not provide an intrinsic operation for creating multiple instances in one round trip.

Armed with an understanding of the `MULTI_QI` structure, the `CoCreateInstanceEx` definition is fairly simple to understand:

```
HRESULT CoCreateInstanceEx(
        [in] REFCLSID rclsid,      // what kind of object?
        [in] IUnknown *pUnkOuter, // for aggregation
        [in] DWORD dwClsCtx,       // locality?
        [in] COSERVERINFO *pcsi,   // host/security info
        [in] ULONG cmqi,           // how many interfaces?
   [out, size_is(cmqi)] MULTI_QI *prgmq); // where to put itfs
```

If all of the requested interfaces are available on the new object, `CoCreateInstanceEx` returns S_OK. If at least one but not all of the requested interfaces are available, then `CoCreateInstanceEx` returns CO_S_ NOTALLINTERFACES, indicating partial success. The caller must then inspect the individual HRESULTs in each `MULTI_QI` structure to determine which interfaces were available and which were not. If `CoCreateInstanceEx` is unable to create an object or none of the requested interfaces are available, then CoCreateInstanceEx returns a SEVERITY_ERROR-based HRESULT indicating why the operation failed.

CoCreateInstanceEx is extremely efficient when multiple types of interfaces are needed. Consider the following additional interface definition:

```
[object,uuid(753A8F7C-A7FF-11d0-8C30-0080C73925BA)]
interface IEgghead : IUnknown {
  import "unknwn.idl";
  HRESULT ContemplateNavel(void);
}
```

Given this interface definition, the client can now bind both types of pointers to a new chimpanzee in one client-server round trip:

```
void CreateChimpEatBananaAndThinkAboutIt(void) {
// declare and initialize an array of MULTI_QI's
  MULTI_QI rgmqi[2] =
      { { &IID_IApe, 0, 0 }, { &IID_IEgghead, 0, 0 } };
  HRESULT hr = CoCreateInstanceEx(
                      CLSID_Chimp, // make a new chimp
                      0,           // no aggregation
                      CLSCTX_ALL,  // any locality
                      0, // no explicit host/security info
                      2, // asking for two interfaces
                      rgmqi); // array of MULTI_QI structs
  if (SUCCEEDED(hr)) {
// hr may be CO_S_NOTALLINTERFACES, so check each result
    if (hr == S_OK || SUCCEEDED(rgmqi[0].hr)) {
// it is safe to blindly cast the resultant ptr to the type
// that corresponds to the IID used to request the interface
        IApe *pApe = reinterpret_cast<IApe*>(rgmqi[0].pItf);
        assert(pApe);
        HRESULT hr2 = pApe->EatBanana();
        assert(SUCCEEDED(hr2));
        pApe->Release();
    }
    if (hr == S_OK || SUCCEEDED(rgmqi[1].hr)) {
      IEgghead *peh =
                reinterpret_cast<IEgghead*>(rgmqi[1].pItf);
      assert(peh);
```

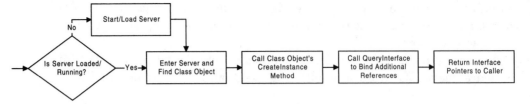

Figure 3.3   CoCreateInstanceEx

```
        HRESULT hr2 = peh->ContemplateNavel();
        assert(SUCCEEDED(hr2));
        peh->Release();
    }
  }
}
```

Figure 3.3 illustrates the steps that are taken by CoCreateInstanceEx to create a new object. It is important to note that both resultant pointers will point to the same object. If two distinct objects are required, then two distinct calls to CoCreateInstanceEx are required.

Using CoCreateInstanceEx is fairly straightforward if only one interface is desired:

```
HRESULT CreateChimpAndEatBanana(void) {
// declare and initialize a MULTI_QI
  MULTI_QI mqi = { &IID_IApe, 0, 0 };
  HRESULT hr = CoCreateInstanceEx(
                    CLSID_Chimp, // make a new chimp
                    0,           // no aggregation
                    CLSCTX_ALL,  // any locality
                    0, // no explicit host/security info
                    1, // asking for one interface
                    &mqi); // array of MULTI_QI structs
  if (SUCCEEDED(hr)) {
    IApe *pApe = reinterpret_cast<IApe*>(mqi.pItf);
    assert(pApe);
// use the new object
    hr = pApe->EatBanana();
// release the interface pointer
    pApe->Release();
  }
```

```
        return hr;
    }
```

If only one interface is needed and no COSERVERINFO will be passed, COM provides a somewhat more convenient version of CoCreateInstanceEx called CoCreateInstance:[10]

```
HRESULT CoCreateInstance(
        [in] REFCLSID rclsid,      // what kind of object?
        [in] IUnknown *pUnkOuter,  // for aggregation
        [in] DWORD dwClsCtx,       // locality?
        [in] REFIID riid,          // what kind of interface
        [out, iid_is(riid)] void **ppv); // where to put itf
```

The preceding example becomes much simpler when CoCreateInstance is used:

```
HRESULT CreateChimpAndEatBanana(void) {
  IApe *pApe = 0;
  HRESULT hr = CoCreateInstance(
                    CLSID_Chimp, // make a new chimp
                    0,           // no aggregation
                    CLSCTX_ALL,  // any locality
                    IID_IApe, // what kind of itf
                    (void**)&pApe); // where to put itf
  if (SUCCEEDED(hr)) {
    assert(pApe);
// use the new object
    hr = pApe->EatBanana();
// release the interface pointer
    pApe->Release();
  }
  return hr;
}
```

---

[10] Technically, CoCreateInstance came first. CoCreateInstanceEx was added in Windows NT 4.0 when it became clear that some developers would want to pass security and host information to COM's activation API functions. In the original prototype for CoGetClassObject, the third parameter was reserved, so NT 4.0 was able to steal the reserved parameter for the COSERVERINFO. Unfortunately, CoCreateInstance had no unused parameters, so CoCreateInstanceEx was created. One could argue that a version of CoGetClassObject that uses MULTI_QI to allow more than one interface to be bound would also be useful, but alas, there is no CoGetClassObjectEx at the time of this writing. A similar argument could be made regarding IMoniker::BindToObject and MULTI_QI.

The previous two examples are functionally equivalent. In fact, the implementation of CoCreateInstance simply calls CoCreateInstanceEx internally:

```
// pseudo-code for implementation of CoCreateInstance API
HRESULT CoCreateInstance(REFCLSID rclsid,
                IUnknown *pUnkOuter, DWORD dwClsCtx,
                REFIID riid, void **ppv) {
    MULTI_QI rgmqi[] = { &riid, 0, 0 };
    HRESULT hr = CoCreateInstanceEx(rclsid, pUnkOuter,
                            dwClsCtx, 0, 1, rgmqi);
    *ppv = rgmqi[0].pItf;
    return hr;
}
```

Although it is possible to issue a remote activation request using CoCreateInstance, the lack of a COSERVERINFO parameter does not allow the caller to specify an explicit host name. Instead, calling CoCreateInstance and specifying only the CLSCTX_REMOTE_SERVER flag informs the SCM to use per-CLSID configuration information to select the host machine that will be used to activate the object.

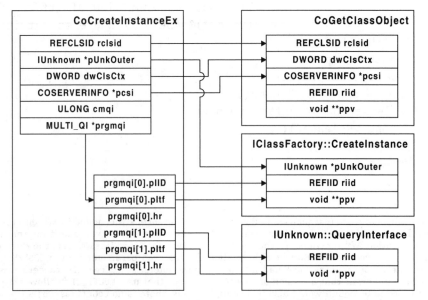

Figure 3.4 CoCreateInstanceEx versus CoGetClassObject

Figure 3.4 shows how the parameters of CoCreateInstanceEx map onto the parameters of CoGetClassObject and IClassFactory::CreateInstance. Contrary to popular belief, CoCreateInstanceEx does not call CoGetClassObject internally. Although there is no logical difference between the two techniques, the implementation of CoCreateInstanceEx will be more efficient when creating one instance, as it avoids the extra client-server round trips that would be required if CoGetClassObject were used. If, however, large numbers of instances will be created, the client can cache the class object pointer and simply call IClassFactory::CreateInstance multiple times. Since IClassFactory::CreateInstance is just a method call and does not go through the SCM, it is somewhat faster than calling CoCreateInstanceEx. The threshold at which it becomes more efficient to cache the class object and bypass CoCreateInstanceEx will vary based on IPC and RPC performance on the host machines and network in use.

Interface and Implementation Again

The previous examples of client-side activation made explicit calls to COM activation API functions. Often, multiple steps may be needed to properly bind to the desired object (*e.g.*, create one type of object, then ask it for a reference to another object based on some query information). To decouple clients from the actual algorithms used for finding or creating objects, COM provides a standard mechanism for resolving arbitrary object names onto the objects to which they refer. This mechanism is based on using locator objects that encapsulate their binding algorithm behind a standard, uniform interface. These locator objects are formally called *monikers* and are simply COM objects that export the IMoniker interface. The IMoniker interface is one of the more complex COM interfaces; however, it exposes one method that is extremely important for this discussion, BindToObject:

```
interface IMoniker : IPersistStream {
  HRESULT BindToObject([in] IBindCtx *pbc,
                       [in, unique] IMoniker *pmkToLeft,
                       [in] REFIID riid,
                       [out, iid_is(riid)] void **ppv);
// remaining methods deleted for clarity
}
```

Recall that interface definitions are abstract and sufficiently vague to allow many interpretations of each method's precise semantics. The abstract semantics of BindToObject are "run your algorithm for finding or creating an object and return a typed interface pointer to the object once it is created or found." When a client calls BindToObject on a moniker, it has no idea of exactly how the moniker will resolve its internal state into a pointer to an object. Given three different monikers, three completely different algorithms may be used. This polymorphic behavior is what makes the moniker idiom so powerful.

Clients get monikers in one of several ways. A client may be given a moniker by some external agent, such as a result from a method call on some object already in use. Clients may call an explicit API function that creates a particular type of moniker. Clients may simply have a text string that is the "stringified" state of the moniker. This last situation is the most interesting, as it allows applications to load and store text-based "object names" using external configuration files or the system registry. If this technique is publicly documented as part of the configuration state of the application, system administrators or sophisticated users could then reconfigure an application to use an alternative strategy for finding objects that may or may not have been anticipated by the original application developer. For example, a moniker that supports load balancing could be reconfigured to use a different policy for selecting host machines simply by changing the textual version of the moniker stored in an application's configuration file.

The textual representation of a moniker is formally called a *display name*. The IMoniker interface exposes a method, GetDisplayName, that allows clients to ask a moniker for its display name. The more interesting problem is how one resolves arbitrary display names onto monikers. This task is somewhat problematic, as the client cannot easily tell what kind of moniker a display name corresponds to. That is the job of MkParseDisplayName, arguably the most important API function in all of COM.

MkParseDisplayName takes an arbitrary display name and resolves it to a moniker:

```
HRESULT MkParseDisplayName(
        [in] IBindCtx *pbc,           // binding info
 [in, string] const OLECHAR *pwszName, // object name
        [out] ULONG *pcchEaten,       // progress on error
        [out] IMoniker **ppmk);       // the resultant moniker
```

The moniker namespace is extensible to support new types of monikers. The top-level parser used by MkParseDisplayName examines the prefix of the display name and tries to match the prefix to a registered ProgID that designates what type of moniker this display name corresponds to. If a match is found, a new moniker of the appropriate type is created and the moniker is given the display name to parse. Because monikers are hierarchical and support composition, the resultant moniker may actually be a composite of two or more monikers. This is an implementation detail that is of no concern to the client. The client simply uses the resultant IMoniker interface pointer (which may or may not point to a composite moniker) to find the object in question.

Recall that the initial entry point into a COM class is through its class object. To connect to a class object, the moniker type that is needed is a Class Moniker. Class Monikers are a built-in moniker type that is provided by COM. Class Monikers keep a CLSID as their internal state and can be created either by using the explicit COM API function CreateClassMoniker:

```
HRESULT CreateClassMoniker([in] REFCLSID rclsid,
                           [out] IMoniker **ppmk);
```

or by passing the display name form of the Class Moniker to MkParse-DisplayName:[11]

```
clsid:571F1680-CC83-11d0-8C48-0080C73925BA:
```

Note that the prefix "clsid" is the ProgID for the Class Moniker.

The following code demonstrates using MkParseDisplayName to create a Class Moniker, which is then used to connect to the class object for Gorillas:

```
HRESULT GetGorillaClass(IApeClass * &rpgc) {
   rpgc = 0;
// declare the CLSID for Gorilla as a display name
   const OLECHAR pwsz[] =
      OLESTR("clsid:571F1680-CC83-11d0-8C48-0080C73925BA:");
// create a new binding context for parsing and binding
// the moniker
   IBindCtx *pbc = 0;
   HRESULT hr = CreateBindCtx(0, &pbc);
   if (SUCCEEDED(hr)) {
      ULONG cchEaten;
      IMoniker *pmk = 0;
```

---

[11] Although using MkParseDisplayName will be somewhat less efficient, it allows much more flexibility. As noted previously, the display name could be read from a file or even from the user interface. Microsoft's Internet Explorer is a great example of an application that allows users to type in arbitrary object names (URLs) that are resolved to monikers (using the extended API function, MkParseDisplayNameEx).

```
// ask COM to convert the display name to a moniker object
    hr = MkParseDisplayName(pbc, pwsz, &cchEaten, &pmk);
    if (SUCCEEDED(hr)) {
// ask the moniker to find or create the object that it
// refers to
        hr = pmk->BindToObject(pbc, 0, IID_IApeClass,
                                (void**)&rpgc);
// we now have a pointer to the desired object, so release
// the moniker and the binding context
        pmk->Release();
    }
    pbc->Release();
  }
  return hr;
}
```

The binding context that is passed to both MkParseDisplayName and
IMoniker::BindToObject is simply a helper object that allows auxiliary parameters to be passed to the moniker parsing and binding machinery. For this
simple example, all that is needed is a new binding context to act as a place-
holder, which is acquired by calling the COM API function CreateBindCtx.[12]

Windows NT 4.0 introduced an API function that simplifies calling
MkParseDisplayName and IMoniker::BindToObject:

```
HRESULT CoGetObject(
            [in, string] const OLECHAR *pszName,
            [in, unique] BIND_OPTS *pBindOptions,
            [in] REFIID riid,
            [out, iid_is(riid)] void **ppv);
```

This API function is implemented as follows:

```
// pseudo-code from OLE32.DLL
HRESULT CoGetObject(const OLECHAR *pszName, BIND_OPTS *pOpt,
                    REFIID riid, void **ppv) {
```

---

[12] Bind contexts are used by composite monikers to optimize parsing and binding operations. Bind
contexts also allow clients to specify CLSCTX flags as well as a COSERVERINFO, although the current implementation of the Class Moniker will ignore both of these attributes. The Class Moniker
instead assumes that it will be composed with a moniker that references an implementation of the
IClassActivator interface, which provides much greater flexibility.

```
// prepare for failure
  *ppv = 0;
// create a bind context
  IBindCtx *pbc = 0;
  HRESULT hr = CreateBindCtx(0, &pbc);
  if (SUCCEEDED(hr)) {
// set bind options if provided
    if (pOpt)
      hr = pbc->SetBindOptions(pOpt);
    if (SUCCEEDED(hr)) {
// convert the display name into a moniker
      ULONG cch;
      IMoniker *pmk = 0;
      hr = MkParseDisplayName(pbc, pszName, &cch, &pmk);
      if (SUCCEEDED(hr)) {
// ask the moniker to bind to the named object
        hr = pmk->BindToObject(pbc, 0, riid, ppv);
        pmk->Release();
      }
    }
    pbc->Release();
  }
  return hr;
}
```

Given this function, creating new gorillas is now a simple matter of finding the class object and invoking the CreateInstance method:

```
HRESULT CreateAGorillaAndEatBanana() {
  IClassFactory *pcf = 0;
// declare the CLSID for Gorilla as a display name
  const OLECHAR pwsz[] =
    OLESTR("clsid:571F1680-CC83-11d0-8C48-0080C73925BA:");
// find the class object via the gorilla's class moniker
  HRESULT hr = CoGetObject(pwsz, 0, IID_IClassFactory,
                           (void**)&pcf);
  if (SUCCEEDED(hr)) {
    IApe *pApe = 0;
// use the class object to create a gorilla
    hr = pcf->CreateInstance(0, IID_IApe, (void**)&pApe);
    if (SUCCEEDED(hr)) {
```

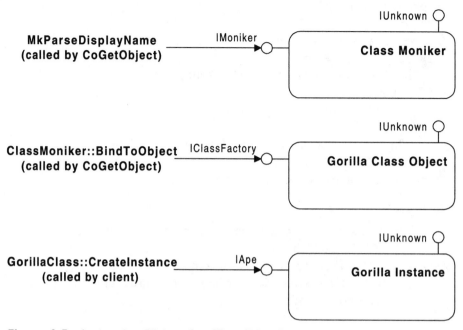

Figure 3.5 Activation Using the Class Moniker

```
// tell the new gorilla to eat a banana
        hr = pApe->EatBanana();
        pApe->Release();
    }
    pcf->Release();
}
    return hr;
}
```

Figure 3.5 illustrates which objects are created or found by each operation.

Visual Basic exposes the functionality of the CoGetObject API routine via the intrinsic function GetObject. The following Visual Basic code also creates a new Gorilla and tells it to eat a banana:

```
Sub CreateGorillaAndEatBanana()
    Dim gc as IApeClass
    Dim ape as IApe
    Dim sz as String
    sz = "clsid:571F1680-CC83-11d0-8C48-0080C73925BA:"
```

```
' get the class object for gorillas
  Set gc = GetObject(sz)
' ask gorilla class object to create a new gorilla
  Set ape = gc.CreateApe()
' ask gorilla to eat a banana
  ape.EatBanana
End Sub
```

Note that the Visual Basic version of this function uses the IApeClass inter-face to instantiate the object. This is because Visual Basic cannot use the IClassFactory interface due to restrictions of the language.

Monikers and Composition

Monikers are often composed from other monikers to allow object hierarchies to be navigated based on a textual description of a path. To support this type of navigation easily, COM provides a standard moniker implementation that, when composed to the right of another moniker, asks the object to bind a reference to another object in the hierarchy. This moniker is called the Item Moniker, and it uses the object's IOleItemContainer interface to resolve an object name to an interface pointer.

The following display name demonstrates the Item Moniker used in tandem with the Class Moniker:

```
clsid:571F1680-CC83-11d0-8C48-0080C73925BA:!Ursus
```

Note the use of the "!" character to delimit the Class Moniker's display name from the item name "Ursus". When parsed, MkParseDisplayName will first use the prefix "clsid" as a ProgID to contact the implementation of the Class Moniker. MkParseDisplayName will then ask the Class Moniker implementation to parse as much of the string as it recognizes. This means that after the Class Moniker has parsed its GUID from the string, the following fragment will still need to be parsed:

```
!Ursus
```

Because this name is meaningful only in the scope of the object named by the moniker to its left, MkParseDisplayName will actually bind the leftmost moniker (the Class Moniker) and ask the object it names (the Gorilla class object) to parse the remainder of the string. To support parsing display names, COM defines the standard interface IParseDisplayName:

```
[ object,uuid(0000011a-0000-0000-C000-000000000046) ]
interface IParseDisplayName : IUnknown {
// convert display name to a moniker
  HRESULT ParseDisplayName(
         [in, unique] IBindCtx *pbc,
         [in] LPOLESTR pszDisplayName,
         [out] ULONG *pchEaten,
         [out] IMoniker **ppmkOut
  );
}
```

In the case of the display name used in this example, the Gorilla class object would need to implement IParseDisplayName and convert the string "!Ursus" to a moniker that MkParseDisplayName will compose to the right of the Class Moniker. Because the standard Item Moniker is desired, the following implementation would suffice:

```
STDMETHODIMP GorillaClass::ParseDisplayName(IBindCtx *pbc,
             LPOLESTR pszDisplayName, ULONG *pchEaten,
             IMoniker **ppmkOut) {
// create an item moniker using explicit API function
  HRESULT hr = CreateItemMoniker(OLESTR("!"),
                                  pszDisplayName + 1,
                                  ppmkOut);
// indicate how many characters were parsed
  if (SUCCEEDED(hr))
    *pchEaten = wcslen(pszDisplayName);
  else
    *pchEaten = 0;
  return hr;
}
```

Note that this example does not attempt to validate the name it is parsing. It simply shears off the leading "!" and creates a new Item Moniker from the remaining display name.

Once the two monikers have been parsed, MkParseDisplayName will couple the two monikers together using a generic composite moniker. Generic composite monikers simply hold two monikers together. The generic composite moniker's implementation of BindToObject simply binds the moniker on the right first, passing the pointer to the moniker on the left as the pmkToLeft parameter. The following pseudocode illustrates this:

```
// pseudo-code from OLE32.DLL
STDMETHODIMP GenericComposite::BindToObject (IBindCtx *pbc,
              IMoniker *pmkToLeft,
              REFIID riid, void **ppv) {
   return m_pmkRight->BindToObject(pbc, m_pmkLeft, riid, ppv);
}
```

This implementation illustrates that the moniker on the right is meaningful only in the scope of the moniker to its left. In the case of the Class!Item Moniker used in this example, the Item Moniker will receive the Class Moniker as its pmkToLeft parameter at bind time.

As stated earlier, the Item Moniker uses the IOleItemContainer interface to bind an interface pointer. The following is the pseudocode for the Item Moniker's BindToObject implementation:

```
// pseudo-code from OLE32.DLL
STDMETHODIMP ItemMoniker::BindToObject(
              IBindCtx *pbc, IMoniker *pmkToLeft,
              REFIID riid, void **ppv) {
// assume failure
   *ppv = 0;
   if (pmkToLeft == 0) // requires a scope
     return E_INVALIDARG;
// first bind moniker to left
   IOleItemContainer *poic = 0;
   HRESULT hr = pmkToLeft->BindToObject(pbc, 0,
                   IID_IOleItemContainer, (void**)&poic);
   if (SUCCEEDED(hr)) {
// cache the bound object in binding context
     pbc->RegisterObjectBound(poic);
// get bind speed from Bind Context
     DWORD dwBindSpeed = this->MyGetSpeedFromCtx(pbc);
// ask object for named sub-object
       hr = poic->GetObject(m_pszItem, dwBindSpeed, pbc,
                     riid, ppv);
     poic->Release();
   }
}
```

This implementation implies that the following code:

```
HRESULT GetUrsus(IApe *&rpApe) {
  const OLECHAR pwsz[] =
OLESTR("clsid:571F1680-CC83-11d0-8C48-0080C73925BA:!Ursus");
  return CoGetObject(pwsz, 0, IID_IApe, (void**)&rpApe);
}
```

is equivalent to

```
HRESULT GetUrsus(IApe *&rpApe) {
  IOleItemContainer *poic = 0;
  HRESULT hr = CoGetClassObject(CLSID_Gorilla, CLSCTX_ALL,
                  0, IID_IOleItemContainer, (void**)&poic);
  if (SUCCEEDED(hr)) {
    hr = poic->GetObject(OLESTR("Ursus"), BINDSPEED_INFINITE,
                    0, IID_IApe, (void**)&rpApe);
    poic->Release();
  }
  return hr;
}
```

Note that the level of indirection afforded by using CoGetObject allows the client to change the binding policy simply by reading a different display name from a configuration file or registry key.

Monikers and Persistence

No discussion of monikers would be complete without a discussion of the File Moniker. Recall that COM supports three activation primitives: binding to class objects, binding to new class instances, and binding to persistent objects stored in files. This chapter has explored the first two of these primitives in detail. The third primitive is based on the COM API function CoGetInstanceFromFile:

```
HRESULT CoGetInstanceFromFile(
     [in, unique] COSERVERINFO *pcsi, // host/security info
     [in, unique] CLSID       *pClsid, // explicit CLSID (opt)
     [in, unique] IUnknown *punkOuter,// for aggregation
     [in] DWORD dwClsCtx,             // locality?
     [in] DWORD grfMode,              // file open mode
     [in] OLECHAR *pwszName,          // file name of object
```

```
    [in] DWORD cmqi,                      // how many interfaces?
    [out, size_is(cmqi)] MULTI_QI *prgmq // where to put itfs
);
```

This routine accepts as input a filename that refers to the persistent state of an object.[13] CoGetInstanceFromFile ensures that the object is running and then returns one or more interface pointers to the [re]activated object. To perform this task, CoGetInstanceFromFile first needs to determine the CLSID of the object. The CLSID is needed for two reasons. If the object is not running, COM will need this CLSID to create a new instance to be initialized from the persistent image. Second, if the caller does not specify an explicit host name to forward the activation call to, COM will use the CLSID to determine which machine to activate the object at.[14]

If the CLSID is not passed explicitly by the caller, the CoGetInstance-FromFile derives the CLSID from the file itself by calling the COM API function GetClassFile:

```
HRESULT GetClassFile([in, string] OLECHAR *pwszFileName,
                     [out] CLSID *pclsid);
```

GetClassFile uses header information in the file as well as registry information to determine what type of object is contained in the file.

Once the class and host machine are determined, COM examines the Running Object Table (ROT) on the target host machine to determine whether the object has already been activated. The ROT is a facility of the SCM that maps arbitrary monikers onto running instances on the local host machine. Persistent objects are expected to register themselves at load time in the local ROT. To represent the persistent object's filename as a moniker, COM provides a standard moniker type called the File Moniker that wraps a filename behind the IMoniker interface. File monikers can be created either by passing the file name to MkParseDisplayName or by calling the explicit API function CreateFileMoniker:

```
HRESULT CreateFileMoniker(
        [in, string] const OLECHAR *pszFileName,
        [out] IMoniker **ppmk);
```

---

[13] An alternative version of this API function, CoGetInstanceFromIStorage, accepts a pointer to a hierarchical storage medium instead of a filename.

[14] In addition to the normal rerouting of CLSIDs to host machines that is used by CoGetClassObject/CoCreateInstanceEx, CoGetInstanceFromFile can use the UNC host name of the file to reroute the activation request to the host machine where the file resides. This activation mode is referred to by the COM Specification as "AtBits" activation and is designated using the "ActivateAtStorage" registry setting described in Chapter 6.

If the persistent object has already registered its File Moniker in the ROT, CoGetInstanceFromFile simply returns a pointer to the already running object. If the object is not found in the ROT, COM creates a new instance of the file's class and initializes it from the persistent image via the instance's IPersistFile::Load method:

```
[ object, uuid(0000010b-0000-0000-C000-000000000046) ]
interface IPersistFile : IPersist {
// called by CoGetInstanceFromFile to initialize object
  HRESULT Load(
      [in, string] const OLECHAR * pszFileName,
      [in] DWORD grfMode
  );
// remaining methods deleted for clarity
}
```

It is the responsibility of the object implementation to load any persistent state from the file as well as to register itself with the local ROT to ensure that only one instance per file is running at a time:

```
STDMETHODIMP Gorilla::Load(const OLECHAR *pszFileName,
                          DWORD grfMode) {
// read in persisted object state
  HRESULT hr = this->MyReadStateFromFile(pszFile, grfMode);
  if (FAILED(hr)) return hr;
// get pointer to ROT from SCM
  IRunningObjectTable *prot = 0;
  hr = GetRunningObjectTable(0, &prot);
  if (SUCCEEDED(hr)) {
// create a file moniker to register in ROT
    IMoniker *pmk = 0;
    hr = CreateFileMoniker(pszFileName, &pmk);
    if (SUCCEEDED(hr)) {
// register self in ROT
      hr = prot->Register(0, this, pmk, &m_dwReg);
      pmk->Release();
    }
    prot->Release();
  }
  return hr;
}
```

The newly created instance's `IPersistFile::Load` method will be called by the SCM during the execution of `CoGetInstanceFromFile`. The example above uses the COM API function `GetRunningObjectTable` to get an `IRunningObjectTable` interface pointer into the SCM. It then uses this interface to register its moniker in the ROT so that subsequent calls to `CoGetInstanceFromFile` using the same filename will not create new objects but instead will return references to this object.[15]

The File Moniker exists for two reasons. One reason is to allow objects to register themselves in the ROT so that `CoGetInstanceFromFile` can find them. The second reason is to hide the use of `CoGetInstanceFromFile` from the client behind the `IMoniker` interface. The File Moniker's implementation of `BindToObject` simply calls `CoGetInstanceFromFile`:

```
// pseudo-code from OLE32.DLL
STDMETHODIMP FileMoniker::BindToObject(IBindCtx *pbc,
                IMoniker *pmkToLeft,
                REFIID riid, void **ppv) {
// assume failure
   *ppv = 0;
   HRESULT hr = E_FAIL;
   if (pmkToLeft == 0) { // no moniker to left
     MULTI_QI mqi = { &riid, 0, 0 };
     COSERVERINFO *pcsi;
     DWORD grfMode;
     DWORD dwClsCtx;
// these three parameters are attributes of the BindCtx
     this->MyGetFromBindCtx(pbc, &pcsi, &grfMode, &dwClsCtx);
     hr = CoGetInstanceFromFile(pcsi, 0, 0, dwClsCtx,
                                grfMode, this->m_pszFileName,
                                1, &mqi);
     if (SUCCEEDED(hr))
       *ppv = mqi.pItf;
   }
   else { // there's a moniker to the left
     // ask object to left for IClassActivator
     // or IClassFactory
   }
```

---

[15] Technically, the ROT is not a machine-wide table but rather a Winstation-wide table, which means that by default, not all logon sessions will have access to the object. To ensure that the object is visible to all possible clients, the object should specify the ROTFLAGS_ALLOWANYCLIENT flag when calling `IRunningObjectTable::Register`.

```
      return hr;
  }
```

Given the behavior of the File Moniker, the following function that calls CoGetInstanceFromFile:

```
HRESULT GetCornelius(IApe * &rpApe) {
  OLECHAR *pwszObject =
              OLESTR("\\\\server\\public\\cornelius.chmp");
  MULTI_QI mqi = { &IID_IApe, 0, 0 };
  HRESULT hr = CoGetInstanceFromFile(0, 0, 0, CLSCTX_SERVER,
                      STGM_READWRITE, pwszObject, 1, &mqi);
  if (SUCCEEDED(hr))
    rpApe = mqi.pItf;
  else
    rpApe = 0;
  return hr;
}
```

could be simplified by calling CoGetObject instead:

```
HRESULT GetCornelius(IApe * &rpApe) {
  OLECHAR *pwszObject =
              OLESTR("\\\\server\\public\\cornelius.chmp");
  return CoGetObject(pwszObject,0,IID_IApe, (void**)&rpApe);
}
```

As was the case when the Class Moniker was used previously, the level of indirection afforded by CoGetObject allows the client to specify arbitrarily complex activation policies without changing one line of code.

Server Lifetime

Previous sections have illustrated how COM automatically loads DLLs to bring object implementations into the address space of client programs. What has not been discussed is exactly how and when these DLLs are unloaded. In general, server DLLs can prevent premature unloading, but it is the client that chooses the moment that DLLs are actually freed. Clients that wish to free idle DLLs call the COM API function CoFreeUnusedLibraries:

```
void CoFreeUnusedLibraries(void);
```

This routine is typically called by clients at idle time to garbage-collect their address space. When CoFreeUnusedLibraries is called, COM queries each DLL that has been loaded to discover unneeded DLLs. It does this by calling each DLL's DllCanUnloadNow function, which must be explicitly exported from the DLL.

The DllCanUnloadNow routine that each server DLL exports must conform to the following signature:

```
HRESULT DllCanUnloadNow(void);
```

If the DLL wishes to be freed, it returns S_OK. If the DLL wishes to remain loaded, it returns S_FALSE. Server DLLs must remain loaded *at least* as long as there are extant interface pointers to its objects. This means that the DLL will need to keep a count of all extant object references. To simplify this implementation, most DLLs keep a single lock count variable and use two functions to increment and decrement the lock count automatically:

```
LONG g_cLocks = 0;
void LockModule(void) { InterlockedIncrement(&g_cLocks); }
void UnlockModule(void) { InterlockedDecrement(&g_cLocks); }
```

Given the presence of these routines, the implementation of DllCanUnloadNow is extremely simple:

```
STDAPI DllCanUnloadNow(void)
{ return g_cLocks == 0 ? S_OK : S_FALSE; }
```

All that remains is to call the LockModule and UnlockModule routines at the appropriate time.

There are two basic forces that must keep a server DLL loaded: outstanding references to class instances and class objects and outstanding calls to IClassFactory::LockServer. Adding support for DllCanUnloadNow to class instances and class objects is fairly straightforward. Heap-based objects (such as class instances) simply increment the server lock count at the first call to AddRef:

```
STDMETHODIMP_(ULONG) Chimp::AddRef(void) {
  if (m_cRef == 0)
    LockModule();
  return InterlockedIncrement(&m_cRef);
}
```

and decrement the server lock count at the final call to Release:

```
STDMETHODIMP_(ULONG) Chimp::Release(void) {
  LONG res = InterlockedDecrement(&m_cRef);
  if (res == 0) {
    delete this;
    UnlockModule();
  }
  return res;
}
```

Because non-heap-based objects (such as class objects) do not keep a reference count, each call to AddRef and Release should increment or decrement the lock count:

```
STDMETHODIMP_(ULONG) ChimpClass::AddRef(void) {
  LockModule();
  return 2;
}

STDMETHODIMP_(ULONG) ChimpClass::Release(void) {
  UnlockModule();
  return 1;
}
```

Class objects that implement IClassFactory should adjust their server's lock count in calls to IClassFactory::LockServer:

```
STDMETHODIMP ChimpClass::LockServer(BOOL bLock) {
  if (bLock)
    LockModule();
  else
    UnlockModule();
  return S_OK;
}
```

As discussed in Chapter 6, IClassFactory::LockServer exists primarily for out-of-process servers, but it is simple enough to implement in in-process servers.

It is worth noting that there is an inherent race condition in the CoFreeUnusedLibraries/DllCanUnloadNow protocol. It is possible that one thread may be executing the final release on the last instance exported from a DLL while a second thread is simultaneously executing the CoFreeUnused-Libraries routine. COM takes every possible precaution to avoid this situation. In particular, the Windows NT 4.0 Service Pack 2 implementation of COM added a special facility to address this potential race condition. The Service Pack 2 version of the COM library detects that a server DLL has been accessed from multiple threads and, instead of unloading the DLL immediately from within CoFreeUnusedLibraries, COM enqueues the DLL onto a list of DLLs that need to be freed. COM will then wait an unspecified period of time before it will allow these idle server DLLs to be freed by a subsequent call to CoFreeUnusedLibraries, ensuring that no residual Release calls are still being executed.[16] This means that in multithreaded environments, it may take considerably longer for a DLL to unload from its client than is expected.

Classes and IDL

As noted early in this chapter, COM treats interfaces and classes as distinct entities. In light of this, COM classes (like COM interfaces) should be defined in IDL to provide a language-neutral description of the concrete data types a server may export. The IDL definition of a COM class contains the list of interfaces that instances of the class export *barring catastrophic failure*:

```
[uuid(753A8A7D-A7FF-11d0-8C30-0080C73925BA)]
coclass Gorilla {
   interface IApe;
   interface IWarrior;
}
```

IDL coclass definitions always appear in the context of a library definition. In IDL, library definitions are used to group a collection of data types (*e.g.*, interfaces, coclasses, typedefs) into a logical unit or namespace. All data types that appear in the context of an IDL library definition will be tokenized into the resultant type library. Type libraries are used in lieu of IDL files by environments such as Visual Basic and Java.

An IDL file can have at most one library statement, and all data types defined or used inside the library definition will appear in the generated type library:

---

[16] It is likely that Windows NT 5.0 will provide additional support for ensuring that DLLs are released promptly and safely. Consult the SDK documentation for more details.

```
// apes.idl //////////////////////////////////

// bring in IDL definitions of ape interfaces
import "apeitfs.idl";
[
  uuid(753A8A80-A7FF-11d0-8C30-0080C73925BA), // LIBID
  version(1.0),  // version number of library
  lcid(9),       // locale ID of library (english)
  helpstring("Library of the Apes") // title of library
]
library ApeLib
{
  importlib("stdole32.tlb"); // bring in std defs.

  [uuid(753A8A7D-A7FF-11d0-8C30-0080C73925BA)]
  coclass Gorilla {
    [default] interface IApe;
    interface IWarrior;
  }

  [uuid(753A8A7E-A7FF-11d0-8C30-0080C73925BA)]
  coclass Chimpanzee {
    [default] interface IApe;
    interface IEgghead;
  }

  [uuid(753A8A7F-A7FF-11d0-8C30-0080C73925BA)]
  coclass Orangutan {
    [default] interface IApe;
    interface IKeeperOfTheFaith;
  }
}
```

The [default] attribute indicates which interface most closely represents the intrinsic type of the class. In languages that recognize this attribute, [default] allows the programmer to declare object references using only the COM coclass name:

```
Dim ursus as Gorilla
```

Based on the IDL definition of Gorilla, this statement is equivalent to

```
Dim ursus as IApe
```

because IApe is the default interface for the class Gorilla. In either case, the programmer could call the methods EatBanana and SwingFromTree on the variable ursus. If the [default] attribute is not specified, it is implicitly added to the first interface in the coclass definition.

Given the preceding IDL library definition, the resultant header file apes.h would use the C preprocessor to include the file apesitfs.h. The file apesitfs.h would contain the abstract base class definitions of the four COM interfaces IApe, IWarrior, IKeeperOfTheFaith, and IEgghead. The file apes.h also would contain the declarations for each of the classes' GUIDs:

```
extern "C" const CLSID CLSID_Gorilla;
extern "C" const CLSID CLSID_Chimpanzee;
extern "C" const CLSID CLSID_Orangutan;
```

The corresponding apes_i.c file would contain the definitions of these CLSIDs. The generated type library, apes.tlb, would contain the descriptions of each of the interfaces and classes, allowing Visual Basic programmers to write the following:

```
Dim ape As IApe
Dim warrior as IWarrior
Set ape = New Gorilla ' ask COM for a new Gorilla
Set warrior = ape
```

Alternately, the following is the Java version of the same code:

```
IApe ape;
IWarrior warrior;
ape = new Gorilla(); // no cast needed for [default]
warrior = (IWarrior)ape;
```

Both of these code fragments tell the underlying virtual machine to use the CLSID of Gorilla to indicate to CoCreateInstanceEx what type of object to create.

In the preceding IDL, the interfaces IApe, IWarrior, IEgghead, and IKeeperOfTheFaith are each referred to from within the library definition. This causes their definitions to be present in the generated type library despite the fact that they are defined outside the scope of the library definition. In fact, any data types that are used as parameters or as base interfaces for these interfaces will also be present in the generated library. It is good practice to define an implementation's library statement in a separate IDL file that imports any interface definitions that it needs from an external IDL file that contains only interface definitions. This practice is mandatory on large projects with multiple IDL files, as it is an error for an IDL file that contains a library definition to import another IDL file that also contains a library definition. By segregating library definitions into distinct IDL files, the interfaces used by a library can be cleanly imported into other projects without having to worry about multiple library definitions. If this practice is not used, then the only way to import an interface definition from an IDL file that contains a library definition is to import the generated type library using the importlib directive:

```
// humans.idl ////////////

// apeitfs.idl DOESN'T have a library statement, so import
import "apeitfs.idl";
[
   uuid(753A8AC9-A7FF-11d0-8C30-0080C73925BA),
   version(1.0), lcid(9), helpstring("Humans that need apes")
]
library HumanLib {
   importlib("stdole32.tlb"); // bring in std defs.
// Dogs.idl DOES have a library definition, so importlib
// its corresponding type library
   importlib("dogs.tlb");

   [uuid(753A8AD1-A7FF-11d0-8C30-0080C73925BA)]
   coclass DogApe {
      interface IDog;
      interface IApe;
   }
}
```

Simple projects often use a single IDL file to define both the interfaces and classes exported from a project. For simple interfaces, this is reasonable, as the generated type library will contain one-to-one mappings of the original IDL definitions, allowing users of the library to use importlib with no loss of information. Unfortunately, for complex interfaces, many of the original IDL-isms are lost in the resultant type library, and using importlib will not work as expected. A future version of the MIDL compiler may be able to generate type libraries that contain *all* of the original IDL.

Class Emulation

It is often the case that class implementors wish to deploy new versions of an existing class to repair defects or to add enhanced functionality. It is useful to give these new implementations new CLSIDs to allow clients to indicate explicitly which version is required. For example, consider what happens when a second version of a class is deployed. If a new CLSID is used to identify the new class (*e.g.*, CLSID_Chimp2), clients that explicitly wish to use the new version would use the new CLSID at activation time:

```
// new client
IApe *pApe = 0;
hr = CoCreateInstance(CLSID_Chimp2, 0, CLSCTX_ALL,
                      IID_Ape, (void**)&pApe);
```

The use of a second CLSID ensures that clients do not accidentally get old versions of the Chimp class. However, legacy clients still make activation requests using the old CLSID:

```
// old client
IApe *pApe = 0;
hr = CoCreateInstance(CLSID_Chimp, 0, CLSCTX_ALL,
                      IID_Ape, (void**)&pApe);
```

To continue to support legacy clients, the Chimp implementor needs to keep the original CLSID in the Registry in order to satisfy these activation requests. If the semantics of the class have changed, then the original server would also need to remain available for these clients. However, it is often the case that the semantics are simply extended. In this case, it would be preferable simply to reroute the legacy activation requests to create instances of the new class.

To allow the implementor of the new version of the class to satisfy activation requests for other CLSIDs transparently, COM supports the notion of class emulation. Class emulation allows a component implementor to indicate that an old CLSID has been replaced by a new alternative CLSID that emulates the original class's semantics. This allows legacy clients that make activation calls using the original CLSID to get instances of the new updated class. To indicate that a class has a new alternative version, COM provides the following API function:

```
HRESULT CoTreatAsClass([in] REFCLSID rclsidOld,
                       [in] REFCLSID rclsidNew);
```

Assuming that Chimp2 is a new version of the class Chimp, the following code informs COM to alter activation requests for Chimp to become activation requests for Chimp2:

```
// cause Chimp activation calls to activate Chimp2
HRESULT hr = CoTreatAsClass(CLSID_Chimp, CLSID_Chimp2);
```

This API routine inserts the following registry key:

```
[HKCR\CLSID\{CLSID_Chimp}\TreatAs]17
@={CLSID_Chimp2}
```

Calling CoTreatAsClass with CLSID_NULL as the second parameter removes the TreatAs setting:

```
// cause Chimp activation calls to activate Chimps
HRESULT hr = CoTreatAsClass(CLSID_Chimp, CLSID_NULL);
```

This call restores the original implementation of the class to its preemulation status. Clients can interrogate the emulation setting of a given class using the CoGetTreatAsClass API function:

```
HRESULT CoGetTreatAsClass([in] REFCLSID rclsidOld,
                          [out] REFCLSID *pclsidNew);
```

If the requested class is being emulated by another class, the emulating class's CLSID will be returned through the second parameter and the routine will return S_OK. If the requested class is not being emulated by another class, the original CLSID will be returned through the second parameter and the routine will return S_FALSE. It is worth noting that, at the time of this writing, class emulation does not work as expected for remote activation requests.

---

[17] Note that *CLSID_Chimp* and *CLSID_Chimp2* are shorthand notation for the actual 32-digit GUIDs in canonical form.

Component Categories

As this chapter has emphasized, the basic COM activation primitives require the caller to know the precise class name in order to create new instances. However, it is sometimes useful simply to request that any class that adheres to some semantic constraint is suitable. In addition, it could be useful to know what services a class requires from its clients prior to issuing an activation request to avoid creating objects that the client is not prepared to support properly. These problems motivate the concept of *component categories*.

COM allows implementors to group related COM classes into logical groups or component categories. Often, all classes within a category will implement the same set of interfaces. However, simply partitioning the class space based on which interfaces each class implements does not provide the proper granularity for many applications. Component categories act as metainformation that indicates which classes are compatible with particular semantic constraints.

A component category is a group of logically related COM classes that share a common category ID or CATID. CATIDs are GUIDs that are stored in the Registry as attributes of a class. Each class can have two subkeys: `Implemented Categories` and `Required Categories`. Assume that there are two categories of components: Simians and Mammals. These two categories would each have a unique CATID (`CATID_Simians` and `CATID_Mammals`, respectively). Assuming that the class `Chimp` is a member of each of these categories, the `Chimp`'s `Implemented Categories` registry key would contain each GUID as an individual subkey:

```
[HKCR\CLSID\{CLSID_Chimp}\Implemented Categories\{CATID_Mammals}]
```

```
[HKCR\CLSID\{CLSID_Chimp}\Implemented Categories\{CATID_Simians}]
```

These registry entries are typically added at self-registration time. Each known component category on a system has an entry under

```
HKEY_CLASSES_ROOT\Component Categories
```

Each category has its own unique subkey named by its CATID. Underneath its subkey, each category has one or more named values that contain the human-readable description of the category. For example, the two categories shown would require the following registry entries:

```
[HKCR\Component Categories\{CATID_Mammals}]
409="Bears live young"

[HKCR\Component Categories\{CATID_Simians}]
409="Eats Bananas"
```

Note that this example uses the 409 value, which is the LCID for U.S. English. Other locales can be supported by adding additional named values.

It is also possible for classes to indicate that they require particular types of functionality from the client. This support typically comes in the form of site interfaces that the client will provide to the object once activated. To allow these client-provided services to be categorized independent of any particular interface, COM allows classes to advertise a second type of category ID that can be used by clients to ensure that they do not activate a component that they cannot properly host. Assume the following two categories of client-provided services: CATID_HasOxygen and CATID_HasWater. Since chimpanzees need oxygen and water to survive, the Chimp implementor might advertise that these two categories of client-provided services are required for activation. This is done by using the Required Categories subkeys:

```
[HKCR\CLSID\{CLSID_Chimp}\Required Categories\{CATID_HasOxygen}]

[HKCR\CLSID\{CLSID_Chimp}\Required Categories\{CATID_HasWater}]
```

These two category IDs would need to be registered under

```
HKEY_CLASSES_ROOT\Component Categories
```

as well. Given these entries, it is the client's responsibility to ensure that it meets the required categories prior to activation. COM does not enforce client conformance.

Component category entries can be registered using either explicit registry functions or the COM-supplied component category manager. COM's component category manager is exposed as an instantiable COM class (CLSID_StdComponentCategoriesMgr) that implements the ICatRegister interface for registering category information and the ICatInformation interface for querying category information. The ICatRegister interface allows server DLLs easily to add the requisite entries to the Registry:

```
[ object, uuid(0002E012-0000-0000-C000-000000000046) ]
interface ICatRegister : IUnknown {
```

```
// description info for a category
  typedef struct tagCATEGORYINFO {
    CATID        catid;
    LCID         lcid;
    OLECHAR szDescription[128];
  } CATEGORYINFO;
// register cCts category descriptions
  HRESULT RegisterCategories([in] ULONG cCts,
          [in, size_is(cCts)] CATEGORYINFO rgCatInfo[]);
// unregister cCategories category descriptions
  HRESULT UnRegisterCategories([in] ULONG cCategories,
          [in, size_is(cCategories)] CATID rgcatid[]);
// indicate a class implements one or more categories
  HRESULT RegisterClassImplCategories([in] REFCLSID rclsid,
          [in] ULONG cCategories,
          [in, size_is(cCategories)] CATID rgcatid[]);
// deindicate a class implements one or more categories
  HRESULT UnRegisterClassImplCategories([in] REFCLSID rclsd,
          [in] ULONG cCategories,
          [in, size_is(cCategories)] CATID rgcatid[]);
// indicate a class requires one or more categories
  HRESULT RegisterClassReqCategories([in] REFCLSID rclsid,
          [in] ULONG cCategories,
          [in, size_is(cCategories)] CATID rgcatid[]);
// deindicate a class requires one or more categories
  HRESULT UnRegisterClassReqCategories([in] REFCLSID rclsid,
          [in] ULONG cCategories,
          [in, size_is(cCategories)] CATID rgcatid[]);
}
```

There is no need for user-defined COM classes to implement this interface. It exists solely to allow servers to self-register their component categories using the COM-provided category manager implementation.

In the case of the Chimp example, the following code would register the correct information regarding each category:

```
// get the standard category manager
ICatRegister *pcr = 0;
HRESULT hr = CoCreateInstance(
              CLSID_StdComponentCategoriesMgr, 0,
              CLSCTX_ALL, IID_ICatRegister, (void**)&pcr);
```

```
if (SUCCEEDED(hr)) {
// build descriptions of each category
  CATEGORYINFO rgcc[4];
  rgcc[0].catid = CATID_Simian;
  rgcc[1].catid = CATID_Mammal;
  rgcc[2].catid = CATID_HasOxygen;
  rgcc[3].catid = CATID_HasWater;
  rgcc[0].lcid = rgcc[1].lcid
    = rgcc[2].lcid = rgcc[3].lcid = 0x409;
  wcscpy(rgcc[0].szDescription, OLESTR("Eats Bananas"));
  wcscpy(rgcc[1].szDescription, OLESTR("Bears live young"));
  wcscpy(rgcc[2].szDescription, OLESTR("Provides Oxygen"));
  wcscpy(rgcc[3].szDescription, OLESTR("Provides Water"));
// register information regarding categories
  pcr->RegisterCategories(4, rgcc);

// note that Chimps are Simians and mammals
  CATID rgcid[2];
  rgcid[0] = CATID_Simian; rgcid[1] = CATID_Mammal;
  pcr->RegisterClassImplCategories(CLSID_Chimp, 2, rgcid);

// note that Chimps require Oxygen and Water
  rgcid[0] = CATID_HasOxygen; rgcid[1] = CATID_HasWater;
  pcr->RegisterClassReqCategories(CLSID_Chimp, 2, rgcid);
  pcr->Release();
}
```

Note that this code makes no raw registry API calls but instead uses the standard category manager to manipulate the Registry.

The standard category manager also allows applications to query the registry to find information regarding categories. This functionality is exposed via the ICatInformation interface:

```
[ object, uuid(0002E013-0000-0000-C000-000000000046) ]
interface ICatInformation : IUnknown {
// get list of known categories
  HRESULT EnumCategories([in] LCID lcid,
        [out] IEnumCATEGORYINFO** ppeci);
// get description of a particular category
  HRESULT GetCategoryDesc([in] REFCATID rcatid,
        [in] LCID lcid,
```

```
            [out] OLECHAR ** ppszDesc);
// get list of classes compatible with specified categories
    HRESULT EnumClassesOfCategories(
            [in] ULONG cImplemented, // -1 indicates ignore
            [in,size_is(cImplemented)] CATID rgcatidImpl[],
            [in] ULONG cRequired,    // -1 indicates ignore
            [in,size_is(cRequired)] CATID rgcatidReq[],
            [out] IEnumCLSID** ppenumClsid);
// verify class is compatible with specified categories
    HRESULT IsClassOfCategories([in] REFCLSID rclsid,
            [in] ULONG cImplemented,
            [in,size_is(cImplemented)] CATID rgcatidImpl[],
            [in] ULONG cRequired,
            [in,size_is(cRequired)] CATID rgcatidReq[]);
// get list of class's implemented categories
    HRESULT EnumImplCategoriesOfClass([in] REFCLSID rclsid,
            [out] IEnumCATID** ppenumCatid);
// get list of class's required categories
    HRESULT EnumReqCategoriesOfClass([in] REFCLSID rclsid,
            [out] IEnumCATID** ppenumCatid);
}
```

Most of these methods return cursors to lists of category or class IDs. These cursors are called enumerators and are described in detail in Chapter 7.

The following code demonstrates how to extract the list of classes that are members of the Mammal category:

```
// get the standard category manager
ICatInformation *pci = 0;
HRESULT hr = CoCreateInstance(
            CLSID_StdComponentCategoriesMgr, 0,
            CLSCTX_ALL, IID_ICatInformation, (void**)&pci);
if (SUCCEEDED(hr)) {
// get the classes that are Simians (ignore required cat.s)
    IEnumCLSID *pec = 0;
    CATID rgcid[1];
    rgcid[0] = CATID_Simian;
    hr = pci->EnumClassesOfCategories(1, rgcid, -1, 0, &pec);
    if (SUCCEEDED(hr)) {
// walk list of CLSIDs 64 at a time
        enum { MAX = 64 };
```

```
        CLSID rgclsid[MAX];
        do {
          ULONG cActual = 0;
          hr = pec->Next(MAX, rgclsid, &cActual);
          if (SUCCEEDED(hr)) {
            for (ULONG i = 0; i < cActual; i++)
              DisplayClass(rgclsid[i]);
          }
        } while (hr == S_OK);
        pec->Release();
      }
    pci->Release();
  }
```

This code fragment ignores the fact that the client program may not support the required categories of the resultant list of classes. Had the client been aware of its supported site categories, it could have specified the list of all supported categories.

Consider the following call to EnumClassesOfCategories:

```
CATID rgimpl[1]; rgimpl[0] = CATID_Simians;
CATID rgreq[3]; rgreq[0] = CATID_HasWater;
rgreq[1] = CATID_HasOxygen; rgreq[2] = CATID_HasMilk;
hr =pci->EnumClassesOfCategories(1, rgimpl, 3, rgreq, &pec);
```

The resultant list of classes would contain all Simians that require *no more than* Oxygen, Water, and Milk from the client's environment. In the case of the Chimp class registered previously, Chimp would be a compatible class, as it implements the specified category Simian and requires a subset of the specified categories used in the query.

One final aspect of component categories that bears discussion is the notion of a default class for a category. COM allows a CATID to be registered as a CLSID under

```
HKEY_CLASSES_ROOT\CLSID
```

To map a CATID to a default CLSID, the TreatAs facility introduced by emulation is used. To indicate that the Gorilla class is the default class of Simian, one would add the following registry key:

```
[HKCR\CLSID\{CATID_Simian}\TreatAs]
@={CLSID_Gorrila}
```

This simple convention allows clients simply to use CATIDs where CLSIDs are expected:

```
// create an instance of the default Simian class
hr = CoCreateInstance(CATID_Simian, 0, CLSCTX_ALL,
                      IID_IApe, (void**)&pApe);
```

If no default class is registered for the specified category, the activation call will fail, returning REGDB_E_CLASSNOTREG.

Where Are We?

This chapter presented the concept of a COM class. COM classes are named concrete data types that export one or more interfaces and are the primary abstraction used in object activation in COM. COM supports three activation primitives. CoGetClassObject binds a reference to a class object, which is a class-wide singleton that represents the instance-independent functionality of a class. CoCreateInstanceEx binds a reference to a new class instance, and CoGetInstanceFromFile binds a reference to a persistent instance in a file. Monikers are used as a uniform abstraction for exposing binding and activation policies to clients, with MkParseDisplayName acting as the entry point into the namespace of COM.

CHAPTER

4 | Objects

```
class object
{
public:
  template <class T> virtual
  T * dynamic_cast(const type_info& t = typeid(T) )
};
```
Anonymous, 1995

Chapter 2 discussed the fundamentals of COM interfaces in general and the IUnknown interface in particular. The notion that objects can expose more than one kind of functionality by deriving from additional interfaces was presented, and the mechanism through which clients interrogate objects to discover available functionalities was shown as well. This mechanism, QueryInterface, was framed as a language/compiler-neutral version of C++'s dynamic_cast operator.

The previous chapter demonstrated that QueryInterface could be implemented directly by using static typecasts to limit the scope of an object's this pointer to the interface type requested by the client. At the physical level, this technique simply mapped interface identifiers to the appropriate offset into the object, which is the technique used by every C++ compiler's implementation of dynamic_cast.

Although the implementations of QueryInterface from the previous chapters are completely legal COM, the rules of IUnknown allow the object implementor a great deal more flexibility than has been illustrated so far. This chapter will investigate these rules and demonstrate the implementation techniques that they imply.

IUnknown Revisited

IUnknown has no default implementation that is part of the COM system call interface. The SDK header files contain no base classes, macros, or templates that provide implementations of QueryInterface, AddRef, and Release that must be used in all C or C++ programs. Instead, the Component Object Model Specification provides very precise rules regarding the assumptions that clients and objects can make about these three methods. This collection of rules forms the protocol of IUnknown and allows each object implementor to map the three IUnknown methods onto whatever makes sense for his or her object.

Chapter 2 presented the de facto C++ implementations of these three methods, but COM in no way mandates that objects use them. All COM requires is that every implementation adhere to the basic rules of IUnknown. How this is accomplished is ultimately of no concern to COM. This makes COM extremely unobtrusive, as it does not require that an object make system calls, derive from system-provided implementations, or do anything other than expose COM-compliant vptrs. In fact, as is shown later in this chapter, it is possible to expose IUnknown-derived vptrs from classes that do not derive from any COM interfaces.

The rules of IUnknown collectively define what it means to be a COM object. To understand the rules of IUnknown, it helps to start from a concrete example. Consider the following interface hierarchy:

```
import "unknwn.idl";

[object, uuid(CD538340-A56D-11d0-8C2F-0080C73925BA)]
interface IVehicle : IUnknown {
  HRESULT GetMaxSpeed([out, retval] long *pMax);
}

[object, uuid(CD538341-A56D-11d0-8C2F-0080C73925BA)]
interface ICar : IVehicle {
  HRESULT Brake(void);
}

[object, uuid(CD538342-A56D-11d0-8C2F-0080C73925BA)]
interface IPlane : IVehicle {
  HRESULT TakeOff(void);
}

[object, uuid(CD538343-A56D-11d0-8C2F-0080C73925BA)]
interface IBoat : IVehicle {
  HRESULT Sink(void);
}
```

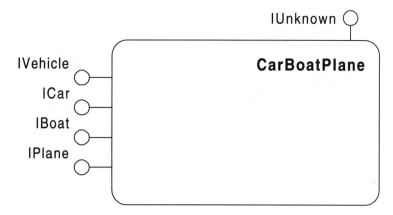

Figure 4.1 CarBoatPlane

COM uses a standard technique for visually representing objects. This technique adheres to the COM philosophy of separation of interface from implementation and does not betray any implementation details of the object other than the list of interfaces it exposes. This technique also visually reinforces many of the rules of IUnknown. Figure 4.1 shows the standard notation for a class CarBoatPlane that implements each of the interfaces just defined. Note that the only inference one can make from this diagram is that, barring catastrophic failure, CarBoatPlane objects will expose the five interfaces IBoat, IPlane, ICar, IVehicle, and IUnknown.

The first rule of IUnknown that bears investigation is the Symmetric/ Transitive/Reflexive requirement of QueryInterface. This requirement defines the relationship between all of an object's interface pointers and begins to define the notion of object identity in COM. Like all IUnknown rules, these requirements must be adhered to at all times *barring catastrophic failure* in order to be considered a valid COM object.

QueryInterface Is Symmetric

The COM Specification requires that if a QueryInterface request for interface *B* is satisfied through an interface pointer of type *A*, then a QueryInterface request for interface *A* through the resultant interface pointer of type *B* on the same object must never fail. This means that if

```
QI(A)->B
```

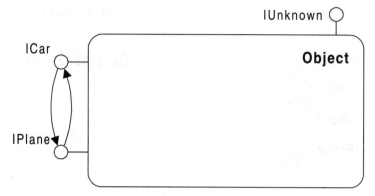

Figure 4.2 QueryInterface and Symmetry

is true, then

```
QI(QI(A)->B)->A
```

must be true as well.

This property is illustrated in Figure 4.2 and implies that the assertion in the following code must always be true:

```
void AssertSymmetric(ICar *pCar) {
  if (pCar) {
    IPlane *pPlane = 0;
// request a second type of interface
    HRESULT hr  = pCar->QueryInterface(IID_IPlane,
                                 (void**)&pPlane);
      if (SUCCEEDED(hr)) {
        ICar *pCar2 = 0;
// request original type of interface
      hr = pPlane->QueryInterface(IID_ICar,
                            (void**)&pCar2);

// if the following assertion fails, pCar
// did not point to a valid COM object
        assert(SUCCEEDED(hr));
        pCar2->Release();
    }
    pPlane->Release();
  }
}
```

The fact that `QueryInterface` is symmetric means that clients do not need to be concerned with which interface to acquire first, as any two interface types can be acquired in either order.

QueryInterface Is Transitive

The COM Specification also requires that if a `QueryInterface` request for interface B is satisfied through an interface pointer of type A and a second `QueryInterface` for interface C is satisfied through the pointer of type B, then a `QueryInterface` request for interface C through the original pointer of type A must succeed as well. This means that if

```
QI(QI(A)->B)->C
```

is true, then

```
QI(A)->C
```

must be true as well.

This requirement is illustrated in Figure 4.3 and implies that the assertion in the following code must always be true:

```
void AssertTransitive(ICar *pCar) {
  if (pCar) {
```

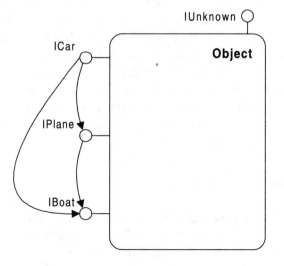

Figure 4.3 `QueryInterface and Transitivity`

```
        IPlane *pPlane = 0;
// request intermediate type of interface
        HRESULT hr  = pCar->QueryInterface(IID_IPlane,
                                    (void**)&pPlane);
        if (SUCCEEDED(hr)) {
        IBoat *pBoat1 = 0;
// request terminal type of interface
        hr = pPlane->QueryInterface(IID_IBoat,
                                (void**)&pBoat1);
        if (SUCCEEDED(hr)) {
        IBoat *pBoat2 = 0;
// request terminal type through the original pointer
        hr = pCar->QueryInterface(IID_IBoat,
                                (void**)&pBoat2);
// if the following assertion fails, pCar
// did not point to a valid COM object
        assert(SUCCEEDED(hr));
        pBoat2->Release();
    }
    pBoat1->Release();
  }
  pPlane->Release();
 }
}
```

The fact that QueryInterface is transitive implies that all interfaces that an object exposes are equivalent peers and do not need to be acquired in any particular sequence. If this were not the case, clients would need to be concerned about which pointer to an object to use for different QueryInterface requests. The transitivity and symmetry of QueryInterface imply that any interface pointer to an object will yield the same yes/no answer for any QueryInterface request. The only case not covered by transitivity and symmetry is asking for the same interface more than once. This situation requires QueryInterface also to be reflexive.

QueryInterface Is Reflexive

The COM Specification requires that a QueryInterface request through an interface pointer must always succeed if the requested type matches the type of pointer used to make the request. This means that

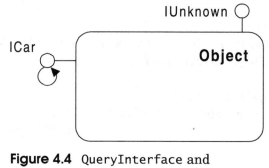

Figure 4.4 QueryInterface and Reflexiveness

```
QI(A)->A
```

must always be true.

This requirement is illustrated in Figure 4.4 and illustrated in the following code fragment:

```
void AssertReflexive(ICar *pCar) {
   if (pCar) {
     ICar *pCar2 = 0;
// request same type of interface
     HRESULT hr = pCar->QueryInterface(IID_ICar,
                            (void**)&pCar2);

// if the following assertion fails, pCar
// did not point to a valid COM object
     assert(SUCCEEDED(hr));
     pCar2->Release();
   }
}
```

The implication of this code is that all implementations of ICar must be capable of satisfying additional QueryInterface requests for ICar through an ICar interface pointer. If this were not true, it would not be possible to pass strongly typed interfaces through base-type parameters without forever losing the original type:

```
extern void GetCar(ICar **ppcar);
extern void UseVehicle(IVehicle *pv);
```

```
ICar *pCar;
GetCar(&pCar);
UseVehicle(pCar); // ICar-ness is syntactically lost
void UseVehicle(IVehicle *pv) {
   ICar *pCar = 0;
// try to regain syntactic ICar-ness
   HRESULT hr = pv->QueryInterface(IID_ICar,
                                          (void**)&pCar);

      :

}
```

Because the pointer value used in the UseVehicle function has the same value as the ICar pointer passed by the caller, it would seem counterintuitive if the type could not be regained inside the function.

The fact that QueryInterface is symmetric, reflexive, and transitive implies that any interface pointer to an object must yield the same yes/no answer to a given QueryInterface request. This allows clients to view the type hierarchy of an object as a simple graph in which all nodes are directly connected to one another (and themselves) by explicit vertices. Figure 4.5 shows such a graph. Note that any node in the graph can be reached from any other node in the graph by traversing only one vertex.

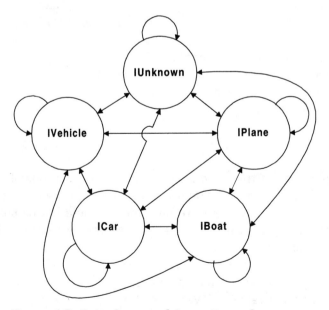

Figure 4.5 Interfaces and QueryInterface

Objects Have Static Type

One corollary that can be inferred from the three `QueryInterface` requirements is that the set of interfaces supported by an object cannot change over time. The COM Specification explicitly requires that this corollary hold true for all objects. This requirement implies that the type hierarchy of an object is static despite the fact that clients must interrogate objects dynamically to determine the set of supported data types. If an object says "yes" to a request for an interface of type *A*, it must say "yes" from that point on. If an object says "no" to a request for an interface of type *A*, it must say "no" from that point on. The phrase "from that point on" literally translates to "as long as there is at least one outstanding interface pointer on the object." This normally corresponds to the lifecycle of the underlying C++ object, but the COM Specification's language is loose enough to allow implementors a certain amount of flexibility (*e.g.*, a global variable's type hierarchy could change once all pointers were released).

That all COM objects have static type hierarchies implies that the assertion in the following code must never be false no matter what interface identifier is used for the second parameter:

```
void AssertStaticType(IUnknown *pUnk, REFIID riid) {
   IUnknown *pUnk1 = 0, *pUnk2 = 0;
   HRESULT hr1 = pUnk->QueryInterface(riid,
                                       (void**)&pUnk1);
   HRESULT hr2 = pUnk->QueryInterface(riid,
                                       (void**)&pUnk2);
// both requests for the same interface should
// yield the same yes/no answer
   assert(SUCCEEDED(hr1) == SUCCEEDED(hr2));
   if (SUCCEEDED(hr1)) pUnk1->Release();
   if (SUCCEEDED(hr2)) pUnk2->Release();
}
```

This requirement means that the following programming techniques are prohibited in COM:

1. Using temporal information to decide whether or not to satisfy a `QueryInterface` request (*e.g.*, giving out the `IMorning` interface only before 12:00 PM).

2. Using transient state information to decide whether or not to satisfy a `QueryInterface` request (*e.g.*, giving out the `INotBusy` interface only when the number of outstanding interface pointers is less than ten).

3. Using the caller's security token to decide whether or not to satisfy a `QueryInterface` request. As Chapter 6 will explain, this does not afford any real security anyway because of the wire protocol used by COM.

4. Using the success of a dynamic resource acquisition to decide whether or not to satisfy a `QueryInterface` request (*e.g.,* giving out the `IHaveTonsOfMemory` interface only if `malloc(4096*4096)` succeeds).

This last technique can be relaxed somewhat if the object implementor is willing to exercise the "barring catastrophic failure" clause of the COM Specification.

These restrictions do not mean that two objects of the same implementation class cannot give different yes/no answers when asked for the same interface. For example, a class could implement the `ICar`, `IBoat`, and `IPlane` interfaces shown previously but allow only one interface to be used on any particular object. These restrictions also do not mean that an object cannot use state or temporal information to decide the *initial* yes/no answer for a given interface. In the example of the class that only allows one of three interfaces, the following idiom would be perfectly legal:

```
class CBP : public ICar, public IPlane, public IBoat{
   enum TYPE { CAR, BOAT, PLANE, NONE };
   TYPE m_type;
   CBP(void) : m_type(NONE) {}
   STDMETHODIMP QueryInterface(REFIID riid,
                               void **ppv) {
     if (riid == IID_ICar) {
// 1st QI initializes type of object
       if (m_type == NONE) m_type = CAR;
// only satisfy request if this object is a car
       if (m_type == CAR)
         *ppv = static_cast<ICar*>(this);
       else
         return (*ppv = 0), E_NOINTERFACE;
     }
     else if (riid == IID_IBoat)
// similar treatment for IBoat and IPlane
};
```

The requirement that the set of supported interfaces is static simply implies that object implementors are prohibited from building designs based on one object giving two different yes/no answers for a particular interface. One reason that the type hierarchy of an object should be considered immutable throughout its lifecycle is that COM does not guarantee that all client QueryInterface requests will be forwarded to the object when it is accessed remotely. This allows client-side proxies to cache the results of QueryInterface to avoid excessive client-object communications. This optimization is critical for COM to be performant but breaks designs that use QueryInterface to communicate *dynamic* semantic information to the caller.

Uniqueness and Identity

The previous section referred to QueryInterface requests as giving their callers yes/no answers. Of course, QueryInterface really returns S_OK (yes) or E_NOINTERFACE (no). When QueryInterface returns S_OK, however, it also returns an interface pointer to the object. COM has a very specific requirement for this pointer value that allows clients to determine whether two interface pointers in fact point to the same object.

QueryInterface and IUnknown

The reflexive property of QueryInterface guarantees that any interface pointer will be able to satisfy requests for IUnknown, because all interface pointers are of type IUnknown implicitly. The COM Specification is a bit more restrictive when describing the results of QueryInterface requests for IUnknown in particular. Not only does an object always have to say "yes" to the request, it must also return *exactly the same pointer value for each request*. This means that both of the assertions in the following code must always be true:

```
void AssertSameObject(IUnknown *pUnk) {
   IUnknown *pUnk1 = 0, *pUnk2 = 0;
   HRESULT hr1 = pUnk->QueryInterface(IID_IUnknown,
                                      (void**)&pUnk1);
   HRESULT hr2 = pUnk->QueryInterface(IID_IUnknown,
                                      (void**)&pUnk2);
// QueryInterface(IUnknown) must always succeed
   assert(SUCCEEDED(hr1) && SUCCEEDED(hr2));

// two requests for IUnknown must always yield the
// same pointer values
   assert(pUnk1 == pUnk2);
```

```
            pUnk1->Release();
            pUnk2->Release();
        }
```

This requirement allows clients to compare any two interface pointers to
determine whether they point to the same *object identity*.

```
        bool IsSameObject(IUnknown *pUnk1, IUnknown *pUnk2) {
          assert(pUnk1 && pUnk2);
          bool bResult = true;
          if (pUnk1 != pUnk2)     {
            HRESULT hr1, hr2;
            IUnknown *p1 = 0, *p2 = 0;
            hr1 = pUnk1->QueryInterface(IID_IUnknown,
                                        (void**)&p1);
            assert(SUCCEEDED(hr1));
            hr2 = pUnk2->QueryInterface(IID_IUnknown,
                                        (void**)&p2);
            assert(SUCCEEDED(hr1));
        // compare the two pointer values, as these
        // represent the identity of the object
            bResult = (p1 == p2);
            p1->Release();   p2->Release();
          }
          return bResult;
        }
```

As will be discussed in Chapter 5, the notion of identity is a fundamental concept that is used by the COM remoting architecture to represent interface
pointers on the network efficiently.

Armed with the knowledge of the rules of IUnknown, it is useful to examine
an object implementation and verify that it adheres to all of the requirements.
The following implementation exposes each of the four vehicle interfaces and
IUnknown:

```
        class CarBoatPlane : public ICar,
                             public IBoat,
                             public IPlane {
        public:
        // IUnknown methods
          STDMETHODIMP QueryInterface(REFIID, void**);
          STDMETHODIMP_(ULONG) AddRef(void);
```

```
   STDMETHODIMP_(ULONG) Release(void);
// IVehicle methods
   STDMETHODIMP GetMaxSpeed(long *pMax);
// ICar methods
   STDMETHODIMP Brake(void);
// IBoat methods
   STDMETHODIMP Sink(void);
// IPlane methods
   STDMETHODIMP TakeOff(void);
};
```

The following is the de facto implementation of CarBoatPlane's Query-Interface:

```
STDMETHODIMP QueryInterface(REFIID riid, void **ppv){
   if (riid == IID_IUnknown)
     *ppv = static_cast<ICar*>(this);
   else if (riid == IID_IVehicle)
     *ppv = static_cast<ICar*>(this);
   else if (riid == IID_ICar)
     *ppv = static_cast<ICar*>(this);
   else if (riid == IID_IIBoat)
     *ppv = static_cast<IBoat*>(this);
   else if (riid == IID_IPlane)
     *ppv = static_cast<IPlane*>(this);
   else
     return (*ppv = 0), E_NOINTERFACE;
   ((IUnknown*)*ppv)->AddRef();
   return S_OK;
}
```

To be a COM object, CarBoatPlane's QueryInterface implementation must adhere completely to the rules of IUnknown presented in this chapter.

The CarBoatPlane class only exposes interfaces of type ICar, IPlane, IBoat, IVehicle, and IUnknown. Each CarBoatPlane vtbl will refer to the single implementation of QueryInterface just shown. Any supported interface can be acquired through this QueryInterface implementation, so it is impossible to find two interfaces that are not symmetric, that is, there are no two interfaces A and B for which the following does not hold true:

```
If QI(A)->B Then QI(QI(A)->B)->A
```

By the same logic, because all five interfaces share the same `QueryInterface` implementation, there are no three interfaces A, B, and C for which the following does not hold true:

```
If QI(QI(A)->B)->C Then QI(A)->C
```

Finally, because the implementation of `QueryInterface` always satisfies requests for the five possible interface pointers that a client could hold, the following must be true for each of the five supported interfaces:

```
QI(A)->A
```

Because multiple inheritance yields a single implementation of `QueryInterface` for all interfaces on an object, it is actually very difficult to violate the requirements of symmetry, transitivity, and reflexivity.

The implementation also correctly implements COM's identity rule of only returning one pointer value when asked for `IUnknown`:

```
if (riid == IID_IUnknown)
    *ppv = static_cast<ICar*>(this);
```

Had the implementation of `QueryInterface` returned a different vptr for each request:

```
if (riid == IID_IUnknown) {
  int n = rand() % 3;
  if (n == 0)
    *ppv = static_cast<ICar*>(this);
  else if (n == 1)
    *ppv = static_cast<IBoat*>(this);
  else if (n == 2)
    *ppv = static_cast<IPlane*>(this);
}
```

the implementation would have been correct in terms of pure C++ type relationships (*i.e.*, all three interfaces are type compatible with the requested type `IUnknown`). However, this is not a legal COM implementation as the identity rule of `QueryInterface` has been violated.

Multiple Interfaces and Method Names

Multiple inheritance is a very efficient and straightforward technique for implementing COM interfaces in a C++ class. It requires very little explicit coding, as the compiler and linker do most of the work in terms of building COM-compliant vptrs and vtbls. If a method name appears in more than one base class with identical parameter types, then the compiler and linker happily populate each vtbl entry to point to the class's one implementation of the method. This behavior applies to methods such as QueryInterface, AddRef, and Release, as all COM interfaces begin with these methods and yet the class implementor needs to write each method only once (this is good). The same behavior also applies to methods in arbitrary interfaces that happen to share the same name and signature. Therein lies the one potential pitfall of multiple inheritance.

The vehicle interface hierarchy in this chapter has a name collision. The ICar interface has a method called GetMaxSpeed. The IBoat and IPlane interfaces also have methods named GetMaxSpeed with identical signatures. This means that when using multiple inheritance, the class implementor writes the GetMaxSpeed method once, and the compiler and linker initialize the ICar, IBoat, and IPlane-compatible vtbls to point to this one implementation.

This may be perfectly reasonable behavior for a large number of implementations. But what if the object needed to return a different maximum speed depending on the interface on which the request was made? Because the name and signatures are identical, unusual measures must be taken to allow multiple implementations of the clashing method. One common technique is to build an intermediate C++ class that derives from an interface and implements the clashing method by making a pure virtual call on a nonclashing name:

```
struct IXCar : public ICar {
// add new non-clashing method as pure virtual
   virtual HRESULT STDMETHODCALLTYPE
                    GetMaxCarSpeed(long *pval) = 0;


// implement clashing method by upcalling
// non-clashing implementation in derived class
   STDMETHODIMP GetMaxSpeed(long *pval)
   { return GetMaxCarSpeed(pval); }
};
```

Assuming that the IBoat and IPlane interfaces received similar treatment, one could now implement different versions of GetMaxSpeed simply by deriving from the extended versions of the interfaces and overriding the non-clashing versions of each GetMaxSpeed method:

```
class CarBoatPlane : public IXCar,
                     public IXBoat,
                     public IXPlane {
public:
// IUnknown methods
    STDMETHODIMP QueryInterface(REFIID, void**);
    STDMETHODIMP_(ULONG) AddRef(void);
    STDMETHODIMP_(ULONG) Release(void);
// IVehicle methods
    // do not override GetMaxSpeed!
// ICar methods
    STDMETHODIMP Brake(void);
// IBoat methods
    STDMETHODIMP Sink(void);
// IXPlane methods
    STDMETHODIMP TakeOff(void);


// upcalled from IXCar::GetMaxSpeed
    STDMETHODIMP GetMaxCarSpeed(long *pval);
// upcalled from IXBoat::GetMaxSpeed
    STDMETHODIMP GetMaxBoatSpeed(long *pval);
// called from IXPlane::GetMaxSpeed
    STDMETHODIMP GetMaxPlaneSpeed(long *pval);
}
```

Figure 4.6 illustrates this class's layout and vtbl formats. Note that the clashing method, GetMaxSpeed, is not implemented in this class. Because each of CarBoatPlane's base classes overrides this pure virtual method, CarBoatPlane does not need to provide its own implementation. In fact, if CarBoatPlane were to override GetMaxSpeed, its one implementation of this method would override the upcall versions from each of the base classes, defeating the purpose of using IXCar, IXBoat, and IXPlane. Because of this problem, this technique is suitable only for situations in which it can be guaranteed that the implementation class (or any potential derived classes) will never override the clashing method.

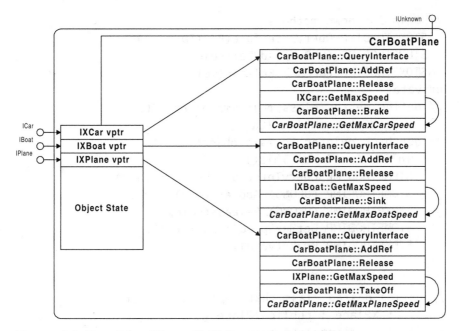

Figure 4.6 Resolving Name Collisions across Interfaces

A different technique for providing multiple implementations of clashing methods is to leverage the rules of IUnknown. The COM Specification does not require an object to be implemented as a C++ class. Although there is a very natural mapping between COM objects and C++ classes based on multiple inheritance, this is only one possible implementation technique. Any programming technique that produces properly formatted vtbls that adhere to COM's QueryInterface rules can be used to build a COM object. One common technique for resolving name clashes is to implement the interfaces with clashing names as distinct C++ classes and compose the target C++ class from instances of these distinct classes. To guarantee that each of these composite data members appears to the outside world as a single COM object, it is common practice to have one master implementation of QueryInterface to which each composite data member will delegate. The following code demonstrates this technique:

```
class CarPlane {
  LONG m_cRef;
  CarPlane(void) : m_cRef(0) {}
public:
```

```
      // Main IUnknown methods
        STDMETHODIMP QueryInterface(REFIID, void**);
        STDMETHODIMP_(ULONG) AddRef(void);
        STDMETHODIMP_(ULONG) Release(void);
    private:
    // define nested class that implements ICar
        struct XCar : public ICar {
    // get back pointer to main object
            inline CarPlane* This();
            STDMETHODIMP QueryInterface(REFIID, void**);
            STDMETHODIMP_(ULONG) AddRef(void);
            STDMETHODIMP_(ULONG) Release(void);
            STDMETHODIMP GetMaxSpeed(long *pval);
            STDMETHODIMP Brake(void);
        };

    // define nested class that implements IPlane
        struct XPlane : public IPlane {
    // Get back pointer to main object
            inline CarPlane* This();
            STDMETHODIMP QueryInterface(REFIID, void**);
            STDMETHODIMP_(ULONG) AddRef(void);
            STDMETHODIMP_(ULONG) Release(void);
            STDMETHODIMP GetMaxSpeed(long *pval);
            STDMETHODIMP TakeOff(void);
        };
    // declare instances of nested classes
        XCar m_xCar;
        XPlane m_xPlane;
    };
```

The use of nested classes is optional but emphasizes that these subordinate classes make no sense outside the context of the class CarPlane. Figure 4.7 illustrates the binary layout of this class and the corresponding vtbl layouts.

Note that there are two nested class definitions, one for each interface that is implemented. This allows the object implementor to provide two distinct implementations of GetMaxSpeed:

```
STDMETHODIMP CarPlane::XCar::GetMaxSpeed(long *pn){
   // set *pn to max speed for cars
}
```

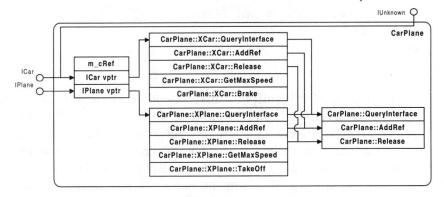

Figure 4.7 Implementation Based on Composition

```
STDMETHODIMP CarPlane::XPlane::GetMaxSpeed(long *pn){
  // set *pn to max speed for planes
}
```

The fact that the two implementations of GetMaxSpeed occur in different nested class definitions allows the method to be defined twice and also ensures that the ICar and IPlane-compliant vtbls will have distinct entries for GetMaxSpeed.

It is also worth noting that although the top-level class CarPlane implements the methods of IUnknown, it does not derive from any IUnknown-derived classes. Instead, CarPlane objects have data members that derive from COM interfaces. This means that instead of using static_cast to shear into the object to find a particular vptr, the implementation of the CarPlane's QueryInterface must now return a pointer to the data member that implements the requested interface:

```
STDMETHODIMP CarPlane::QueryInterface(REFIID riid,
                                       Void **ppv) {
  if (riid == IID_IUnknown)
    *ppv = static_cast<IUnknown*>(&m_xCar);
  else if (riid == IID_IVehicle)
    *ppv = static_cast<IVehicle*>(&m_xCar);
  else if (riid == IID_ICar)
    *ppv = static_cast<ICar*>(&m_xCar);
  else if (riid == IID_IPlane)
    *ppv = static_cast<IPlane*>(&m_xPlane);
  else
```

```
            return (*ppv = 0), E_NOINTERFACE;
         ((IUnknown*)(*ppv))->AddRef();
         return S_OK;
      }
```

To ensure that object identity is maintained, each of the CarPlane's data members must either mimic this code in its own implementation of QueryInterface or simply delegate to the master QueryInterface of CarPlane. To do this, a mechanism is needed for getting to the main object from a member function of the composite data member. The class definition of CarPlane::XCar contains an inline routine that uses fixed offsets to calculate the main object's this pointer from the this pointer of the composite data member.

```
inline CarPlane CarPlane::XCar::This(void) {
   return (CarPlane*)((char*)this // ptr to composite
                    - offsetof(CarPlane, m_xCar));
}

inline CarPlane CarPlane::XPlane::This(void) {
   return (CarPlane*)((char*)this // ptr to composite
                    - offsetof(CarPlane, m_xPlane));
}
```

This technique for back-pointer calculation is portable as well as being extremely efficient, as it requires no explicit data members to find the main object from within a data member's method implementation. With these back-pointer routines in place, the composite QueryInterface implementation is trivial:

```
STDMETHODIMP CarPlane::XCar::QueryInterface(REFIID r,
                                                  void**p){
   return This()->QueryInterface(r, p);
}

STDMETHODIMP CarPlane::XPlane::QueryInterface(
                               REFIID r, void**p){
   return This()->QueryInterface(r, p);
}
```

This same delegation would be required for AddRef and Release to maintain a unified notion of object lifetime across the composite data members.

The technique based on using composition to implement interfaces requires considerably more code than simply using multiple inheritance. Also, the quality of the generated code is likely to be no better (and perhaps somewhat worse) than when using multiple inheritance. The fact that the CarPlane class did not need to derive from any COM interfaces does imply that composition is a reasonable technique for mapping COM onto legacy class libraries (*e.g.,* the Microsoft Foundation Classes [MFC] use this technique). The motivation for using composition when implementing new classes is to have distinct implementations of a method that is defined identically in more than one interface. Fortunately, the standard interfaces defined by COM have very few such collisions, and the few that do occur almost always map to semantically equivalent functionality. To solve collisions like those in the GetMaxSpeed scenario, composition is probably overkill, as the first approach's use of intermediate classes to map collisions to unique upcalls is straightforward, efficient, and requires virtually no additional coding. The primary motivation for using composition in new code is to implement per-interface reference counting.

It is sometimes desirable to allocate resources in an object on the basis of the interfaces currently in use. However, using multiple inheritance to implement COM interfaces implies that only one implementation of AddRef and Release will be used in each vtbl. Although one can detect the first request for a given interface and allocate the resources on demand:

```
STDMETHODIMP QueryInterface(REFIID riid, void **ppv){
  if (riid == IID_IBoat) {
// allocate resource the first time through
    if (m_pTonsOfMemory == 0)
      m_pTonsOfMemory = new char[4096 * 4096];
    *ppv = static_cast<IBoat*>(this);
  }
  else if ...
}
```

there is no way to detect when there are no more outstanding IBoat interface pointers, as the Release call that a client makes through the IBoat interface is indistinguishable from a Release call made through any other interface on the object. This is normally what is desired, but in this case, the AddRef and Release calls through the IBoat interfaces need to be treated differently. Had the IBoat interface been implemented using composition, it would have its own unique AddRef and Release implementations, in which it could maintain its own reference count distinct from that of the main object:

```
      class CarBoatPlane : public ICar, public IPlane {
        LONG m_cRef;
        char *m_pTonsOfMemory;
        CarBoatPlane(void): m_cRef(0), m_pTonsOfMemory(0){}
      public:
      // IUnknown methods
        STDMETHODIMP QueryInterface(REFIID, void**);
        STDMETHODIMP_(ULONG) AddRef(void);
        STDMETHODIMP_(ULONG) Release(void);
      // IVehicle methods
        STDMETHODIMP GetMaxSpeed(long *pMax);
      // ICar methods
        STDMETHODIMP Brake(void);
      // IPlane methods
        STDMETHODIMP TakeOff(void);

      // define nested class that implements IBoat
        struct XBoat : public IBoat {
      // get back pointer to main object
          inline CarBoatPlane* This();
          LONG m_cBoatRef; // per-interface ref count
          XBoat(void) : m_cBoatRef(0) {}
          STDMETHODIMP QueryInterface(REFIID, void**);
          STDMETHODIMP_(ULONG) AddRef(void);
          STDMETHODIMP_(ULONG) Release(void);
          STDMETHODIMP GetMaxSpeed(long *pval);
          STDMETHODIMP Sink(void);
        };
        XBoat m_xBoat;
      };
```

The implementation of IBoat's AddRef and Release can now track the number of references of type IBoat and deallocate the resource when it is no longer needed:

```
STDMETHODIMP_(ULONG) CarBoatPlane::XBoat::AddRef() {
  ULONG res = InterlockedIncrement(&m_cBoatRef);
   if (res == 1) { // first AddRef
// allocate resource and forward AddRef to object
      This()->m_pTonsOfMemory = new char[4096*4096];
      This()->AddRef();
```

```
    }
    return res;
  }

STDMETHODIMP_(ULONG) CarBoatPlane::XBoat::Release() {
    ULONG res = InterlockedDecrement(&m_cBoatRef);
    if (res == 0) { // last Release
// free resource and forward Release to object
      delete [] This()->m_pTonsOfMemory;
      This()->Release();
    }
    return res;
  }
```

For this technique to work, all interface pointer users adhere to the COM Specification's requirement that `Release` must be called through the pointer that the corresponding `AddRef` is called on. This is why the canonical tail of `QueryInterface` ends like this:

```
    ((IUnknown*)(*ppv))->AddRef(); // use exact ptr
    return S_OK;
```

instead of this:

```
    AddRef(); // just call this->AddRef
    return S_OK;
```

The former ensures that when the client writes the following correct code

```
    IBoat *pBoat = 0;
    HRESULT hr = pUnk->QueryInterface(IID_IBoat,
                                      (void**)&pBoat);
    if (SUCCEEDED(hr)) {
      hr = pBoat->Sink();
      pBoat->Release();
    }
```

exactly the same pointer value is used for both `AddRef` and `Release`.

It is possible to support composition in the context of a table-driven `QueryInterface` implementation. Based on the family of preprocessor macros presented in the previous chapter, all that is needed is one additional macro to designate that a data member instead of a base class is used and another macro to implement the IUnknown methods in the composite:

```
class CarBoatPlane : public ICar, public IPlane {
public:
  struct XBoat : public IBoat {
// composite QI/AddRef/Release/This()
    IMPLEMENT_COMPOSITE_UNKNOWN(CarBoatPlane,
                                XBoat, m_xBoat)
    STDMETHODIMP GetMaxSpeed(long *pval);
    STDMETHODIMP Sink(void);
  };
  XBoat m_xBoat;

// IVehicle methods
  STDMETHODIMP GetMaxSpeed(long *pMax);
// ICar methods
  STDMETHODIMP Brake(void);
// IPlane methods
  STDMETHODIMP TakeOff(void);

// standard heap-based QI/AddRef/Release
  IMPLEMENT_UNKNOWN(CarBoatPlane)
  BEGIN_INTERFACE_TABLE(CarBoatPlane)
    IMPLEMENTS_INTERFACE_AS(IVehicle, ICar)
    IMPLEMENTS_INTERFACE(ICar)
    IMPLEMENTS_INTERFACE(IPlane)
// macro that calculates offset of data member
    IMPLEMENTS_INTERFACE_WITH_COMPOSITE(IBoat,
                                XBoat,m_xBoat)
  END_INTERFACE_TABLE()
};
```

All that are missing from the preceding class definition are definitions of the object's methods beyond QueryInterface, AddRef and Release. The two new macros used in the class definition are defined as follows:

```
// inttable.h // (book-specific header file) ///
#define COMPOSITE_OFFSET(ClassName, BaseName,\
                         MemberType, MemberName) \
(DWORD(static_cast<BaseName*>(\
```

```
reinterpret_cast<MemberType*>(0x10000000 + \
offsetof(ClassName, MemberName)))) - 0x10000000)

#define IMPLEMENTS_INTERFACE_WITH_COMPOSITE(Req,\
                 MemberType, MemberName) \
{ &IID_##Req,ENTRY_IS_OFFSET, COMPOSITE_OFFSET(_IT,\

 Req, MemberType, MemberName) },

// impunk.h // (book-specific header file) ///
#define IMPLEMENT_COMPOSITE_UNKNOWN(OuterClassName,\
                  InnerClassName, DataMemberName) \
OuterClassName *This() \
{ return (OuterClassName*)((char*)this - \
offsetof(OuterClassName, DataMemberName)); }\
STDMETHODIMP QueryInterface(REFIID riid, void **ppv)\
{ return This()->QueryInterface(riid, ppv); }\
STDMETHODIMP_(ULONG) AddRef(void) \
{ return This()->AddRef(); }\
STDMETHODIMP_(ULONG) Release(void) \
{ return This()->Release(); }\
```

These preprocessor macros simply replicate the de facto implementations of QueryInterface, AddRef, and Release used in composition.

Dynamic Composition

When multiple inheritance or composition is used to implement an interface in a C++ class, each object of that class will carry four bytes worth of vptr overhead per supported interface (assuming that sizeof(void*) == 4). If the number of interfaces an object exports is small, this overhead is negligible, especially in light of the benefits provided by the COM programming model. However, if the number of supported interfaces is large, then this vptr overhead can actually grow to dwarf the non-COM-related size of the object. If every one of these interfaces will be used at all times, this overhead is unavoidable. If, however, these interfaces may never be used or will be used only for a short time, it is possible to take advantage of a loophole in the COM Specification to optimize away some of an object's vptrs when they are not in use.

Recall the rule that indicated that all QueryInterface requests on an object asking for IUnknown must return exactly the same pointer value. This is how object identity is established in COM. However, the COM Specification explicitly allows implementations to return *different* pointer values from QueryInterface requests for any type of interface other than IUnknown. This means that for infrequently used interfaces, an object can dynamically allocate the memory for the vptr on demand without having to worry about returning the same dynamically allocated block of memory each time a particular interface is requested. This technique of transiently allocating composites was first documented in the Microsoft white paper *The COM Programmer's Cookbook* by Crispin Goswell (http://www.microsoft.com/oledev). This white paper referred to these transient interfaces as *tearoffs*.

Implementing an interface as a tearoff is similar to implementing an interface using composition. A second class must be defined for the tearoff that derives from the interface it will implement. The tearoff's QueryInterface must delegate to the main class's QueryInterface in order to maintain identity. The two primary differences are that (1) the main object dynamically allocates the tearoff instead of having an instance data member and (2) the tearoff composite must maintain an explicit back pointer to the main object, as the fixed offset technique used in composition does not work because the tearoff is discontiguous with the main object. The following class implements IBoat as a tearoff:

```
class CarBoat : public ICar {
  LONG m_cRef;
  CarBoat (void): m_cRef(0) {}
public:
// IUnknown methods
  STDMETHODIMP QueryInterface(REFIID, void**);
  STDMETHODIMP_(ULONG) AddRef(void);
  STDMETHODIMP_(ULONG) Release(void);
// IVehicle methods
  STDMETHODIMP GetMaxSpeed(long *pMax);
// ICar methods
  STDMETHODIMP Brake(void);
// define nested class that implements IBoat
  struct XBoat : public IBoat {
    LONG m_cBoatRef;
// back pointer to main object is explicit member
    CarBoat *m_pThis;
    inline CarBoat* This() { return m_pThis; }
    XBoat(CarBoat *pThis);
    ~XBoat(void);
    STDMETHODIMP QueryInterface(REFIID, void**);
```

```
      STDMETHODIMP_(ULONG) AddRef(void);
      STDMETHODIMP_(ULONG) Release(void);
      STDMETHODIMP GetMaxSpeed(long *pval);
      STDMETHODIMP Sink(void);
    };
// note: no data member of type XBoat
};
```

The QueryInterface for the main object needs to allocate a new tearoff dynamically each time IBoat is requested:

```
STDMETHODIMP CarBoat::QueryInterface(REFIID riid,
                                            void **ppv) {
  if (riid == IID_IBoat)
    *ppv = static_cast<IBoat*>(new XBoat(this));
  else if (riid == IID_IUnknown)
    *ppv = static_cast<IUnknown*>(this);
       :     :     :
```

Each time a request for an IBoat interface is received, a new tearoff is allocated. Based on the standard QueryInterface practice of calling AddRef through the resultant pointer:

```
((IUnknown*)*ppv)->AddRef();
```

only the tearoff will be AddRefed directly from QueryInterface. It is important that the main object stay in memory as long as the tearoff is in existence. The easiest way to ensure this is to have the tearoff itself represent an outstanding reference. This can be implemented in the constructor and destructor of the tearoff:

```
CarBoat::XBoat::XBoat(CarBoat *pThis)
  : m_cBoatRef(0), m_pThis(pThis) {
  m_pThis->AddRef();
}

CarBoat::XBoat::~XBoat(void) {
  m_pThis->Release();
}
```

As is the case with composition, the QueryInterface method of the tearoff needs to maintain object identity by delegating to the main object's implementation. However, the tearoff can detect requests for the interface(s) it implements and simply return an AddRefed pointer to itself:

```
STDMETHODIMP
CarBoat::XBoat::QueryInterface(REFIID riid,
                                void**ppv) {
  if (riid != IID_IBoat)
    return This()->QueryInterface(riid, ppv);
  *ppv = static_cast<IBoat*>(this);
  reinterpret_cast<IUnkown*>(*ppv)->AddRef();
  return S_OK;
}
```

Because the tearoff needs to destroy itself when it is no longer in use, it should maintain a reference count of its own and delete itself when this count reaches zero. As noted earlier, the destructor of the tearoff will release the main object prior to vanishing from memory:

```
STDMETHODIMP_(ULONG) CarBoat::XBoat::AddRef(void) {
  return InterlockedIncrement(&m_cRef);
}

STDMETHODIMP_(ULONG) CarBoat::XBoat::Release(void) {
  ULONG res = InterlockedDecrement(&m_cBoatRef);
  if (res == 0)
    delete this; // dtor releases main object
  return res;
}
```

As was the case with composition, the This() method can be used in any of the tearoff's methods that need to access the state of the main object. The difference is that tearoffs require an explicit back pointer, whereas normal composites could use fixed offsets, saving four bytes per composite.

At first glance, tearoffs seem like the best of all possible worlds. When an interface is not used, the object has zero bytes of interface-specific overhead. When the interface is in use, the object indirectly pays 4 bytes worth of overhead in the tearoff. This perception is based on several fallacious assumptions. First, the cost of the tearoff when in use is not just the 4 bytes of memory for its vptr. The tearoff also requires a back pointer and a reference count.[1] Second,

---

[1] The overhead of the reference count can be optimized away *if* the implementor is willing to restrict the client's usage of AddRef. This is a very dangerous optimization given the increasing popularity of smart pointers, which often result in redundant (but harmless) AddRef/Release pairs.

unless a custom memory allocator is used, the tearoff will require at least 4 additional bytes due to padding and/or arena headers used by the C runtime library's implementation of malloc/operator new. This means that although the object indeed saves 4 bytes when the interface is not in use, when the interface is in use, the tearoff consumes a minimum of 12 bytes if a custom memory allocator is used and 16 bytes if the default, operator new, is used. If the interface is rarely requested, this may be a reasonable optimization, especially if the client releases the interface soon after it is acquired. If, however, the client holds on to the tearoff interface for the lifetime of the object, then the benefits of the tearoff interface are lost on that particular instance.

Unfortunately, the tearoff story gets even worse. Based on the implementation shown earlier, if the object receives two QueryInterface requests for the same tearoff interface, two copies of the tearoff will be created, as the pointer to the first tearoff is completely forgotten by the main object once it is returned to the caller. This means that the tearoff now consumes at least 24 to 32 bytes, as two tearoff vptrs are in memory, one per QueryInterface request. This memory will not be reclaimed until the client releases each tearoff. The case in which two QueryInterface requests hold on to the pointer for the lifetime of the object is especially relevant, because this is exactly what happens when an object is accessed remotely. COM's remoting layer will QueryInterface an object twice for the same interface and hold on to both results for the lifetime of the object. This makes tearoffs especially risky for objects that may be accessed remotely.

Given all of the potential pitfalls of tearoffs, a logical question might be, "when *are* tearoffs appropriate?" There is no absolute answer; however, tearoffs are a great technique for supporting a large number of mutually exclusive interfaces. Consider the case in which, in addition to the three vehicle interfaces shown previously, there are interfaces ITruck, IMonsterTruck, IMotorcycle, IBicycle, IUnicycle, ISkateboard, and IHelicopter, all of which derive from IVehicle. If a generic vehicle class wanted to be able to support any of these interfaces, but only one of them for any given instance, then tearoffs would be a great way to do this, *provided the main object caches a pointer to the first tearoff.* The main object's class definition would look like this:

```
class GenericVehicle : public IUnknown {
  LONG m_cRef;
  IVehicle *m_pTearOff; // cached ptr to tearoff
  GenericVehicle(void) : m_cRef(0), m_pTearOff(0){}
// IUnknown methods
  STDMETHODIMP QueryInterface(REFIID, void**);
  STDMETHODIMP_(ULONG) AddRef(void);
```

```
        STDMETHODIMP_(ULONG) Release(void);
// define tearoff classes
    class XTruck : public ITruck { ... };
    class XMonsterTruck : public IMonsterTruck { ... };
    class XBicycle : public IBicycle { ... };
      :       :       :
};
```

In this class, when none of the interfaces are in use, the object only pays an additional four bytes for the empty cached pointer. When a QueryInterface request arrives for one of the ten vehicle interfaces, the memory is allocated for the new tearoff *once* and cached for later use:

```
STDMETHODIMP
GenericVehicle::QueryInterface(REFIID riid,void**ppv)
{
    if (riid == IID_IUnknown)
      *ppv = static_cast<IUnknown*>(this);
    else if (riid == IID_ITruck) {
      if (m_pTearOff == 0) // no tearoff yet, make one
        m_pTearOff = new XTruck(this);
      if (m_pTearOff) // tearoff exists, let tearoff QI
        return m_pTearOff->QueryInterface(riid, ppv);
      else  // memory allocation failure
        return (*ppv = 0), E_NOINTERFACE;
    } else if (riid == IID_IMonsterTruck) {
      if (m_pTearOff == 0) // no tearoff yet, make one
        m_pTearOff = new XMonsterTruck(this);
      if (m_pTearOff) // tearoff exists, let tearoff QI
        return m_pTearOff->QueryInterface(riid, ppv);
      else  // memory allocation failure
        return (*ppv = 0), E_NOINTERFACE;
    } else ...
      :   :   :
}
```

Based on the QueryInterface implementation shown here, there will be at most one tearoff per object. This means that if no vehicle interfaces are requested, the object will consume 12 bytes total (IUnknown vptr + reference count + cached pointer to tearoff). If a vehicle interface is requested, then the object will consume 24 to 28 bytes total (original 12 bytes + IVehicle-derived vptr + reference count + back pointer to main object + (opt) malloc overhead).

Had tearoffs not been used in this case, the class definition would have looked like this:

```
class GenericVehicle
: public ITruck, public IHelicopter, public IBoat,
  public ICar, public IMonsterTruck, public IBicycle,
  public IMotorcycle, public ICar, public IPlane,
  public ISkateboard {
  LONG m_cRef;
// IUnknown methods
  :    :    :
};
```

This class would result in objects that always consume 44 bytes (ten vptrs + reference count). Although the generic vehicle class may seem a bit contrived, COM persistence interfaces fall into a similar category, as there are currently eight different persistence interfaces but an object typically exposes only one of them per instance. However, the class implementor cannot always predict which interface (if any) will be requested by a particular client. Also, each of the eight interfaces requires a different set of supporting data members to implement the interface's methods correctly. If these data members were made part of the tearoff instead of the main object, then only one set of data members would be allocated per object. This type of scenario is perfect for tearoffs, but again, to be most effective, the pointer to the tearoff needs to be cached in the main object.

Binary Composition

Composition and tearoffs are two source-level techniques for implementing COM objects in C++. Both techniques require the object implementor to have the C++ source code definitions of each composite or tearoff class in order to instantiate the subobject prior to returning it via QueryInterface. For many situations, this is perfectly reasonable. However, there are instances in which it would be convenient to package a reusable implementation of one or more interfaces into a *binary* component that could be instantiated across DLL boundaries without requiring the source code of the subcomponent. This would allow the subcomponent to be reused by a wider audience without the tight coupling associated with source-code reuse described in Chapter 1. However, for binary composites or tearoffs to be possible, the reusable component needs to participate in the overall object identity.

To grasp the problems related to unifying identity across component boundaries, consider the following simple implementation of ICar:

```
class Car : public ICar {
  LONG m_cRef;
  Car(void) : m_cRef(0) {}
  STDMETHODIMP QueryInterface(REFIID, void **);
  STDMETHODIMP_(ULONG) AddRef(void);
  STDMETHODIMP_(ULONG) Release(void);
  STDMETHODIMP GetMaxSpeed(long *pn);
  STDMETHODIMP Brake(void);
};

STDMETHODIMP Car::QueryInterface(REFIID riid,
                                        Void **ppv) {
  if (riid == IID_IUnknown)
    *ppv = static_cast<IUnknown*>(this);
  else if (riid == IID_IVehicle)
    *ppv = static_cast<IVehicle*>(this);
  else if (riid == IID_ICar)
    *ppv = static_cast<ICar*>(this);
  else
    return (*ppv = 0), E_NOINTERFACE;
  ((IUnknown*)*ppv)->AddRef();
  return S_OK;
}
// car class object's IClassFactory::CreateInstance
STDMETHODIMP CarClass::CreateInstance(IUnknown *pUnkOuter,
                                        REFIID riid,void **ppv){
  Car *pCar = new Car;
  if (!pCar) return (*ppv = 0), E_OUTOFMEMORY;
  pCar->AddRef();
  HRESULT hr = pCar->QueryInterface(riid, ppv);
  pCar->Release();
  return hr;
}
```

This class simply uses the de facto implementations for QueryInterface, AddRef, and Release.

Consider the following second C++ class that tries to use the Car implementation as a binary composite:

```
class CarBoat : public IBoat {
  LONG m_cRef;
  IUnknown *m_pUnkCar;
  CarBoat(void);
  virtual ~CarBoat(void);
  STDMETHODIMP QueryInterface(REFIID, void **);
  STDMETHODIMP_(ULONG) AddRef(void);
  STDMETHODIMP_(ULONG) Release(void);
  STDMETHODIMP GetMaxSpeed(long *pn);
  STDMETHODIMP Sink(void);
};
```

To emulate composition, the constructor would create the Car subobject and the destructor would release the pointer to the subobject:

```
CarBoat::CarBoat(void) : m_cRef(0) {
    HRESULT hr = CoCreateInstance(CLSID_Car, 0, CLSCTX_ALL,
                        IID_IUnknown, (void**)&m_pUnkCar);
    assert(SUCCEEDED(hr));
}

CarBoat::~CarBoat(void) {
  if (m_pUnkCar)
    m_pUnkCar->Release();
}
```

An interesting problem arises in the implementation of QueryInterface:

```
STDMETHODIMP CarBoat::QueryInterface(REFIID riid,
                                        void **ppv) {
  if (riid == IID_IUnknown)
    *ppv = static_cast<IUnknown*>(this);
  else if (riid == IID_IVehicle)
    *ppv = static_cast<IVehicle*>(this);
  else if (riid == IID_IBoat)
    *ppv = static_cast<IBoat*>(this);
  else if (riid == IID_ICar) // forward request...
    return m_pUnkCar->QueryInterface(riid, ppv);
  else
    return (*ppv = 0), E_NOINTERFACE;
  ((IUnknown*)*ppv)->AddRef();
```

```
        return S_OK;
    }
```

Because the Car subobject has no idea that it is part of another object's identity, it will fail any QueryInterface requests for IBoat. This means that:

```
    QI(IBoat)->ICar
```

would succeed, but

```
    QI(QI(IBoat)->ICar)->IBoat
```

would fail, resulting in a QueryInterface that is not symmetric. In addition,
QueryInterface requests for IUnknown via the ICar and IBoat interface pointers would return distinct values, implying two distinct object identities. These
violations of the IUnknown protocol imply that CarBoat objects are simply not
legal COM objects.

The idea of composing an object from binary composites is fairly sound. In
fact, the COM Specification explicitly details how to implement this idea in a
standard predictable manner. The technique of exposing a binary subcomponent to a client directly via QueryInterface is called COM aggregation. COM
aggregation is a set of rules that define the relationships between the outer
object (the aggregator) and the inner object (the aggregatee). COM aggregation is simply a set of IUnknown rules that allow more than one binary component to appear as a single COM identity.

COM aggregation is by no means the primary vehicle for reuse in COM. It
is far more common simply to instantiate an object and use its methods in the
implementation of another object's methods. It is rare that one would want to
expose the interfaces of another object directly to the client *as part of the same
identity*. Consider the following scenario:

```
    class Handlebar : public IHandlebar { ... };
    class Wheel : public IWheel {};

    class Bicycle : public IBicycle {
      IHandlebar * m_pHandlebar;
      IWheel *m_pFrontWheel;
      IWheel *m_pBackWheel;
    };
```

It would be counterintuitive for the Bicycle class to give out an IHandlebar or
IWheel interface in its QueryInterface method. QueryInterface is reserved

for expressing *is-a* relationships, and clearly a bicycle is *not* a wheel or handlebar. If the Bicycle designer wanted to provide direct access to these aspects of the object, then the IBicycle interface should have explicit property accessors for this purpose:

```
[object, uuid(753A8A60-A7FF-11d0-8C30-0080C73925BA)]
interface IBicycle : IVehicle {
  HRESULT GetHandlebar([out,retval] IHandlebar**pph);
  HRESULT GetWheels([out] IWheel **ppwFront,
                    [out] IWheel **ppwBack);
}
```

The bicycle implementation could then simply return pointers to its subobjects:

```
STDMETHODIMP Bicycle::GetHandlebar(IHandlebar**pph){
  if (*pph = m_pHandlebar)
    (*pph)->AddRef();
  return S_OK;
}
STDMETHODIMP Bicycle::GetWheels(IWheel **ppwFront,
                                IWheel **ppwBack){
  if (*ppwFront = m_pFrontWheel)
    (*ppwFront)->AddRef();
  if (*ppwBack = m_pBackWheel)
    (*ppwBack)->AddRef();
  return S_OK;
}
```

When this technique is used, the client still gets direct access to the subobjects. However, because the pointers are acquired via explicit methods and not via QueryInterface, no identity relationship is implied between the various components.

Despite this example, there are still scenarios in which it is desirable to provide an implementation of an interface that can be merged into another object's identity. To support this, COM aggregation requires that the inner object (the aggregatee) be notified at creation time that it is being created as part of another object's identity. This means that the creation function used to create an object requires one additional parameter: an IUnknown pointer to the identity that the aggregate must delegate to in its QueryInterface, AddRef, and Release methods. Note the definition of the CreateInstance method of the IClassFactory interface:

```
HRESULT CreateInstance([in] IUnknown *pUnkOuter,
        [in] REFIID riid, [out, iid_is(riid)] void **ppv);
```

This method (and the corresponding API functions CoCreateInstanceEx and CoCreateInstance) is overloaded to support creation of stand-alone objects and aggregates. If a caller passes a null pointer for the first parameter of CreateInstance (pUnkOuter), then the resultant object will be a stand-alone identity unto itself. If instead the caller passes a non-null pointer for the first parameter, then the resultant object will be an aggregate of the identity referred to by pUnkOuter. In the case of aggregation, the aggregate must forward all QueryInterface, AddRef, and Release requests directly to pUnkOuter unconditionally. This is vital for maintaining object identity.

Given the function prototype shown above, the CarBoat class needs only slight modification to adhere to the rules of aggregation:

```
CarBoat::CarBoat(void) : m_cRef(0) {
// need to pass identity of self to Create routine
// to notify car object it is an aggregate
    HRESULT hr = CoCreateInstance(CLSID_Car, this,
            CLSCTX_ALL, IID_IUnknown, (void**)&m_pUnkCar);
    assert(SUCCEEDED(hr));
}
```

CarBoat's implementation of QueryInterface simply forwards the request for ICar to the inner aggregate:

```
STDMETHODIMP CarBoat::QueryInterface(REFIID riid,
                                        void **ppv) {
  if (riid == IID_IUnknown)
    *ppv = static_cast<IUnknown*>(this);
  else if (riid == IID_ICar) // forward request...
    return m_pUnkCar->QueryInterface(riid, ppv);
  else if (riid == IID_IBoat)
    :   :   :
```

In theory, this should work, as the aggregate will always forward any subsequent QueryInterface requests back to the main object, thereby maintaining object identity.

In the preceding scenario, the Car class's CreateInstance method returns an IUnknown-derived interface pointer to the outer object. If this interface pointer were simply to delegate to the IUnknown of the outer object, there would be no way to (1) notify the aggregate that it is no longer needed or (2) request interface pointers to give out to the main object's clients. In fact, the QueryInterface implementation shown above would result in an infinite loop, as the outer is delegating to the inner, which is delegating back to the outer.

To address this problem, the initial interface pointer that is returned to the outer object must not delegate back to the outer object's IUnknown implementation. This means that objects that support COM aggregation must have two implementations of IUnknown. The delegating implementation forwards all QueryInterface, AddRef, and Release requests to an external implementation. This is the default implementation that is referred to by all of the object's vtbls and is the version seen by external clients. The object must also have a nondelegating implementation of IUnknown that is exposed only to the aggregating outer object.

There are several ways to provide two distinct implementations of IUnknown from a single object. The most direct technique[2] is to use composition and use a data member to implement the nondelegating IUnknown methods. The following is an aggregatable implementation of Car:

```
class Car : public ICar {
  LONG m_cRef;
  IUnknown *m_pUnkOuter;
public:
  Car(IUnknown *pUnkOuter);
// non-delegating IUnknown methods
  STDMETHODIMP InternalQueryInterface(REFIID,
                                      void **);
  STDMETHODIMP_(ULONG) InternalAddRef(void);
  STDMETHODIMP_(ULONG) InternalRelease(void);
// delegating IUnknown methods
  STDMETHODIMP QueryInterface(REFIID, void **);
  STDMETHODIMP_(ULONG) AddRef(void);
  STDMETHODIMP_(ULONG) Release(void);
  STDMETHODIMP GetMaxSpeed(long *pn);
  STDMETHODIMP Brake(void);

// composite to map distinguished IUnknown vptr to
// non-delegating InternalXXX routines in main object
```

---

[2] The author once believed that using method coloring to provide two implementations of IUnknown was the superior technique. Over time, the technique shown in this book has proved to be more maintainable and no less efficient.

```
class XNDUnknown : public IUnknown {
  Car* This() { return (Car*)((BYTE*)this -
                   offsetof(Car, m_innerUnknown));}
  STDMETHODIMP QueryInterface(REFIID r, void**p)
  { return This()->InternalQueryInterface(r,p); }
  STDMETHODIMP_(ULONG) AddRef(void)
  { return This()->InternalAddRef(); }
  STDMETHODIMP_(ULONG) Release(void)
  { return This()->InternalRelease(); }
};
XNDUnknown m_innerUnknown; // composite instance
};
```

The binary layout of this object is shown in Figure 4.8. The class's delegating methods are extremely simple:

```
STDMETHODIMP Car::QueryInterface(REFIID riid,
                                  void **ppv)
{ return m_pUnkOuter->QueryInterface(riid, ppv); }

STDMETHODIMP_(ULONG) Car::AddRef(Void)
{ return m_pUnkOuter->AddRef(); }

STDMETHODIMP_(ULONG) Car::Release(Void)
{ return m_pUnkOuter->Release(); }
```

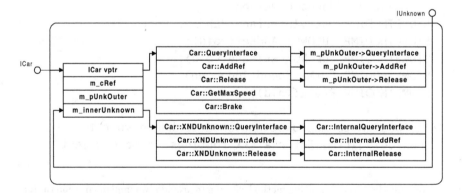

Figure 4.8 An Aggregatable Car

These routines are the versions that will populate all of the object's interface vtbls, so that no matter which interface a client is accessing, the IUnknown methods always delegate to the main identity of the object.

To allow the object to be used in both aggregation and stand-alone scenarios, the constructor of the object must set its m_pUnkOuter data member to point to its own nondelegating IUnknown when used in stand-alone mode:

```
Car::Car(IUnknown *pUnkOuter)
{
  if (pUnkOuter) // delegate to pUnkOuter
    m_pUnkOuter = pUnkOuter;
  else  // delegate to non-delegating self
    m_pUnkOuter = &m_innerUnknown;
}
```

The constructor ensures that in either case, m_pUnkOuter points to the correct implementation of the QueryInterface, AddRef, and Release for this object.

The normal nondelegating implementations of QueryInterface, AddRef, and Release are very regular and predictable:

```
STDMETHODIMP Car::InternalQueryInterface(REFIID riid,
                                  void **ppv) {
  if (riid == IID_IUnknown)
    *ppv = static_cast<IUnknown*>(&m_innerUnknown);
  else if (riid == IID_IVehicle)
    *ppv = static_cast<IVehicle*>(this);
  else if (riid == IID_ICar)
    *ppv = static_cast<ICar*>(this);
  else
    return (*ppv = 0), E_NOINTERFACE;
  ((IUnknown*)*ppv)->AddRef();
  return S_OK;
}

STDMETHODIMP_(ULONG) Car::InternalAddRef(void) {
  return InterlockedIncrement(&m_cRef);
}

STDMETHODIMP_(ULONG) Car::InternalRelease(void) {
  ULONG res = InterlockedDecrement(&m_cRef);
  if (res == 0)
```

```
      delete this;
   return res;
  }
```

The only distinctive aspect of these three methods (besides their names) is the fact that `InternalQueryInterface` returns the pointer to the nondelegating unknown when asked for `IUnknown`. This is simply a requirement mandated by the COM Specification that must be adhered to.

Finally, the creation routine for Car needs to be modified to support COM aggregation:

```
STDMETHODIMP CarClass::CreateInstance(IUnknown *pUnkOuter,
                              REFIID riid, void **ppv){
// verify that aggregator only requests IUnknown as
// initial interface
  if (pUnkOuter != 0 && riid != IID_IUnknown)
    return (*ppv = 0), E_INVALIDARG;

// create new object/aggregate

  Car *p = new Car(pUnkOuter);
  if (!p) return (*ppv = 0), E_OUTOFMEMORY;
// return resultant pointer
  p->InternalAddRef();
  HRESULT hr = p->InternalQueryInterface(riid, ppv);
  p->InternalRelease();
  return hr;
  }
```

Note that the nondelegating versions of `QueryInterface`, `AddRef`, and `Release` are used. If a stand-alone identity is being created, this is certainly appropriate. If an aggregate is being created, this is necessary to ensure that the inner object is AddRefed, not the outer object. Also note that the outer object must request IUnknown as the initial interface. This is mandated by the COM Specification. If the outer object could request any initial interface, then the inner object would essentially need to keep two duplicate sets of vptrs, one set that delegated its `QueryInterface`, `AddRef`, and `Release` implementations and another set that did not. By restricting the initial interface to IUnknown, the object implementor needs to isolate only one vptr to act as the nondelegating IUnknown.

One potential hazard that occurs when programming with COM aggregation is related to reference counting. Note that the constructor of the inner object duplicates the pointer to the controlling outer object but does not call AddRef. Calling AddRef in this particular situation is prohibited, because if both entities AddRef each other, a cycle occurs that can never be broken. The reference counting rules of aggregation mandate that the outer object holds a reference counted pointer to the inner object's nondelegating IUnknown (this is the pointer returned by the object's creation routine). The inner object holds a nonreference counted pointer to the IUnknown of the controlling outer. Technically, this relationship is covered by the special knowledge clause of COM's reference counting guidelines. In general, the technique of using nonreference counted pointers should not be used, as it is impossible to implement when objects are accessed remotely. A more effective way to deal with reference counting cycles is to introduce intermediate object identities whose reference counts do not affect the lifetime of either entity.

One additional problem that can occur when programming aggregation arises when communication between the inner and outer objects is needed. For the inner object to communicate with the outer object, a call to QueryInterface through the controlling IUnknown must be made. However, this QueryInterface request will call AddRef through the resultant pointer, which has the net effect of AddRefing the outer object. If the inner object were to hold this pointer as a data member, then a cycle would be created, as the inner has now implicitly AddRefed the outer object. This means that the inner object must use one of two strategies. The inner object can acquire and release the pointer on demand, holding on to the pointer only as long as it is needed:

```
STDMETHODIMP Inner::MethodX(void) {
   ITruck *pTruck = 0;
// outer object will be AddRefed after this call...
   HRESULT hr = m_pUnkOuter->QueryInterface(IID_ITruck,
                                            (void**)&pTruck);
   if (SUCCEEDED(hr)) {
     pTruck->ShiftGears();
     pTruck->HaulDirt();
// release reference to outer object
     pTruck->Release();
   }
}
```

A second technique is to acquire the pointer once at initialization time and release the corresponding outer object immediately after acquisition.

```
    HRESULT Inner::Initialize(void) {
// outer object will be AddRefed after this call...
   HRESULT hr = m_pUnkOuter->QueryInterface(IID_ITruck,
                                   (void**)&m_pTruck);
// release reference to outer object here and DO NOT
// release it later in the object's destructor
  if (SUCCEEDED(hr))
     m_pTruck->Release();
}
```

This technique works because the inner object's lifetime is a proper subset of the outer object's lifetime. This means that m_pTruck will theoretically always point to a valid object. Of course, if the outer object implemented ITruck as a tearoff, all bets are off, as the Release call will destroy the tearoff.

Objects that aggregate other objects need to be aware of the problems related to inner aggregates requesting interface pointers. In addition to the caveat regarding tearoffs already mentioned, one other potential hazard is related to object stabilization. When an object is accessed by clients, it must be in a stable state. In particular, its reference count must be nonzero. In general, this is not a problem, as clients can acquire interface pointers only via QueryInterface, which always performs an AddRef prior to returning. However, if an object creates an aggregate in its constructor while its reference count is still zero, the inner object initialization code shown above would execute the final release on the outer object, forcing the outer object to destroy itself prematurely. To avoid this problem, objects that aggregate other objects temporarily raise their reference count to one while the aggregates are being created:

```
    Outer::Outer(void) {
  ++m_cRef; // protect against delete this
  CoCreateInstance(CLSID_Inner, this, CLSCTX_ALL,
                   IID_IUnknown, (void**)&m_pUnkInner);
  --m_cRef; // allow delete this
}
```

This stabilization technique prevents premature destruction when the inner object releases pointers that it may acquire in its initialization code. This technique is so common that most COM programming frameworks provide an explicit overridable method that executes inside the scope of an increment/decrement pair. MFC calls this method CreateAggregates, ATL calls this method FinalConstruct.

Because the techniques shown earlier for implementing an aggregatable object do not require any additional base classes to be added to the C++ class, an alternative form of the IMPLEMENT_UNKNOWN macro can transparently implement the bifurcated IUnknown implementation. The original class definition:

```
class Car : public ICar {
  Car(void);
  IMPLEMENT_UNKNOWN(Car)
  BEGIN_INTERFACE_TABLE(Car)
    IMPLEMENTS_INTERFACE(ICar)
    IMPLEMENTS_INTERFACE(IVehicle)
  END_INTERFACE()
// IVehicle methods
  STDMETHODIMP GetMaxSpeed(long *pn);
// ICar methods
  STDMETHODIMP Brake(void);
};
```

simply translates to the following:

```
class Car : public ICar {
  Car(void);
// indicate that aggregation is required
  IMPLEMENT_AGGREGATABLE_UNKNOWN(Car)
  BEGIN_INTERFACE_TABLE(Car)
    IMPLEMENTS_INTERFACE(ICar)
    IMPLEMENTS_INTERFACE(IVehicle)
  END_INTERFACE()
// IVehicle methods
  STDMETHODIMP GetMaxSpeed(long *pn);
// ICar methods
  STDMETHODIMP Brake(void);
};
```

The inline expansion of the IMPLEMENT_AGGREGATABLE_UNKNOWN macro is included in the code that accompanies this book.

Containment

Not all classes are aggregatable. To expose nonaggregatable classes as part of another object's identity requires the outer object to explicitly forward method calls to the inner object. This technique is often called COM containment. As

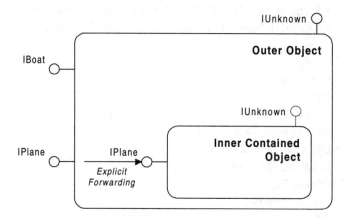

Figure 4.9 COM Containment

shown in Figure 4.9, containment does not require any participation on the part of the inner object. It does, however, require the outer object to provide implementations of each interface that the inner object exposes. These outer implementations simply forward the client's request to the inner object. COM containment requires no special care with regard to the identity rules of COM, as the inner object is never directly accessible to the client and therefore never directly mingles with the outer object's type hierarchy. Although COM containment is part of the vocabulary of COM, it requires no unusual programming techniques. In fact, the object being contained cannot detect that the outer object is forwarding its method calls from the actual client.

Where Are We?

This chapter discussed the identity laws of COM. These laws define what it means to be a COM object. The identity laws of COM allow object implementors tremendous flexibility in terms of how to partition an object implementation. Composition was presented as a technique for implementing per-interface reference counting. Tearoffs were presented as a technique for reducing vptr bloat and more efficiently managing object state. Aggregation was then shown as a technique for composing a single identity from two or more binary components. Each of these techniques allows more than one object to appear as a single COM identity. Each technique has its advantages, and the use of any or all of these techniques is completely hidden from the object's clients.

CHAPTER

5 | Apartments

```
STDMETHODIMP CMyClass::MethodX(void) {
  EnterCriticalSection(&m_cs);
  if (TryToPerformX() == false)
    return E_UNEXPECTED;
  LeaveCriticalSection(&m_cs);
  return S_OK;
}
```
Anonymous, 1996

The previous chapter discussed the fundamentals of COM identity and formally defined what distinguishes COM objects from random memory. The rules of IUnknown were presented, in addition to techniques for leveraging these rules to afford the object implementor maximum flexibility. This chapter refines the definition of COM identity to take into account basic operating system primitives (*e.g.*, threads, processes) and distributed access. This marriage of system primitives and distribution forms the basis for the COM remoting architecture.

Interface and Implementation Revisited

Some developers make extensive use of multithreaded programming techniques and are able to write amazingly sophisticated software using the thread synchronization primitives available from the operating system. Other developers are more concerned with solving domain-specific problems and cannot be bothered with the nuisance of writing thread-safe or thread-hot code. Still other developers have special threading constraints due to the fact that many windowing systems (including Windows) have very strict rules regarding how threads and windowing primitives relate. Yet another class of developer may make extensive use of a legacy class library that is thread hostile and cannot tolerate any multithreaded access whatsoever. All four types of developers need to be able to use each other's objects without having to rearchitect their threading strategy to accommodate all possible scenarios. To facilitate transparent usage of an object irrespective of its thread awareness, COM treats an object's concurrency constraints as yet another implementation detail that the client has no business worrying about. To decouple the client from an object's concurrency and reentrancy constraints, COM has a very formal abstraction that models how objects are related to both processes and threads. This abstraction is formally called an apartment.[1] Apartments define a logical grouping of objects that share a common set of concurrency and reentrancy constraints. Every COM object belongs to exactly one apartment; however, one apartment can be shared by multiple objects. The apartment an object belongs to is implicitly part of an object's identity.

An apartment is neither a process nor a thread; however, apartments share some of the properties of both. Every process that uses COM has one or more apartments; however, an apartment is contained in exactly one process. This means that every process that uses COM has at least one group of objects that share concurrency and reentrancy requirements; however, two objects that reside in the same process may belong to two different apartments and therefore could have different concurrency and reentrancy constraints. This principle allows libraries with wildly different thread awareness to interoperate peacefully in a single process.

A thread executes in exactly one apartment at a time. Before a thread can use COM, it must first enter an apartment. When a thread enters an apartment, COM stores information about the apartment in thread local storage (TLS), and this information remains associated with the thread until the thread exits the apartment. COM mandates that objects may be accessed only by threads executing in the apartment of the object. This means that if a thread is executing in the same process as an object, it may be prohibited from accessing the object even though the memory that the object occupies is fully visible and accessible. COM defines an HRESULT (RPC_E_WRONG_THREAD) that certain system-level objects will return when directly accessed from foreign apartments. It is legal for user-defined objects to return this HRESULT as well; however, few developers are willing to go to this length to ensure proper usage of their objects.

The Windows NT 4.0 release of COM defines two types of apartments: multithreaded apartments (MTAs) and singlethreaded apartments (STAs). Each process has at most one MTA; however, a process can contain multiple STAs. As their names imply, multiple threads can execute in an MTA concurrently, whereas only one thread can execute in an STA. More precisely, only

---

[1] Apartments are the more modern term for what the COM Specification originally referred to as an execution context.

one thread can *ever* execute in a given STA, which means not only that objects that reside in an STA will never be accessed concurrently but also that only one *particular* thread will ever execute the object's methods. This thread affinity allows object implementors to safely store intermediate state in TLS between method calls, as well as to hold locks that have thread affinity (*e.g.,* Win32-critical sections and mutexes) across method invocations.

These practices lead to disaster when used by MTA-based objects as there are no guarantees which thread will execute any given method invocation. The disadvantage of an STA is that it allows only one method call to execute concurrently, no matter how many objects belong to the apartment. In an MTA, threads can be dynamically allocated based on the current demand with no correlation with the number of objects in the apartment. To build concurrent server processes using only singlethreaded apartments, multiple apartments are necessary, which can cause excessive thread overhead if care is not taken. Also, the degree of concurrency in an STA-based server process cannot exceed the total number of objects in the process. If the server process contains only a small number of coarse-grained objects, then only a small number of threads can be utilized, even if each object lives in its own private STA.

A future release of COM may introduce a third type of apartment, the rentalthreaded apartment (RTA). Like an MTA, RTAs allow more than one thread to enter an apartment. Unlike an MTA, when the thread enters an RTA, it acquires an apartment-wide lock (hence, it *rents* the apartment) that keeps other threads from entering the apartment concurrently. This apartment-wide lock is released when the thread exits the RTA, allowing the next thread to enter. In this respect, an RTA is like an MTA except that all method calls are serialized. This makes RTAs much more suitable for classes that are not known to be thread safe. Although all calls in an STA are also serialized, RTA-based objects differ in that they do not have thread affinity; that is, arbitrary threads can execute inside the RTA, not just the initial thread that created the apartment. This lack of thread affinity makes RTA-based objects more flexible and efficient than STA-based objects, as any thread can conceivably call into the object simply by entering the object's RTA. At the time of this writing, the details of how RTA apartments will be created and entered had not been finalized. Consult the SDK documentation for more details.

When a thread is first created by the operating system as a result of calling either `CreateProcess` or `CreateThread`, the newly created thread has no associated apartment.[2] Prior to using COM, the new thread must first enter an apartment by calling one of the following three API functions:

---

[2] This fact is subject to change under Windows NT 5.0. Consult the SDK documentation for more details.

```
HRESULT CoInitializeEx(void *pvReserved, DWORD dwFlags);
HRESULT CoInitialize(void *pvReserved);
HRESULT OleInitialize(void *pvReserved);
```

For all three API functions just listed, the first parameter is reserved and must be zero.

CoInitializeEx is the lowest level API function and allows the caller to specify which type of apartment to enter. To enter the process-wide MTA, the caller must use the COINIT_MULTITHREADED flag:

```
HRESULT hr = CoInitializeEx(0, COINIT_MULTITHREADED);
```

To enter a newly created STA, the caller must specify the COINIT_ APARTMENTTHREADED flag:

```
HRESULT hr = CoInitializeEx(0, COINIT_APARTMENTTHREADED);
```

Each thread in a process that calls CoInitializeEx with COINIT_ MULTITHREADED executes in the same apartment. Each thread that calls CoInitializeEx with COINIT_APARTMENTTHREADED executes in a private apartment that no other threads can enter. CoInitialize is a legacy routine that simply calls CoInitializeEx using the COINIT_APARTMENTTHREADED flag. OleInitialize first calls CoInitialize and then initializes several subsystems used in OLE applications, such as OLE Drag and Drop and the OLE Clipboard. In general, it is preferable to call CoInitialize or CoInitializeEx if these higher level services will not be used.

Each of these three API functions can be called more than once per thread. The first call on each thread will return S_OK. Subsequent calls will simply reenter the same apartment and return S_FALSE. For each successful call to CoInitialize or CoInitializeEx, a call to CoUninitialize must be made from the same thread. For each successful call to OleInitialize, a call to OleUninitialize must be made from the same thread. These uninitialization routines have very simple signatures:

```
void CoUninitialize(void);
void OleUninitialize(void);
```

Failing to call these routines prior to thread or process termination may delay the reclamation of resources. Once a thread enters an apartment, it is illegal to change apartment types using CoInitializeEx. Attempts to do so will result in the HRESULT RPC_E_CHANGED_MODE. However, once a thread completely exits an apartment using CoUninitialize, it may enter another apartment by calling CoInitializeEx again.

Objects, Interfaces, and Apartments

Clients want to call methods on objects. Objects simply want to expose their methods to clients. The fact that an object may have different concurrency constraints than those implied by the client's apartment is an implementation detail that the client should not care about. Similarly, if the object implementor chooses to deploy an object implementation only on a small set of host machines that are distinct from the host machine where the client program is located, this again is an implementation detail that the client should not care about. However, in either case, the object must reside in an apartment distinct from that of the client.

From a programming perspective, apartment membership is an interface pointer attribute, not an object attribute. When an interface pointer is returned from a COM API call or from a method invocation, the thread that invoked the API call or method determines which apartment the resultant interface pointer belongs to. If the call returns a pointer to the actual object, then the object itself resides in the calling thread's apartment. Often, the object cannot reside in the caller's apartment, either because the object already exists in a different process or host machine or because the concurrency requirements of the object are incompatible with the client's apartment. In these cases, the client receives a pointer to a proxy.

In COM, a proxy is an object that is semantically identical to an object in another apartment. In a sense, a proxy represents another object's identity in a different apartment. A proxy exposes the same set of interfaces as the object it represents, however the proxy's implementation of each of the interface's methods simply forwards the calls to the object, ensuring that the object's methods always execute in the object's apartment. Irrespective of whether the client receives a pointer to an object or a pointer to a proxy, any interface pointer that a client receives from an API call or a method call is valid for all threads in the caller's apartment.

Object implementors decide the types of apartments in which their objects can execute. As is discussed in Chapter 6, out-of-process servers explicitly decide their apartment type by calling CoInitializeEx with the appropriate parameter. For in-process servers, a different approach is needed, as the client will already have called CoInitializeEx by the time the object is created. To allow in-process servers to control their apartment type, COM allows each CLSID to have its own distinct threading model that is advertised in the local registry using the ThreadingModel named value:

```
[HKCR\CLSID\{96556310-D779-11d0-8C4F-0080C73925BA}\InprocServer32]
@="C:\racer.dll"
ThreadingModel="Free"
```

Each CLSID in a DLL can have its own distinct ThreadingModel. Under Windows NT 4.0, COM allows four possible ThreadingModels for a CLSID. ThreadingModel="Both" indicates that the class can execute in either an MTA or an STA. ThreadingModel="Free" indicates that the class can execute only in an MTA. ThreadingModel="Apartment" indicates that the class can execute only in an STA. The absence of a ThreadingModel value implies that the class can run only on the main STA. The main STA is defined as the first STA to be initialized in the process.

If the client's apartment is compatible with the CLSID's threading model, then all in-process activation requests for that CLSID will instantiate the object directly in the apartment of the client. This is by far the most efficient scenario, as no intermediate proxy is needed.[3] If the client's apartment is incompatible with the CLSID's threading model, then in-process activation requests for that CLSID will force COM to silently instantiate the object in a distinct apartment, and a proxy will be returned to the client. In the case of STA-based clients activating ThreadingModel="Free" classes, the class object (and subsequent instances) will execute in the MTA. In the case of MTA-based clients activating ThreadingModel="Apartment" classes, the class object (and subsequent instances) will execute in a COM-created STA. In the case of any type of client activating main STA-based classes, the class object (and subsequent instances) must execute in a main STA of the process. If the client happens to be the main STA thread, then the object will be accessed directly. Otherwise, the client will get back a proxy. If no STAs exist in the process (that is, if no threads have called CoInitializeEx with the COINIT_APARTMENTTHREADED flag), then COM will create a new STA to act as the main STA for the process.

Class implementors that do not mark a threading model for their classes can largely ignore threading issues, as their DLL will be accessed from only one thread, the main STA thread. Implementors that mark their classes as supporting any explicit threading model are implicitly indicating that multiple apartments in a process (which implies the potential for multiple threads) may each contain instances of the class. Because of this, the implementor must protect any resources that are shared by more than one instance of the class against concurrent access. This means that all global and static

---

[3] The performance cost of an interapartment method invocation can potentially be thousands of times greater than that of an intraapartment method call due to thread-switching overhead.

variables must be protected using an appropriate thread synchronization primitive. For a COM in-process server, the global lock count that keeps track of the server's lifetime must be protected using `InterlockedIncrement/InterlockedDecrement`, as demonstrated in Chapter 3. Any other server-specific state needs to be protected as well.

Implementors that mark their classes as ThreadingModel="Apartment" are stating that their instances must be accessed from only one thread for the lifetime of the object. This implies that there is no need to protect instance state, only the state that is shared by multiple instances of the class, as mentioned previously. Implementors that mark their classes as either ThreadingModel="Free" or ThreadingModel="Both" are making the statement that instances of their class may run in the MTA, which means that a single instance of the class may be accessed concurrently. Because of this, implementors must protect all resources that are used by a single instance against concurrent access. This applies not only to shared static variables but also to instance data members. For heap-based objects, this implies that the reference count data member must be protected using `InterlockedIncrement/InterlockedDecrement`, as demonstrated in Chapter 2. Any other class-specific instance state needs to be protected as well.

At first glance, it is less than obvious why ThreadingModel="Free" exists, because the requirements of running in an MTA are often seen as a superset of the requirements for STA compatibility. If an object implementor plans on creating worker threads that will need access to the object, it is highly advantageous to prevent the object from being created in an STA. This is because the worker threads cannot enter the STA where the object lives and therefore must run in a different apartment. If a class is marked ThreadingModel="Both" and an activation request is made from an STA-based thread, the object will live in an STA. This means that the worker threads (which will run in the MTA) must access the object using interapartment method calls, which are considerably less efficient than intraapartment method invocation. However, if the class is marked ThreadingModel="Free," then any STA-based activation requests will force the new instance to be created in the MTA, where any worker threads could access the object directly. This means that when the STA-based client invokes methods on the object, the performance will be diminished; however, the worker threads will experience much better performance. This is a reasonable trade-off if the object will be accessed by the worker threads more often than by the actual STA-based client. It is tempting simply to relax the rules of COM and note that some objects may be directly accessed from more than one apartment without causing faults. However, in the general case, this is not true, especially for objects that use other objects to perform their work.

Cross-Apartment Access

To allow objects to reside in apartments that are distinct from the client's apartment, COM allows interfaces to be exported from one apartment and imported into another. To make an object's interfaces visible outside the object's apartment is to *export* the interface. To make an external interface visible inside an apartment is to *import* an interface. When an interface is imported, the resultant interface pointer refers to a proxy that can be legally accessed by any thread in the importing apartment.[4] It is the job of the proxy to pass control back to the object's apartment, ensuring that all method calls execute in the correct apartment. This passing of control from one apartment to another is referred to as *method remoting* and is how all cross-thread, cross-process, and cross-host communications occur in COM.

By default, method remoting uses the COM Object RPC (ORPC) communications protocol. COM ORPC is a lightweight protocol that is layered over MS-RPC, a DCE derivative. MS-RPC is a protocol-independent communications mechanism that can be extended to support new transport protocols (via dynamically loadable transport DLLs) and new authentication packages (via dynamically loadable Security Support Provider DLLs). COM uses the most efficient transport protocol available based on the proximity and types of the importing and exporting apartments. When communicating off host, COM prefers the User Datagram Protocol (UDP), although most common network protocols are supported.[5] When communicating locally, COM uses one of several transports, each of which is optimized for a particular apartment type.

COM allows interface pointers to be passed across apartment boundaries using a technique called marshaling. Marshaling an interface pointer simply transforms the interface pointer into a transmissible byte stream whose contents uniquely identify the object and its owning apartment. This byte stream is the marshaled state of the interface pointer and allows any apartment to import the interface pointer and make method calls on the object. Note that because COM deals exclusively with interface pointers, not the objects themselves, this marshaled state does not represent the state of the *object* but rather the serialized state of an apartment-independent reference to the

---

[4] If the importing apartment is the apartment that the object belongs to, no proxy will be used and the imported pointer will point directly to the object.

[5] UDP is preferred over TCP due to the excessive overhead of TCP connection establishment. COM, like DCE RPC, piggybacks its security and protocol synchronization information in the packet headers used to transmit the first RPC request. Because COM-based systems tend to set up and tear down many transient connections, UDP is the superior choice. When using datagram transports such as UDP, the RPC runtime library reimplements the error correction and flow/congestion control algorithms of TCP.

object. These marshaled object references simply contain connection establishment information that is completely independent of the object's state.

Normally, interface pointers are marshaled implicitly as part of the normal operation of COM. When an in-process activation request is made for a class with an incompatible threading model, COM implicitly marshals the interface from the object's apartment and unmarshals a proxy in the client's apartment. When an out-of-process or off-host activation request is made, COM also marshals the resultant pointer from the apartment of the object and unmarshals a proxy for the client. When method calls are performed on proxies, any interface pointers that are passed as method parameters will be marshaled in order to make the object references available in both the client's and the object's apartments. Occasionally, it is necessary to marshal interfaces explicitly from one apartment to another outside the context of an activation request or a method call. To support this, COM provides a low-level API function, CoMarshalInterface, to marshal interface pointers explicitly.

CoMarshalInterface takes an interface pointer on input and writes the serialized representation of the pointer to a caller-provided byte stream. This byte stream can then be passed to another apartment, where the CoUnmarshalInterface API function uses the byte stream to return an interface pointer that is semantically equivalent to the original object yet can be legally accessed in the apartment that executes the CoUnmarshalInterface call. When calling CoMarshalInterface, the caller must indicate how far away the importing apartment is expected to be. COM defines an enumeration for expressing this distance:

```
typedef enum tagMSHCTX {
   MSHCTX_INPROC = 4,              // in-process/same host
   MSHCTX_LOCAL = 0,              // out-of-process/same host
   MSHCTX_NOSHAREDMEM = 1,        // 16/32 bit/same host
   MSHCTX_DIFFERENTMACHINE = 2, // off-host
} MSHCTX;
```

It is legal to specify a greater distance than required, but it is more efficient to use the correct MSHCTX when possible. CoMarshalInterface also allows the caller to specify the marshaling semantics using the following marshal flags:

```
typedef enum tagMSHLFLAGS {
   MSHLFLAGS_NORMAL,       // marshal once, unmarshal once
   MSHLFLAGS_TABLESTRONG,  // marshal once, unmarshal many
   MSHLFLAGS_TABLEWEAK,    // marshal once, unmarshal many
```

```
    MSHLFLAGS_NOPING = 4,    // suppress dist. garbage collection
} MSHLFLAGS;
```

Normal marshaling (sometimes called call marshaling) indicates that the marshaled object reference must be unmarshaled only once, and if additional proxies are needed, additional calls to CoMarshalInterface are required. Table marshaling indicates that the marshaled object reference may be unmarshaled zero or more times without requiring additional calls to CoMarshalInterface. The details of table marshaling are described later in this chapter.

To allow interface pointers to be marshaled to a variety of media, CoMarshalInterface serializes the interface pointer through a caller-supplied interface of type IStream. The IStream interface models an arbitrary I/O device and exposes Read and Write methods. CoMarshalInterface simply calls the Write method on the caller-provided IStream interface without concern for where the actual bytes will be stored. Callers can get an IStream wrapper to raw memory by calling the API function CreateStreamOnHGlobal:

```
HRESULT CreateStreamOnHGlobal(
        [in] HGLOBAL hglobal,  // pass null to autoalloc
        [in] BOOL bFreeMemoryOnRelease,
        [out] IStream **ppStm);
```

Given the semantics of IStream, the following code fragment:

```
void UseRawMemoryToPrintString(void) {
  void *pv = 0;
// alloc memory
  pv = malloc(13);
  if (pv != 0) {
// write a string to the underlying memory
    memcpy(pv, "Hello, World", 13);
    printf((const char*)pv);
// free all resources
    free (pv);
  }
}
```

is equivalent to this code fragment that uses an IStream interface instead of memcpy:

```
void UseStreamToPrintString(void) {
  IStream *pStm = 0;
```

```
// alloc memory and wrap behind an IStream interface
  HRESULT hr = CreateStreamOnHGlobal(0, TRUE, &pStm);
  if (SUCCEEDED(hr)) {
// write a string to the underlying memory
    hr = pStm->Write("Hello, World", 13, 0);
    assert(SUCCEEDED(hr));
// suck out the memory
    HGLOBAL hglobal = 0;
    hr = GetHGlobalFromStream(pStm, &hglobal);
    assert(SUCCEEDED(hr));
    printf((const char*)GlobalLock(hglobal));
// free all resources
    GlobalUnlock(hglobal);
    pStm->Release();
  }
}
```

The API function GetHGlobalFromStream allows the caller to extract a handle to the memory that was allocated in CreateStreamOnHGlobal. The use of HGLOBALs is historic and in no way implies shared memory.

Armed with an understanding of each of its parameter types, the CoMarshalInterface API function is fairly simple:

```
HRESULT CoMarshalInterface(
    [in] IStream *pStm,     // where to write marshaled state
    [in] REFIID riid,       // type of ptr being marshaled
[in,iid_is(riid)] IUnknown *pItf,// pointer being marshaled
    [in] DWORD dwDestCtx,   // MSHCTX for destination apt.
    [in] void *pvDestCtx,   // reserved, must be zero
    [in] DWORD dwMshlFlags  // normal vs. table marshal
);
```

The following code marshals an interface pointer into a block of memory suitable for transmitting to any apartment on the network:

```
HRESULT WritePtr(IRacer *pRacer, HGLOBAL& rhglobal) {
  IStream *pStm = 0; rhglobal = 0;
// alloc and wrap block of memory
  HRESULT hr = CreateStreamOnHGlobal(0, FALSE, &pStm);
  if (SUCCEEDED(hr)) {
// write marshaled object reference to memory
```

```
        hr = CoMarshalInterface(pStm, IID_IRacer, pRacer,
                                MSHCTX_DIFFERENTMACHINE, 0,
                                MSHLFLAGS_NORMAL);
// extract handle to underlying memory
    if (SUCCEEDED(hr))
        hr = GetHGlobalFromStream(pStm, &rhglobal);
    pStm->Release();
  }
  return hr;
}
```

Figure 5.1 illustrates the relationship between the interface pointer and the underlying memory that contains the marshaled object reference. After calling CoMarshalInterface, the object's apartment is now ready to receive a connection request from a foreign apartment. Because the MSHCTX_DIFFERENTMACHINE flag was used, the importing apartment can potentially be on a different host machine.

To decode the marshaled object reference created in the previous code fragment into a valid interface pointer, the importing apartment will need to call the CoUnmarshalInterface API function:

```
HRESULT CoUnmarshalInterface(

    [in] IStream *pStm,        // where to read marshaled state
    [in] REFIID riid,          // type of ptr being unmarshaled
```

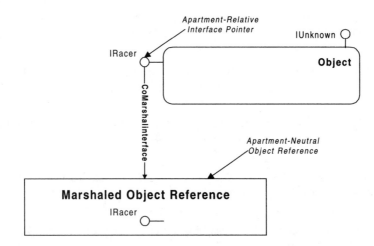

Figure 5.1 Marshaled Object Reference

```
    [out,iid_is(riid)] void **ppv// where to put unmarshaled ptr
);
```

CoUnmarshalInterface simply reads a serialized object reference and returns a pointer to the original object that can be legally accessed in the calling thread's apartment. If the importing apartment is different from the apartment that originally exported the interface, then the resultant pointer will be a pointer to a proxy. If for some reason the CoUnmarshalInterface call is issued from the original apartment where the object resides, then a pointer to the actual object will be returned and no proxy will be created. The following code translates a marshaled object reference into a valid interface pointer:

```
HRESULT ReadPtr(HGLOBAL hglobal, IRacer * &rpRacer) {
    IStream *pStm = 0; rpRacer = 0;
// wrap block of existing memory passed on input
    HRESULT hr = CreateStreamOnHGlobal(hglobal, FALSE, &pStm);
    if (SUCCEEDED(hr)) {
// get a pointer to the object that is legal in this apt.
        hr = CoUnmarshalInterface(pStm,
                                IID_IRacer, (void**)&rpRacer);
        pStm->Release();
    }
    return hr;
}
```

The resultant proxy will implement each of the interfaces that the object exports by forwarding the method requests to the object's apartment.

Prior to the Windows NT 4.0 release of COM, the format of a marshaled object reference was undocumented. To allow third parties to build COM-aware network products, the format was publicly documented in 1996 and submitted as an Internet draft standard. Figure 5.2 shows the format of a marshaled object reference. The header of the marshaled object reference begins with a distinguished signature ('MEOW')[6] and a flags field indicates the marshaling technique used (*e.g.,* standard marshaling, custom marshaling) as well as the IID of the interface contained in the reference. Assuming standard marshaling is used, a subheader of the object reference indicates how many external references this marshaled reference represents. This external reference count is part

---

[6] A Microsoft Program Manager who shall remain anonymous claims that MEOW stands for *Microsoft Extended Object Wire* representation. The author, while somewhat gullible, is skeptical of this story but is willing to give the aforementioned source the benefit of the doubt.

MEOW	*Signature*
FLAGS	*Standard/Custom/Handler Flags*
IID	*IID of Marshaled Interface*
STD FLAGS	*Standard Marshal-Specific Flags (no-ping)*
cPublicRefs	*Count of References Represented by OBJREF*
OXID	*Apartment Identifier of Exporting Apartment*
OID	*Object Identifier of Identity*
IPID	*Process-relative Identifier of Interface Pointer*
cch | **secOffset**	*Character Count/Security Offset of Host/Sec Info*
Host Addresses	*Host Addresses of OXID Resolver*
Security Package Info	*Security Packages Used by Object Exporter*

Figure 5.2 Standard Marshal Object Reference

of COM's distributed garbage collection protocol and does not directly correspond to the AddRef/Release reference count that the object may implement. The interesting elements of the object reference are the OXID/OID/IPID tuple that uniquely identify an interface pointer. Each apartment in the network is assigned a unique Object Exporter Identifier (OXID) at apartment creation time. This OXID is used to find network/IPC addressing information when a proxy first connects to the object. The Object Identifier (OID) uniquely identifies a COM identity in the network and is used by CoUnmarshalInterface to maintain the COM identity laws for proxies. The Interface Pointer Identifier (IPID) uniquely identifies an interface pointer *in an apartment* and is placed in the header of each subsequent method request. The IPID is used to efficiently dispatch ORPC requests to the correct interface pointer in the object's apartment.

Although OXIDs are interesting as logical identifiers, by themselves they are useless, as the proxy will need to use some IPC mechanism or network protocol to contact the object's apartment. To translate OXIDs into fully qualified network or IPC addresses, each COM-enabled host machine provides an OXID Resolver (OR) service. Under Windows NT 4.0, the OR is implemented as part of the RPCSS service. When an apartment is first initialized, COM allocates an OXID and registers it with the local OR. This means that each OR knows of all running apartments on the local system. The OR also keeps track of the local IPC port for each apartment. When `CoUnmarshalInterface` needs to connect a new proxy to the object's apartment, the local OR is consulted to resolve the OXID into a valid IPC or network address. If the unmarshal occurs on the same machine as the object's apartment, then the OR simply looks up the OXID in its local OXID table and returns a local IPC address. If the unmarshal occurs on a host machine other than that of the object, the local OR first checks to see if it has encountered the OXID in the recent past by consulting a cache of recently resolved remote OXIDs. If the OXID has not been encountered recently, it forwards the request to the OR on the host machine of the object using RPC. Note that the marshaled object reference contains the object's host address in a format suitable for a variety of network protocols, so the unmarshal-side OR knows where to forward the request.

To allow distributed OXID resolution, the OR service on each host machine listens for remote OXID resolution requests on a well-known endpoint (port 135 for TCP and UDP) for each supported network protocol. When an OXID resolution request is received from the network, the local OXID table is consulted. The resolution request will indicate which network protocols the client machine supports. If the requested apartment's process has not yet started to use one of the requested protocols, the OR will contact the COM library in the object's apartment using local IPC and cause the object's process to start using the requested protocol. Once this occurs, the OR will note the new network address of the apartment in the local OXID table. After the new network address is recorded, the address is returned to the unmarshal-side OR, where it is cached to avoid additional network requests for commonly used apartments. Although it may seem odd not just to write out the object's fully qualified network addresses in the marshaled object reference, the level of indirection afforded by protocol-independent apartment IDs (OXIDs) allows a COM-based process to postpone using network protocols until they are needed. This is especially important because COM can operate over a variety of different protocols (not just TCP), and requiring every process to listen for requests using all supported protocols would be extremely inefficient. In fact, if a COM-based process never exports pointers to off-host clients, it will never consume any network resources whatsoever.

In-Process Marshaling Helpers

Although the WritePtr and ReadPtr code fragments from the previous section are fairly straightforward to implement, COM recognizes that most explicit calls to CoMarshalInterface will be used to pass an interface pointer from one thread to another in the same process. To simplify this task, COM provides two wrapper functions that implement the required boilerplate code around CoMarshalInterface and CoUnmarshalInterface. The COM API function CoMarshalInterThreadInterfaceInStream

```
HRESULT CoMarshalInterThreadInterfaceInStream(
    [in] REFIID riid,
    [in, iid_is(riid)] IUnknown *pItf,
    [out] IStream **ppStm
);
```

provides a simple wrapper around CreateStreamOnHGlobal and CoMarshal-Interface, as shown here:

```
// from OLE32.DLL (approx.)
HRESULT CoMarshalInterThreadInterfaceInStream(
    REFIID riid, IUnknown *pItf, IStream **ppStm) {
  HRESULT hr = CreateStreamOnHGlobal(0, TRUE, ppStm);
  if (SUCCEEDED(hr))
    hr = CoMarshalInterface(*ppStm, riid, pItf,
                    MSHCTX_INPROC, 0, MSHLFLAGS_NORMAL);
  return hr;
}
```

COM also provides a wrapper around CoUnmarshalInterface:

```
HRESULT CoGetInterfaceAndReleaseStream(
            [in] IStream *pStm,
            [in] REFIID riid,
            [out, iid_is(riid)] void **ppv
);
```

which is a very thin veneer over CoUnmarshalInterface:

```
// from OLE32.DLL (approx.)
HRESULT CoGetInterfaceAndReleaseStream(
                IStream *pStm, REFIID riid, void **ppv) {
```

```
      HRESULT hr = CoUnmarshalInterface(pStm, riid, ppv);
      pStm->Release();
      return hr;
    }
```

Neither of these two routines is especially enabling, but they are somewhat more convenient than their lower level counterparts.

The following code fragment could be used to pass an interface pointer to another apartment in the same process using a global variable to hold the intermediate marshaled object reference:

```
HRESULT WritePtrToGlobalVariable(IRacer *pRacer) {
// where to write the marshaled ptr
  extern IStream *g_pStmPtr;
// thread synchronization for read/write
  extern HANDLE g_heventWritten;
// write marshaled object reference to global variable
  HRESULT hr = CoMarshalInterThreadInterfaceInStream(
                    IID_IRacer, pRacer, &g_pStmPtr);
// signal other thread that ptr is now available
  SetEvent(g_heventWritten);
  return hr;
}
```

The corresponding code would correctly unmarshal the object reference into the caller's apartment provided it is in the same process:

```
HRESULT ReadPtrFromGlobalVariable(IRacer * &rpRacer) {
// where to write the marshaled ptr
  extern IStream *g_pStmPtr;
// thread synchronization for read/write
  extern HANDLE g_heventWritten;
// wait for other thread to signal that ptr is available
  WaitForSingleObject(g_heventWritten, INFINITE);
// read marshaled object reference from global variable
  HRESULT hr = CoGetInterfaceAndReleaseStream(
                    g_pStmPtr, IID_IRacer, (void**)&rpRacer);
// MSHLFLAGS_NORMAL means no more unmarshals are legal
  g_pStmPtr = 0;
  return hr;
}
```

The preceding code is required when passing a pointer from one apartment to another.[7] Note that to pass a pointer from a thread executing in an MTA or RTA to another thread executing in the same apartment, no marshaling calls are required. However, it is common practice for the writer of the interface pointer to call AddRef prior to handing off a copy to the reader thread. The reader thread would of course need to call Release when it is done using the pointer.

Note that the preceding reader code set the global variable g_pStmPtr to null after the unmarshal. This is because the object reference was marshaled using the MSHLFLAGS_NORMAL flag and can be unmarshaled only once. For many scenarios, this is not a problem. However, there are many scenarios in which it is desirable to marshal a pointer from one thread and have multiple worker threads unmarshal the interface pointer when it is needed. If the worker threads all run in the MTA, this is not a problem, as only one of the threads needs to perform the unmarshal on behalf of all of the threads running in the MTA. However, if the worker threads run in arbitrary apartments, this approach would not work, as each worker thread would need to unmarshal the object reference independently. Most developers turn to the MSHLFLAGS_TABLESTRONG flag at this point, hoping to marshal once and unmarshal as many times as necessary (once per apartment). Unfortunately, table marshaling (unlike normal marshaling) is not supported if the original pointer is a proxy, which is often the case, especially in distributed applications. To address this need, the Windows NT 4.0 Service Pack 3 release of COM introduced the Global Interface Table.

The Global Interface Table (GIT) is an optimization of CoMarshalInterface/CoUnmarshalInterface that allows interface pointers to be accessed by all apartments in a process. COM internally implements one GIT per process. The GIT contains marshaled interface pointers that can be efficiently unmarshaled multiple times within the same process. This is the semantic equivalent of using table marshaling, but the GIT can be used with both objects and proxies. The GIT exposes the IGlobalInterfaceTable interface:

```
[ uuid(00000146-0000-0000-C000-000000000046),object,local ]
interface IGlobalInterfaceTable : IUnknown {
// marshal an interface into the GIT
```

---

[7] It may seem odd that the global variable is an interface pointer that is initialized in the writer's apartment and used from the reader's apartment. This inconsistency is addressed by the documentation for CoMarshalInterThreadInterfaceInStream, which states that the resultant IStream interface pointer can be accessed from any apartment in the process.

```
    HRESULT RegisterInterfaceInGlobal(
            [in, iid_is(riid)] IUnknown *pItf,
            [in] REFIID riid,
            [out] DWORD *pdwCookie);
// destroy the marshaled object reference
    HRESULT RevokeInterfaceFromGlobal(
            [in] DWORD dwCookie);
// unmarshal an interface from the GIT
    HRESULT GetInterfaceFromGlobal (
            [in] DWORD dwCookie
            [in] REFIID riid,
            [out, iid_is(riid)] void **ppv);
}
```

Clients gain access to the GIT for their process by calling CoCreateInstance using the class CLSID_StdGlobalInterfaceTable. Each call to CoCreateInstance using this CLSID returns a pointer to the single GIT of the process. Like the IStream interface returned by CoMarshalInterThreadInterfaceInStream, interface pointers to the GIT can be accessed from any apartment without requiring marshaling.

To make an interface pointer available to all apartments in the process, the apartment that owns the interface pointer must register it with the GIT by calling the RegisterInterfaceInGlobal method. The GIT will return a DWORD to the caller that represents the pointer globally across all apartments in the process. This DWORD can be used from any apartment in the process to unmarshal a new proxy by calling the GetInterfaceFromGlobal method. This DWORD can be used to unmarshal proxies repeatedly until a call to RevokeInterfaceFromGlobal invalidates the global interface pointer. Applications that use the global interface table usually bind a single process-wide interface pointer at startup:

```
IGlobalInterfaceTable *g_pGIT = 0;
HRESULT InitOnce(void) {
    assert(g_pGIT == 0);
    return CoCreateInstance(CLSID_StdGlobalInterfaceTable, 0,
                    CLSCTX_INPROC_SERVER,
                    IID_IGlobalInterfaceTable,
                    (void**)&g_pGIT);
}
```

Once the global interface table is available, passing an interface pointer to another apartment simply means registering the pointer with the global interface table:

```
HRESULT WritePtrToGlobalVariable(IRacer *pRacer) {
// where to write the marshaled ptr
  extern DWORD g_dwCookie;
// thread synchronization
  extern HANDLE g_heventWritten;
// write marshaled object reference to global variable
  HRESULT hr = g_pGIT->RegisterInterfaceInGlobal(
                    pRacer, IID_IRacer, &g_dwCookie);
// signal other thread that ptr is now available
  SetEvent(g_heventWritten);
  return hr;
}
```

The following code correctly unmarshals the object reference and can be called from any apartment in the same process:

```
HRESULT ReadPtrFromGlobalVariable(IRacer * &rpRacer,
                                  bool bLastUnmarshal) {
// where to write the marshaled ptr
  extern DWORD g_dwCookie;
// thread synchronization
  extern HANDLE g_heventWritten;
// wait for other thread to signal that ptr is available
  WaitForSingleObject(g_heventWritten, INFINITE);
// read marshaled object reference from global variable
  HRESULT hr = g_pGIT->GetInterfaceFromGlobal(
                    g_dwCookie, IID_IRacer, (void**)&rpRacer);
// if we are the last to unmarshal, revoke the pointer
  if (bLastUnmarshal)
    g_pGIT->RevokeInterfaceFromGlobal(g_dwCookie);
  return hr;
}
```

Note that a critical difference between these code fragments and the examples using CoMarshalInterThreadInterfaceInStream is that the GIT-based code supports unmarshaling more than one proxy.

Standard Marshaling Architecture

As mentioned previously in this chapter, COM uses the ORPC protocol for all cross-apartment access. This fact may be interesting architecturally, but few developers want to program low-level communications code. To take advantage of ORPC communications, COM objects need to do nothing beyond implement `IUnknown` to facilitate ORPC-based cross-apartment access. By default, when `CoMarshalInterface` is first called on an object, the object is asked whether it wishes to handle its own cross-apartment communications. This question comes in the form of a `QueryInterface` request for the `IMarshal` interface. Most objects do not implement the `IMarshal` interface and fail this `QueryInterface` request, indicating that they are perfectly happy to let COM handle all communications via ORPC calls. Objects that do implement the `IMarshal` interface are indicating that ORPC is inappropriate and that the object implementor would prefer to handle all cross-apartment communications via a custom proxy. When an object implements the `IMarshal` interface all references to the object will be *custom marshaled*. Custom marshaling is discussed later in this chapter. When an object does not implement the `IMarshal` interface, all references to the object will be *standard marshaled*. Most objects elect to use standard marshaling, and that is the focus of this section.

When `CoMarshalInterface` first determines that an object wishes to use standard marshaling, a special COM object called the *stub manager* is created. The stub manager acts as the network-wide identity of the object and is uniquely identified by an Object Identifier (OID) that represents the object's identity across all apartments. There is a one-to-one correspondence between stub managers and COM object identities. Each stub manager refers to exactly one COM object. Each COM object that is using standard marshaling will have exactly one stub manager. The stub manager holds at least one outstanding reference to the object, which keeps the object's resources in memory. In this respect, the stub manager is yet another in-process client to the object. The stub manager keeps track of the number of outstanding external references and will remain alive as long as there is at least one outstanding reference somewhere in the network. Most external references are simply proxies, although intermediate marshaled object references can hold the stub running to ensure that the object is still alive when the first proxy is created. When outstanding proxies/references are destroyed, the stub manager is notified and it decrements its count of external references. When the last external reference to the stub manager is destroyed, the stub manager destroys itself, releasing its outstanding references to the actual object. This simulates the effect of having client-side references keeping the object alive. Techniques for explicitly controlling the lifetime of the stub will be discussed later in the chapter.

The stub manager simply acts as the network identity of the object and does not understand how to handle incoming ORPC requests that are destined for the object.[8] To translate incoming ORPC requests into actual method invocations on the object, the stub manager requires a helper object that knows the details of the interface's method signatures. This helper object is called an *interface stub* and must properly unmarshal the [in] parameters that are present in the ORPC request message, call the method on the actual object, and marshal the HRESULT and any [out] parameters into the ORPC response message. Interface stubs are identified internally using Interface Pointer Identifiers (IPIDs) that are unique within an apartment. Like the stub manager, each interface stub holds a reference to the object; however, the interface held will be a typed interface, not simply IUnknown. Figure 5.3 shows the relationship between the stub manager, interface stubs, and the object. Note that some interface stubs know how to decode more than one interface type, whereas others understand only one interface.

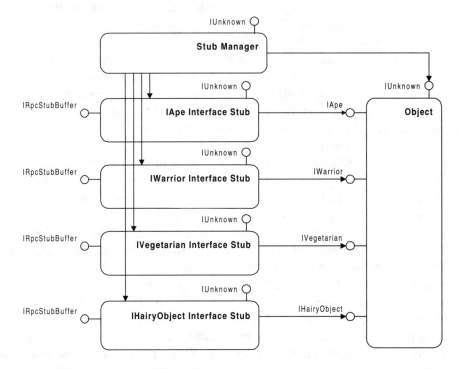

Figure 5.3 Stub Architecture

---

[8] Logically, the stub manager handles remote calls to IUnknown methods; however, this task is actually implemented by the apartment object that exposes the IRemUnknown interface.

When `CoUnmarshalInterface` unmarshals a standard marshaled object reference, it technically returns a pointer to the *proxy manager.* The proxy manager acts as the client-side identity of the object and, like the stub manager, does not have any a priori understanding of any COM interfaces. The proxy manager does, however, know how to implement the three methods of `IUnknown`. Any redundant calls to `AddRef` or `Release` simply increment or decrement an internal reference count in the proxy manager and are never transmitted using ORPC. The final `Release` on the proxy manager does destroy the proxy, sending a disconnect request to the object's apartment. `QueryInterface` requests on the proxy manager are handled somewhat differently. Like the stub manager, the proxy manager has no a priori knowledge of COM interfaces. Instead, the proxy manager must load *interface proxies* that expose the actual interface being remoted. The interface proxy translates method invocations into ORPC calls. Unlike the stub manager, the proxy manager is directly visible to programmers, and to maintain the correct identity relationships, the interface proxies are aggregated into the proxy manager's identity. This gives the client the illusion that all of the interfaces are exposed from a single COM object. Figure 5.4 shows the relationship between the proxy manager, interface proxies, and the stub.

As Figure 5.4 illustrates, the proxy communicates with the stub via a third object called the channel. The channel is a COM-supplied wrapper around the RPC runtime layer. The channel exposes the `IRpcChannelBuffer` interface:

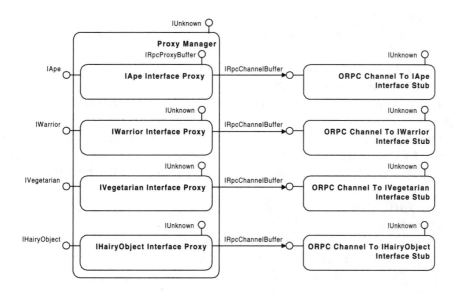

Figure 5.4   Proxy Architecture

```
[ uuid(D5F56B60-593B-101A-B569-08002B2DBF7A),local,object ]
interface IRpcChannelBuffer : IUnknown {
// programmatic representation of ORPC message
  typedef struct tagRPCOLEMESSAGE {
      void              *reserved1;
      unsigned long      dataRepresentation; // endian/ebcdic
      void              *Buffer;              // payload goes here
      ULONG              cbBuffer;            // length of payload
      ULONG              iMethod;             // which method?
      void              *reserved2[5];
      ULONG              rpcFlags;
  } RPCOLEMESSAGE;

// allocate a transmission buffer
  HRESULT GetBuffer([in] RPCOLEMESSAGE *pMessage,
                    [in] REFIID riid);
// send an ORPC request and receive an ORPC response
  HRESULT SendReceive([in,out] RPCOLEMESSAGE *pMessage,
                      [out] ULONG *pStatus);
// deallocate a transmission buffer
  HRESULT FreeBuffer([in] RPCOLEMESSAGE *pMessage);
// get distance to destination for CoMarshalInterface
  HRESULT GetDestCtx([out] DWORD *pdwDestCtx,
                     [out] void **ppvDestCtx);
// check for explicit disconnects
  HRESULT IsConnected(void);
}
```

Interface proxies use the SendReceive method on this interface to cause the
channel to send ORPC request messages and receive ORPC response messages.

Interface proxies and stubs are simply COM in-process objects that are
created by the proxy and stub managers using normal COM activation techniques. The interface stub must expose the IRpcStubBuffer interface:

```
[ uuid(D5F56AFC-593B-101A-B569-08002B2DBF7A),local,object ]
interface IRpcStubBuffer : IUnknown {
// called to connect stub to object
  HRESULT Connect([in] IUnknown *pUnkServer);
// called to inform stub to release object
  void    Disconnect(void);
```

```
  // called when ORPC request arrives
  HRESULT Invoke([in] RPCOLEMESSAGE *pmsg,
                 [in] IRpcChannelBuffer *pChannel);
  // used to support multiple itf types per stub
  IRpcStubBuffer *IsIIDSupported([in] REFIID riid);
  // used to support multiple itf types per stub
  ULONG   CountRefs(void);
  // used by ORPC debugger to find pointer to object
  HRESULT DebugServerQueryInterface(void **ppv);
  // used by ORPC debugger to release pointer to object
  void    DebugServerRelease(void *pv);
}
```

The Invoke method will be called by the COM library when an ORPC request arrives for the object. On input, the RPCOLEMESSAGE will contain the marshaled [in] parameters, and on output, the stub must marshal the method's HRESULT and any [out] parameters that will be returned in the ORPC response message.

The interface proxy must expose the interface(s) it is responsible for remoting in addition to the IRpcProxyBuffer interface:

```
[ uuid(D5F56A34-593B-101A-B569-08002B2DBF7A),local,object ]
interface IRpcProxyBuffer : IUnknown {
  HRESULT Connect([in] IRpcChannelBuffer *pChannelBuffer);
  void    Disconnect(void);
}
```

The IRpcProxyBuffer interface must be the nondelegating unknown of the interface proxy. All other interfaces the interface proxy exposes must delegate their IUnknown methods to the proxy manager. It is in the method implementations of these other interfaces that the interface proxy must use the channel to send ORPC requests to the interface stub's Invoke method, which then executes the method in the object's apartment.

Interface proxies and interface stubs are dynamically bound and share a single CLSID for both the proxy and stub. This bifurcated implementation is often called an interface marshaler. The class object of the interface marshaler exposes the IPSFactoryBuffer interface:

```
[ uuid(D5F569D0-593B-101A-B569-08002B2DBF7A),local,object ]
interface IPSFactoryBuffer : IUnknown {
  HRESULT CreateProxy(
```

```
        [in] IUnknown *pUnkOuter, // ptr to proxy manager
        [in] REFIID riid,         // the requested itf to remote
        [out] IRpcProxyBuffer **ppProxy, // ptr. to proxy itf.
        [out] void **ppv          // ptr to remoting interface
    );
    HRESULT CreateStub(
        [in] REFIID riid,          // the requested itf to remote
        [in] IUnknown *pUnkServer, // ptr to actual object
        [out] IRpcStubBuffer **ppStub // ptr to stub on output
    );
}
```

The proxy manager calls the CreateProxy method to aggregate a new interface proxy. The stub manager calls the CreateStub method to create a new interface stub.

When a new interface is requested on an object, the proxy and stub managers must resolve the requested IID onto the CLSID of the interface marshaler. Under Windows NT 5.0, the class store maintains these mappings in the NT directory, and they are cached at each host machine in the local registry. The machine-wide IID-to-CLSID mappings are cached at

```
HKEY_CLASSES_ROOT\Interface
```

and the per-user mappings are cached at

```
HKEY_CURRENT_USER\Software\Classes\Interface
```

One or both of these keys will contain a subkey for each known interface. Under Windows NT 4.0 or earlier, there is no class store and only the HKEY_CLASSES_ROOT\Interface area of the local registry is used.

If the interface has an interface marshaler installed, there will be an additional subkey (ProxyStubClsid32) that indicates the CLSID of the interface marshaler. The following illustrates the required registry keys for a marshalable interface:

```
[HKCR\Interface\{1A3A29F0-D87E-11d0-8C4F-0080C73925BA}]
@="IRacer"
[HKCR\Interface\{1A3A29F0-D87E-11d0-8C4F-0080C73925BA}\ProxyStubClsid32]
@="{1A3A29F3-D87E-11d0-8C4F-0080C73925BA}"
```

These registry entries state that there is an in-process server with a CLSID of {1A3A29F3-D87E-11d0-8C4F-0080C73925BA} that implements the interface proxy and stub for interface IRacer ({1A3A29F0-D87E-11d0-8C4F-0080C73925BA}). This implies that HKCR\CLSID will have a subkey for the interface marshaler mapping the CLSID onto the appropriate DLL filename. Again, under Windows NT 5.0, this mapping may exist in the class store, which can dynamically populate the local registry. Because interface marshalers must run in the same apartment as the proxy manager or the stub manager, they must use ThreadingModel="Both" to ensure that they can always load into the correct apartment.

Implementing Interface Marshalers

The previous section illustrated the four interfaces used by the standard marshaling architecture. Although it is possible to implement interface marshalers using manual C++ coding techniques, it is rarely done in practice. This is because the IDL compiler can automatically generate the C source code for an interface marshaler based on the IDL definition of an interface. MIDL-generated interface marshalers serialize method parameters using the Network Data Representation (NDR) protocol, which allows the parameters to be unmarshaled on a variety of host architectures. NDR takes into account differences in byte ordering, floating point formats, character sets, and alignment issues. NDR supports virtually all C-compatible data types. To support passing interface pointers as parameters, MIDL generates calls to CoMarshalInterface/CoUnmarshalInterface to marshal any interface pointer parameters. If the parameter is a statically typed interface pointer:

```
HRESULT Method([out] IRacer **ppRacer);
```

the generated marshaling code will marshal the ppRacer parameter by passing the IID of IRacer (IID_IRacer) to the CoMarshalInterface/CoUnmarshalInterface calls. If instead the interface pointer is dynamically typed:

```
HRESULT Method([in] REFIID riid,
               [out, iid_is(riid)] void **ppv);
```

then the generated marshaling code will marshal the interface using the IID passed at runtime in the first method parameter.

MIDL generates interface marshaler source code for every nonlocal interface defined *outside* the scope of the library statement. In the following pseudo-IDL:

```
// sports.idl
[local, object] interface IBoxer : IUnknown { ... }
[object] interface IRacer : IUnknown { ... }
[object] interface ISwimmer : IUnknown { ... }
[helpstring("Sports Lib")]
library SportsLibrary {
  interface IRacer; // include def. of IRacer in TLB
  [object] interface IWrestler : IUnknown { ... }
}
```

only the IRacer and ISwimmer interfaces would have interface marshaler source code. MIDL would not generate marshaling code for IBoxer because the [local] attribute suppresses marshaling. MIDL also would not generate a marshaler for IWrestler because it is defined inside the scope of a library statement.

When presented with the IDL just shown, the MIDL compiler would generate five files. The file sports.h would contain the C/C++ definitions of the interfaces, sports_i.c would contain the definitions of the IIDs and LIBIDs, and sports.tlb would contain the tokenized IDL for IRacer and IWrestler suitable for use in COM-aware development environments. The file sports_p.c would contain the actual interface proxy and stub method implementations that perform the method call-to-NDR transformations. This file would also contain the C-based vtable definitions for the interface proxy and stub along with other MIDL-specific management code. Because interface marshalers are COM in-process servers, the standard four entry points (DllGetClassObject *et al*) must also be defined. These four methods are defined in the fifth file, dlldata.c.

All that is needed to build an interface marshaler from these generated files is to write a makefile that compiles the three C source files (sports_i.c, sports_p.c, dlldata.c) and links them together to build the DLL. The four standard COM entry points must be explicitly exported using either a module definition file or linker switches. Note that by default, dlldata.c contains only definitions of DllGetClassObject and DllCanUnloadNow. This is because the supporting RPC runtime library under Windows NT 3.50 supported only these two routines. If the interface marshaler will be used only under Windows NT 3.51 or later (or under Windows 95), the C preprocessor symbol REGISTER_PROXY_DLL should be defined when compiling the dlldata.c file to compile the standard self-registration entry points as well. Once the interface marshaler is built, it should be installed into the local registry and/or the class store.

The Windows NT 4.0 implementation of the COM library introduced support for fully interpretive marshaling. Depending on the interface, using the interpretive marshaler can vastly improve the performance of an application by reducing the working set size. The preinstalled interface marshalers for all COM standard interfaces use the interpretive marshaler. Microsoft Transaction Server requires interface marshalers to use the interpretive marshaler.[9] To enable the interpretive marshaler, simply run the MIDL compiler using the /Oicf command-line switch:

```
midl.exe /Oicf sports.idl
```

At the time of this writing, the MIDL compiler would not overwrite a preexisting _p.c file, so this file must be deleted when changing this setting. Because /Oicf-based interface marshalers will not work on pre-Windows NT 4.0 versions of COM, the C preprocessor symbol _WIN32_WINNT must be defined to some integer greater than or equal to 0x400 when the marshaler's source code is compiled. The C compiler will enforce this at compile time.

A third technique for generating interface marshalers is supported for a limited class of interfaces. If an interface uses only the primitive data types supported by VARIANTs,[10] the universal marshaler can be used. Adding the [oleautomation] attribute to an interface definition enables the universal marshaler:

```
[ uuid(F99D19A3-D8BA-11d0-8C4F-0080C73925BA), version(1.0) ]
library SportsLib {
  importlib("stdole32.tlb");
  [
    uuid(F99D1907-D8BA-11d0-8C4F-0080C73925BA), object,
    oleautomation
  ]
  interface IWrestler : IUnknown {
    import "oaidl.idl";
    HRESULT HalfNelson([in] double nmsec);
  }
}
```

---

[9] MTS also requires the marshaler to be built using a special runtime library that allows MTS to find out information about an interface based on its interpretive format.

[10] Variants are a data type used by scripting environments and are described in Chapter 2.

The presence of the [oleautomation] attribute informs the RegisterTypeLib function to add the following additional registry entries when registering the type library:

```
[HKCR\Interface\{F99D1907-D8BA-11d0-8C4F-0080C73925BA}]
@="IWrestler"

[HKCR\Interface\{F99D1907-D8BA-11d0-8C4F-0080C73925BA}\ProxyStubClsid32]
@="{00020424-0000-0000-C000-000000000046}"

[HKCR\Interface\{F99D1907-D8BA-11d0-8C4F-0080C73925BA}\ProxyStubClsid]
@="{00020424-0000-0000-C000-000000000046}"

[HKCR\Interface\{F99D1907-D8BA-11d0-8C4F-0080C73925BA}\TypeLib]
@="{F99D19A3-D8BA-11d0-8C4F-0080C73925BA}"
Version="1.0"
```

The CLSID {00020424-0000-0000-C000-000000000046} corresponds to the universal marshaler, which is preinstalled on all platforms that support COM, including 16-bit Windows.

The primary advantage of using the universal marshaler is that it is the only supported technique for standard marshaling between 16-bit and 32-bit applications. The universal marshaler is also compatible with Microsoft Transaction Server. A side benefit of the universal marshaler is that if the type library is installed on both the client and object host machines, no additional interface marshaler DLL will be needed. The primary disadvantage of using the universal marshaler is the limited support for parameter data types. This is exactly the same as the limitation imposed by dynamic invocation and scripting environments, but it is a serious limitation for designing low-level systems programming interfaces.[11] Under Windows NT 4.0, the initial cost of calling CoMarshalInterface/CoUnmarshalInterface will be somewhat greater using the universal marshaler. However, once the interface proxy and stub are instantiated, the method invocation performance is identical to /Oicf-based marshalers.

---

[11] It is likely that future implementations of the COM library will remove this restriction. Consult your local documentation for more details.

Standard Marshaling, Threads, and Protocols

The details of how COM actually maps ORPC requests onto threads are undocumented and subject to change as the implementation of the COM library evolves. The descriptions contained in this section are accurate at the time of this writing, but certain implementation details may change in subsequent releases of COM.

When the first apartment is initialized in a process, COM enables the RPC runtime layer, turning the process into an RPC server. If the apartment type is an MTA or RTA, the ncalrpc RPC protocol sequence is used, which is a wrapper around Windows NT LPC ports. If the apartment type is an STA, a private protocol sequence is used that is based on Windows MSG queues. As objects that reside in the process are first accessed by off-host clients, additional network protocol sequences are registered in the process. When a process first begins to use protocols *other than the Windows MSG protocol,* the RPC thread cache is started. This thread cache begins with one thread that listens for incoming connection requests, RPC requests, or other protocol-specific activity. When any of these events happen, the RPC thread cache will dispatch a thread to service the request and continue to wait for additional activity. To avoid excessive thread creation/destruction overhead, these threads return to the thread cache, where they will wait for additional work. If no additional work arrives, the threads will destroy themselves after a predefined period of inactivity. The net effect is that the RPC thread cache grows and shrinks based on the busyness of the objects that are exported from the process' apartments. From a programming perspective, the important observation is that the RPC thread cache dynamically allocates threads based on ORPC requests that arrive on all protocols *except* the Windows MSG protocol, which will be discussed later in this section.

When an incoming ORPC request is dispatched to a thread from the cache, the thread extracts the IPID from the header of the ORPC call and finds the corresponding stub manager and interface stub. The thread determines the type of apartment the object resides in, and if the object is in the MTA or an RTA, the thread enters the object's apartment and calls the IRpcStubBuffer::Invoke method on the interface stub. If the apartment is an RTA, subsequent threads will be held at bay for the duration of the method call. If the apartment is the MTA, then subsequent threads may access the object concurrently. For intraprocess RTA/MTA communications, the channel is able to shortcut the RPC thread cache and reuse the client thread simply by entering the object's apartment temporarily. If MTAs and RTAs were the only types of apartment, this would be all that is required.

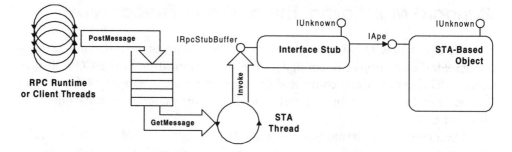

Figure 5.5 Singlethreaded Apartment Call Dispatching

Dispatching calls to an STA is more complex, simply because no other threads can enter an existing STA. Unfortunately, when ORPC requests arrive from off-host clients, they are dispatched using threads from the RPC thread cache, which by definition cannot execute in the object's STA. To enter the STA and dispatch the call to the STA's thread, the RPC thread uses the PostMessage API function to enqueue a message onto the STA thread's MSG queue as shown in Figure 5.5. This queue is the same FIFO queue used by the windowing system. This means that to finish dispatching the call, the STA thread must service the queue via some variation on the following code:

```
MSG msg;
while (GetMessage(&msg, 0, 0, 0))
   DispatchMessage(&msg);
```

This code implies that the STA thread has at least one window that can receive messages. When a thread enters a new STA by calling CoInitializeEx, COM creates a new invisible window by calling CreateWindowEx. This window is associated with a COM-registered window class whose WndProc looks for a predefined window message and services the corresponding ORPC request by calling the IRpcStubBuffer::Invoke method on the interface stub. Note that because windows, like STA-based objects, have thread affinity, the WndProc will execute in the apartment of the object. To avoid excessive thread switching, the Windows 95 release of COM introduced an RPC transport that bypasses the RPC thread cache and calls PostMessage from the thread of the caller. This transport is available only when the client is on the same host as the object, because the PostMessage API does not work over the network.

To help prevent deadlock, all COM apartment types support reentrancy.[12] When a thread in an apartment makes a call through a proxy to an object out-

---

[12] At the time of this writing, COM provided no non-reentrant apartment types. It is possible that future versions of COM could provide new apartment types that do not support reentrancy.

side the caller's apartment, incoming method requests can continue to be serviced while the caller's thread is waiting for the ORPC response from the original call. Without this support, it would be impossible to build systems based on collaborating objects. In the following code, assume that CLSID_Callback is an in-process server that supports the threading model of the calling thread and that CLSID_Object is a class that is configured to activate on a remote machine:

```
ICallback *pcb = 0;
HRESULT hr = CoCreateInstance(CLSID_Callback, 0, CLSCTX_ALL,
                             IID_ICallback, (void**)&pcb);
assert(SUCCEEDED(hr)); // callback object lives in this apt.
IObject *po = 0;
hr = CoCreateInstance(CLSID_Object, 0, CLSCTX_REMOTE_SERVER,
                      IID_IObject, (void**)&po);
assert(SUCCEEDED(hr)); // object lives in different apt.
// make a call to remote object, marshaling a reference to
// the callback object as an [in] parameter
hr = po->UseCallback(pcb);
// clean up resources
pcb->Release();
pco->Release();
```

As shown in Figure 5.6, if the caller's apartment did not support reentrancy, then the following implementation of the UseCallback method would cause a deadlock:

```
STDMETHODIMP Object::UseCallback(ICallback *pcb) {
    HRESULT hr = pcb->GetBackToCallersApartment();
```

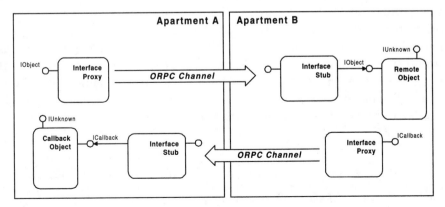

Figure 5.6 Interapartment Callbacks

```
        assert(SUCCEEDED(hr));
        return S_OK;
    }
```

Recall that when an [in] parameter is passed to the proxy's UseCallback method, the proxy calls CoMarshalInterface to marshal the ICallback interface pointer. Because the pointer refers to an object that resides in the caller's apartment, the caller's apartment becomes an object exporter and any cross-apartment calls on the callback object must be serviced in the caller's apartment. When the IObject interface stub unmarshals the ICallback interface, it creates a proxy to pass to the UseCallback method implementation. This proxy represents a transient connection to the callback object that lives for the duration of the call. The lifetime of this proxy/connection can exceed the scope of the call if the method implementation simply calls AddRef on the proxy:[13]

```
    STDMETHODIMP Object::UseCallback(ICallback *pcb) {
        if (!pcb) return E_INVALIDARG;
    // hold onto proxy for later use
        (m_pcbMyCaller = pcb)->AddRef();
        return S_OK;
    }
```

The connection back to the client's apartment will last until the proxy is released by the object. Because all COM apartments can receive ORPC requests, the object can call back into the client's apartment whenever it chooses.

Reentrancy is implemented differently for each apartment type. The MTA implementation is the simplest, as MTAs make no concurrency guarantees, nor do they address which thread will service any given method call. When a reentrant call arrives while an MTA thread is blocked in the channel waiting for the ORPC response, the RPC thread that receives the reentrant request simply enters the MTA and services the call using the RPC thread. The fact that another thread in the apartment is blocked waiting for an ORPC response is not relevant to call dispatching. In the case of the RTA implementation, when a thread executing in an RTA makes a cross-apartment call through a proxy, the channel yields control of the apartment, releasing the RTA-wide lock and allowing incoming calls to be serviced. Again, because RTA-based objects do not have thread affinity, an RPC thread that receives an ORPC request can simply enter the RTA and service the call once the RTA-wide lock is acquired.

---

[13] It is a common misconception that Connection Points are required to enable bidirectional communication or callbacks. As described in Chapter 7, Connection Points are required only for supporting event handlers in Visual Basic and scripting environments.

The implementation of reentrancy for STAs is more complex. Because STA-based objects have thread affinity, when a thread makes a cross-apartment call from an STA, COM cannot allow the thread to make a blocking call that would prevent incoming ORPC requests from being serviced. When the caller's thread enters the channel's SendReceive method to send the ORPC request and receive the ORPC response, the channel steals the caller's thread and places it in an internal windows MSG loop. This is not unlike what happens when a thread creates a modal dialog box. In both cases the caller's thread is needed to service certain classes of window messages while the operation is in progress. In the case of modal dialog boxes, the thread is needed to service basic window messages to ensure that the overall user interface does not appear frozen. In the case of a cross-apartment COM method call, the thread is needed to service not only normal user-interface window messages but also window messages that correspond to incoming ORPC requests. By default, the channel will allow all incoming ORPC calls to be serviced while the client thread waits for an ORPC response. This behavior is customizable by installing a custom message filter for the thread.

Message filters are unique to STAs. A message filter is a per-STA COM object that is used to decide whether or not to dispatch incoming ORPC requests. Message filters are also used to determine the disposition of pending user-interface messages when the STA's thread is waiting for an ORPC response inside the channel. Message filters expose the IMessageFilter interface:

```
[ uuid(00000016-0000-0000-C000-000000000046),local,object ]
interface IMessageFilter : IUnknown {
  typedef struct tagINTERFACEINFO {
    IUnknown     *pUnk;        // which object?
    IID          iid;          // which interface?
    WORD         wMethod;      // which method?
  } INTERFACEINFO;

// called when an incoming ORPC request arrives in an STA
  DWORD HandleInComingCall(
    [in] DWORD dwCallType,
    [in] HTASK dwThreadIdCaller,
    [in] DWORD dwTickCount,
    [in] INTERFACEINFO *pInterfaceInfo
  );

// called when another STA rejects or postpones
// an ORPC request
```

```
    DWORD RetryRejectedCall(
       [in] HTASK dwThreadIdCallee,
       [in] DWORD dwTickCount,
       [in] DWORD dwRejectType
    );

// called when a non-COM MSG arrives while the thread is
// awaiting an ORPC response
    DWORD MessagePending(
       [in] HTASK dwThreadIdCallee,
       [in] DWORD dwTickCount,
       [in] DWORD dwPendingType
    );
}
```

To install a custom message filter, COM provides the API function
CoRegisterMessageFilter:

```
HRESULT CoRegisterMessageFilter([in] IMessageFilter *pmfNew,
                                [out] IMessageFilter **ppmfOld);
```

CoRegisterMessageFilter associates the provided message filter with the
current STA. The previous message filter is returned to allow the caller to re-
store the prior message filter at a later time.

Whenever an incoming ORPC request arrives on an STA thread, the message filter's HandleIncomingCall method is called, giving the apartment an
opportunity to either accept, reject, or postpone the call. HandleIncomingCall
is used both for reentrant and non-reentrant calls. The dwCallType parameter
indicates which type of call was received:

```
typedef enum tagCALLTYPE {
  CALLTYPE_TOPLEVEL, // STA not in outbound call
  CALLTYPE_NESTED,   // callback on behalf of outbound call
  CALLTYPE_ASYNC,    // asynchronous call
  CALLTYPE_TOPLEVEL_CALLPENDING, // new call while waiting
  CALLTYPE_ASYNC_CALLPENDING    // async call while waiting
} CALLTYPE;
```

Nested (reentrant) and toplevel callpending (non-reentrant) calls occur while
the thread is waiting in the channel for an ORPC response. Toplevel calls
occur when there are no active calls in the apartment.

COM defines an enumeration that the implementation of HandleIncoming-Call must return to indicate the disposition of the call:

```
typedef enum tagSERVERCALL {
SERVERCALL_ISHANDLED, // accept call and forward to stub
SERVERCALL_REJECTED,  // tell caller that call is rejected
SERVERCALL_RETRYLATER // tell caller that call is postponed
} SERVERCALL;
```

If the message filter's HandleIncomingCall returns SERVERCALL_ISHANDLED, the call will be forwarded to the interface stub for unmarshaling. The default message filter always returns SERVERCALL_ISHANDLED. If HandleIncomingCall returns SERVERCALL_REJECTED or SERVERCALL_RETRYLATER, then the caller's message filter will be informed of the disposition of the call and the ORPC request will be discarded.

When a message filter rejects or postpones a call, the caller's message filter is informed via the RetryRejectedCall method. This call happens in the context of the caller's apartment, and the message filter's implementation of RetryRejectedCall can decide whether or not to retry a postponed call. The dwRejectType parameter indicates whether the call was rejected or postponed. The caller's channel implementation will decide what action to take based on the value returned by RetryRejectedCall. If RetryRejectedCall returns –1, then the channel will assume that no retries are desired and will immediately cause the proxy to return the HRESULT RPC_E_CALL_REJECTED. The default message filter always returns –1. Any other value returned by RetryRejectedCall is interpreted as the number of milliseconds to wait until retrying the call. Because this negotiation happens inside the channel, the ORPC request does not need to be regenerated by the proxy. In fact, interface marshalers are completely oblivious to the activities of the message filter.

When an STA-based thread is blocked in the channel waiting for an ORPC response, non-COM-related window messages may arrive on the thread's MSG queue. When this occurs, the STA's message filter is notified via the MessagePending method. The default message filter allows certain window messages to be dispatched in order to keep the overall windowing system from appearing frozen; however, input events (*e.g.,* mouse clicks, key presses) are discarded to prevent the end-user from beginning new user interactions. As has already been stated, message filters are unique to STA apartments and are not supported for RTAs or MTAs. Message filters simply allow better integration of COM with user-interface threads. This implies that all user-interface threads should run in singlethreaded apartments. Most user-interface threads will want to install a custom message filter to ensure that incoming calls are not dispatched while the application is in a critical phase where reentrancy could cause semantic errors. Message filters should *not* be used as a general-purpose flow control mechanism. The implementation of message filters is notoriously inefficient when calls are rejected or postponed, making them poorly suited as a flow control mechanism for high-throughput applications.

Lifecycle Management and Marshaling

Earlier in this chapter, the relationship between the stub manager and the object was discussed. A stub manager is created the first time CoMarshalInterface is called on a particular object identity. The stub manager holds outstanding references to the object it represents, and the stub manager stays alive as long as there is at least one outstanding external reference to the stub. These external references are usually proxies, although marshaled object references are counted as well, as they represent potential proxies. When all external references to a stub manager are destroyed, the stub manager deletes itself and releases all references it holds on the actual object. This default behavior exactly simulates the normal in-process semantics of AddRef and Release. Many objects do not have any special lifecycle requirements and are perfectly satisfied with this default behavior. Some objects wish to customize the relationships between external references, the stub manager, and the object. Fortunately, COM provides ample hooks into the lifecycle of the stub manager, to allow a variety of policies to be implemented. To understand how stub lifecycle management works, it is first necessary to examine COM's distributed garbage collection algorithm.

When a stub manager is created, its Object Identifier (OID) is registered with COM's distributed garbage collector, which currently is implemented by the OXID Resolver service. The OR keeps track of which OIDs are exported from each apartment on the local host machine. When a proxy manager is created, CoUnmarshalInterface informs the local OR that an object reference is being imported into an apartment. This means that the local OR also knows which OIDs have been imported by each apartment on the local host machine. When a particular OID is first imported on a host machine, the importing host's OR establishes a ping relationship with the exporting host's OR. The import-side OR will then send a periodic ping message via RPC, indicating that the importing host machine is still operational and is reachable on the network. The current implementation sends this ping message once every two minutes. If no additional OIDs have been imported in the last ping interval, then a simple ping notification is sent. If new references have been imported or existing references have been released, then a more complex ping message will be sent, indicating the delta between the previous set of held references and the current set.

Under the Windows NT 4.0 implementation of COM, if three consecutive ping intervals (six minutes) elapse without receiving a ping notification from a particular host, the OR will assume that the host has either crashed or become unreachable due to a network failure. At this time, the OR will inform each stub manager that had been imported by the now-dead host that the outstanding references are now invalid and should be released. If a particular object had been used only by clients on the now-dead host, then the stub manager will have no more outstanding references and will delete itself, which in turn will release the COM references to the object.

The previous scenario describes what happens when a host machine becomes unreachable on the network. The more interesting scenario is what happens when a process prematurely exits while holding outstanding proxies. If a process exits without calling CoUninitialize the appropriate number of times (*e.g.*, the process simply crashes), the COM library has no chance to clean up the leaked references. When this happens, the local OR will eventually detect the death of the process and will remove its imported references from subsequent ping messages, which will cause the exporter's OR to eventually release the held references. If the process held imported references to objects on the local machine, these can be released soon after detecting the death of the client.[14]

The COM distributed garbage collector is sometimes criticized for being inefficient. In reality, if objects need to detect client liveness reliably, the COM approach is likely to be much more efficient than ad hoc application-specific solutions. This is because COM's garbage collector can aggregate keep-alive messages for all references held on a particular machine into a single periodic message. Application-specific techniques do not have the same global knowledge and would likely result in a different keep-alive handshake per application, not per host machine. For scenarios in which COM's garbage collector actually affects performance, pinging can be disabled for a particular stub manager by using the MSHLFLAGS_NOPING flag; however, the default behavior of the garbage collector is suitable for most applications and will outperform many application-specific solutions.

The stub manager keeps track of how many external references are outstanding. When the stub is created, this count begins at zero. When a call to CoMarshalInterface is made using MSHLFLAGS_NORMAL, this count is increased by some number n that is written to the marshaled object reference. When the proxy manager unmarshals the reference, it adds n to its count of held

---

[14] Technically, the local OR waits for a short period of time to ensure that any extant marshaled object references created by the dead client have a chance to be unmarshaled.

references. If `CoMarshalInterface` is called on the proxy manager to pass a copy of the reference to another apartment, the proxy manager is free to give out some number of references in order to initialize the second proxy. If a proxy has only one remaining reference, it must go back to the stub manager to request additional references.

It is often useful to store marshaled interface references in a central location that can be accessed by one or more clients. The Running Object Table used by some moniker implementations is the canonical example of this. If the marshaled interface pointer were to be created using MSHLFLAGS_NORMAL, then only one client could ever unmarshal the object reference. If multiple clients are expected to unmarshal the object reference, then the reference needs to be marshaled using either MSHLFLAGS_TABLESTRONG or MSHLFLAGS_TABLEWEAK. In either case, the marshaled object reference can be unmarshaled multiple times.

The difference between strong and weak table marshaling revolves around the relationship between the marshaled object reference and the stub manager. When a marshaled object reference is created using MSHLFLAGS_ TABLEWEAK, the external reference count in the stub manager is not incremented. This means that the marshaled object reference will contain zero references, and each proxy manager will need to contact the stub manager to acquire one or more external references. Because the weak table-marshaled reference does not represent a *counted* external reference on the stub manager, when the last proxy manager disconnects from the stub manager, the stub manager will destroy itself and, of course, release any held COM references on the object. If no proxy managers ever connect to the stub manager, the stub manager will remain alive indefinitely. The net effect is that the outstanding marshaled object reference does not force the lifecycle of the stub manager or the object to remain alive. Conversely, when a marshaled object reference is created using MSHLFLAGS_TABLESTRONG, the external reference count in the stub manager is incremented. This means that the marshaled object reference represents a counted external reference on the stub manager. As with a weak table marshal, each proxy manager will need to contact the stub manager to acquire one or more additional external references. Because the strong table-marshaled reference does represent an external reference count on the stub manager, when the last proxy manager disconnects from the stub manager, the stub manager will *not* destroy itself and will in fact continue to hold COM references on the object. The net effect of strong table marshaling is that the outstanding marshaled object reference does affect the lifecycle of the stub manager or the object. This means that there must be some mechanism to release the references held by the strong table-marshaled object reference. COM provides an API function, `CoReleaseMarshalData`, that informs the stub manager that a marshaled object reference is being destroyed:

```
HRESULT CoReleaseMarshalData([in] IStream *pStm);
```

Like `CoUnmarshalInterface`, `CoReleaseMarshalData` takes an `IStream` interface pointer to a marshaled object reference. `CoReleaseMarshalData` must be called to revoke a table marshal when it is no longer needed. `CoReleaseMarshalData` should also be called if for some reason a normal-marshaled object reference will not be unmarshaled by `CoUnmarshalInterface`.

Object implementors can access the external reference count of the stub manager manually to ensure that the stub manager stays alive during critical phases of an object's lifecycle. COM provides a function, `CoLockObjectExternal`, that increments or decrements the stub manager's external reference count:

```
HRESULT CoLockObjectExternal([in] IUnknown *pUnkObject,
                             [in] BOOL bLock,
                             [in] BOOL bLastUnlockKillsStub);
```

The first parameter to `CoLockObjectExternal` must point to the actual object; it cannot point to a proxy. The second parameter, `bLock`, indicates whether to increment or decrement the stub manager's external reference count. The third parameter indicates whether or not the stub manager should be destroyed if this call removes the last external reference. To understand why `CoLockObjectExternal` is necessary, consider an object that monitors some hardware device and is registered in the Running Object Table using weak table marshaling. While the object is actively monitoring, it wants to ensure that its stub manager remains valid so that new clients can connect to the object to check the state of the hardware. However, if the object is not actively monitoring, it would like the stub manager to disappear unless there are outstanding proxies connected to it. To implement this functionality, the object might have a method that begins monitoring:

```
STDMETHODIMP Monitor::StartMonitoring(void) {
// ensure that stub manager/object stays alive
  HRESULT hr = CoLockObjectExternal(this, TRUE, FALSE);
// start hardware monitoring
  if (SUCCEEDED(hr))
    hr = this->EnableHardwareProbe();
  return hr;
}
```

and another method that tells the object to end its monitoring activity:

```
STDMETHODIMP Monitor::StopMonitoring(void) {
// stop hardware monitoring
  this->DisableHardwareProbe();
// allow stub manager/object to die when no clients exist
  hr = CoLockObjectExternal(this, FALSE, TRUE);
  return hr;
}
```

Assuming that the object was originally marshaled using weak table marshaling, the preceding code ensures that the stub manager and the object remain alive as long as there is at least one outstanding proxy *or* the object is actively monitoring the underlying hardware.

In addition to allowing object implementors to adjust the external reference count on the stub manager, COM allows object implementors to explicitly destroy the stub manager irrespective of the number of outstanding object references. COM provides an API function, CoDisconnectObject, that finds an object's stub manager and destroys it, disconnecting any extant proxies:

```
HRESULT CoDisconnectObject(
    [in] IUnknown * pUnkObject,   // ptr. to object
    [in] DWORD dwReserved);       // reserved, must be zero
```

Like CoLockObjectExternal, CoDisconnectObject must be called from within the process of the actual object and cannot be called on a proxy. To apply CoDisconnectObject to the hardware monitor object presented earlier, consider what would happen if the state of the object were to become corrupted. To prevent additional method invocations on the object that might return erroneous results, the object could call CoDisconnectObject to rudely disconnect any extant proxies:

```
STDMETHODIMP Monitor::GetSample(/*[out]*/ SAMPLEDATA *ps) {
  HRESULT hr = this->GetSampleFromProbe(ps);
  if (FAILED(hr)) // probe or object may be corrupted
    CoDisconnectObject(this, 0);
  return hr;
}
```

CoDisconnectObject is also used when a process wishes to shut down while one or more of its objects may have outstanding proxies. By explicitly calling CoDisconnectObject prior to destroying any objects that may have extant proxies, there is no risk that incoming ORPC requests will be serviced after the object is destroyed. If an incoming ORPC request were to arrive after the object is destroyed but while the stub manager remains alive, the interface stub would blithely invoke the corresponding method on the memory formerly known as the object, causing unnecessary suffering due to futile debugging efforts.

CoLockObjectExternal and CoDisconnectObject are both techniques that an object implementor can use to manipulate the stub manager. It is often useful to know whether any extant proxies or strong marshals exist on the stub manager. To inform objects that there are outstanding external references on the stub manager, COM defines an interface, IExternalConnection, that objects can export:

```
[ uuid(00000019-0000-0000-C000-000000000046),object,local ]
interface IExternalConnection : IUnknown {
  DWORD AddConnection(
    [in] DWORD extconn,  // type of reference
    [in] DWORD reserved  // reserved, must be zero
  );
  DWORD ReleaseConnection(
    [in] DWORD extconn,  // type of reference
    [in] DWORD reserved, // reserved, must be zero
    [in] BOOL fLastReleaseCloses // should kill stub?
  );
}
```

When the stub manager first attaches to an object, it asks the object if it would like to be notified when external references are created or destroyed. It does this via a QueryInterface request for the IExternalConnection interface. If the object does not implement IExternalConnection, then the stub manager will use its own reference count to decide when to destroy the stub manager. If the object elects to implement IExternalConnection, then the stub manager will live until the object explicitly destroys it via a call to CoDisconnectObject.

Objects that implement IExternalConnection are expected to maintain a lock count that records the number of calls to AddConnection and ReleaseConnection. For efficiency, COM does not call AddConnection each time a proxy is created. This means that if the object maintains a lock count based on calls to AddConnection and ReleaseConnection, the object's lock count will not accurately reflect the number of extant object references. However, COM does guarantee that the nonzeroness of the lock count does indicate that at least one outstanding reference exists and the zeroness of the lock count will indicate that no outstanding references exist. Calls to CoLockObjectExternal will affect this count as well. This information is especially useful for objects that care about the existence of external clients. For example, assume that the hardware monitoring object presented earlier spawns a thread to do background logging of sample data. Also assume that sample error might occur if logging were to take place while the object is actively monitoring data or being controlled by external clients. To avoid this problem, the logging thread could check the lock count maintained by the object's IExternalConnection implementation and perform the logging operation only when no external references exist. This assumes that the object implements IExternalConnection as follows:

```
class Monitor : public IExternalConnection,
                public IMonitor {
  LONG m_cRef;     // normal COM reference count
  LONG m_cExtRef; // external reference count
  Monitor(void) : m_cRef(0), m_cExtRef(0) { ... }

  STDMETHODIMP_(DWORD) AddConnection(DWORD extconn, DWORD) {
    if (extconn & EXTCONN_STRONG) // must check for this bit
      return InterlockedIncrement(&m_cExtRef);
  }

  STDMETHODIMP_(DWORD) ReleaseConnection(DWORD extconn, DWORD,
                            BOOL bLastUnlockKillsStub) {
    DWORD res = 0;
    if (extconn & EXTCONN_STRONG){ //must check for this bit
      res = InterlockedDecrement(&m_cExtRef);
      if (res == 0 && bLastUnlockKillsStub)
        CoDisconnectObject(this, 0);
    }
    return res;
  }
  :    :    :
  :    :    :
}
```

Given this implementation, the thread routine could check the state of the object and decide whether or not to perform the logging operation based on the activity level of the object:

```
DWORD WINAPI ThreadProc(void *pv) {
// assume ptr to real object is passed to CreateThread
   Monitor *pm = (Monitor*)pv;
   while (1) {
// sleep for 10 seconds
      Sleep(10000);
// if object is not in use, perform a log operation
      if (pm->m_cExtRef == 0)
         pm->TryToLogSampleData();
   }
   return 0;
}
```

Assuming that the object's TryToLogSampleData method handles concurrency correctly, this thread procedure will log data only when the object is not in use by external clients or actively monitoring (recall that when monitoring, the object raises the external reference count via CoLockObjectExternal). Although this example may seem somewhat contrived, there are cases in which tracking external references is critical to correct operation. One classic example is described in Chapter 6 and is related to registering class objects in out-of-process servers.

Custom Marshaling

So far, this chapter has focused on standard marshaling and ORPC-based method remoting. For a large class of objects, this is all that is needed to achieve the proper balance between performance, semantic correctness, and simplicity of implementation. There are objects for which the default behavior of ORPC method remoting is inefficient to the point of being unusable. For these objects, COM supports custom marshaling. As mentioned earlier in this chapter, custom marshaling allows the object implementor to provide a custom proxy implementation that will be created in the importing apartment. Objects indicate that they wish to support custom marshaling by exporting the IMarshal interface:

```
[ uuid(00000003-0000-0000-C000-000000000046),local,object ]
interface IMarshal : IUnknown {

// get CLSID for custom proxy (CoMarshalInterface)
   HRESULT GetUnmarshalClass(
```

```
        [in] REFIID riid, [in, iid_is(riid)] void *pv,
        [in] DWORD dwDestCtx, [in] void *pvDestCtx,
        [in] DWORD mshlflags, [out] CLSID *pclsid);

// get size of custom marshaled objref (CoGetMarshalSizeMax)
  HRESULT GetMarshalSizeMax(
        [in] REFIID riid, [in, iid_is(riid)] void *pv,
        [in] DWORD dwDestCtx, [in] void *pvDestCtx,
        [in] DWORD mshlflags, [out] DWORD *pSize);

// write out custom marshaled objref (CoMarshalInterface)
  HRESULT MarshalInterface([in] IStream *pStm,
        [in] REFIID riid, [in, iid_is(riid)] void *pv,
        [in] DWORD dwDestCtx, [in] void *pvDestCtx,
        [in] DWORD mshlflags);

// read objref and return proxy (CoUnmarshalInterface)
  HRESULT UnmarshalInterface([in] IStream *pStm,
                        [in] REFIID riid,
                [out,iid_is(riid)] void **ppv);

// revoke a marshal (CoReleaseMarshalData)
  HRESULT ReleaseMarshalData([in] IStream *pStm);

// tear down connection-state (CoDisconnectObject)
  HRESULT DisconnectObject([in] DWORD dwReserved);
}
```

The comments that precede the method definitions indicate which COM APIs call each method.

When CoMarshalInterface is called on an object that supports custom marshaling, the marshaled object reference has a somewhat different format, as shown in Figure 5.7. Note that after the standard MEOW header, the marshaled object reference simply contains a CLSID used to create the custom proxy and an opaque array of bytes that will be used to initialize the custom proxy. CoMarshalInterface discovers the custom proxy's CLSID by calling the IMarshal::GetUnmarshalClass method on the object. CoMarshalInterface fills the opaque byte array by calling the object's IMarshal::MarshalInterface implementation. It is in MarshalInterface that the object gets its one and only chance to send an initialization message to the new custom proxy simply by writing the message to the supplied byte

MEOW	*Signature*
FLAGS	*Standard/Custom/Handler Flags*
IID	*IID of Marshaled Interface*
CLSID	*CLSID for Custom Proxy*
cb	*Custom Marshal Data Byte Count*
Custom Marshal Data	*Initialization Data for Custom Proxy*

Figure 5.7 Custom Marshal Object Reference

stream. When `CoUnmarshalInterface` is called, this message will be given to a newly created custom proxy via the proxy's `IMarshal::UnmarshalInterface` method. This means that both the object and the custom proxy must implement `IMarshal`. The object's `MarshalInterface` method writes the initialization message. The proxy's `UnmarshalInterface` reads the initialization message. Once the `UnmarshalInterface` method returns, COM is no longer involved in any proxy/object communications. It is the job of the custom proxy to implement the interface methods in a way that is semantically correct. If a method call needs to be remoted to the object, then it is the proxy's job to do this. If the method can be implemented in the client's apartment, then the proxy can do this as well.

One of the benefits of custom marshaling is that the client is oblivious that it is being used. In fact, the client cannot reliably detect whether an interface is a standard proxy, a custom proxy, or the actual object. Custom marshaling is an object-by-object decision. Two instances of the same class could elect to use standard or custom marshaling independently. When an object elects to implement custom marshaling, it must do so for all interfaces. If an object wishes to custom marshal only for a subset of all possible marshaling contexts (*e.g.,* in-process, local, different machine), the object can get an instance of the standard marshaler and forward its `IMarshal` methods for unsupported contexts so that all contexts can be supported. In fact, if an object were simply to forward all `IMarshal` methods to the standard marshaler unconditionally, the object would in effect always use standard marshaling.

To get a pointer to the standard marshaler, objects can call the `CoGetStandard-Marshal` method:

```
HRESULT CoGetStandardMarshal(
    [in]REFIID riid,          // type of itf marshaled?
[in, iid_is(riid)] IUnknown *pUnk, // the itf to marshal
    [in] DWORD dwDestCtx,   // MSHCTX
    [in] void *pvDestCtx,   // reserved
    [in] DWORD mshlflags,   // normal vs. table
    [out] IMarshal **ppMarshal); // ptr to std. Marshal
```

Assume that an object uses a technique for custom marshaling that works only on the local host but not when communicating with off-host apartments. The object's implementation of `GetMarshalSizeMax` would look something like this:

```
STDMETHODIMP CustStd::GetMarshalSizeMax(ULONG *pcb,
                REFIID riid, void *pv, DWORD dwDestCtx,
                void *pvDestCtx,  DWORD mshlflags) {
// if context is supported, do work!
  if (dwDestCtx==MSHCTX_LOCAL || dwDestCtx==MSHCTX_INPROC)
    return this->MyCustomMarshalingRoutine(pcb);

// unsupported context, delegate to std marshal
  IMarshal *pMsh = 0;
  HRESULT hr = CoGetStandardMarshal(riid, pv, dwDestCtx,
                                    pvDestCtx, mshlflags,
                                    &pMsh);
  if (SUCCEEDED(hr)) {
    hr = pMsh->GetMarshalSizeMax(pcb, riid, pv, dwDestCtx,
                                 pvDestCtx, mshlflags);
    pMsh->Release();
  }
  return hr;
}
```

What isn't shown in this code fragment is how to write the initialization message when custom marshaling is actually desired. This is because there is no standard implementation of any of the `IMarshal` methods (hence the term *custom* marshaling). However, there are several common scenarios in which custom marshaling is extremely beneficial and implementing `IMarshal` in these scenarios is somewhat regular. By far the most common application of IMarshal is to implement marshal-by-value.

Marshal-by-value is most useful for objects that never change their state once initialized. COM wrappers to structures are a common example of an object that is simply initialized, passed to another object to be queried, and then destroyed. Such an object is a prime candidate for custom marshaling. To implement marshal-by-value, the object implementation is almost always an in-process server. This allows the object and proxy to share the same implementation class. The idea behind marshal-by-value is that the custom proxy becomes a clone of the original object. This implies that the marshaled object reference must contain the entire state of the original object and (for simplicity) that the CLSID for the custom proxy must be the same as that of the original object.

Assume the following class definition of a COM wrapper around a simple two-dimensional point:

```
class Point : public IPoint, public IMarshal {
  long m_x; long m_y;
public:
  Point(void) : m_x(0), m_y(0) {}
  IMPLEMENT_UNKNOWN(Point)
  BEGIN_INTERFACE_TABLE(Point)
    IMPLEMENTS_INTERFACE(IPoint)
    IMPLEMENTS_INTERFACE(IMarshal)
  END_INTERFACE_TABLE()
// IPoint methods
// IMarshal methods
};
```

To support marshal-by-value, the class's MarshalInterface method would need to serialize the state of the object as the initialization message for the proxy:

```
STDMETHODIMP Point::MarshalInterface(IStream *pStm, REFIID,
                 void *, DWORD, void *, DWORD) {
// write out endian header
  DWORD dw = 0xFF669900;
  HRESULT hr = pStm->Write(&dw, sizeof(DWORD), 0);
  if (FAILED(hr)) return hr;
  dw = m_x;
  hr = pStm->Write(&dw, sizeof(DWORD), 0);
  if (FAILED(hr)) return hr;
  dw = m_y;
```

```
      return pStm->Write(&dw, sizeof(DWORD), 0);
}
```

Assuming that the object's class is implemented as an in-process server, the custom proxy can simply be a second instance of the same class, which implies the following implementation of GetUnmarshalClass:

```
STDMETHODIMP Point::GetUnmarshalClass(REFIID, void *, DWORD,
                              void *, DWORD, CLSID *pclsid) {
  *pclsid = CLSID_Point; // this class's CLSID
  return hr;
}
```

To ensure that enough room is allocated for the initialization message, the object's GetMarshalSizeMax method needs to return the correct byte count:

```
STDMETHODIMP Point::GetMarshalSizeMax(REFIID, void *, DWORD,
                              void *, DWORD, DWORD *pcb) {
  *pcb = 3 * sizeof(DWORD); // m_x + m_y + header
  return hr;
}
```

When the marshaled object reference is unmarshaled by CoUnmarshal-Interface, the fact that the marshaled object reference is a custom marshal will cause a new custom proxy to be created. The object reference contains the custom proxy's CLSID that the original object returned in its GetUnmarshalClass method. Once a new custom proxy is created, its UnmarshalInterface method is given the initialization message that the object wrote in its MarshalInterface implementation:

```
STDMETHODIMP Point::UnmarshalInterface(IStream *pStm,
                              REFIID riid, void ** ppv) {
  *ppv = 0;
// read endian header
  DWORD dw; ULONG cbRead;
  HRESULT hr = pStm->Read(&dw, sizeof(DWORD), &cbRead);
  if (FAILED(hr) || cbRead != sizeof(DWORD))
    return RPC_E_INVALID_DATA;
  bool bSwapEndian = dw == 0x009966FF;
// read m_x and m_y
  hr = pStm->Read(&dw, sizeof(DWORD), &cbRead);   m_x = dw;
```

```
   if (FAILED(hr) || cbRead != sizeof(DWORD))
     return RPC_E_INVALID_DATA;
   hr = pStm->Read(&dw, sizeof(DWORD), &cbRead); m_y = dw;
   if (FAILED(hr)) || cbRead != sizeof(DWORD))
     return RPC_E_INVALID_DATA;
// byte swap members if necessary
   if (bSwapEndian)
     byteswapdata(&m_x, &m_y);
// return pointer to this object
   return this->QueryInterface(riid, ppv);
}
```

Note that the implementation of MarshalInterface and UnmarshalInterface need to ensure that the marshaled state is readable on any platform. This means manually dealing with alignment, byte ordering, and data type size differences.

The preceding implementation of UnmarshalInterface simply returns a pointer to the newly created custom proxy. For a simple marshal-by-value object, this may be satisfactory. However, more generic implementations of UnmarshalInterface may want to detect multiple unmarshals that correspond to the same COM identity and return a pointer to the same proxy identity to maintain the identity relationship of the proxy to the object. This not only can save resources but also keeps the programming model cleaner.

The FreeThreaded Marshaler

When a class is marked ThreadingModel="both," it is indicating that its instances and class object can safely reside in either an STA or an MTA. However, according to the rules of COM, any given instance will reside on only one apartment. If an object implementor has gone to the length of ensuring that an object can safely reside in an MTA, it might be the case that the object does not care about apartments at all. Such an object could be accessed concurrently not only by multiple threads in the MTA but also by non-MTA-based threads (*e.g.,* threads that are executing in an STA). However, it is impossible for clients to know that such access is safe for a particular object, so all cross-apartment interface pointer sharing must be established using an explicit marshaling technique. This means that access to an in-process object will be via ORPC calls unless the caller is executing in the apartment that originally created the object.

Unlike clients, objects do know about their relationship to apartments, concurrency, and reentrancy. Objects that are satisfied with ORPC calls when accessed from multiple apartments in the same process get this behavior by default. However, an object that is not satisfied with ORPC-based access has the opportunity to bypass this by implementing custom marshaling. Custom marshaling could be used fairly easily to bypass the stub manager and simply serialize a raw pointer to the object into the marshaled object reference. When using this technique, the custom proxy implementation could simply read the raw pointer from the marshaled object reference and pass it to the caller in the importing apartment. The client threads would still pass the interface pointer across the apartment boundary by calling CoMarshalInterface/ CoUnmarshalInterface either explicitly or implicitly; however, the object would conspire with a custom proxy to simply pass a raw pointer to the actual object. Although this technique will work perfectly for intraprocess marshaling, it will fail miserably for interprocess marshaling. Fortunately, the object implementation can simply delegate to the standard marshaler for any marshaling context other than MSHCTX_INPROC.

Because the behavior just described is useful to a large class of objects, COM provides an aggregatable implementation of IMarshal that accomplishes exactly what was described. This implementation is called the FreeThreaded Marshaler (FTM) and can be created using the CoCreateFreeThreadedMarshaler API call:

```
HRESULT CoCreateFreeThreadedMarshaler(
                [in] IUnknown *pUnkOuter,
                [out] IUnknown **ppUnkInner);
```

A class that wishes to use the FTM simply aggregates an instance either at initialization time or on demand at the first QueryInterface request for IMarshal. The following class preinstantiates the FTM at construction time:

```
class Point : public IPoint {
  LONG m_cRef;  IUnknown *m_pUnkFTM;
  long m_x; long m_y;
  Point(void) : m_cRef(0), m_x(0), m_y(0) {
    HRESULT hr = CoCreateFreeThreadedMarshaler(this,
                                               &m_pUnkFTM);
    assert(SUCCEEDED(hr));
  }
  virtual ~Point(void) { m_pUnkFTM->Release(); }
};
```

The corresponding QueryInterface implementation would simply request the IMarshal interface from the FTM:

```
STDMETHODIMP Point::QueryInterface(REFIID riid, void **ppv) {
  if (riid == IID_IUnknown || riid == IID_IPoint)
    *ppv = static_cast<IPoint*>(this);
  else if (riid == IID_IMarshal)
    return m_pUnkFTM->QueryInterface(riid, ppv);
  else
    return (*ppv = 0), E_NOINTERFACE;
  ((IUnknown*)*ppv)->AddRef();
  return S_OK;
}
```

Once the FTM is in place, whenever references to Point objects are marshaled across intraprocess apartment boundaries, no proxies will ever be used. This applies to explicit calls to CoMarshalInterface/CoUnmarshalInterface, as well as when references to Point objects are passed as method parameters to intraprocess proxies to non-Point objects.

The FTM consumes at least 16 bytes of memory. Because many in-process objects are never used outside their original apartment, preallocating the FTM may not be the best use of available resources. It is highly likely that the object will already have some thread synchronization primitive. If this is the case, then the FTM can be lazy-aggregated at the first QueryInterface for IMarshal. To achieve this, assume the following class definition:

```
class LazyPoint : public IPoint {
  LONG m_cRef;  IUnknown *m_pUnkFTM;
  long m_x; long m_y;
  LazyPoint(void) : m_cRef(0),m_pUnkFTM(0),m_x(0),m_y(0) {}
  virtual ~LazyPoint(void)
  { if (m_pUnkFTM) m_pUnkFTM->Release(); }
  void Lock(void);    // acquire object-specific lock
  void Unlock(void); // release object-specific lock
    :     :     :
};
```

Based on the preceding class definition, the following QueryInterface implementation will correctly aggregate the FTM on demand:

```
STDMETHODIMP Point::QueryInterface(REFIID riid, void **ppv) {
  if (riid == IID_IUnknown || riid == IID_IPoint)
    *ppv = static_cast<IPoint*>(this);
  else if (riid == IID_IMarshal) {
    this->Lock();
```

```
            HRESULT hr = E_NOINTERFACE; *ppv = 0;
            if (m_pUnkFTM == 0) // acquire FTM first time through
                CoCreateFreeThreadedMarshaler(this, &m_pUnkFTM);
            if (m_pUnkFTM != 0) // by here, FTM is acquired
                hr = m_pUnkFTM->QueryInterface(riid, ppv);
            this->Unlock();
            return hr;
        }
        else
            return (*ppv = 0), E_NOINTERFACE;
        ((IUnknown*)*ppv)->AddRef();
        return S_OK;
    }
```

The disadvantage of this approach is that all QueryInterface requests for
IMarshal will be serialized; however, if IMarshal is never requested, then
fewer resources will be acquired.

Given the relative ease of using the FTM, it is interesting to consider when
the FTM is inappropriate. Certainly objects that can live only in singlethreaded apartments should not use the FTM, as they are highly unlikely to
be expecting concurrent access. This does not mean, however, that all objects
capable of running in the MTA should use the FTM. Objects that have interface
pointers as data members must use caution when using the FTM. Consider the
following class that uses other COM objects to perform its operations:

```
    class Rect : public IRect {
      LONG m_cRef;
      IPoint *m_pPtTopLeft;
      IPoint *m_pPtBottomRight;
      Rect(void) : m_cRef(0) {
        HRESULT hr = CoCreateInstance(CLSID_Point, 0,
                CLSCTX_INPROC, IID_IPoint, (void**)&m_pPtTopLeft);
        assert(SUCCEEDED(hr));
        hr = CoCreateInstance(CLSID_Point, 0, CLSCTX_INPROC,
                        IID_IPoint, (void**)&m_pPtBottomRight);
        assert(SUCCEEDED(hr));
      }
      :   :   :
    }
```

Assume that the class Rect is an in-process class and is marked Threading-
Model="Both." The constructor for a given Rect object will always execute in

the apartment of the thread that calls CoCreateInstance (CLSID_Rect). This means that the two calls to CoCreateInstance (CLSID_Point) will also execute in the client's apartment. The rules of COM indicate that the data members m_pPtTopLeft and m_pPtBottomRight can be accessed only from the apartment that executes the CoCreateInstance calls.

It is likely that at least one of the Rect methods uses the two interface pointer data members to perform its work:

```
STDMETHODIMP Rect::get_Area(long *pn) {
    long top, left, bottom, right;
    HRESULT hr = m_pPtTopLeft->GetCoords(&left, &top);
    assert(SUCCEEDED(hr));
    hr = m_pPtBottomRight->GetCoords(&right, &bottom);
    assert(SUCCEEDED(hr));
    *pn = (right - left) * (bottom - top);
    return S_OK;
}
```

If the class Rect were to use the FTM, then it would be possible to invoke this method from apartments other than the apartment that made the initial CoCreateInstance calls. Unfortunately, this would cause the get_Area method to violate the rules of COM, because the two interface pointer data members are valid only in the original apartment. If the Point class also happened to use the FTM, then this would technically not be a problem. However, in general, clients (such as the Rect class) should not make assumptions about this very specific implementation detail. In fact, if the Point objects did not use the FTM and happened to be created in a different apartment due to ThreadingModel incompatibilities, the Rect object would be holding pointers to proxies. Proxies are notorious for enforcing the rules of COM and correctly return RPC_E_WRONG_THREAD when accessed from the wrong apartment.

This leaves the Rect implementor with one of two choices. One choice would be not to use the FTM and simply accept the fact that when clients pass Rect object references between apartments, ORPC will be used to access instances of class Rect. This is certainly the easiest solution, as it involves no additional code and will simply work without requiring any thought. The other choice is no longer to keep raw interface pointers as data members but instead to keep some marshaled form of an interface pointer as a data member. This is exactly what the Global Interface Table is intended for. To implement this approach, the Rect class would keep DWORD cookies as data members in lieu of raw interface pointers:

```
class SafeRect : public IRect {
  LONG m_cRef;              // COM reference count
  IUnknown *m_pUnkFTM;      // cache for FTM lazy aggregate
  DWORD m_dwTopLeft;        // GIT cookie for top/left
  DWORD m_dwBottomRight;    // GIT cookie for bottom/right
  :   :   :
}
```

The constructor would still create two instances of Point, but instead of holding the raw pointers, the constructor would register the interface pointers with the global interface table:

```
SafeRect::SafeRect(void) : m_cRef(0), m_pUnkFTM(0) {
// assume ptr to GIT is initialized elsewhere
  extern IGlobalInterfaceTable *g_pGIT; assert(g_pGIT != 0);
  IPoint *pPoint = 0;
// create instance of class Point
  HRESULT hr = CoCreateInstance(CLSID_Point, 0,
          CLSCTX_INPROC, IID_IPoint, (void**)&pPoint);
  assert(SUCCEEDED(hr));
// register interface pointer in GIT
  hr = g_pGIT->RegisterInterfaceInGlobal(pPoint, IID_IPoint,
                                       &m_dwTopLeft);
  assert(SUCCEEDED(hr));
  pPoint->Release(); // reference is now held in GIT

// create instance of class point
  hr = CoCreateInstance(CLSID_Point, 0, CLSCTX_INPROC,
                        IID_IPoint, (void**)&pPoint);
  assert(SUCCEEDED(hr));
// register interface pointer in GIT
  hr = g_pGIT->RegisterInterfaceInGlobal(pPoint, IID_IPoint,
                                       &m_dwBottomRight);
  assert(SUCCEEDED(hr));
  pPoint->Release(); // reference is now held in GIT
}
```

Note that as long as the interface pointer is registered in the GIT, no additional references must be held by the interface pointer user.

Once the class has been converted to use the GIT instead of raw interface pointers, it must unmarshal a new proxy in each method call that needs access to the registered interfaces:

```
STDMETHODIMP SafeRect::get_Area(long *pn) {
   extern IGlobalInterfaceTable *g_pGIT; assert(g_pGIT != 0);
// unmarshal the two interface pointers from the GIT
   IPoint *ptl = 0, *pbr = 0;
   HRESULT hr = g_pGIT->GetInterfaceFromGlobal(m_dwPtTopLeft,
                                    IID_IPoint, (void**)&ptl);
   assert(SUCCEEDED(hr));
   hr = g_pGIT->GetInterfaceFromGlobal(m_dwPtBottomRight,
                                    IID_IPoint, (void**)&pbr);
// use temp ptrs to implement method
   long top, left, bottom, right;
   hr = ptl->GetCoords(&left, &top);
   assert(SUCCEEDED(hr));
   hr = pbr->GetCoords(&right, &bottom);
   assert(SUCCEEDED(hr));
   *pn = (right - left) * (bottom - top);
// release temp ptrs.
   ptl->Release();
   pbr->Release();
   return S_OK;
}
```

Because the implementation of SafeRect uses the FTM, it is pointless to try to keep the unmarshaled interface pointers across method invocations, because it is not known whether the next method invocation will happen in the same apartment.

The GIT will keep any registered interface pointers alive until they are explicitly removed from the GIT. This means that the SafeRect class must explicitly revoke the GIT entries for its two data members:

```
SafeRect::~SafeRect(void) {
   extern IGlobalInterfaceTable *g_pGIT; assert(g_pGIT != 0);
   HRESULT hr=g_pGIT->RevokeInterfaceFromGlobal(m_dwTopLeft);
   assert(SUCCEEDED(hr));
   hr = g_pGIT->RevokeInterfaceFromGlobal(m_dwBottomRight);
   assert(SUCCEEDED(hr));
}
```

Removing an interface pointer from the GIT releases any references held on the object.

Note that using the GIT and FTM together implies that many, many calls to the GIT will be made to create temporary interface pointers for use in each individual method. Although the GIT is optimized to support this exact usage pattern, the code is still tedious. The following simple C++ class wraps the usage of GIT cookies behind a convenient type-safe interface:

```
template <class Itf, const IID* piid>
class GlobalInterfacePointer {
  DWORD m_dwCookie; // the GIT cookie
// prevent misuse
  GlobalInterfacePointer(const GlobalInterfacePointer&);
  void operator =(const GlobalInterfacePointer&);
public:
// start as invalid cookie
  GlobalInterfacePointer(void) : m_dwCookie(0) { }

// start with auto-globalized local pointer
  GlobalInterfacePointer(Itf *pItf, HRESULT& hr)
    : m_dwCookie(0) { hr = Globalize(pItf); }

// auto-unglobalize
  ~GlobalInterfacePointer(void)
  { if (m_dwCookie) Unglobalize(); }

// register an interface pointer in GIT
  HRESULT Globalize(Itf *pItf) {
    assert(g_pGIT != 0 && m_dwCookie == 0);
    return g_pGIT->RegisterInterfaceInGlobal(pItf,
                                   *piid, &m_dwCookie);
  }

// revoke an interface pointer in GIT
  HRESULT Unglobalize(void) {
    assert(g_pGIT != 0 && m_dwCookie != 0);
    HRESULT hr=g_pGIT->RevokeInterfaceFromGlobal(m_dwCookie);
    m_dwCookie = 0;
    return hr;
  }
// get a local interface pointer from GIT
  HRESULT Localize(Itf **ppItf) const {
    assert(g_pGIT != 0 && m_dwCookie != 0);
    return g_pGIT->GetInterfaceFromGlobal(m_dwCookie,
                                 *piid,(void**)ppItf);
```

```
    }
// convenience methods
    bool IsOK(void) const { return m_dwCookie != 0; }
    DWORD GetCookie(void) const { return m_dwCookie; }
};
#define GIP(Itf) GlobalInterfacePointer<Itf, &IID_##Itf>
```

Given this class definition and macro, the SafeRect class now holds GlobalInterfacePointers instead of raw DWORDs:

```
class SafeRect : public IRect {
    LONG m_cRef;                    // COM reference count
    IUnknown *m_pUnkFTM;            // cache for FTM lazy aggregate
    GIP(IPoint) m_gipTopLeft;       // GIT cookie - top/left
    GIP(IPoint) m_gipBottomRight;   // GIT cookie - bottom/right
        :    :    :
}
```

To initialize the GlobalInterfacePointer member, the constructor (which executes in the object's apartment) simply registers the managed pointers by calling the Globalize method on each GlobalInterfacePointer:

```
SafeRect::SafeRect(void) : m_cRef(0), m_pUnkFTM(0) {
    IPoint *pPoint = 0;
// create instance of class Point
    HRESULT hr = CoCreateInstance(CLSID_Point, 0,
            CLSCTX_INPROC, IID_IPoint, (void**)&pPoint);
    assert(SUCCEEDED(hr));
// register interface pointer in GIT
    hr = m_gipTopLeft.Globalize(pPoint);
    assert(SUCCEEDED(hr));
    pPoint->Release(); // reference is now held in GIT

// create instance of class point
    hr = CoCreateInstance(CLSID_Point, 0, CLSCTX_INPROC,
                        IID_IPoint, (void**)&pPoint);
    assert(SUCCEEDED(hr));
// register interface pointer in GIT
    hr = m_gipBottomRight.Globalize(pPoint);
    assert(SUCCEEDED(hr));
    pPoint->Release(); // reference is now held in GIT
}
```

Methods that need access to the globalized pointers can import a local copy via the GlobalInterfacePointer's Localize method:

```
STDMETHODIMP SafeRect::get_Top(long *pVal) {
  IPoint *pPoint = 0; // local imported pointer
  HRESULT hr = m_gipTopLeft.Localize(&pPoint);
  if (SUCCEEDED(hr)) {
    long x;
    hr = pPoint->get_Coords(&x, pVal);
    pPoint->Release();
  }
  return hr;
}
```

Note that because the FreeThreaded Marshaler is in use, the raw interface pointer cannot be cached and must be imported in each method invocation to avoid access from the wrong apartment.

The previous code fragment can be automated even further. Because most method invocations on the GlobalInterfacePointer class will be to localize a temporary pointer in a method invocation, the following class automates the importing of the temporary pointer and its subsequent release, much like a smart pointer:

```
template <class Itf, const IID* piid>
class LocalInterfacePointer {
    Itf *m_pItf; // temp imported pointer
// prevent misuse
    LocalInterfacePointer(const LocalInterfacePointer&);
    operator = (const LocalInterfacePointer&);
public:
  LocalInterfacePointer(const GlobalInterfacePointer<Itf,
                        piid>& rhs,HRESULT& hr) {
    hr = rhs.Localize(&m_pItf);
  }

  LocalInterfacePointer(DWORD dwCookie, HRESULT& hr) {
    assert(g_pGIT != 0);
    hr = g_pGIT->GetInterfaceFromGlobal(dwCookie, *piid,
                                (void**)&m_pItf);
  }
```

```
~LocalInterfacePointer(void)
  { if (m_pItf) m_pItf->Release(); }

class SafeItf : public Itf {
  STDMETHOD_(ULONG, AddRef)(void) = 0;  // hide
  STDMETHOD_(ULONG, Release)(void) = 0; // hide
};


SafeItf *GetInterface(void) const
{ return (SafeItf*)m_pItf; }


SafeItf *operator ->(void) const
{ assert(m_pItf != 0); return GetInterface();  }
};
#define LIP(Itf) LocalInterfacePointer<Itf, &IID_##Itf>
```

Given this second C++ class, managing imported pointers becomes much simpler:

```
STDMETHODIMP SafeRect::get_Area(long *pn) {
  long top, left, bottom, right;
  HRESULT hr, hr2;
// import pointers
  LIP(IPoint) lipTopLeft(m_gipTopLeft, hr);
  LIP(IPoint) lipBottomRight(m_gipBottomRight, hr2);
  assert(SUCCEEDED(hr) && SUCCEEDED(hr2));
// use temp local pointers
  hr = lipTopLeft->GetCoords(&left, &top);
  hr2 = lipBottomRight->GetCoords(&right, &bottom);
  assert(SUCCEEDED(hr) && SUCCEEDED(hr2));
  *pn = (right - left) * (bottom - top);
  return S_OK;
// LocalInterfacePointer auto-releases temp ptrs.
}
```

The GIP and LIP macros make using the GIT and FTM together much less cumbersome. Prior to the availability of the GIT, using the FTM in a class with interface pointers was far more difficult than any of the code shown in this section.

Where Are We?

This chapter described the apartment abstraction as a logical grouping of objects that share concurrency and reentrancy constraints. Processes have one or more apartments. Threads execute in exactly one apartment at a time. Each COM object belongs to exactly one apartment, and to allow interapartment communications, COM supports marshaling of object references across apartment boundaries. A proxy is a local representation of an object that resides in another apartment. Standard proxies use ORPC to transmit method requests to the remote object. Custom proxies do whatever they like to provide the correct semantics. The apartment is the fundamental abstraction that is used throughout the COM remoting architecture.

CHAPTER 6 | Applications

```
int process_id = fork();
if (process_id == 0)
  exec("../bin/serverd");
```
Anonymous, 1981

The previous chapter presented the fundamentals of COM apartments and illustrated the COM remoting architecture in a fair amount of detail. The rules of managing COM object references in a multithreaded environment were examined, as were techniques for implementing thread-aware COM classes and objects. This chapter will examine the issues related to process and application management in COM, focusing on how apartments relate to fault isolation, trust, and security context.

In-Process Activation Pitfalls

So far, COM servers have been presented as in-process units of code that are loaded into the activator's process to create objects and execute their methods. For a large class of objects, this is a reasonable deployment strategy. However, this strategy is not without its shortcomings. One pitfall of running an object in the client's process is the lack of fault isolation. If the object causes an access violation or other fatal runtime error, the client's process will terminate with the object. Likewise, if the client program somehow causes a fault, all objects that were created in its address space will be instantly destroyed without warning. This problem also applies to clients that decide to exit normally, such as when an end-user shuts down an application. When the client process exits, any objects that were created in the client's address space will be destroyed, even if external clients outside the process hold valid imported references. Clearly, when activated in process, object lifetime can be terminated prematurely when the client process exits.

Another potential pitfall of running in the client's process is the shared security context. When a client activates an object in process, the object's methods execute using the security credentials of the client. This means that objects created by privileged users can do a substantial amount of damage. This also means that objects created by relatively untrusted users may not have sufficient privileges to access resources that are critical to the object's correct operation. Unfortunately, there is no straightforward way to give an in-process object its own security context.

One other pitfall of in-process activation is that it does not enable distributed computation. If an object must be activated in the client's address space, then by definition it shares the CPU and other local resources with the client. In-process activation also makes it difficult for multiple client processes to share a single object. Although the notion of apartments does allow object references to be exported from any process (including what traditionally would be considered client processes), the activation semantics for sharing an in-process instance are hard to imagine.

To address these issues, COM allows classes to be activated in distinct processes. When activated in a distinct process, each class (or group of classes) can have its own distinct security context. This means that the class implementor is in control of which users are allowed to communicate with its objects. The class implementor is also in control of which set of security credentials the process should use. Depending on how the class is actually packaged, the class implementor is also in control over when (if ever) the surrounding process will terminate. Finally, activating a class in a distinct process provides a degree of fault isolation that insulates the client and the objects from each other's terminal errors.

Activation and the SCM

The COM Service Control Manager (SCM) supports associating CLSIDs with server processes in the registry. This allows the SCM to start a server process on demand based on client activation requests. Assuming that the code for a class will be packaged as a process image (an EXE) rather than as a DLL, all that is needed is to use the LocalServer32 registry key in lieu of the InprocServer32 key, as shown in the following example:

```
[HKCR\CLSID\{27EE6A26-DF65-11d0-8C5F-0080C73925BA}]
@="Gorilla"

[HKCR\CLSID\{27EE6A26-DF65-11d0-8C5F-0080C73925BA}\LocalServer32]
@="C:\ServerOfTheApes.exe"
```

It is expected that the out-of-process server will install these keys at self-installation time. Unlike their in-process counterparts, out-of-process servers do not export the well-known exports DllRegisterServer and DllUnregisterServer.

Instead, an out-of-process server must check the command line for the distinguished command-line switches /RegServer and /UnregServer.[1] Given the preceding registry entries, the SCM will start a new server process using the ServerOfTheApes.exe file the first time an activation request is made for the Gorilla class. It is then the responsibility of the server process to notify the SCM which classes are actually available from the new process.

As discussed in Chapter 3, processes can communicate with the SCM to bind references to class objects, class instances, and persistent instances. COM provides three activation functions to facilitate this (CoGetClassObject, CoCreateInstanceEx, and CoGetInstanceFromFile), as well as higher level monikers to hide the details of how each binding policy is implemented. For each of these three activation policies, the class object is used to bring the object to life. As Chapter 3 discussed, when activating an object in process, the class's DLL is loaded by COM and the well-known entry point DllGetClassObject is used to fetch the appropriate class object. What was not discussed was how objects can be activated across process boundaries.

A process becomes the server process for a particular class by explicitly registering itself with the SCM. Upon registering with the SCM, any activation requests for the class that require out-of-process activation will be dispatched to the registered server process.[2] Server processes register themselves with the SCM using the CoRegisterClassObject API function:

```
HRESULT CoRegisterClassObject(
        [in] REFCLSID rclsid,               // which class?
        [in] IUnknown *pUnkClassObject,     // ptr to class object
        [in] DWORD dwClsCtx,                // locality
        [in] DWORD dwRegCls,                // activation flags
        [out] DWORD *pdwReg);               // association ID
```

When calling CoRegisterClassObject, the COM library holds a reference to the class object provided as the second parameter and associates the class object with its CLSID in an internally maintained table. Depending on the activation flags used in the call, the COM library may also notify the local SCM that the caller's process is now the server process for the designated class. CoRegisterClassObject returns a DWORD that represents the CLSID/Class Object association. This DWORD can be used to terminate the association

---

[1] Well-implemented servers also check for -RegServer and -UnregServer. All four switches are case insensitive.

[2] Depending on how the class is configured in the local registry, the server process's registration may apply to all client processes or just to client processes that execute with the same security credentials and/or window station.

(and potentially inform the SCM that the caller is no longer the CLSID's server process) by calling the CoRevokeClassObject API function:

```
HRESULT CoRevokeClassObject(
        [in] DWORD dwReg); // association ID
```

Many of the subtleties of CoRegisterClassObject revolve around the two DWORD parameters that give the caller control over how and when the class object is available.

The activation flags that are passed as the fourth parameter to CoRegisterClassObject allow the caller to determine when its class object will be made available and for how long. COM provides the following constants for use in this parameter:

```
typedef enum tagREGCLS {
    REGCLS_SINGLEUSE         = 0, // give out class object once
    REGCLS_MULTIPLEUSE       = 1, // give out class object many
    REGCLS_MULTI_SEPARATE    = 2, // give out class object many
    REGCLS_SUSPENDED         = 4, // do not notify SCM (flag)
    REGCLS_SURROGATE         = 8  // used with DLL Surrogates
} REGCLS;
```

The REGCLS_SURROGATE value is used in DLL surrogate implementations, which are discussed later in this chapter. The two primary values are REGCLS_SINGLEUSE and REGCLS_MULTIPLEUSE. The former tells the COM library to use a class object to service only one activation request. Once the first activation request occurs, COM removes the registered class object from public view. If a second activation request is made, COM must use a different registered class object. If no other class object with the same CLSID is available, COM will create another server process to satisfy the request.

In contrast, the REGCLS_MULTIPLEUSE flag indicates that the class object may be used multiple times until a call to CoRevokeClassObject removes its entry from the COM library's class table. The flag REGCLS_MULTI_SEPARATE addresses subsequent in-process activation requests that may occur in the caller's process. If the caller registers a class object using REGCLS_MULTIPLEUSE, COM assumes that any in-process activation requests from the caller's process should *not* load a distinct in-process server but should, instead, just use the registered class object. This means that even if the caller only registered the class object using the CLSCTX_LOCAL_SERVER flag, the registered class object will be used to satisfy in-process requests from the same process. If this behavior is unacceptable, the caller can register the class object using the REGCLS_MULTI_SEPARATE flag, which informs COM to use the registered class object for in-process requests only *if* the CLSCTX_INPROC_SERVER flag was used to register the class. This means that the following call to CoRegisterClassObject:

```
hr = CoRegisterClassObject(CLSID_Me, &g_coMe,
            CLSCTX_LOCAL_SERVER, REGCLS_MULTIPLEUSE, &dw);
```

is equivalent to

```
hr = CoRegisterClassObject(CLSID_Me, &g_coMe,
            CLSCTX_LOCAL_SERVER|CLSCTX_INPROC,
            REGCLS_MULTI_SEPARATE, &dw);
```

In either case, if the following call were made from the caller's process:

```
hr = CoGetClassObject(CLSID_Me, CLSCTX_INPROC, 0,
                    IID_IUnknown, (void**)&pUnkCO);
```

no DLL would be loaded; instead, COM would satisfy the request using the class object registered using CoRegisterClassObject. If, however, the server process had called CoRegisterClassObject as follows:

```
hr = CoRegisterClassObject(CLSID_Me, &g_coMe,
                    CLSCTX_LOCAL_SERVER,
                    REGCLS_MULTI_SEPARATE, &dw);
```

any in-process activation requests for CLSID_Me issued from within the server process would force a DLL to be loaded.

CoRegisterClassObject associates the registered class object with the apartment of the caller. This means that all incoming method requests will execute in the caller's apartment. If the class object exports the IClassFactory interface, this specifically means that the CreateInstance method will execute in the caller's apartment. The results of the CreateInstance method will be marshaled from the class object's apartment, which means that instances of the class will belong to the same apartment as the class object.[3]

Server processes can register class objects for more than one class. If the class objects are registered to run in the MTA of the process, this means that incoming activation requests may be serviced as soon as the first call to

---

[3] It is technically possible for the CreateInstance method to force the object to be created in a distinct apartment using standard multiapartment programming techniques. However, the de facto implementation of CreateInstance simply instantiates a new object while executing in the current apartment.

CoRegisterClassObject completes. In many MTA-based server processes, this can cause problems as the process may have further initialization to perform. To avoid this problem, the Windows NT 4.0 release of COM introduced the REG-CLS_SUSPENDED flag. When adding this flag to a CoRegisterClassObject call, the COM library does not notify the SCM that the class is available. This prevents incoming activation requests from arriving in the server process. The COM library does associate the CLSID with the class object; however, it marks the entry in the library's class table as suspended. To remove this designation, COM provides an API function, CoResumeClassObjects:

```
HRESULT CoResumeClassObjects(void);
```

CoResumeClassObjects does two things. First, it marks all suspended class objects as valid for use. Second, it sends a single notification to the SCM informing the SCM that all of the formerly suspended class objects are now available in the server process. This notification is atomic; that is, it updates the SCM's machine-wide class table en masse for all classes that were registered by the caller.

Given the three API functions just described, it is simple to create a server process that exports one or more classes. The following is a simple program that exports three classes from the server's MTA:

```
int WINAPI WinMain(HINSTANCE, HINSTANCE, LPSTR, int) {
// define a singleton class object for each class
  static GorillaClass s_gorillaClass;
  static OrangutanClass s_orangutanClass;
  static ChimpClass s_chimpClass;
  DWORD rgdwReg[3];
  const DWORD dwRegCls= REGCLS_MULTIPLEUSE|REGCLS_SUSPENDED;
  const DWORD dwClsCtx = CLSCTX_LOCAL_SERVER;
// enter the MTA
  HRESULT hr = CoInitializeEx(0, COINIT_MULTITHREADED);
  assert(SUCCEEDED(hr));

// register class objects with COM library's class table
  hr = CoRegisterClassObject(CLSID_Gorilla, &s_gorillaClass,
                             dwClsCtx, dwRegCls, rgdwReg);
  assert(SUCCEEDED(hr));
  hr = CoRegisterClassObject(CLSID_Orangutan,
          &s_orangutanClass, dwClsCtx, dwRegCls, rgdwReg + 1);
  assert(SUCCEEDED(hr));
  hr = CoRegisterClassObject(CLSID_Chimp, &s_chimpClass,
                             dwClsCtx, dwRegCls, rgdwReg + 2);
```

```
  assert(SUCCEEDED(hr));
// notify the SCM
  hr = CoResumeClassObjects();
  assert(SUCCEEDED(hr));
// keep process alive until event is signaled
  extern HANDLE g_heventShutdown;
  WaitForSingleObject(g_heventShutdown, INFINITE);
// remove entries from COM library's class table
  for (int n = 0; n < 3; n++)
    CoRevokeClassObject(rgdwReg[n]);
// leave the MTA
  CoUninitialize();
  return 0;
}
```

This code fragment assumes that a Win32 Event object will be initialized somewhere else in the process as follows:

```
HANDLE g_heventShutdown = CreateEvent(0, TRUE, FALSE, 0);
```

With this event in place, the server can be shut down in an orderly fashion simply by calling the SetEvent API function:

```
SetEvent(g_heventShutdown);
```

which will trigger the shutdown sequence in the main thread. Had the server been implemented as an STA-based server, it would be necessary for the main thread to run a windows message pump in lieu of waiting for a Win32 Event. This is required to allow incoming ORPC requests to enter the apartment of the main thread.

Server Lifetime Revisited

The example shown in the previous section did not address exactly how and when a server process should shut down. In general, a server process controls its own lifetime and can elect to shut down at any time it chooses. Although it is legal for a server process to remain running indefinitely, most server processes elect to shut down when there are no outstanding references to their objects or class objects. This is similar to the policy used by most in-process servers in their implementation of DllCanUnloadNow. Recall from Chapter 3 that a server typically implemented two routines that were called as interface pointers were acquired or released by external clients:

```
// reasons to remain loaded
LONG g_cLocks = 0;
// called from AddRef + IClassFactory::LockServer(TRUE)
void LockModule(void)
{ InterlockedIncrement(&g_cLocks); }
// called from Release + IClassFactory::LockServer(FALSE)
void UnlockModule(void)
{ InterlockedDecrement(&g_cLocks); }
```

This made the implementation of DllCanUnloadNow extremely simple:

```
STDAPI DllCanUnloadNow() {return g_cLocks ? S_FALSE : S_OK;}
```

The DllCanUnloadNow routine would be called when the client elected to garbage-collect its address space by calling CoFreeUnusedLibraries.

There are several differences in how EXE-based servers handle server shutdown. First, it is the job of the server process to initiate its own shutdown proactively. Unlike in-process servers, there is no garbage collector that will query an out-of-process server if it would like to be shut down. Instead, the server process must explicitly initiate its own shut down when appropriate. If a Win32 Event is used to shut down the server, then the process must call the SetEvent API function:

```
void UnlockModule(void) {
  if (InterlockedDecrement(&g_cLocks) == 0) {
    extern HANDLE g_heventShutdown;
    SetEvent(g_heventShutdown);
  }
}
```

If instead the server's main thread is servicing a Windows MSG queue, some API must be used to terminate the loop. The most direct technique is to use PostThreadMessage to post a WM_QUIT message to the main thread:

```
void UnlockModule(void) {
  if (InterlockedDecrement(&g_cLocks) == 0) {
    extern DWORD g_dwMainThreadID; // set from main thread
    PostThreadMessage(g_dwMainThreadID, WM_QUIT, 0, 0);
  }
}
```

If an STA-based server process knows it will never create additional threads, it can use the somewhat simpler PostQuitMessage API function:

```
void UnlockModule(void) {
  if (InterlockedDecrement(&g_cLocks) == 0)
    PostQuitMessage(0);
}
```

This technique works only if called from the main thread of the server process.

Another difference between in-process and out-of-process server lifetime management is related to the forces that must keep the server loaded or running. In an in-process server, there are two forces: outstanding references to objects and outstanding calls to IClassFactory::LockServer(TRUE). The first of these forces needs to be examined in the context of an out-of-process server.

Certainly, a server should remain available while external clients have outstanding references to a server's class objects. For an in-process server, this is implemented as follows:

```
STDMETHODIMP_(ULONG) MyClassObject::AddRef(void) {
  LockModule(); // note outstanding reference
  return 2;      // non-heap-based object
}
STDMETHODIMP_(ULONG) MyClassObject::Release(void) {
  UnlockModule(); // note destroyed reference
  return 1;       // non-heap-based object
}
```

This is the mandatory behavior, because if a DLL is unloaded while there are outstanding references to class objects, subsequent calls to even the Release method would cause the client process to crash.

Unfortunately, the preceding implementation of AddRef and Release is inappropriate for out-of-process servers. Recall that after entering a COM apartment, the first thing a typical out-of-process server does is register its class objects with the COM library by calling CoRegisterClassObject. However, while the class table holds a class object, there is at least one outstanding COM reference to the class object. This means that after registering its class objects, the module-wide lock count will be nonzero. These self-imposed references will not be released until the server process calls CoRevokeClassObject. Unfortunately, a typical server process will not call CoRevokeClassObject until the module-wide lock count reaches zero, which means that the server process will never shut down.

To break the cyclical relationship between the class table and the server's lifetime, most out-of-process implementations of class objects simply ignore outstanding calls to AddRef and Release:

```
STDMETHODIMP_(ULONG) MyClassObject::AddRef(void) {
  // ignore outstanding reference
  return 2;      // non-heap-based object
}


STDMETHODIMP_(ULONG) MyClassObject::Release(void) {
  // ignore destroyed reference
  return 1;          // non-heap-based object
}
```

This means that after registering its class objects, the module-wide lock count will remain at zero.

At first glance, this implementation implies that the server process may terminate while outstanding references to its class objects exist. This behavior actually depends on the implementation of the class object. Recall that the server should remain running as long as there are *external* references to its class objects. The preceding AddRef and Release modifications affect only the *internal* references held by the COM library's class table and are therefore ignored. When an external client requests a reference to one of the server process's class objects, the SCM enters the class object's apartment to retrieve a reference to the class object. At this time, a call to CoMarshalInterface is made to serialize an object reference for use by the client. If the class object implements the IExternalConnection interface, it can note when external references are outstanding and use this information to control server lifetime. Assuming that a class object implements the IExternalConnection interface, the following would achieve the desired effect:

```
STDMETHODIMP_(DWORD) MyClassObject::AddConnection(
                                    DWORD extconn, DWORD) {
  DWORD res = 0;
  if (extconn&EXTCONN_STRONG) {
    LockModule(); // note external reference
    res = InterlockedIncrement(&m_cExtRef);
  }
  return res;
}
STDMETHODIMP_(DWORD) MyClassObject::ReleaseConnection(
        DWORD extconn, DWORD, BOOL bLastReleaseKillsStub){
  DWORD res = 0;
  if (extconn&EXTCONN_STRONG) {
    UnlockModule(); // note external reference
    res = InterlockedDecrement(&m_cExtRef);
    if (res == 0 & bLastReleaseKillsStub)
```

```
        CoDisconnectObject((IExternalConnection*)this, 0);
    }
    return res;
}
```

Note that the module-wide lock count will be nonzero as long as there are outstanding *external* references to the class object, but *internal* references held by the COM library are ignored.

Although the technique of using IExternalConnection on class objects has worked since the early days of COM, few implementors actually used this technique. Instead, most servers would typically ignore outstanding external references to class objects and prematurely terminate their server processes. This situation was encouraged by the presence of the method LockServer on the IClassFactory interface, which lulled developers into thinking that clients could actually ensure that a server would remain running. While most server implementors would properly lock their module in their LockServer methods, there was no reliable way for a client to call this method. Consider the following client code:

```
IClassFactory *pcf = 0;
HRESULT hr = CoGetClassObject(CLSID_You,CLSCTX_LOCAL_SERVER,
                     0, IID_IClassFactory, (void**)&pcf);
if (SUCCEEDED(hr))
  hr = pcf->LockServer(TRUE); // keep server running?
```

Under the original releases of COM, this code fragment has a serious race condition. Note that there is a gap between the calls to CoGetClassObject and IClassFactory::LockServer. During this gap of time, it is possible for another client to destroy the last remaining instance of the class. Because the outstanding reference to the class object is ignored by naive server implementations, the server process will shut down prior to the original client's call to LockServer. In theory, this could be addressed as follows:

```
IClassFactory *pcf = 0;
HRESULT hr = S_OK;
do {
  if (pcf) pcf->Release();
  hr = CoGetClassObject(CLSID_You,CLSCTX_LOCAL_SERVER,
                     0, IID_IClassFactory, (void**)&pcf);
  if (FAILED(hr))
    break;
  hr = pcf->LockServer(TRUE); // keep server running?
} while (FAILED(hr));
```

Note that this code fragment repeatedly tries to attach to a class object and lock it until the call to LockServer is successful. If the server prematurely terminates between a call to CoGetClassObject and LockServer, the LockServer call will return an error indicating a disconnected proxy, which forces the sequence to repeat. Under Windows NT 3.51 or earlier, this grotesque code was the only reliable way to acquire a reference to a class object.

Acknowledging that many server implementations were not using IExternalConnection to manage server lifetime properly, the Windows NT 4.0 release of COM introduced the following enhancement to compensate for these naive implementations. When marshaling a reference to a class object in response to a CoGetClassObject call, the SCM will call the class object's IClassFactory::LockServer method. Since the vast majority of servers implement IClassFactory on their class objects, this enhancement to the COM runtimes repairs most defects. However, if a class object does not export the IClassFactory interface *or* if the server must also execute on pre-Window NT 4.0 releases of COM, the IExternalConnection technique must be used.

One additional issue related to server lifetime must be discussed. Note that when a server elects to shut down, it signals that the main thread of the server application should begin its shutdown sequence prior to exiting the process. Part of this shutdown sequence includes calling CoRevokeClassObject to unregister its class objects. However, if the implementations of UnlockModule shown previously are used, there is a serious race condition. It is possible for additional activation requests to arrive at the server process between the time the server signals the main thread via a call to SetEvent or PostThreadMessage and the time the server revokes its class objects via calls to CoRevokeClassObject. If new objects are created during this interval of time, there is no way to signal to the main thread that shutdown is a bad idea and that the process now has new objects to service. To eliminate this race condition, COM provides the following two API functions:

```
ULONG CoAddRefServerProcess(void);
ULONG CoReleaseServerProcess(void);
```

These two routines manage a module-wide lock count on behalf of the caller. These routines temporarily block all access to the COM library to ensure that no new activation requests will be serviced while the lock count is being adjusted. In addition, if CoReleaseServerProcess detects that it is removing the last lock on the process, it will internally mark all of the process's class objects as suspended and notify the SCM that the process is no longer the server for its CLSIDs.

The following routines correctly implement server lifetime in an out-of-process server:

```
void LockModule(void) {
  CoAddRefServerProcess(); // COM maintains lock count
}
void UnlockModule(void) {
  if (CoReleaseServerProcess() == 0)
    SetEvent(g_heventShutdown);
}
```

Note that it is still the responsibility of the caller to shut its process down in an orderly fashion. However, once the decision is made to shut down, no new activation requests will be serviced by this process.

Even when CoAddRefServerProcess/CoReleaseServerProcess is used, there are still possibilities for race conditions. While CoReleaseServerProcess is executing, it is possible that the RPC layer will receive an incoming activation request from the SCM. If the call from the SCM is dispatched after CoReleaseServerProcess releases its lock on the COM library, the activation request will note that the class object has been marked as suspended and a distinguished error code will be returned to the SCM (CO_E_SERVER_STOPPING). When the SCM detects this distinguished error code, it simply starts a new instance of the server process and retries the request once the new server process registers itself. Despite the safeguards used by the COM library, there are still possibilities that an incoming activation request will execute concurrently with the final CoReleaseServerProcess call. To address this, a server can explicitly return CO_E_SERVER_STOPPING from both IClassFactory::CreateInstance and IPersistFile::Load if it detects that a request has been made after issuing a shutdown request. The following code demonstrates this technique:

```
STDMETHODIMP MyClassObject::CreateInstance(IUnknown *puo,
                          REFIID riid, void **ppv) {
  LockModule(); // ensure we don't shut down while in call
  HRESULT hr; *ppv = 0;
// shutdown initiated?
  DWORD dw = WaitForSingleObject(g_heventShutdown,0);
  if (dw == WAIT_OBJECT_0) hr = CO_E_SERVER_STOPPING;
  else {
    // normal CreateInstance implementation
  }
  UnlockModule();
  return hr;
}
```

At the time of this writing, no commercial COM class libraries implement this technique.

Application IDs

The Windows NT 4.0 release of COM introduced the concept of COM applications. COM applications are identified by a GUID (called an AppID in this context) and represent a server process for one or more classes. Each CLSID can be associated with exactly one Application ID. This association appears in the local registry using the AppID named value:

```
[HKCR\CLSID\{27EE6A4E-DF65-11d0-8C5F-0080C73925BA}]
@="Gorilla"
AppID="{27EE6A4D-DF65-11d0-8C5F-0080C73925BA}"
```

All of the classes that belong to the same COM application will have the same AppID and will share the same remote activation and security settings. These settings are stored in the local registry under the key:

```
HKEY_CLASSES_ROOT\AppID
```

Like CLSIDs, AppIDs can be registered on a per-user basis under Windows NT 5.0 or greater. Because servers implemented prior to the release of Windows NT 4.0 do not explicitly register their AppIDs, COM configuration tools (*e.g.,* DCOMCNFG.EXE, OLEVIEW.EXE) will automatically create a new AppID for these legacy servers. To synthesize an AppID for legacy servers, these tools automatically add the AppID named value to all of the CLSIDs exported by a particular local server. When adding these named values, DCOMCNFG or OLEVIEW simply uses the first CLSID it encounters for a particular server as an AppID. Applications that are developed after the release of Windows NT 4.0 can (and should) use a distinct GUID for their AppID.

Most AppID settings can be manipulated using DCOMCNFG.EXE, which is a standard component of Windows NT 4.0 or greater. DCOMCNFG.EXE provides administrators with an easy-to-use interface for controlling remoting and security settings. A more powerful tool, OLEVIEW.EXE, subsumes most of the functionality of DCOMCNFG.EXE in addition to providing a very COM-centric view of the registry. Both tools are extremely intuitive to use and both are essential for COM development work.

The simplest AppID setting is RemoteServerName. This named value indicates which host machine to use for remote activation requests that do not explicitly indicate a remote host name using COSERVERINFO. Consider the following registry settings:

```
[HKCR\AppID\{27EE6A4D-DF65-11d0-8C5F-0080C73925BA}]
@="Ape Server"
RemoteServerName="www.apes.com"

[HKCR\CLSID\{27EE6A4E-DF65-11d0-8C5F-0080C73925BA}]
@="Gorilla"
AppID="{27EE6A4D-DF65-11d0-8C5F-0080C73925BA}"

[HKCR\CLSID\{27EE6A4F-DF65-11d0-8C5F-0080C73925BA}]
@="Chimp"
AppID="{27EE6A4D-DF65-11d0-8C5F-0080C73925BA}"
```

If the client issues an activation request as follows:

```
IApeClass *pac = 0;
HRESULT hr = CoGetClassObject(CLSID_Chimp,
     CLSCTX_REMOTE_SERVER, 0, IID_IApeClass, (void**)&pac);
```

the client-side SCM will forward the request to the SCM on www.apes.com, where the request will be treated as a local activation request. Note that if the client provides an explicit host name:

```
IApeClass *pac = 0;
COSERVERINFO csi; ZeroMemory(&csi, sizeof(csi));
csi.pwszName = OLESTR("www.dogs.com");
HRESULT hr = CoGetClassObject(CLSID_Chimp,
    CLSCTX_REMOTE_SERVER, &csi, IID_IApeClass, (void**)&pac);
```

the `RemoteServerName` setting is ignored and the request is forwarded to www.dogs.com.

The more common situation is one in which clients do not explicitly specify a host name or a locality preference. Consider the following call to `CoGetClassObject`:

```
IApeClass *pac = 0;
HRESULT hr = CoGetClassObject(CLSID_Chimp,
     CLSCTX_ALL, 0, IID_IApeClass, (void**)&pac);
```

Because no host name is specified, the SCM will first look for the following key in the local Registry:

```
[HKCR\CLSID\{27EE6A4F-DF65-11d0-8C5F-0080C73925BA}]
```

If this key is not available locally, COM will then consult the Windows NT 5.0 class store if available. If at this point the class's registry key is available, the SCM will then look for the `InprocServer32` subkey:

```
[HKCR\CLSID\{27EE6A4F-DF65-11d0-8C5F-0080C73925BA}\InprocServer32]
@="C:\somefile.dll"
```

If this key is found, the class will be activated by loading the DLL indicated in the Registry. If this key is not found, the SCM looks for the `InprocHandler32` subkey:

```
[HKCR\CLSID\{27EE6A4F-DF65-11d0-8C5F-0080C73925BA}\InprocHandler32]
@="C:\somefile.dll"
```

If the class has a handler key, again, the class will be activated by loading the DLL indicated in the Registry. If neither in-process subkey is available, the SCM assumes the activation request must be out of process. At this point, the SCM checks to see if a server process has a class object currently registered for the requested CLSID.[4] If so, the SCM reaches into the server process and marshals an object reference from the appropriate class object and returns this to the caller's apartment, where it is unmarshaled prior to returning control to the caller. If the class object was registered by the server process using the flag `REGCLS_SIN-GLEUSE`, the SCM then forgets that the class is available in the server process and will not use it for subsequent activation requests.

The scenario just described is correct if a server process is already running. If, however, the SCM receives an out-of-process activation request but no server process has registered itself for the requested CLSID, the SCM will start a server process if one is not already running. COM supports three process models for creating servers: NT Services, normal processes, and surrogate processes. NT services and normal processes are very similar, and the exact reasons one might favor one over the other are discussed later in this chapter. Surrogate processes are used primarily to host legacy in-process servers in distinct server processes. This provides the benefits of remote activation and fault isolation for legacy DLLs or classes that must be packaged as a DLL (*e.g.*, the Java virtual machine). Irrespective of which model is used to create a server process, the server process has 120 seconds (or 30 seconds under Windows NT Service Pack 2 or earlier) to register the requested class object using `CoRegisterClassObject`. If the server process fails to register itself in time, the SCM will fail the caller's activation request.

---

[4] Technically, there must be a class object registered that is valid in the caller's security context.

When creating a server process, the SCM first checks to see if the requested class's corresponding AppID has a LocalService named value:

```
[HKCR\AppID\{27EE6A4D-DF65-11d0-8C5F-0080C73925BA}]
LocalService="apesvc"
```

If this named value is present, the SCM uses the NT Service Control Manager to start the NT service designated in the Registry (*e.g.*, apesvc). If the LocalService named value is not present, the SCM then looks for the LocalServer32 subkey at the designated CLSID key:

```
[HKCR\CLSID\{27EE6A4F-DF65-11d0-8C5F-0080C73925BA}\LocalServer32]
@="C:\somefile.exe"
```

If this key is present, the SCM will use the CreateProcess (or CreateProcessAsUser) API function to start the server process. If no LocalService or LocalServer32 entry is present, the SCM then looks to see if a surrogate process has been designated for the class's AppID:

```
[HKCR\AppID\{27EE6A4D-DF65-11d0-8C5F-0080C73925BA}]
DllSurrogate=""
```

If the DllSurrogate named value is present but empty, the SCM will start the default surrogate process (dllhost.exe). If the DllSurrogate named value is present but refers to a valid filename:

```
[HKCR\AppID\{27EE6A4D-DF65-11d0-8C5F-0080C73925BA}]
DllSurrogate="C:\somefile.exe"
```

the SCM will start the designated server process. In either case, the surrogate process registers itself with the COM library (and SCM) as a surrogate process using the CoRegisterSurrogate API function:

```
HRESULT CoRegisterSurrogate([in] ISurrogate *psg);
```

This API function expects the surrogate process to provide an implementation of the ISurrogate interface:

```
[ uuid(00000022-0000-0000-C000-000000000046), object ]
interface ISurrogate : IUnknown {
// SCM asking surrogate to load inprocess class object and
// call CoRegisterClassObject using REGCLS_SUSPENDED
```

```
  HRESULT LoadDllServer([in] REFCLSID rclsid);
// SCM asking surrogate to shut down
  HRESULT FreeSurrogate();
}
```

The ISurrogate interface provides COM with a mechanism for requesting the surrogate process to register class objects and to shut down. The surrogate mechanism exists primarily to support remote activation of legacy in-process servers. In general, surrogates should be used only when in-process servers cannot be rebuilt as out-of-process servers.

Finally, if none of these registry keys or values is present, the SCM will look for a RemoteServerName entry under the class's corresponding AppID key:

```
[HKCR\AppID\{27EE6A4D-DF65-11d0-8C5F-0080C73925BA}]
RemoteServerName="www.apes.com"
```

If this value is present, the activation request will be forwarded to the SCM on the designated host machine. Note that even if the client specified only the CLSCTX_LOCAL_SERVER flag in the initial activation request, the request will be forwarded *if no local server processes are registered.*

One additional factor that can reroute activation requests applies only to CoGetInstanceFromFile requests (including calls to BindToObject on a file moniker). By default, if the filename used to name a persistent object refers to a file on a remote file system, COM will use the algorithm just described to determine where to activate the object. If, however, the class's AppID has an ActivateAtStorage named value and its value is "Y" or "y," COM will forward the activation request to the machine on which the file resides provided the caller did not pass an explicit host name via the COSERVERINFO structure. This ensures that only one instance will exist on the entire network.

COM and Security

The original version of COM did not address security. This could be seen as an oversight, as many nonremotable NT primitives (*e.g.,* processes, threads) can be secured, even though they cannot be manipulated remotely. The release of Windows NT 4.0 forced security to be added to COM, as it became possible for server processes to be accessed from potentially any machine on the network. Fortunately, because COM uses RPC as its transport, COM security simply leverages the existing security infrastructure of RPC.

COM security can be broken down into three categories: *authentication, access control,* and *token management.* Authentication deals with ensuring that a message is authentic, that is, that the sender is indeed who he says he is and that a given message is indeed from the sender. Access control addresses who is allowed to access a server's objects and who is allowed to start a server process. Token management is required to control which credentials are used when starting server processes and when executing inside a method call. COM provides *somewhat* reasonable defaults for each of these three aspects of security, making it theoretically possible to write COM applications without considering security. These defaults are based on the principle of least surprise; that is, if a programmer does nothing explicit with security, it is unlikely that any holes in the NT security model will be introduced. However, building even a simple distributed COM-based application requires that each aspect of security be given a nontrivial amount of attention.

Most aspects of COM security can be configured by placing the correct information in the Registry. The DCOMCNFG.EXE program allows administrators to adjust most (but not all) of the settings related to COM security. For most (but not all) of these settings, the application programmer can elect to override the registry settings using explicit API functions. In general, most applications use a combination of DCOMCNFG.EXE settings and explicit API functions. The former is easier for system administrators to debug, while the latter provides both greater flexibility as well as insulation from DCOMCNFG.EXE abuse.

COM security uses the underlying RPC facilities for authentication and impersonation. Recall that RPC uses loadable transport modules to allow new network protocols to be added to the system after the fact. These transport modules are named using protocol sequences (*e.g.,* "ncadg_ip_udp") that are mapped in the registry to a specific transport DLL. This allows third parties to install support for new transport protocols without modifying the COM library. Similarly, RPC supports loadable security packages to allow new security protocols to be added to the system after the fact. These security packages are named using integers that are mapped in the Registry to a specific security package DLL. These DLLs must conform to the Security Support Provider Interface (SSPI), which was derived from the Internet Draft Standard GSSAPI.

The system header files define several constants for known security packages. The following is the current list of known security packages at the time of this writing:

```
enum {
    RPC_C_AUTHN_NONE = 0,              // no authentication package
    RPC_C_AUTHN_DCE_PRIVATE = 1,       // DCE private key (not used)
    RPC_C_AUTHN_DCE_PUBLIC = 2,        // DCE public key (not used)
    RPC_C_AUTHN_DEC_PUBLIC = 4,        // Digital Equip. (not used)
    RPC_C_AUTHN_WINNT = 10,            // NT Lan Manager
```

```
        RPC_C_AUTHN_GSS_KERBEROS,
        RPC_C_AUTHN_MQ = 100,                // MS Message Queue package
        RPC_C_AUTHN_DEFAULT = 0xFFFFFFFFL
    };
```

RPC_C_AUTHN_WINNT indicates that the NT LAN Manager (NTLM) authentication protocol should be used. RPC_C_AUTHN_GSS_KERBEROS indicates that the Kerberos authentication protocol should be used. Under Windows NT 4.0, only NTLM is supported unless a third-party SSP is installed. Windows NT 5.0 will ship with support for at least NTLM and Kerberos. Consult the current documentation for availability information regarding additional authentication packages.

Each interface proxy can be configured independently to use a different security package. When an interface proxy is configured to use a security protocol, the corresponding SSP DLL is loaded into the client process. To allow the secure connection request to be accepted, the server process must have registered and loaded the corresponding SSP DLL prior to receiving the first ORPC call from the client. When a connection is configured to use a security package, the corresponding SSP DLL works in conjunction with the RPC runtime layer and is given an opportunity to see every packet that is transmitted and received on behalf of the particular connection. SSP DLLs can send additional security-specific information in each packet as well as modify the marshaled parameter state to allow encryption. DCE RPC (and COM) allows six levels of authentication protection, which vary from no protection to full encryption of all parameter state:

```
    enum {
      RPC_C_AUTHN_LEVEL_DEFAULT,        // use default level for pkg
      RPC_C_AUTHN_LEVEL_NONE,           // no authentication
      RPC_C_AUTHN_LEVEL_CONNECT,        // only authenticate credentials
      RPC_C_AUTHN_LEVEL_CALL,           // protect message headers
      RPC_C_AUTHN_LEVEL_PKT,            // protect packet headers
      RPC_C_AUTHN_LEVEL_PKT_INTEGRITY,  // protect parameter state_
      RPC_C_AUTHN_LEVEL_PKT_PRIVACY,    // encrypt parameter state
    };
```

Each successive level of authentication subsumes the previous level's functionality. RPC_C_AUTHN_LEVEL_NONE indicates that no authentication will take place. RPC_C_AUTHN_LEVEL_CONNECT indicates that at the first method call, the client's credentials must be authenticated at the server. If the client does not have valid credentials, the ORPC call will fail with E_ACCESSDENIED. How these credentials are validated is dependent on the SSP in use. Under NTLM, the server process issues a *challenge* to the client process. The challenge is simply an unpredictable large random number. The client uses an encoded version of the caller's password to encrypt the challenge, which is then sent back to the server as the *response*. The server then encrypts the original challenge with what it thinks the encoded password is and then compares the result with the response it received from the client. If the client's response matches the server's encrypted challenge, then the client's identity is assumed to be authentic. Because the NTLMSSP piggybacks the challenge-response handshake onto the initial packets that are sent by the RPC runtime to synchronize sequence numbers, no additional client-server network traffic is generated. Depending on the type of account (domain, local), there may or may not be additional traffic to a domain controller to support pass-through authentication.

When the RPC_C_AUTHN_LEVEL_CONNECT level is used, no additional security-specific information is exchanged once the initial credentials are verified. This means that malicious programs can conceivably intercept messages on the network and replay RPC calls simply by modifying the DCE sequence numbers in the packet headers. To add protection against call replay, the RPC_C_AUTHN_LEVEL_CALL level should be used. This informs the SSP DLLs to also protect the RPC header of the first packet of each RPC request or response message by concatenating a one-way hash key in the transmitted packet. Because an RPC request or response may need to be fragmented into more than one network packet, the RPC API also supports the RPC_C_AUTHN_LEVEL_PKT level. This level protects against replay at the network packet level, which, because an RPC message may transcend two or more packets, is greater protection than the RPC_C_AUTHN_LEVEL_CALL level.

Up to and including the RPC_C_AUTHN_LEVEL_PKT level, the SSP DLL more or less ignores the actual payload of the RPC packets and protects only the integrity of the RPC headers. To ensure that the marshaled parameter state is not modified by a malicious agent on the network, RPC provides the RPC_C_AUTHN_LEVEL_PKT_INTEGRITY level. This level causes the SSP DLLs also to perform a checksum on the marshaled parameter state and verify that the contents of the packet have not been modified in transit. Because this level of authentication requires each transmitted byte to be processed by the SSP DLL, it is considerably slower than the RPC_C_AUTHN_LEVEL_PKT level and should be used only for security-sensitive situations.

Up to and including the RPC_C_AUTHN_LEVEL_PKT_INTEGRITY level, the actual payload of the RPC packets is sent as clear text (*e.g.,* unencrypted). To ensure that the marshaled parameter state cannot be seen by a malicious agent on the network, RPC provides the RPC_C_AUTHN_LEVEL_PKT_PRIVACY level. This level causes the SSP DLLs to encrypt the marshaled parameter state prior to transmission. Like all other authentication levels, RPC_C_AUTHN_LEVEL_PKT_PRIVACY subsumes the protection of each level below it. As with RPC_C_AUTHN_LEVEL_PKT_INTEGRITY, each transmitted byte must be processed by the SSP DLL and should be used only for security-sensitive situations to avoid excessive overhead.

The most important API function in COM security is CoInitializeSecurity. Every process that uses COM calls CoInitializeSecurity exactly once, either explicitly or implicitly. CoInitializeSecurity establishes the *automatic* security settings. These settings apply to all imported and exported object references unless explicitly overridden using additional API calls. CoInitializeSecurity configures the underlying RPC runtime to use one or more security packages, and also sets the default authentication level for a process. In addition, CoInitializeSecurity allows the caller to specify which users are allowed to make ORPC calls to the objects exported from the current process. CoInitializeSecurity has a fairly large number of parameters:

```
HRESULT CoInitializeSecurity(
  [in] PSECURITY_DESCRIPTOR pSecDesc, // access control
  [in] LONG   cAuthSvc, // # of sec pkgs (-1 == use defaults)
  [in] SOLE_AUTHENTICATION_SERVICE *rgsAuthSvc, // SSP array
  [in] void   *pReserved1,     // reserved MBZ
  [in] DWORD dwAuthnLevel,     // auto. AUTHN_LEVEL
  [in] DWORD dwImpLevel,       // auto. IMP_LEVEL
  [in] void   *pReserved2,     // reserved MBZ
  [in] DWORD dwCapabilities,   // misc flags
  [in] void   *pReserved3      // reserved MBZ
);
```

Some of these parameters apply only when the process acts as an exporter/server. Others apply only when the process acts as an importer/client. Others apply in both cases.

The first parameter to CoInitializeSecurity, pSecDesc, is applicable only when the process is acting as an exporter. It is used to control which security principals are allowed to access objects exported from this process. This parameter is discussed in detail later in this chapter. The second and third parameters to CoInitializeSecurity, cAuthSvc and rgsAuthSvc, are used when the process acts as an exporter to register one or more authentication packages with the COM library. These two parameters refer to an array of security package descriptions:

```
typedef struct tagSOLE_AUTHENTICATION_SERVICE {
  DWORD     dwAuthnSvc; // which authentication package?
  DWORD     dwAuthzSvc; // which authorization service?
  OLECHAR *pPrincipalName; // server principal name?
```

```
   HRESULT  hr;                    // result of registration
} SOLE_AUTHENTICATION_SERVICE;
```

Under Windows NT 4.0, the only installed authentication service is
RPC_C_AUTHN_WINNT (NTLM). When using NTLM authentication, the autho-
rization service must be RPC_C_AUTHZ_NONE and the server principal name is
not used and must be null.[5] For processes that simply wish to use the default
security package(s) on a particular machine, the values of -1 (cAuthSvc) and
null (rgsAuthSvc) should be used.

The fifth parameter to CoInitializeSecurity, dwAuthnLevel, applies to
both exported and imported object references. The value specified for this
parameter sets the low-watermark authentication level for object references
exported from this process. This means that incoming ORPC calls must use
at least this level of authentication; otherwise, the call will automatically be
rejected. This value also specifies the minimum authentication used by new
interface proxies returned by COM API functions or methods. When COM creates a new interface proxy at unmarshal time, COM discovers the exporter's
low watermark as part of OXID resolution. COM then sets the authentication
level on the new proxy to either the exporter's low watermark or the current
process's low watermark, depending on which is higher. If the process that imports the object reference has an authentication level lower than that of the
exporting process, the exporter's low watermark is used to set the authentication level. This ensures that any ORPC requests that are sent by the interface
proxy will get past the exporter's low watermark. As discussed later in this
chapter, it is possible to change the authentication level explicitly for a particular interface proxy for finer grained control.[6]

The sixth parameter to CoInitializeSecurity, dwImpLevel, applies to imported object references. The value specified for this parameter sets the impersonation level used by all object references returned by CoUnmarshalInterface.
The impersonation level represents the degree of trust the client has toward
the server. This parameter must be one of the following four impersonation
levels:

---

[5] It is possible that these two parameters will be used for other authentication packages.

[6] A particular security package may choose to increase the client/server-specified level depending on the transport protocol used. In particular, NTLM will use RPC_C_AUTHN_LEVEL_PRIVACY for all same-machine calls. In
addition, NTLM will promote RPC_AUTHN_LEVEL_CONNECT and RPC_C_AUTHN_LEVEL_CALL to
RPC_C_AUTHN_LEVEL_PKT for datagram transports (*e.g.*, UDP), and will promote RPC_C_AUTHN_LEVEL_CALL
to RPC_C_AUTHN_LEVEL_PKT for connection-oriented transports (*e.g.*, TCP).

```
enum {
// hide credentials of caller from object
  RPC_C_IMP_LEVEL_ANONYMOUS = 1,
// allow object to query credentials of caller
  RPC_C_IMP_LEVEL_IDENTIFY = 2,
// allow use of caller's credentials up to one-hop away
  RPC_C_IMP_LEVEL_IMPERSONATE = 3,
// allow use of caller's credentials across multiple hops
  RPC_C_IMP_LEVEL_DELEGATE = 4
};
```

The RPC_C_IMP_LEVEL_ANONYMOUS level prevents the object implementation from discovering the security identifier of the caller.[7] The RPC_C_IMP_LEVEL_IDENTIFY level of trust indicates that the object implementation can programmatically determine the caller's security identifier. The RPC_C_IMP_LEVEL_IMPERSONATE level of trust indicates that the server can not only determine the caller's security identifier but also execute OS-level operations using the caller's credentials. This level of trust limits objects to accessing only local resources while using the caller's credentials.[8] In contrast, the RPC_C_IMP_LEVEL_DELEGATE level of trust allows the server to access both local and remote resources using the caller's credentials. This level of trust is not supported by the NTLM authentication protocol but is supported by the Kerberos authentication protocol.

The eighth parameter to CoInitializeSecurity, dwCapabilities, applies to both imported and exported object references. This parameter is a bitmask that can consist of zero or more of the following bits:

```
typedef enum tagEOLE_AUTHENTICATION_CAPABILITIES {
  EOAC_NONE              = 0x0,
  EOAC_MUTUAL_AUTH       = 0x1,
// These are only valid for CoInitializeSecurity
  EOAC_SECURE_REFS       = 0x2,
  EOAC_ACCESS_CONTROL    = 0x4,
  EOAC_APPID             = 0x8
} EOLE_AUTHENTICATION_CAPABILITIES;
```

---

[7] At the time of this writing, both the NTLM and Kerberos SSPs happily accept this value but silently promote it to RPC_C_IMP_LEVEL_IDENTIFY if the connection is to a remote machine.

[8] Technically, RPC_C_IMP_LEVEL_IMPERSONATE allows the caller's credentials to be passed across, at most, one network hop. This effectively limits remote objects to accessing only resources on the object's local machine.

Mutual authentication (EOAC_MUTUAL_AUTH) is not supported under NTLM. It is used to verify that the server is running as the expected security principal. Secure references (EOAC_SECURE_REFS) indicate that COM's distributed reference counting calls will be authenticated to ensure that no malicious agents can tamper with the reference count used by the OR and stub managers to implement life cycle management. EOAC_ACCESS_CONTROL and EOAC_APPID are used to control the semantics of the first parameter to CoInitializeSecurity and are discussed later in this chapter.

As stated earlier in this section, CoInitializeSecurity is called once per process, either explicitly or implicitly. Applications that wish to call CoInitializeSecurity explicitly must do so after the first call to CoInitializeEx but before the "first interesting COM call." The phrase "first interesting COM call" refers to any API function that may require an OXID. This includes CoMarshalInterface and CoUnmarshalInterface and any API calls that implicitly call them. Because calls to CoRegisterClassObject associate class objects with apartments, CoInitializeSecurity must be called prior to registering class objects. The activation APIs (*e.g.,* CoCreateInstanceEx) are an interesting exception. Activation APIs for certain *internal* classes that are part of the COM API (*e.g.,* the global interface table, COM's default access control object) may be called prior to calling CoInitializeSecurity. However, CoInitializeSecurity must be called before any activation calls that actually consult the Registry and load other DLLs or contact other servers. If an application does not explicitly call CoInitializeSecurity, COM will call it implicitly at the first interesting COM call.

When COM implicitly calls CoInitializeSecurity, it reads the values of most of the parameters from the Registry; some of the parameters are stored in a machine-wide registry key, while others are stored under the specific AppID of the application. To derive the AppID of the application, COM looks up the filename of the application process under the

```
HKEY_CLASSES_ROOT\AppID
```

registry key. If COM finds the filename there, it derives the AppID from the AppID named value:

```
[HKCR\AppID\ServerOfTheApes.exe]
AppID="{27EE6A4D-DF65-11d0-8C5F-0080C73925BA}"
```

If no mapping exists, COM assumes the application has no specific security settings in the Registry.

Implicit calls to CoInitializeSecurity find the first parameter, pSecDesc, by looking for a serialized NT SECURITY_DESCRIPTOR at the following named value:

```
[HKCR\AppID\{27EE6A4D-DF65-11d0-8C5F-0080C73925BA}]
AccessPermission=<serialized NT security descriptor>
```

If this named value is not found, COM then looks for the following machine-wide entry:

```
[HKEY_LOCAL_MACHINE\Software\Microsoft\OLE]
DefaultAccessPermission=<serialized NT security descriptor>
```

Both of the registry entries can be easily modified using DCOMCNFG.EXE. If neither of these registry entries is found, COM will create a security descriptor granting access to only the caller's principal and the built-in account SYSTEM. COM uses this security descriptor to grant or deny access to the objects exported from this process using the Win32 API function AccessCheck.

Implicit calls to CoInitializeSecurity use -1 and null for the second and third parameters (cAuthSvc and rgsAuthSvc), indicating that the default security packages should be used. Implicit calls to CoInitializeSecurity find the values for the fifth and sixth parameters (dwAuthnLevel and dwImpLevel) at the following machine-wide registry entry:

```
[HKEY_LOCAL_MACHINE\Software\Microsoft\OLE]
LegacyAuthenticationLevel = 0x5
LegacyImpersonationLevel = 0x3
```

The numeric values 5 and 3 correspond to RPC_C_AUTHN_LEVEL_PKT_INTEGRITY and RPC_C_IMP_LEVEL_IMPERSONATE, respectively. If these named values are missing, the values RPC_C_AUTHN_LEVEL_CONNECT and RPC_C_IMP_LEVEL_IDENTIFY are used. Of the flags used by the eighth parameter to CoInitializeSecurity, dwCapabilities, only EOAC_SECURE_REFS is currently read from the machine-wide registry entry:

```
[HKEY_LOCAL_MACHINE\Software\Microsoft\OLE]
LegacySecureRefs = "Y"
```

If this named value is present and contains either "Y" or "y," then COM will use the EOAC_SECURE_REFS flag; otherwise, COM uses the EOAC_NONE flag. Each of these three legacy authentication settings can be easily modified using DCOMCNFG.EXE.

Programmatic Security

The settings made using CoInitializeSecurity are called the *automatic* security settings because they apply to all marshaled object references automatically. It is often the case that a small number of object references need to use security settings that deviate from the process-wide defaults. The most common scenario arises when a fairly low authentication level is used for performance reasons but one particular interface requires encryption. Rather than force the entire process to use encryption, it is preferable simply to apply encryption to object references that need it.

To allow developers to override the automatic security settings on an interface proxy basis, the proxy manager exposes the IClientSecurity interface:

```
[ local,object,uuid(0000013D-0000-0000-C000-000000000046) ]
interface IClientSecurity : IUnknown {
// get security settings for interface proxy pProxy
  HRESULT QueryBlanket([in]  IUnknown *pProxy,
    [out] DWORD *pAuthnSvc, [out] DWORD *pAuthzSvc,
    [out] OLECHAR **pServerPrincName,
    [out] DWORD *pAuthnLevel, [out] DWORD *pImpLevel,
    [out] void **pAuthInfo, [out] DWORD  *pCapabilities
  );
// change security settings for interface proxy pProxy
  HRESULT SetBlanket([in] IUnknown  *pProxy,
    [in] DWORD AuthnSvc, [in] DWORD AuthzSvc,
    [in] OLECHAR *pServerPrincName,
    [in] DWORD AuthnLevel, [in] DWORD ImpLevel,
    [in] void *pAuthInfo, [in] DWORD Capabilities
  );
// duplicate an interface proxy
  HRESULT CopyProxy([in]   IUnknown  *pProxy,
                    [out] IUnknown **ppCopy
  );
}
```

The second, third, and fourth parameters to SetBlanket and QueryBlanket correspond to the three members of the SOLE_AUTHENTICATION_SERVICE data structure. Under Windows NT 4.0, the only legal values are RPC_C_AUTHN_WINNT, RPC_C_AUTHZ_NONE, and null, respectively.

As shown in Figure 6.1, each individual interface proxy has its own authentication settings. The IClientSecurity::SetBlanket method allows a caller to change these settings for a particular interface proxy. The

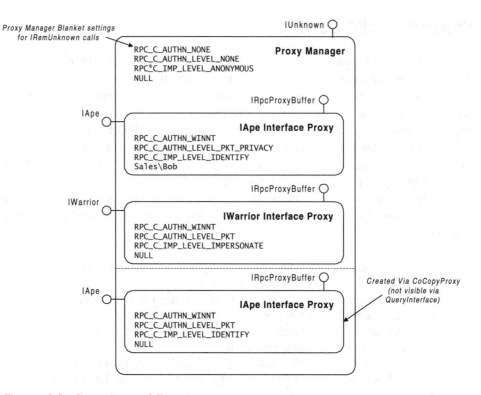

Figure 6.1 Security and Proxies

IClientSecurity::QueryBlanket method allows a caller to read these settings for a particular interface proxy. For parameters that the caller does not care about, null pointers can be passed. The IClientSecurity::CopyProxy method allows a caller to duplicate an interface proxy. This allows modifications to be made on a duplicate version of the interface that will not be returned by subsequent calls to QueryInterface on the proxy manager. Ideally, security settings should be made only on duplicated interface proxies to isolate the modified proxy from the proxy manager's normal QueryInterface implementation, as well as to allow multiple threads to independently change security blanket settings between method invocations.

All the parameters to IClientSecurity::SetBlanket and IClient-Security::QueryBlanket correspond to parameters to CoInitialize-Security with one notable exception. The seventh parameter (pAuthInfo) points to a set of client credentials. The exact form of these credentials is security package specific. For the NTLM security package, this parameter can point to a COAUTHIDENTITY structure:

```
typedef struct _COAUTHIDENTITY {
   OLECHAR *User;            // user account name
   ULONG    UserLength;      // wcslen(User)
   OLECHAR *Domain;          // Domain/Machine name
   ULONG    DomainLength;    // wcslen(Domain)
   OLECHAR *Password;        // cleartext password
   ULONG    PasswordLength;  // wcslen(Password)
   ULONG    Flags; // must be SEC_WINNT_AUTH_IDENTITY_UNICODE
} COAUTHIDENTITY;
```

This structure allows clients to make COM method calls as arbitrary security principals *provided they know the clear-text passwords for the desired account*.[9] If a null pointer is passed instead of a pointer to an explicit COAUTHIDENTITY, then each outbound call will be made using the credentials of the calling process.[10]

One of the more common uses of `IClientSecurity::SetBlanket` is to raise the authentication level for a particular proxy. The following code demonstrates this technique:

```
HRESULT Encrypt(IApe *pApe) {
   IClientSecurity *pcs = 0;
// ask proxy manager for IClientSecurity interface
   HRESULT hr = pApe->QueryInterface(IID_IClientSecurity,
                                     (void**)&pcs);
   if (SUCCEEDED(hr)) {
      hr = pcs->SetBlanket(pApe, RPC_C_AUTHN_WINNT,
                     RPC_C_AUTHZ_NONE, 0,
                     RPC_C_AUTHN_LEVEL_PKT_PRIVACY,
                     RPC_C_IMP_LEVEL_IDENTIFY,
                     0, EOAC_NONE);
      pcs->Release();
   }
   return hr;
}
```

Ideally, the caller will pass this function a duplicated interface proxy. Alternatively, the function could be modified to perform the duplication as follows:

---

[9] It is important to note that at the time of this writing, COAUTHIDENTITY is not supported for same-machine communications. It does work reliably for remote host communications.

[10] Under Windows NT 5.0, support for delegation-level impersonation may change this behavior to use the calling thread's token. Consult the current documentation for more information.

```
HRESULT DupeAndEncrypt(IApe *pApe, IApe * &rpSecretApe) {
  rpSecretApe = 0;
  IClientSecurity *pcs = 0;
// ask proxy manager for IClientSecurity interface
  HRESULT hr = pApe->QueryInterface(IID_IClientSecurity,
                                    (void**)&pcs);
  if (SUCCEEDED(hr)) {
    hr = pcs->CopyProxy(pApe, (IUnknown**)&rpSecretApe);
    if (SUCCEEDED(hr))
    hr = pcs->SetBlanket(rpSecretApe, RPC_C_AUTHN_WINNT,
                         RPC_C_AUTHZ_NONE, 0,
                         RPC_C_AUTHN_LEVEL_PKT_PRIVACY,
                         RPC_C_IMP_LEVEL_IDENTIFY,
                         0, EOAC_NONE);
    pcs->Release();
  }
  return hr;
}
```

For convenience, the COM API provides wrapper functions around each of the three IClientSecurity methods that internally call QueryInterface to find the corresponding IClientSecurity interface and then calls the appropriate method:

```
// get security settings for interface proxy pProxy
HRESULT CoQueryProxyBlanket([in]  IUnknown *pProxy,
    [out] DWORD *pAuthnSvc, [out] DWORD *pAuthzSvc,
    [out] OLECHAR **pServerPrincName,
    [out] DWORD *pAuthnLevel, [out] DWORD *pImpLevel,
    [out] void **pAuthInfo, [out] DWORD *pCapabilities);

// change security settings for interface proxy pProxy
HRESULT CoSetProxyBlanket([in] IUnknown  *pProxy,
    [in] DWORD AuthnSvc, [in] DWORD AuthzSvc,
    [in] OLECHAR *pServerPrincName,
    [in] DWORD AuthnLevel, [in] DWORD ImpLevel,
    [in] void *pAuthInfo, [in] DWORD Capabilities);

// duplicate an interface proxy
HRESULT CoCopyProxy([in]  IUnknown  *pProxy,
                    [out] IUnknown **ppCopy);
```

The following is a modified version of the previous function that uses these convenience routines:

```
HRESULT DupeAndEncrypt(IApe *pApe, IApe * &rpSecretApe) {
   rpSecretApe = 0;
   HRESULT hr = CoCopyProxy(pApe, (IUnknown**)&rpSecretApe);
   if (SUCCEEDED(hr))
      hr = CoSetProxyBlanket(rpSecretApe, RPC_C_AUTHN_WINNT,
                             RPC_C_AUTHZ_NONE, 0,
                             RPC_C_AUTHN_LEVEL_PKT_PRIVACY,
                             RPC_C_IMP_LEVEL_IDENTIFY,
                             0, EOAC_NONE);
      return hr;
}
```

The former version is somewhat more efficient, as only one call to QueryInterface is used to find the IClientSecurity interface. The latter version requires less coding and is therefore somewhat less error prone.

It is important to note that the IClientSecurity methods can only be applied to interfaces that use interface proxies. This means that interfaces that are implemented locally by the proxy manager (*e.g.*, IMultiQI, IClientSecurity) cannot be used with IClientSecurity methods. The IUnknown interface is a special case. IUnknown is technically a local interface implemented by the proxy manager. However, the proxy manager often needs to communicate with the server's apartment to request new interfaces and to release resources held by the corresponding stub manager. This communication happens via a private interface (IRemUnknown) that is implemented internally by the COM library on a per-apartment basis. Developers can control the security blanket used for these IRemUnknown calls by passing the proxy manager's IUnknown implementation to IClientSecurity::SetBlanket (like an interface proxy, the proxy manager uses the process-wide automatic security settings if SetBlanket is not called).[11] Because all interface proxies are aggregated by the proxy manager, this, in effect, means that QueryInterface, AddRef, and Release are not affected by calls to IClientSecurity::SetBlanket on any particular interface proxy. Rather, they are affected by the settings applied to the proxy manager's IUnknown implementation. To get a pointer to the proxy manager's IUnknown implementation, one can simply QueryInterface an interface proxy for IID_IUnknown. The following code fragment demonstrates this technique by disabling security for both an interface proxy and its proxy manager:

---

[11] This statement requires two slight qualifications. First, if the client process was configured to use secure references in its call to CoInitializeSecurity, calls to IRemUnknown::RemAddRef and IRemUnknown::RemRelease will be issued using the process' security principal, not the principal specified in IClientSecurity::SetBlanket. Second, prior to the release of Windows NT 4.0 Service Pack 4, *all* calls to IRemUnknown::RemAddRef and IRemUnknown::RemRelease were issued using the process' security principal independent of the blanket settings made to the proxy manager.

```
                  void TurnOffAllSecurity(IApe *pApe) {
                    IUnknown *pUnkProxyManager = 0;
                  // get a pointer to the proxy manager
                    HRESULT hr = pApe->QueryInterface(IID_IUnknown,
                                              (void**)&pUnkProxyManager);
                    assert(SUCCEEDED(hr));
                  // set blanket for proxy manager
                    hr = CoSetProxyBlanket(pUnkProxyManager,
                                  RPC_C_AUTHN_NONE, RPC_C_AUTHZ_NONE,
                                  0, RPC_C_AUTHN_LEVEL_NONE,
                                  RPC_C_IMP_LEVEL_ANONYMOUS,
                                  0, EOAC_NONE);
                    assert(SUCCEEDED(hr));
                  // set blanket for interface proxy
                    hr = CoSetProxyBlanket(pApe,
                                  RPC_C_AUTHN_NONE, RPC_C_AUTHZ_NONE,
                                  0, RPC_C_AUTHN_LEVEL_NONE,
                                  RPC_C_IMP_LEVEL_ANONYMOUS,
                                  0, EOAC_NONE);
                    assert(SUCCEEDED(hr));
                  // release temporary pointer to proxy manager
                    pUnkProxyManager->Release();
                  }
```

Although it is possible to set and query a security blanket for a proxy manager, it is not possible to duplicate a proxy manager using IClientSecurity:: CopyProxy, as this would violate the identity laws of COM.

When an ORPC request is dispatched to an interface stub, COM creates a call context object that represents various aspects of the call, including the security blanket settings of the interface proxy that issued the request. COM associates this context object with the thread that will execute the method call. The COM library exposes an API function, CoGetCallContext, that allows method implementations to access the context for the current method call:

```
HRESULT CoGetCallContext([in] REFIID riid,
                         [out, iid_is(riid)] void **ppv);
```

In Windows NT 4.0, the only interface that is available to the call context object is the IServerSecurity interface:

```
[ local,object,uuid(0000013E-0000-0000-C000-000000000046) ]
interface IServerSecurity : IUnknown {
// get caller's security settings
  HRESULT QueryBlanket(
```

```
  [out] DWORD    *pAuthnSvc,   // authentication pkg
  [out] DWORD    *pAuthzSvc,   // authorization pkg
  [out] OLECHAR **pServerName, // server principal
  [out] DWORD    *pAuthnLevel, // authentication level
  [out] DWORD    *pImpLevel,   // impersonation level
  [out] void    **pPrivs,      // client principal
  [out] DWORD    *pCaps        // EOAC flags
  );
// start running with credentials of caller
  HRESULT ImpersonateClient(void);
// stop running with credentials of caller
  HRESULT RevertToSelf(void);
// test for impersonation
  BOOL IsImpersonating(void);
}
```

IServerSecurity::QueryBlanket returns the security blanket settings actually used to issue the current ORPC call (which may differ somewhat from the client's settings due to SSP-specific promotion of levels). As was the case with IClientSecurity::QueryBlanket, IServerSecurity::QueryBlanket allows the caller to pass null for parameters that are not interesting. The following is an example of a method implementation that ensures that the caller has enabled encryption prior to processing the call:

```
STDMETHODIMP Gorilla::SwingFromTree(/*[in]*/ long nTreeID) {
// get current call context
  IServerSecurity *pss = 0;
  HRESULT hr = CoGetCallContext(IID_IServerSecurity,
                                (void**)&pss);
  DWORD dwAuthnLevel;
  if (SUCCEEDED(hr)) {
// get authentication level of current call
    hr = pss->QueryBlanket(0, 0, 0, &dwAuthnLevel, 0, 0, 0);
    pss->Release();
  }
// verify proper authentication level
  if (FAILED(hr) ||
      dwAuthnLevel != RPC_C_AUTHN_LEVEL_PKT_PRIVACY)
    hr = APE_E_NOPUBLICTREE;
  else
    hr = this->ActuallySwingFromTree(nTreeID);
  return hr;
}
```

As was the case with IClientSecurity, each IServerSecurity method is available as a convenience API function. The following method implementation uses the convenience routine instead of the explicit IServerSecurity interface:

```
STDMETHODIMP Gorilla::SwingFromTree(/*[in]*/ long nTreeID) {
  DWORD dwAuthnLevel;
// get authentication level of current call
  HRESULT hr = CoQueryClientBlanket(0, 0, 0, &dwAuthnLevel,
                                    0, 0, 0);
// verify proper authentication level
  if (FAILED(hr) ||
      dwAuthnLevel != RPC_C_AUTHN_LEVEL_PKT_PRIVACY)
    hr = APE_E_NOPUBLICTREE;
  else
    hr = this->ActuallySwingFromTree(nTreeID);
  return hr;
}
```

Again, the latter version requires less coding and is therefore somewhat less error prone.

The IServerSecurity::QueryBlanket method also allows the object implementor to discover the security identifier of the caller via the pPrivs parameter. As was the case with credentials passed to IClientSecurity:: SetBlanket, the exact format of this identifier is security package specific. For NTLM, the format is simply a string in the form

```
Authority\AccountName
```

The following method implementation fetches the security identifier of the caller using the CoQueryClientBlanket API function:

```
STDMETHODIMP Gorilla::EatBanana( ) {
  OLECHAR *pwszClientPrincipal = 0;
// get security identifier of caller
  HRESULT hr = CoQueryClientBlanket(0, 0, 0, 0, 0,
                      (void**)&pwszClientPrincipal, 0);
// log user name
  if (SUCCEEDED(hr)) {
    this->LogCallerIDToFile(pwszClientPrincipal);
    hr = this->ActuallyEatBanana();
  }
  return hr;
}
```

For the call to CoQueryClientBlanket to successfully return the caller's security identifier, the caller must have specified (1) at least RPC_C_IMP_LEVEL_ IDENTIFY as the automatic (or explicit) impersonation level and (2) at least RPC_C_AUTHN_LEVEL_CONNECT as the automatic (or explicit) authentication level. If the caller explicitly changed the calling principal using a COAUTHIDENTITY in the proxy's blanket settings, the explicitly provided principal name will be returned instead.

Just as it is possible to completely control the security settings used when making a method call using the IClientSecurity interface, it is also useful to control the security settings used when making an activation call. Unfortunately, activation calls are global API functions with no corresponding proxy manager to get an IClientSecurity interface from. To allow callers to specify security settings for activation calls, each activation call accepts a COSERVERINFO structure:

```
typedef struct _COSERVERINFO {
  DWORD           dwReserved1;
  LPWSTR          pwszName;
  COAUTHINFO *    pAuthInfo;
  DWORD           dwReserved2;
} COSERVERINFO;
```

As was noted in an earlier chapter, the pwszName data member allows the caller to control explicitly which host machine will service the activation request. The third data member, pAuthInfo, points to a data structure that allows the caller to control the security settings used to make the activation call. This parameter is a pointer to a COAUTHINFO structure, which is defined as follows:

```
typedef struct _COAUTHINFO {
  DWORD               dwAuthnSvc;
  DWORD               dwAuthzSvc;
  LPWSTR              pwszServerPrincName;
  DWORD               dwAuthnLevel;
  DWORD               dwImpersonationLevel;
  COAUTHIDENTITY *    pAuthIdentityData;
  DWORD               dwCapabilities;
} COAUTHINFO;
```

These data members correspond to the parameters to IClientSecurity:: SetBlanket but are used only during the activation call and do not affect the resultant interface proxy.[12]

---

[12] It is important to note that since the recipient of an activation call is initially the server-side SCM, some authentication packages may not be supported. The Windows NT 4.0 SCM only supports NTLM. Consult the current documentation for more information on supported packages under Windows NT 5.0.

The following code fragment issues an activation call using the COAUTHINFO structure to force the SCM to use encryption (RPC_C_AUTHN_LEVEL_PKT_PRI-VACY) when it makes the activation request:

```
void CreateSecretChimp(IApe *&rpApe) {
  rpApe = 0;
// create a COAUTHINFO that specifies privacy
  COAUTHINFO cai = {
    RPC_C_AUTHN_WINNT, RPC_C_AUTHZ_NONE, 0,
    RPC_C_AUTHN_LEVEL_PKT_PRIVACY,
    RPC_C_IMP_LEVEL_IDENTIFY,
    0, 0
  };
// issue an activation call using the COAUTHINFO
  COSERVERINFO csi = { 0, 0, &cai, 0 };
  IApeClass *pac = 0;
  hr = CoGetClassObject(CLSID_Chimp, CLSCTX_ALL, &csi,
                        IID_IApeClass, (void**)&pac);
  assert(SUCCEEDED(hr));
// the activation call occurred with encryption,
// but pac is using automatic security settings
  hr = pac->CreateApe(&rpApe);
  pac->Release();
  return hr;
}
```

It is important to note that because the COAUTHINFO structure affects only the activation call itself, the resultant IApeClass interface proxy will use the automatic security settings that were set by an earlier call to CoInitializeSecurity. This means that the call to IApeClass::CreateApe will use the automatic security settings, not those specified in the COAUTHINFO structure. To ensure that encryption is used during the creation or manipulation of the new Chimp, the function needs to be modified also to set the security blanket on both the IApeClass and IApe interface proxies:

```
// encrypt calls on IApeClass reference
CoSetProxyBlanket(pac, RPC_C_AUTHN_WINNT, RPC_C_AUTHZ_NONE,
        0, RPC_C_AUTHN_LEVEL_PKT_PRIVACY,
        RPC_C_IMP_LEVEL_ANONYMOUS, 0, EOAC_NONE);

// issue call to create object
pac->CreateApe(&rpApe);

// encrypt calls on IApe reference
```

```
CoSetProxyBlanket(rpApe, RPC_C_AUTHN_WINNT,RPC_C_AUTHZ_NONE,
    0, RPC_C_AUTHN_LEVEL_PKT_PRIVACY,
    RPC_C_IMP_LEVEL_ANONYMOUS, 0, EOAC_NONE);
```

Using an explicit COAUTHIDENTITY at activation time can allow the caller to create objects in processes that otherwise would be inaccessible to the calling process' principal. However, it is then the caller's responsibility to ensure that the proxy manager uses these same credentials when releasing the interface pointer, otherwise server-side resources will be leaked. As was mentioned earlier in this chapter, the security blanket of the proxy manager is controlled separately by calling IClientSecurity::SetBlanket on the proxy manager's IUnknown implementation.

Access Control

As mentioned earlier in this chapter, each COM process can protect itself against unauthorized access. COM addresses access control at two levels: *launch permissions* and *access permissions*. Launch permissions are used to determine which users can start server processes when making activation calls to the SCM. Access permissions determine which users can access a process' objects once the server is started. Both types of access control can be configured using DCOMCNFG.EXE, but only access permissions can be specified programmatically at runtime (because once the server process starts, it is too late to deny launch permission to a user). Instead, launch permission is enforced by the SCM at activation time.

When the SCM determines that a new server process must be started, it attempts to get an NT SECURITY_DESCRIPTOR that describes which users are allowed to start the server process. The SCM first checks the class's AppID for an explicit launch permission setting. This setting comes in the form of a serialized self-relative NT security descriptor that is stored at the AppID's LaunchPermission named value:

```
[HKCR\AppID\{27EE6A4D-DF65-11d0-8C5F-0080C73925BA}]
LaunchPermission=<serialized NT security descriptor>
```

If this named value is not present, the SCM then attempts to read the machine-wide launch permissions from the following named value:

```
[HKEY_LOCAL_MACHINE\Software\Microsoft\OLE]
DefaultLaunchPermission=<serialized NT security descriptor>
```

Both of these settings can be modified using DCOMCNFG.EXE. If neither of these registry entries is found, COM will deny launch permissions to everyone. Once a SECURITY_DESCRIPTOR is found, the SCM then checks the security identifier of the activating caller (formally called the *activator*) against the SECURITY_DESCRIPTOR's Discretionary Access Control List (DACL) to determine whether or not the activator has permission to start the server. If the activator has not been granted permission, then the activation call fails with the HRESULT E_ACCESSDENIED and no processes are started. Otherwise, the SCM starts the server process and continues processing the activation request.

Launch permission addresses only which users can or cannot cause server processes to start at activation time. This check is always performed by the SCM based on information stored in the Registry. Access permission addresses which users can actually communicate with the server process' objects. This check is performed by the COM library as each connection establishment request is received from a client. To control the access permission settings of a process, developers can use the CoInitializeSecurity API function.

Recall that processes that do not call CoInitializeSecurity explicitly automatically use the access control list stored at the application's AppID registry key:

```
[HKCR\AppID\{27EE6A4D-DF65-11d0-8C5F-0080C73925BA}]
AccessPermission=<serialized NT security descriptor>
```

As explained earlier, if this registry entry is not present, COM looks for a machine-wide default setting, and if this is also not found, a new access control list is created that includes only the server process' principal and the built-in SYSTEM account.

Applications that explicitly call CoInitializeSecurity can manually control which callers are allowed to access objects exported from the current process. By default, the first parameter to CoInitializeSecurity accepts a pointer to an NT SECURITY_DESCRIPTOR. If the caller passes a null pointer for this parameter, COM will not perform any access checks on incoming calls. This allows calls from any authenticated security principal. If both the client and server specify RPC_C_AUTHN_LEVEL_NONE, COM will allow calls from anyone, irrespective of whether they can be authenticated. If the caller provides a valid pointer to a security descriptor, COM will use the security descriptor's DACL to determine which callers are allowed to access the process' objects. The SDK headers define one specific rights flag (COM_RIGHTS_EXECUTE) to use when building the DACL to explicitly grant or deny users permission to connect to the process' objects.

Although it is legal to use the Win32 API to build a SECURITY_DESCRIPTOR to pass to CoInitializeSecurity, this is not the preferred technique for controlling access to a process' objects, largely due to the arcane nature of the original Win32 security API. To simplify programming COM access control, the Windows NT 4.0 Service Pack 2 implementation of COM allows implementors to designate a COM object that COM will use to perform the access check when new connections are established. This object is registered with the COM library at CoInitializeSecurity time and must implement the IAccessControl interface:

```
[ object,uuid(EEDD23E0-8410-11CE-A1C3-08002B2B8D8F) ]
interface IAccessControl : IUnknown {
// add access allowed rights for a list of users
  HRESULT GrantAccessRights(
    [in] PACTRL_ACCESSW                   pAccessList
  );
// explicitly set the access rights for a list of users
  HRESULT SetAccessRights(
    [in] PACTRL_ACCESSW  pAccessList     // users+rights
  );
// set the owner/group IDs of the descriptor
  HRESULT SetOwner(
    [in] PTRUSTEEW      pOwner,          // owner ID
    [in] PTRUSTEEW      pGroup           // group ID
  );
// remove access rights for a list of users
  HRESULT RevokeAccessRights(
    [in] LPWSTR           lpProperty,    // not used
    [in] ULONG            cTrustees,     // how many users
    [in, size_is(cTrustees)] TRUSTEEW prgTrustees[] // users
  );
// get list of users and their rights
  HRESULT GetAllAccessRights(
    [in] LPWSTR           lpProperty,        // not used
    [out] PACTRL_ACCESSW  *ppAccessList,     // users+rights
    [out] PTRUSTEEW      *ppOwner,           // owner ID
    [out] PTRUSTEEW      *ppGroup            // group ID
  );
// called by COM to allow/deny access to an object
  HRESULT IsAccessAllowed(
    [in] PTRUSTEEW      pTrustee,  // caller's ID
    [in] LPWSTR         lpProperty, // not used
    [in] ACCESS_RIGHTS  Rights,     // COM_RIGHTS_EXECUTE
    [out] BOOL          *pbAllowed  // yes/no!
  );
}
```

This interface is designed to allow developers to build access control objects based on static data tables that map principal names to access rights. This interface is based on the new Windows NT 4.0 trustee-based security API. The fundamental data type used by this API is the TRUSTEE:

```
typedef struct _TRUSTEE_W {
    struct _TRUSTEE_W            *pMultipleTrustee;
    MULTIPLE_TRUSTEE_OPERATION  MultipleTrusteeOperation;
    TRUSTEE_FORM                TrusteeForm;
    TRUSTEE_TYPE                TrusteeType;
    [switch_is(TrusteeForm)]
    union {
    [case(TRUSTEE_IS_NAME)]
      LPWSTR                    ptstrName;
    [case(TRUSTEE_IS_SID)]
      SID                       *pSid;
    };
} TRUSTEE_W, *PTRUSTEE_W, TRUSTEEW, *PTRUSTEEW;
```

This data type is used to describe a security principal. The first two parameters (pMultipleTrustee and MultipleTrusteeOperation) allow the caller to distinguish between physical logins and impersonation attempts. The fifth parameter (ptstrName/pSid) contains either the NT security identifier (SID) or a text-based account name being identified, with the third parameter (TrusteeForm) indicating which union member is being used. The fourth parameter (TrusteeType) indicates whether the specified principal is a user or a group account.

To associate a trustee with the permissions it is being granted or refused, the Win32 API also provides the ACTRL_ACCESS_ENTRY data type:

```
typedef struct _ACTRL_ACCESS_ENTRYW {
  TRUSTEE_W       Trustee;              // who?
  ULONG           fAccessFlags;         // allowed/denied?
  ACCESS_RIGHTS   Access;               // which rights?
  ACCESS_RIGHTS   ProvSpecificAccess;   // not used by COM
  INHERIT_FLAGS   Inheritance;          // not used by COM
  LPWSTR          lpInheritProperty;    // not used by COM
} ACTRL_ACCESS_ENTRYW, *PACTRL_ACCESS_ENTRYW;
```

as well as a data type to model lists of trustee/permissions entries:

```
typedef struct _ACTRL_ACCESS_ENTRY_LISTW {
  ULONG                          cEntries;
```

```
        [size_is(cEntries)] ACTRL_ACCESS_ENTRYW   *pAccessList;
      } ACTRL_ACCESS_ENTRY_LISTW, *PACTRL_ACCESS_ENTRY_LISTW;
```

Finally, Win32 provides two additional data types that allow access entry lists to be associated with named properties.

```
      typedef struct _ACTRL_PROPERTY_ENTRYW {
          LPWSTR                        lpProperty; // not used by COM
          ACTRL_ACCESS_ENTRY_LISTW *pAccessEntryList;
          ULONG                         fListFlags; // not used by COM
      } ACTRL_PROPERTY_ENTRYW, *PACTRL_PROPERTY_ENTRYW;

      typedef struct _ACTRL_ALISTW {
        ULONG                    cEntries;
        [size_is(cEntries)]
        ACTRL_PROPERTY_ENTRYW    *pPropertyAccessList;
      } ACTRL_ACCESSW, *PACTRL_ACCESSW;
```

Although COM does not currently use the per-property capabilities implied by these two data types, the ACTRL_ACCESSW data type is still used by IAccessControl to represent access control lists. This is because the interface is also used extensively in the Windows NT 5.0 directory service, where per-property access control is required.

COM provides an implementation of IAccessControl (CLSID_ DCOMAccessControl) that callers can populate with explicit account names and access rights using the NT 4.0 access control data types.[13] The following code fragment uses this implementation to create an access control object that allows access by the built-in account SYSTEM and by users in the Sales\Managers group but prohibits access by the particular user Sales\Bob:

```
      HRESULT CreateAccessControl(IAccessControl * &rpac) {
        rpac = 0;
      // create default access control object
        HRESULT hr = CoCreateInstance(CLSID_DCOMAccessControl,
                        0, CLSCTX_ALL, IID_IAccessControl,
                        (void**)&rpac);
        if (SUCCEEDED(hr)) {
      // build list of users/rights using NT4 security data types
          ACTRL_ACCESS_ENTRYW rgaae[] = {
```

---

[13] This class also implements the IPersistStream interface. Its serialized format is recognized by the SCM for writing to an AccessPermission registry entry at self-registration time.

```
            { {0, NO_MULTIPLE_TRUSTEE, TRUSTEE_IS_NAME,
                TRUSTEE_IS_USER, L"Sales\\Bob" },
                ACTRL_ACCESS_DENIED, COM_RIGHTS_EXECUTE, 0,
                NO_INHERITANCE, 0 },
            { {0, NO_MULTIPLE_TRUSTEE, TRUSTEE_IS_NAME,
                TRUSTEE_IS_GROUP, L"Sales\\Managers" },
                ACTRL_ACCESS_ALLOWED, COM_RIGHTS_EXECUTE, 0,
                NO_INHERITANCE, 0 },
            { {0, NO_MULTIPLE_TRUSTEE, TRUSTEE_IS_NAME,
                TRUSTEE_IS_USER, L"NT AUTHORITY\\SYSTEM" },
                ACTRL_ACCESS_ALLOWED, COM_RIGHTS_EXECUTE, 0,
                NO_INHERITANCE, 0 },
        };
        ACTRL_ACCESS_ENTRY_LISTW aael =
            { sizeof(rgaae)/sizeof(*rgaae), rgaae };
        ACTRL_PROPERTY_ENTRYW ape = { 0, &aael, 0 };
        ACTRL_ACCESSW aa = { 1, &ape };
// present list of users+rights to Access Control object
        hr = rpac->SetAccessRights(&aa);
    }
    return hr;
}
```

Given this function, an application could associate the newly created access control object with its process as follows:

```
IAccessControl *pac = 0;
HRESULT hr = CreateAccessControl(pac);
assert(SUCCEEDED(hr));
hr = CoInitializeSecurity(pac, -1, 0, 0,
        RPC_C_AUTHN_LEVEL_PKT, RPC_C_IMP_LEVEL_IDENTIFY, 0,
        EOAC_ACCESS_CONTROL, // use IAccessControl
        0);
assert(SUCCEEDED(hr));
pac->Release(); // COM holds reference until last CoUninit.
```

The EOAC_ACCESS_CONTROL flag indicates that the first parameter to CoInitializeSecurity is an IAccessControl interface pointer and not a pointer to an NT SECURITY_DESCRIPTOR. At each incoming connection request, COM will use this object's IsAccessAllowed method to determine whether the caller is granted or denied access to the process' objects. It is interesting to note that although this code must be executed prior to the first interesting COM call, the call to CoCreateInstance to get the default implementation of IAccessControl is legal as it is not considered interesting by COM.

If the list of authorized users cannot be known at process start-up time, it is possible to register a custom implementation of IAccessControl that performs some sort of runtime access check in its implementation of IsAccessAllowed. Because COM itself uses only the IsAccessAllowed method, such a custom implementation could safely return E_NOTIMPL for all other IAccessControl methods. The following is a simple implementation of IAccessControl that allows only users with the character "x" in their account names to gain access to a process' objects:

```
class XOnly : public IAccessControl {
// IUnknown methods
  STDMETHODIMP QueryInterface(REFIID riid, void**ppv){
    if (riid == IID_IAccessControl || riid == IID_IUnknown)
       *ppv = static_cast<IAccessControl*>(this);
    else
        return (*ppv = 0), E_NOINTERFACE;
    ((IUnknown*)*ppv)->AddRef();
    return S_OK;
  }
  STDMETHODIMP_(ULONG) AddRef(void)  { return 2; }
  STDMETHODIMP_(ULONG) Release(void) { return 1; }
// IAccessControl methods
  STDMETHODIMP GrantAccessRights(ACTRL_ACCESSW *)
  { return E_NOTIMPL; }
  STDMETHODIMP SetAccessRights(ACTRL_ACCESSW *)
  { return E_NOTIMPL; }
  STDMETHODIMP SetOwner(PTRUSTEEW,PTRUSTEEW)
  { return E_NOTIMPL; }
  STDMETHODIMP RevokeAccessRights(LPWSTR,ULONG, TRUSTEEW [])
  { return E_NOTIMPL; }
  STDMETHODIMP GetAllAccessRights(LPWSTR,
      PACTRL_ACCESSW_ALLOCATE_ALL_NODES *,
      PTRUSTEEW *,PTRUSTEEW *)
  { return E_NOTIMPL; }
// this is the only IAccessControl method called by COM
  STDMETHODIMP IsAccessAllowed(
        PTRUSTEEW pTrustee, LPWSTR lpProperty,
        ACCESS_RIGHTS AccessRights, BOOL *pbIsAllowed) {
// verify that trustee contains a string
    if (pTrustee == 0
        || pTrustee->TrusteeForm != TRUSTEE_IS_NAME)
        return E_UNEXPECTED;
// look for X or x and grant/deny based on presence
    *pbIsAllowed = wcsstr(pTrustee->ptstrName, L"x") != 0
```

```
                             || wcsstr(pTrustee->ptstrName, L"X") != 0;
        return S_OK;
    }
};
```

If an instance of the preceding C++ class is registered with CoInitializeSecurity:

```
XOnly xo; // declare an instance of the C++ class
Hr = CoInitializeSecurity(static_cast<IAccessControl*>(&xo),
        -1, 0, 0, RPC_C_AUTHN_LEVEL_PKT,
        RPC_C_IMP_LEVEL_IDENTIFY, 0,
        EOAC_ACCESS_CONTROL, // use IAccessControl
        0);
assert(SUCCEEDED(hr));
```

no incoming calls will be accepted from users that do not have an "x" in their account names. Because the trustee name contains the domain name as a prefix, this simple test will also grant access to user accounts that belong to domains that have "x" in their names. Although this access test is unlikely to be very useful, it demonstrates the technique of using a custom IAccessControl object with CoInitializeSecurity.

Token Management

Under Windows NT, each process has an access token that represents the credentials of a security principal. This access token is created at process initialization time and contains various pieces of information about a user, including the user's NT security identifier (SID), the list of groups the user belongs to, as well as the list of privileges the user holds (*e.g.,* whether the user can shut down the system, whether the user can change the system clock). When a process attempts to gain access to secure kernel resources (*e.g.,* files, registry keys, semaphores), the NT Security Reference Monitor uses the caller's token for auditing and access control purposes.

When an ORPC request message arrives at a process, COM arranges for the corresponding method call to execute on either an RPC thread (in the case of MTA-based objects) or a user-created thread (in the case of STA-based objects). In either case, the method executes using the access token of the process. In general, this is what is desired, as it allows object implementors to predict what privileges and rights their objects will have irrespective of which user has issued the request. However, it is occasionally useful for a method to execute using the credentials of the client that invoked the method, either to restrict or enhance the normal rights and privileges of the object. To support this style of programming, Windows NT allows access tokens to be assigned to individual threads. When a thread has its own token, the Security Reference Monitor does not use the process token. Instead, the token that is assigned to the thread is used to perform auditing and access control. Although it is possible to create tokens programmatically and assign them to threads, COM provides a much more direct mechanism for creating a token based on the ORPC request being serviced by the current thread. This mechanism is exposed to object implementors via the call context object.

Recall that the call context object is associated with a thread when an ORPC request is dispatched to an interface stub. Object implementors access the call context via the CoGetCallContext API function. The call context object implements the IServerSecurity interface:

```
[ local,object,uuid(0000013E-0000-0000-C000-000000000046) ]
interface IServerSecurity : IUnknown {
// get caller's security settings
  HRESULT QueryBlanket(
     [out] DWORD    *pAuthnSvc,   // authentication pkg
     [out] DWORD    *pAuthzSvc,   // authorization pkg
     [out] OLECHAR **pServerName,// server principal
     [out] DWORD    *pAuthnLevel,// authentication level
     [out] DWORD    *pImpLevel,   // impersonation level
     [out] void     **pPrivs,     // client principal
     [out] DWORD    *pCaps        // EOAC flags
  );
// start running with credentials of caller
  HRESULT ImpersonateClient(void);
// stop running with credentials of caller
  HRESULT RevertToSelf(void);
// test for impersonation
  BOOL IsImpersonating(void);
}
```

An earlier section of this chapter has already examined the QueryBlanket method. The remaining three methods are used to manage thread tokens during method execution. The ImpersonateClient method creates an access token based on the client's credentials and assigns the token to the current thread. Once IServerSecurity::ImpersonateClient returns, all attempts to access OS resources will be allowed or denied based on the client's credentials, not the object's. The RevertToSelf method causes the current thread to revert back to using the process' access token. If the current method call returns while running under impersonation, COM will implicitly revert the

thread back to using the process token. Finally, the ISeverSecurity::
IsImpersonating method indicates whether or not the current thread is using
the client's credentials or the token of the object's process. Like the
QueryBlanket method, two of these ISeverSecurity methods also have convenience wrappers that internally call CoGetCallContext and then call the
corresponding method:

```
HRESULT  CoImpersonateClient(void);
HRESULT  CoRevertToSelf(void);
```

In general, if more than one ISeverSecurity method will be used, it is
slightly more efficient to call CoGetCallContext once and use the resultant
ISeverSecurity interface to call each method.

The following code demonstrates using the call context object to execute a
portion of a method's code using the client's credentials:

```
STDMETHODIMP MyClass::ReadWrite(DWORD dwNew, DWORD *pdwOld){
// execute using server's token to let anyone read the value
  ULONG cb;
  HANDLE hfile = CreateFile("C:\\file1.bin",GENERIC_READ,
               0, 0, OPEN_EXISTING, FILE_ATTRIBUTE_NORMAL, 0);
  if (hfile == INVALID_HANDLE_VALUE)
    return MAKE_HRESULT(SEVERITY_ERROR,FACILITY_WIN32,
                        GetLastError());
  ReadFile(hfile, pdwold, sizeof(DWORD), &cb, 0);
  CloseHandle(hfile);

// get call context object
  IServerSecurity *pss = 0;
  HRESULT hr = CoGetCallContext(IID_IServerSecurity,
                                (void**)&pss);
  if (FAILED(hr)) return hr;
// set thread token to use caller's credentials
  hr = pss->ImpersonateClient();
  assert(SUCCEEDED(hr));

// execute using client's token to let only users that can
// write to the file change the value
  hfile = CreateFile("C:\\file2.bin",
                     GENERIC_READ|GENERIC_WRITE, 0, 0,
                     OPEN_EXISTING, FILE_ATTRIBUTE_NORMAL, 0);
  if (hfile == INVALID_HANDLE_VALUE)
    hr = MAKE_HRESULT(SEVERITY_ERROR,FACILTY_WIN32,
                      GetLastError());
```

```
      else {
        WriteFile(hfile, &dwNew, sizeof(DWORD), &cb, 0);
        CloseHandle(hfile);
      }
  // restore thread to use process-level token
      pss->RevertToSelf();
  // release call context
      pss->Release();
      return hr;
  }
```

Note that the first call to CreateFile executes using the credentials of the object's process, while the second call executes with the client's credentials. If the client has read/write access rights to the underlying file, the second call to CreateFile can succeed even if the object's process does not normally have access to the file.

It is important to note that while IServerSecurity::ImpersonateClient will succeed barring catastrophic failure, the object's client is in control of the impersonation level allowed by the resultant token. Each interface proxy has an impersonation level that must be one of four constants (RPC_C_IMP_LEVEL_ANONYMOUS, RPC_C_IMP_LEVEL_IDENTIFY, RPC_C_IMP_LEVEL_IMPERSONATE, or RPC_C_IMP_LEVEL_DELEGATE). At unmarshal time, COM sets this level to the value specified in the client's call to CoInitializeSecurity; however, this setting can be manually overridden using IClientSecurity::SetBlanket. When an object calls IServerSecurity::ImpersonateClient, the new token will be limited to the level specified in the interface proxy used to issue the call. This means that if the client specified only RPC_C_IMP_LEVEL_IDENTIFY, the object cannot access kernel resources while executing with the client's credentials. However, the object can use the Win32 API functions OpenThreadToken/GetTokenInformation to read information about the client (*e.g.,* the security ID, group membership) from the impersonation token. It is important to note that unless the client specified RPC_C_IMP_LEVEL_DELEGATE, the object cannot access any secure remote resources using the client's credentials. This includes opening files on remote file systems as well as making authenticated COM calls to remote objects. Unfortunately, the NTLM authentication protocol does not support RPC_C_IMP_LEVEL_DELEGATE, so delegation is impossible under Windows NT 4.0.

The previous discussion emphasized that an object's methods normally execute using the access token of the object's process. What has not been discussed is how to control which security principal should be used to create the initial token of a server process. When the SCM starts a server process, it assigns the new server process a token based on the configuration of the AppID's

RunAs named value. If the AppID does not have a RunAs value, it is assumed that the server has not been properly configured for distributed access. To keep this type of server process from introducing security holes into the system, the SCM starts these processes using the security principal that issued the activation request. This type of activation is often called "As Activator" activation, as the server process runs the same security principal as the launching user. As Activator activation is intended for supporting remote activation of legacy servers and has several pitfalls. First, to remain true to the semantics of As Activator, COM will start a separate server process for each activating user account irrespective of the usage of REGCLS_MULTIPLEUSE in CoRegisterClassObject. This has a serious impact on scalability, in addition to making it impossible to keep all instances of a class in the same process. Second, each server process is started with a token that is limited to RPC_C_IMP_LEVEL_IMPERSONATE, which means the server process cannot access any remote resources or objects.[14]

Ideally, server processes are configured to run as a particular security principal. This can be controlled by the presence of an account name at the AppID's RunAs named value:

```
[HKCR\AppID\{27EE6A4D-DF65-11d0-8C5F-0080C73925BA}]
RunAs="DomainX\UserY"
```

If this named value is present, the SCM will use the designated account name to create a new login token and assign the token to the server process. Two things are required for this to work properly. First, the corresponding password must be stored in a distinguished location in the Registry as a Local Security Authority (LSA) secret. Second, the designated user account must have the "Logon as a batch job" privilege. When setting the RunAs value, the DCOMCNFG.EXE utility ensures that both of these conditions are met.[15]

To prevent spoofing of classes by malicious programs, CoRegisterClassObject checks the AppID of the class being registered. If the AppID has a RunAs setting, COM ensures that the caller's principal matches the principal name stored in the Registry. If the caller is not the designated RunAs account for the class' AppID, CoRegisterClassObject will fail and return the distinguished HRESULT CO_E_WRONG_SERVER_IDENTITY. Because COM's configura-

---

[14] This, of course, implies that the caller must have specified at least RPC_C_IMP_LEVEL_IMPERSONATE when making the activation request, either implicitly via CoInitializeSecurity or explicitly using a COAUTHINFO structure.

[15] It is possible to perform both of these operations at self-register time. Consult Mike Nelson's excellent DCOMPERM sample from the Win32 SDK.

tion settings are stored in a secure portion of the registry, only privileged users can modify which classes run as which users.

It is important to note that when an AppID has an explicit RunAs user account, the SCM will always start the server process in its own distinct window station.[16] This means that the server process cannot easily create windows that are visible to the interactive user on the machine, nor can the server process easily read input from the keyboard, mouse, or clipboard. In general, this protection is beneficial, as it keeps naive COM servers from interfering with the user experience of the person currently logged onto the machine.[17] Unfortunately, it is sometimes necessary for a server process to communicate with the currently logged on user. One technique for achieving this is to use the explicit Win32 API functions for managing window stations and desktops to cause a thread to execute temporarily in the interactive desktop. While executing in the interactive desktop, any windows the thread creates will be visible to the interactive user, and the thread can also receive hardware messages from the keyboard and mouse. Alternatively, if all that is needed is a simple yes/no answer from the user, the Win32 API function MessageBox supports the flag MB_SERVICE_NOTIFICATION, which causes the message box to appear in the interactive desktop without additional coding.

If extensive interaction with the interactive user is required, using the Win32 window station API can be fairly cumbersome. A better approach would be to segregate the user-interface components into a second out-of-process server that can run in a window station that is distinct from that of the primary object hierarchy. To force a server process that has user-interface components to run in the interactive user's window station, COM recognizes the distinguished RunAs value "Interactive User":

```
[HKCR\AppID\{27EE6A4D-DF65-11d0-8C5F-0080C73925BA}]
RunAs="Interactive User"
```

When this value is used, COM starts the new server process in the window station of the currently logged on user. To acquire the credentials for the

---

[16] If the AppID does not have a RunAs setting (*i.e.,* the class is configured to use As Activator activation), the SCM starts the server process in the window station of the activator (or a new window station if the activator is a remote client). This means that the server can interact with the interactive user only if the activator happened to be the interactive user.

[17] This isolation does not come without performance cost. Each server process that the SCM starts using a RunAs account consumes a window station and desktop. By default, Windows NT 4.0 is configured to allow only approximately 14 total desktops. This implies that only 14 (or less) RunAs servers can run simultaneously on a default configuration. The Microsoft Knowledge Base article Q171890 explains how to change this limit to a more reasonable number.

new server process, COM simply duplicates the token of the current interactive session when creating the new server process. This means that no password needs to be stored in the registry. Unfortunately, this mode of activation is not without its pitfalls. First, if an activation request arrives while no user is logged onto the host machine, the activation call will fail with E_ACCESSDENIED. In addition, if the interactive user logs off while the server process still has connected clients, the server process will be prematurely terminated, which rudely disconnects any extant proxies. Finally, it is often unpredictable which user will be logged in at activation time, making it difficult to ensure that the object will have sufficient rights and privileges to access all required resources. These limitations restrict the usability of this activation mode to simple user-interface components only.[18]

One interesting variation on controlling the token and window station of a server process relates to NT services. Recall that the presence of the LocalService named value causes the SCM to use the NT Service Control Manager to start a server process in lieu of using CreateProcess or CreateProcessAsUser. When starting server processes as NT services, COM has no control over which principal the process will start as, simply because this is hard-coded into the configuration of the particular NT service being started. In this case COM ignores the RunAs named value, however, to ensure that random processes cannot spoof calls to CoRegisterClassObject; the presence of the LocalService named value requires the caller to be running as an NT service. If the service itself is configured to start as the built-in account SYSTEM, the server process will either run the interactive window station or a predefined window station that is shared by all NT services that run as SYSTEM (depending on how the NT service is configured). If instead the NT service is configured to run as a particular user account, the NT Service Control Manager will always start the service in a new window station that is specific to the server process.

One common motivation for implementing a COM server as an NT service relates to the fact that only NT services can execute using the built-in account SYSTEM. This account typically has greater access to local resources such as files and registry keys. In addition, this account is often the only account that can act as part of the trusted computing base and use low-level security services that would be dangerous if accessible from normal user accounts. Unfortunately, although the SYSTEM account is virtually omnipotent on the local

---

[18] However, this activation mode is required to avoid RPC_E_WRONG_SERVER_IDENTITY errors when debugging the initialization of a server process.

system, it is completely impotent for accessing secure remote resources, in-cluding remote file systems and remote COM objects. This makes the SYSTEM account somewhat less useful than one might expect for building distributed systems. Irrespective of whether a server is deployed as an NT service or as a traditional Win32 process, it is common practice to create a distinguished user account for each COM application that has full network-wide credentials.

Where Are We?

This chapter examined the issues related to segregating classes into distinct server processes. COM supports starting server processes based on activation requests. These server processes must register themselves with the COM li-brary using `CoRegisterClassObject` to make their class objects available to external clients. The COM security architecture integrates tightly with the na-tive security model of the OS and is based on three distinct concepts. Authentication addresses the integrity and authenticity of ORPC messages that are passed between a client and an object. Access control addresses which security principals can access the objects exported from a given process. Token management addresses which credentials are used to start server processes and execute the methods of an object.

```
IChapter *pc = 0;
HRESULT hr = CoGetObject(OLESTR("Chapter:7"), 0,
                         IID_IChapter, (void**)&pc);
if (SUCCEEDED(hr)) {
  hr = pc->IncludeAllTopicsNotCoveredYet();
  pc->Release();
}
```
Author, 1997

The previous chapters have presented the foundations of the COM programming model and remoting architecture. Although various COM interfaces and techniques have been examined throughout the book, there remain a handful of topics that have no affinity to any particular chapter but yet are required to tell the complete story. Rather than simply shoehorn these topics into other chapters that already had a reasonable flow or were already overly long-winded, I reserved this chapter as the repository of "little" topics that don't necessarily fit anywhere else in the book. Except for the introductory sections on pointers, memory management, and arrays, none of these topics are critical for building efficient distributed systems with COM. With this in mind, feel free to let your eyes glaze over as the chapter winds down to an end.

Pointer Basics

COM, like DCE, has its roots in the C programming language. Although few developers use C to develop or use COM components, it is from C that COM inherits the syntax for its interface definition language. One of the most confusing issues in interface design and usage is the management of pointers. Consider the following simple IDL method definition:

```
HRESULT f([in] const short *ps);
```

If a caller were to invoke the method as follows:

```
short s = 10;
HRESULT hr = p->f(&s);
```

the value 10 must be sent to the object. If this method were to be remoted across apartment boundaries, it would be the responsibility of the interface proxy to dereference the pointer and transmit the value 10 in the ORPC request message.

The following client code, while completely legal C, is a somewhat more interesting case:

```
HRESULT hr = p->f(0); // pass a null pointer
```

If the calling thread executes in the apartment of the object, then there is no proxy and the null pointer will be passed directly to the object. But what if the object resides in a different apartment and a proxy is used? What exactly should the interface proxy transmit to represent that a null pointer was passed? Moreover, does this mean that interface proxies and stubs must check each and every pointer for null? It turns out that there are cases in which a pointer must never be null and other cases in which null pointers are extremely useful as rogue values and the fact that a null pointer is passed to an interface proxy must be replicated in the object's apartment by the interface stub.

To address these different requirements, COM allows interface designers to indicate the exact semantics of each pointer parameter. To indicate that a pointer must never be null, the interface designer can use the [ref] attribute:

```
HRESULT g([in, ref] short *ps); // ps cannot be a null ptr.
```

Pointers that use the [ref] attribute are called *reference pointers*. Given the IDL definition above, the following client-side code:

```
HRESULT hr = p->g(0); // danger: passing null [ref] ptr.
```

is illegal and if p points to an interface proxy, the interface proxy will detect the null pointer and return a marshaling error to the caller without ever remoting the method to the actual object. If, instead, a null pointer is a legal parameter value, the IDL definition should use the [unique] attribute:

```
HRESULT h([in, unique] short *ps); // ps can be a null ptr.
```

Pointers that use the [unique] attribute are called *unique pointers*. Given this IDL definition, the following client-side code:

```
HRESULT hr = p->h(0); // relax: passing null [unique] ptr.
```

is completely legal. This means that the interface proxy must explicitly test the pointer prior to dereferencing it. More important, this means that the interface proxy needs to write more than just the dereferenced value to the ORPC request. It must also write a tag indicating whether or not a null pointer was passed. This adds four bytes per pointer to the size of the ORPC message. For most applications, the additional four bytes and the CPU cycles needed to detect the null pointer[1] are negligible relative to the benefits of being able to use null pointers as parameter values.

In the overall scheme of things, the performance differences between [ref] and [unique] are fairly minute. However, one additional problem related to pointers has not yet been discussed. Consider the following IDL fragment:

```
HRESULT j([in] short *ps1, [in] short *ps2);
```

Given this IDL definition, consider the following client-side code:

```
short x = 100;
HRESULT hr = p->j(&x, &x); // note: same ptr. passed twice
```

The question at hand is what the interface proxy should do in the presence of duplicate pointers. If the interface proxy does nothing, then the value 100 will be transmitted twice in the ORPC request: once for *ps1 and once for *ps2. This means that the proxy is sending the same information twice, wasting network bandwidth and affecting performance. Granted, the number of bytes consumed by the value 100 is insignificant, but if ps1 and ps2 pointed to extremely large data structures, the duplicate transmission could have a significant impact on performance. Another side effect of not detecting the duplicate pointer is that the interface stub will unmarshal the values into two distinct memory locations. If the semantics of the method varied based on the equivalence of the two pointers:

---

[1] MIDL-generated interface proxies and stubs do not test [ref] pointers for null. Instead, they blindly dereference the pointer and allow an access violation to occur. Because the MIDL-generated marshalers always execute inside an exception handler, the access violation is caught inside the marshaler and translated into a marshaling error that is returned as the HRESULT of the method.

```
STDMETHODIMP MyClass::j(short *ps1, short *ps2) {
  if (ps1 == ps2)
    return this->OneKindOfBehavior(ps1);
  else
    return this->AnotherKindOfBehavior(ps1, ps2);
}
```

the interface marshaler would violate the semantic contract of the interface, which breaks the remoting transparency of COM.

The pointer attributes [ref] and [unique] both imply that the memory that the pointer refers to is not aliased by any other pointer in the method call and that the interface marshaler should *not* perform duplicate detection. To indicate that a pointer may point to memory aliased by another pointer in the same method call, the IDL designer should use the [ptr] attribute:

```
HRESULT k([in,ptr] short *ps1, [in,ptr] short *ps2);
```

Pointers that use the [ptr] attribute are called *full pointers,* because they come the closest to *full* compliance with the semantics of the C programming language. Given this IDL definition, the following client-side code:

```
short x = 100;
HRESULT hr = p->k(&x, &x); // note: same ptr. passed twice
```

will result in the value 100 being transmitted exactly once, because the [ptr] attribute on the ps1 parameter informs the interface marshaler to perform duplicate detection against all other [ptr] parameters. Since the ps2 parameter also uses the [ptr] attribute, the interface marshaler will detect the duplicate pointer value[2] and dereference and transmit the value of only one of the pointers. The interface stub will note that the transmitted value must be passed as both the ps1 and ps2 parameters, which causes the method to receive the same pointer in both parameters.

Although full pointers can solve a variety of problems and are useful in certain scenarios, they are not the preferred pointer semantics in COM. This is because more often than not, the interface designer knows a priori that no duplicate pointers will be passed. Also, while full pointers result in smaller OPRC messages *when there are duplicate pointers,* the runtime processing costs of finding duplicate pointers can be nontrivial as the number

---

[2] The interface marshaler detects duplicate pointer values (ps1 == ps2), not duplicate dereferenced values (*ps1 == *ps2); however, the latter is implied by the former.

of pointers per method grows. If the interface designer is certain no duplicates will occur, it is preferable to indicate this and use either unique or reference pointers.

Pointers and Memory

The interfaces shown so far in this chapter have been fairly simple and have used only primitive data types. One of the more problematic areas of using complex data types relates to how memory is managed for method parameters. Consider the following IDL function prototype:

```
HRESULT f([out] short *ps);
```

Given this prototype, the following is completely legal C:

```
short s;
HRESULT hr = p->f(&s); // s now contains whatever f wrote
```

For a simple function like this, it should be obvious how the memory is managed. However, often novice (and not so novice) programmers accidentally write code similar to this:

```
short *ps; // the function says it takes a short *, so...
HRESULT hr = p->f(ps);
```

When one considers the following legal implementation of the function:

```
STDMETHODIMP MyClass::f(short *ps) {
  static short n = 0;
  *ps = n++;
  return S_OK;
}
```

it is obvious that it is the caller's responsibility to allocate memory for the short integer and pass a *reference* to the memory as the function argument. Note from the implementation just shown that it is immaterial to the function where this memory comes from (*e.g.,* dynamically allocated from the heap, declared as an auto variable on the stack), as long as the actual argument refers to valid memory. To reinforce this requirement, COM requires [out] parameters that are pointers to be reference pointers.

Things become less clear when user-defined types are used instead of simple integral types. Consider the following IDL:

```
typedef struct tagPoint {
  short x; short y;
} Point;
HRESULT g([out] Point *pPoint);
```

As in the previous example, the correct usage is for the caller to allocate the memory for the values and pass a reference to *caller-allocated* memory:

```
Point pt;
HRESULT hr = p->g(&pt);
```

Had the caller passed an invalid pointer:

```
Point *ppt; // random uninitialized pointer
HRESULT hr = p->g(ppt); // where should proxy copy x & y to?
```

there is no valid memory for the method (or interface proxy) to write the values of x and y.

Things get interesting as the user-defined types become more complex. Consider the following IDL:

```
[ uuid(E02E5345-1473-11d1-8C85-0080C73925BA), object ]
interface IDogManager : IUnknown {
  typedef struct tagHUMAN {
    long nHumanID;
  } HUMAN;
  typedef struct tagDOG {
    long nDogID;
    [unique] HUMAN *pOwner;
  } DOG;
  HRESULT GetFromPound([out] DOG *pDog);
  HRESULT TakeToGroomer([in] const DOG *pDog);
  HRESULT SendToVet([in, out] DOG *pDog);
}
```

The distinctive aspect of this interface is that now the caller must pass a pointer to a memory location that itself will contain a pointer. For the preceding method definition, one could argue that the following code is correct:

```
DOG fido; // argument is a DOG *, so caller needs a DOG
HUMAN dummy; // the DOG refers to an owner, so alloc space?
fido.pOwner = &dummy;
HRESULT hr = p->GetFromPound(&fido); // is this correct?
```

This code assumes that the caller is responsible for allocating the memory for the DOG that is passed by reference. In this respect the code is correct. However, the code also assumes that it is responsible for managing any subordinate memory that may potentially be referred to by the updated value of the DOG object. It is here that this code departs from the COM way of doing things.

COM partitions the pointers involved in a method call into two categories. Any named parameters to a method that are pointers are referred to as *top-level* pointers. Any subordinate pointer that is implied by dereferencing a top-level pointer is referred to as an *embedded* pointer. In the GetFromPound method, the parameter pDog is considered a top-level pointer. The subordinate pointer pDog-> pOwner is considered an embedded pointer. Note that the DOG structure definition uses the [unique] attribute to qualify explicitly the pointer semantics for the structure member pOwner. Had the pointer semantics not been explicitly qualified, the interface designer could have applied an interface-wide default for all embedded pointers using the [pointer_default] attribute:

```
[
    uuid(E02E5345-1473-11d1-8C85-0080C73925BA), object,
    pointer_default(ref) // default embedded ptrs to [ref]
]
interface IUseStructs : IUnknown {
    typedef struct tagNODE {
        long val;
        [unique] struct tagNODE *pNode; // explicitly [unique]
    } NODE;
    typedef struct tagFOO {
        long val;
        long *pVal; // implicitly [ref]
    } FOO;
    HRESULT Method([in] FOO *pFoo, [in, unique] NODE *pHead);
}
```

The [pointer_default] attribute applies only to embedded pointers *whose pointer semantics are not explicitly qualified.* In the preceding interface definition, the only pointer to which this applies is the pVal data member of the FOO structure. The pNode member of the NODE structure is explicitly qualified to be a unique pointer, so it is not affected by the [pointer_default] setting. The method parameters pFoo and pHead are not affected by the [pointer_default] simply because they are top-level pointers and default to [ref] unless explicitly qualified otherwise (as in the case of pHead).

The primary reason embedded pointers are given distinguished status in COM is that they have unique memory management requirements. With respect to memory management, the distinction between top-level and embedded pointers is largely unimportant for [in] parameters, as the caller is providing all of the values to the method and therefore must have allocated memory that these values occupy:

```
HUMAN bob = { 2231 };
DOG fido = { 12288, &bob }; // fido is owned by bob
HRESULT hr = p->TakeToGroomer(&fido);   // this is correct!
```

However, the distinction between top-level and embedded pointers *is* important when it comes to managing memory for [out] and [in,out] parameters. For both [out] and [in,out] parameters, the memory referred to by top-level pointers is managed by the caller, as is the case for [in] parameters. For embedded pointers that appear in [out] or [in,out] parameters, the memory is managed by the *callee* (the method). The reason for this rule is data types can nest arbitrarily deep. For example, given the following type definition:

```
typedef struct tagNODE {
  short value;
  [unique] struct tagNODE *pNext;
} NODE;
```

it is impossible for the caller to anticipate how many subelements will need to be allocated. However, because the callee (the method) will be supplying the data for each node, it can safely allocate the memory for each node that is required.

Given that method implementors must allocate the memory to initialize any embedded pointers, the natural question that arises is, where should methods get this memory from so that callers know how to free it once they are done reading any returned values? The answer is the COM task allocator. The COM task allocator is a per-process memory allocator that is used exclusively for allocating memory for [out] and [in,out] embedded pointers. The simplest way to use the COM task allocator is via these three COM API functions:

```
void *CoTaskMemAlloc(DWORD cb); // allocate cb bytes
void CoTaskMemFree(void *pv); // deallocate memory at *pv
void *CoTaskMemRealloc(void *pv,DWORD cb);// grow/shrink *pv
```

The semantics of these three functions are identical to those of their C run-time library equivalents malloc, free, and realloc. The difference is that they are meant exclusively for allocating memory for [out] and [in,out] embedded pointer parameters. Another important distinction is that C runtime library routines cannot be used to allocate memory in one module and free it in another. This is because the details of how each C runtime library is implemented are proprietary and vary from compiler to compiler. By having all parties agree to use a single COM-provided allocator, there is no problem having a client free memory that is allocated by an object that is compiled in a separate DLL.

To understand how callee-allocated buffers are used in practice, consider the GetFromPound method shown previously:

```
HRESULT GetFromPound([out] DOG *pDog);
```

Whereas the memory for the DOG object must be allocated by the caller (pDog is a top-level pointer), the memory for the HUMAN object must be allocated by the method implementation using the task allocator (pDog->pOwner is an embedded pointer in an [out] parameter). The method implementation would look something like this:

```
STDMETHODIMP GetFromPound(/*[out]*/DOG *pDog) {
  short did = LookupNewDogId();
  short hid = LookupHumanId(did);
  pDog->nDogID = did;
// allocate memory for embedded pointer
  pDog->pOwner = (HUMAN*)CoTaskMemAlloc(sizeof(HUMAN));
  if (pDog->pOwner == 0) // not enough memory
    return E_OUTOFMEMORY;
  pDog->pOwner->nHumanID = hid;
  return S_OK;
}
```

Note that the method returns the distinguished HRESULT E_OUTOFMEMORY, indicating that the operation failed because of insufficient memory.

The caller of the GetFromPound method is responsible for freeing any callee-allocated memory once the values have been consumed:

```
DOG fido;
HRESULT hr = p->GetFromPound(&fido);
if (SUCCEEDED(hr)) {
  printf("The dog %h is owned by %h", fido.nDogID,
         fido.pOwner->nHumanID);
// data has been consumed, so free the memory
  CoTaskMemFree(fido.pOwner);
}
```

Unless otherwise documented, when a method fails, the client can assume that no memory was allocated.

The example just shown used a pure [out] parameter. Managing [in,out] parameters is somewhat more complex. Embedded pointers for [in,out] parameters must be allocated by the *caller* using the task allocator. If the method needs to reallocate the memory passed in by the client, the method must reallocate it using CoTaskMemRealloc. If the caller has no information to pass to the method, it can pass a null pointer on input and the method can still use CoTaskMemRealloc (which happily accepts a null pointer and does the right thing). Likewise, if the method has no information it wishes to pass back to the caller, it can simply deallocate the memory referred to by an embedded pointer. Consider the following IDL method definition:

```
HRESULT SendToVet([in, out] DOG *pDog);
```

Assuming that the caller has a valid HUMAN it wishes to pass as a parameter, the client code would look something like this:

```
HUMAN *pHuman = (HUMAN*)CoTaskMemAlloc(sizeof(HUMAN));
pHuman->nHumanID = 1522;
DOG fido = { 4111, pHuman };
HRESULT hr = p->SendToVet(&fido); // [in, out]
if (SUCCEEDED(hr)) {
  if (fido.pOwner)
    printf("Dog is now owned by %h", fido.pOwner->nHumanID);
  CoTaskMemFree(fido.pOwner); // OK to free null ptr.
}
```

The method implementation could reuse the caller-supplied buffer or allocate a new buffer if the caller passed a null embedded pointer:

```
STDMETHODIMP MyClass::SendToVet(/*[in, out]*/DOG *pDog) {
```

```
   if (fido.pOwner == 0)
     fido.pOwner = (HUMAN*)CoTaskMemAlloc(sizeof(HUMAN));
   if (fido.pOwner == 0) // alloc failed
     return E_OUTOFMEMORY;
   fido.pOwner->nHumanID = 22;
   return S_OK;
}
```

Because of the subtleties of dealing with [in,out] parameters with embedded pointers, it is a common practice to reiterate the rules of memory management for embedded pointers in an interface's documentation.

The preceding code fragments use the most convenient interface to the COM task allocator. Prior to the Windows NT release of COM, the primary interface to the task allocator was via its IMalloc interface:

```
[ uuid(00000002-0000-0000-C000-000000000046),local,object ]
interface IMalloc : IUnknown {
    void *Alloc([in] ULONG cb);
    void *Realloc ([in, unique] void *pv, [in] ULONG cb);
    void  Free([in, unique] void *pv);
    ULONG GetSize([in, unique] void *pv);
    int   DidAlloc([in, unique] void *pv);
    void  HeapMinimize(void);
}
```

To gain access to the task allocator's IMalloc interface, COM provides the API function CoGetMalloc:

```
HRESULT CoGetMalloc(
            [in] DWORD dwMemCtx, // reserved, must be one
            [out] IMalloc **ppMalloc); // put it here!
```

This means that instead of calling the convenient CoTaskMemAlloc:

```
HUMAN *pHuman = (HUMAN*)CoTaskMemAlloc(sizeof(HUMAN));
```

one can use the following less convenient form:

```
IMalloc *pMalloc = 0;
pHuman = 0;
HRESULT hr = CoGetMalloc(1, &pMalloc);
```

```
if (SUCCEEDED(hr)) {
  pHuman = (HUMAN*)pMalloc->Alloc(sizeof(HUMAN));
  pMalloc->Release();
}
```

The advantage of the latter technique is that it is compatible with pre-Windows NT releases of COM. In general, it is preferable to use CoTaskMemAlloc *et al* simply because it requires less coding and is therefore less subject to programmer errors.

The discussion of the task allocator has so far focused on how and when objects allocate memory and clients free memory. What has not been discussed is how this works when the object resides in a different address space from the client. This is largely because there is no difference in the way clients and objects are implemented when interface marshalers are used. To address the fact that the COM task allocator gets its memory from the process' private address space, it is the job of the interface stub and interface proxy to hide the fact that the task allocator cannot straddle the two address spaces. When the interface stub calls a method on an object, it marshals any [out] or [in,out] parameters into the ORPC response message. As shown in Figure 7.1, once this marshaling is complete, the interface stub (which ultimately is the intraapartment client of the object) frees any callee-allocated memory using CoTaskMemFree. This effectively frees all of the method call's task-allocated memory inside the object's address space. Upon receiving the ORPC response message, the interface proxy allocates space for any callee-allocated parameters using

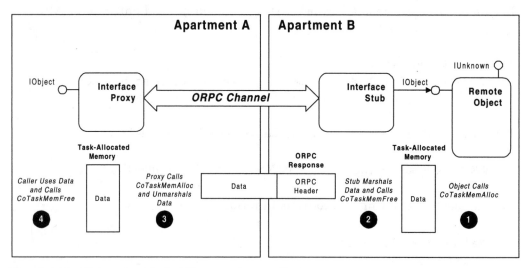

Figure 7.1 Using the Task Allocator Across Processes

CoTaskMemAlloc. When these blocks of memory are freed by the actual client using CoTaskMemFree, this effectively frees all of the method call's task-allocated memory inside the client's address space.

Because programmers are notorious for neglecting to free memory, it is sometimes useful to monitor the activity (or lack of activity) of the task allocator in a process. To facilitate this, COM allows the task allocator to be hooked using a user-defined spy object that will be notified before and after every task allocator call. This user-defined spy object must implement the IMallocSpy interface:

```
[ uuid(0000001d-0000-0000-C000-000000000046),local,object ]
interface IMallocSpy : IUnknown {
  ULONG PreAlloc([in] ULONG cbRequest);
  void  *PostAlloc([in] void *pActual);
  void  *PreFree([in] void *pRequest,[in] BOOL fSpyed);
  void  PostFree([in] BOOL fSpyed);
  ULONG PreRealloc([in] void *pRequest,[in] ULONG cbRequest,
              [out] void **ppNewRequest,[in] BOOL fSpyed);
  void  *PostRealloc([in] void *pActual,[in] BOOL fSpyed);
  void  *PreGetSize([in] void *pRequest,[in] BOOL fSpyed);
  ULONG PostGetSize([in] ULONG cbActual,[in] BOOL fSpyed);
  void  *PreDidAlloc([in] void *pRequest,[in] BOOL fSpyed);
  int   PostDidAlloc([in] void *pRequest,
                    [in] BOOL fSpyed,[in] int fActual);
  void  PreHeapMinimize(void);
  void  PostHeapMinimize(void);
}
```

Note that for each IMalloc method, the IMallocSpy interface has two methods: one that is called by COM prior to the actual allocator doing its work, one that is called by COM just after the actual allocator does its work. In each premethod, the user-provided spy object can modify the parameters passed by the user to the task allocator. In each postmethod, the spy object can modify the results returned by the actual allocator. This allows a spy object to allocate extra memory to add debugging information to each block of memory. COM provides an API function for registering a process-wide malloc spy:

```
HRESULT CoRegisterMallocSpy([in] IMallocSpy *pms);
```

Only one malloc spy can be registered per process (CoRegisterMallocSpy will return CO_E_OBJISREG if another spy is already registered). To remove a malloc spy, COM provides the API function CoRevokeMallocSpy:

```
HRESULT CoRevokeMallocSpy(void);
```

COM will not allow a malloc spy to be revoked while memory allocated using the current spy has not been freed.

Arrays

By default, pointer parameters are assumed to be pointers to single instances, not arrays. To pass an array as a parameter, one can either use the C array syntax and/or use special IDL attributes to indicate various array dimension information. The simplest technique for passing arrays is to specify the dimensions at compile time:

```
HRESULT Method1([in] short rgs[8]);
```

This is formally known as a fixed array and is both the simplest to express in IDL and the simplest and most compact representation at runtime. For this array, the interface proxy will allocate 16 bytes (8 * sizeof(short)) in the ORPC request message and then copy all eight elements into the message. Once the ORPC request is received by the server, the interface stub will use the memory from the received buffer directly as an argument to the function, as shown in Figure 7.2.

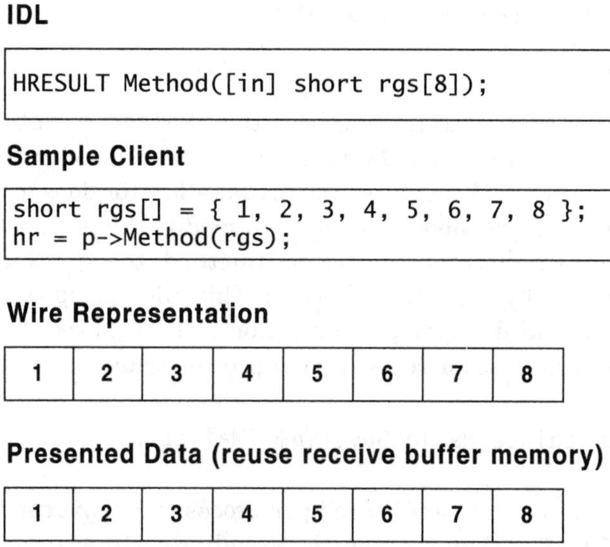

IDL

```
HRESULT Method([in] short rgs[8]);
```

Sample Client

```
short rgs[] = { 1, 2, 3, 4, 5, 6, 7, 8 };
hr = p->Method(rgs);
```

Wire Representation

| 1 | 2 | 3 | 4 | 5 | 6 | 7 | 8 |

Presented Data (reuse receive buffer memory)

| 1 | 2 | 3 | 4 | 5 | 6 | 7 | 8 |

Figure 7.2 Fixed Arrays

Because the size of the array is fixed and the entire contents of the array is already in the received buffer, the interface stub is smart enough to reuse the presented buffer memory as the actual argument to the method.

The method just shown is useful if the only reasonable array length is 8 in all cases. It allows the caller to pass any array of shorts it chooses, provided that the array has only eight elements:

```
void f(IFoo *pFoo) {
    short rgs[8] = { 1, 2, 3, 4, 5, 6, 7, 8 };
    pFoo->Method1(rgs);
}
```

Predicting the appropriate array length in practice is virtually impossible, as guessing too small means that not enough elements will be transmitted and guessing too large will cause the transmitted message to be overly large. Moreover, if the array consists of complex data types, marshaling elements beyond the actual array size could be extremely expensive and/or cause marshaling errors. Nonetheless, fixed arrays are useful when the size of an array is constant and known at interface design time.

To allow arrays to be dimensioned at runtime, IDL (and the underlying wire protocol NDR) allows the caller to specify the capacity of the array at runtime. Arrays of this type are referred to as conformant arrays. The maximum legal index of a conformant array can be specified at either runtime or compile time, and the capacity (known as the array's *conformance*) is transmitted prior to the actual elements, as shown in Figure 7.3. As with a fixed array, conformant arrays can be passed to the method implementation directly from the received buffer without any additional copying, as the entire contents of the array is always present in the received message.

IDL uses the [size_is] attribute to allow the caller to specify the conformance of an array:

```
    HRESULT Method2([in] long cElems,
                    [in, size_is(cElems)] short rgs[*]);
```
or
```
    HRESULT Method3([in] long cElems,
                    [in, size_is(cElems)] short rgs[]);
```
or
```
    HRESULT Method4([in] long cElems,
                    [in, size_is(cElems)] short *rgs);
```

All of these styles are equivalent in terms of the underlying packet format. Any of these methods allow the caller to determine the appropriate array size as follows:

IDL

```
HRESULT Method([in] long cElems, [in, size_is(cElems)] short *prgs);
```

Sample Client

```
short rgs[] = { 1, 2, 3, 4, 5, 6, 7, 8 };
hr = p->Method(sizeof(rgs)/sizeof(*rgs), rgs);
```

Wire Representation

8	1	2	3	4	5	6	7	8

Presented Data (reuse receive buffer memory)

1	2	3	4	5	6	7	8

Figure 7.3 Conformant Arrays

```
void f(IFoo *pFoo) {
    short rgs[] = { 1, 2, 3, 4, 5, 6, 7, 8 };
    pFoo->Method2(8, rgs);
}
```

When used as a parameter attribute as just shown, the expression used by the [size_is] attribute can use any other parameters to the same method and can use arithmetic, logical, and conditional operators. For example, the following IDL is legal, if not easily understood:

```
HRESULT Method5([in] long arg1, [in] long arg2,
    [in] long arg3,
    [in, size_is(arg1 ? (arg3+1) : (arg1&arg2))]
        short *rgs);
```

Function calls or other language constructs that could potentially cause side effects (such as the ++ and −− operators) are prohibited in [size_is] expressions.

When used to describe a conformant array that is embedded inside a struct, the [size_is] attribute can use any other members of the same struct:

```
typedef struct tagCOUNTED_SHORTS {
    long cElems;
```

```
    [size_is(cElems)] short rgs[];
} COUNTED_SHORTS;

HRESULT Method6([in] COUNTED_SHORTS *pcs);
```

which assumes the caller will write code as follows:

```
void SendFiveShorts (IFoo *pFoo) {
  char buffer [sizeof (COUNTED_SHORTS) + 4 * sizeof (short)];
  COUNTED_SHORTS& rcs = *reinterpret_cast<COUNTED_SHORTS*>(buffer);
  rcs.cElems = 5; rcs.rgs[0] = 0; rcs.rgs[1] = 1;
  rcs.rgs[2] = 2; rcs.rgs[3] = 3; rcs.rgs[4] = 4;
  pFoo->Method6(&rcs);
}
```

IDL also supports the [max_is] attribute, which is a stylistic variation on [size_is]. The [size_is] attribute indicates the number of elements an array can contain; the [max_is] attribute indicates the maximum legal index in an array (which is one less than the number of elements an array can contain). This means that the following two declarations are identical:

```
HRESULT Method7([in, size_is(10)] short *rgs);
HRESULT Method8([in, max_is(9)] short *rgs);
```

As a point of interest, although constants can be used in [size_is] attributes as just shown, it is slightly more efficient just to use a fixed array. If a conformant array is used, the conformance dimension must be transmitted in the preceding examples, despite the fact that its value is static and is known by both the interface proxy and interface stub at compile time.

If the contents of arrays were passed only from the caller to the method implementation, the conformant array would be sufficient for almost all uses. There are many cases, however, in which the caller wishes to pass a potentially empty array to the object and have it filled with useful values. It is possible to use conformant arrays as output parameters, as shown in the following:

```
HRESULT Method9([in] long cMax,
                [out, size_is(cMax)] short *rgs);
```

which implies the following caller-side usage:

```
void f(IFoo *pFoo) {
  short rgs[100];
  pFoo->Method9(100, rgs);
}
```

and the following server-side implementation:

```
HRESULT CFoo::Method9(long cMax, short *rgs) {
  for (long n = 0; n < cMax; n++)
    rgs[n] = n * n;
  return S_OK;
}
```

But what if the method implementation cannot correctly fill the entire array with valid elements? In the preceding code fragment, even if the method initializes only the first cMax/2 elements of the array, the server-side stub will still transmit the entire array of cMax elements. This is clearly inefficient, and to address this, IDL and NDR provide a third type of array, the varying array.

A varying array is an array that has a fixed capacity but may contain fewer valid elements than its actual capacity. A single contiguous subset of a varying array's contents will be transmitted, without regard for the actual capacity of the array. To specify the subset of elements to transmit, IDL uses the [length_is] attribute. Unlike the [size_is] attribute, which describes the capacity of the array, the [length_is] attribute describes the actual *contents* of the array. Consider the following IDL:

```
HRESULT Method10([in] long cActual,
          [in, length_is(cActual)] short rgs[1024]);
```

When transmitted, the value of cActual (which is known as the *variance* of the array) will precede the transmitted values. To allow the transmitted region to appear anywhere within the array, not just at the beginning, IDL and NDR also support the [first_is] attribute, which indicates where the transmitted region begins. This offset value will also be transmitted with the array contents so that the unmarshaler will know which subset of the array is being initialized. Just as [size_is] had its stylistic variant, [max_is], [length_is] also has a variant, [last_is], that uses an index in lieu of a count. The following two definitions are equivalent:

```
HRESULT Method11([in, first_is(2), length_is(5)]
                  short rgs[8]);
```

```
HRESULT Method12([in, first_is(2), last_is(6)]
                 short rgs[8]);
```

Both methods instruct the marshaler to transmit only five array elements, but at the unmarshal side, room for eight elements is allocated and the incoming values are copied to the appropriate locations. Any elements not present in the received buffer will be initialized to zero.

Varying arrays can result in reduced network traffic, as only the required elements are transmitted. However, as shown in Figure 7.4, varying arrays are less efficient than conformant arrays in terms of memory copying overhead, as the array that is passed to the method implementation by the server-side stub is allocated as a distinct block of memory on the heap. This block is first initialized filled with zeros and then the contents of the received buffer are copied into the appropriate locations. This causes one or two additional passes over the memory of the array before entering the method, which for large arrays can hurt performance. This is not to say that varying arrays are not useful, but when used as input-only parameters, a varying array will be considerably less efficient than a logically equivalent conformant array.

Like fixed arrays, varying arrays require the interface designer to specify the conformance/capacity at compile time. This makes varying arrays fairly limiting, as it is difficult in practice to anticipate the optimal buffer size for all uses of an interface (*e.g.,* some clients may have extreme limitations on memory usage, others may put a premium on round-trips and would prefer larger

IDL

```
HRESULT Method([in] long cActual, [in] long iFirst,
               [in,length_is(cActual),first_is(iFirst)] short prgs[8]);
```

Sample Client

```
short rgs[8]; rgs[4] = 5; rgs[5] = 6;
hr = p->Method(2, 4, rgs);
```

Wire Representation

4	2	5	6

Presented Data (separate memory block)

0	0	0	0	5	6	0	0

Figure 7.4: Varying Arrays

buffers). Fortunately, IDL and NDR allow both the contents (variance) and capacity (conformance) to be specified for a given array by combining the [size_is] and [length_is] attributes. When both attributes are used, the array is known as a conformant varying array or, more conveniently, an open array. To specify an open array, simply provide the caller with a way of specifying both the capacity and the contents via parameters:

```
HRESULT Method13([in] cMax, [in] cActual,
                 [in,
                  size_is(cMax),
                  length_is(cActual)] short rgs[]);
```

or

```
HRESULT Method14([in] cMax, [in] cActual,
                 [in,
                  size_is(cMax),
                  length_is(cActual)] short rgs[*]);
```

or

```
HRESULT Method15([in] cMax, [in] cActual,
                 [in,
                  size_is(cMax),
                  length_is(cActual)] short *rgs);
```

any of which imply a client-side usage as follows:

```
void f(IFoo *pFoo) {
  short rgs[8];
  rgs[0] = 1; rgs[1] = 2;
  pFoo->Method13(8, 2, rgs);
}
```

As shown in Figure 7.5, when transmitting an open array, the marshaler will first write out the capacity of the array in addition to the offset and length of the actual contents. As with the varying array, the capacity of the array may be greater than the number of elements transmitted. This implies that the contents of the received buffer cannot be passed directly to the caller, so a second block of memory is used, increasing memory overhead.

Conformant arrays are the most useful type of array for input parameters. Open arrays are most useful for output or input/output parameters, as they

IDL

```
HRESULT Method([in] long cMax, [in] long cActual, [in] long iFirst,
[in,size_is(cMax),length_is(cActual),first_is(iFirst)] short *prgs);
```

Sample Client

```
short rgs[8]; rgs[4] = 5; rgs[5] = 6;
hr = p->Method(8, 2, 4, rgs);
```

Wire Representation

8	4	2	5	6

Presented Data (separate memory block)

0	0	0	0	5	6	0	0

Figure 7.5 Open Arrays

allow the caller to allocate an arbitrarily sized buffer and yet only the number of elements actually used will be transmitted. To allow this type of usage, the IDL typically looks something like this:

```
HRESULT Method16([in] long cMax,
                 [out] long *pcActual,
        [out, size_is(cMax), length_is(*pcActual)]
                 short *rgs);
```

which implies the following client-side usage:

```
void f(IFoo *pFoo) {
  short rgs[8];
  long cActual;
  pFoo->Method16(8, &cActual, rgs);
  // .. process first cActual elements of rgs
}
```

and a server-side implementation something like this:

```
HRESULT CFoo::Method16(long cMax, long *pcActual,
                       short *rgs) {
  *pcActual = min(cMax,5); //only write 1st 5 elems
  for (long n = 0; n < *pcActual; n++)
```

```
        rgs[n] = n * n;
      return S_OK;
  }
```

This allows the caller to control the buffer sizing, but the method implementation controls the actual number of elements transmitted.

If an open array will be used as an input-output parameter, the variance of the array needs to be specified in each direction. If the number of elements on input may not be the same as on output, the variance parameter must be an input-output parameter as well:

```
HRESULT Method17([in] long cMax,
                 [in, out] long *pcActual,
         [in, out, size_is(cMax), length_is(*pcActual)]
                      short *rgs);
```

which implies the following client-side usage:

```
void f(IFoo *pFoo) {
  short rgs[8];
  rgs[0] = 0; rgs[1] = 1;
  long cActual = 2;
  pFoo->Method17(8, &cActual, rgs);
  // .. process first cActual elements of rgs
}
```

If the number of elements on input will match the number of elements on output, a conformant array would suffice:

```
HRESULT Method18([in] long cElems,
     [in, out, size_is(cElems)] short *rgs);
```

This method benefits from the efficiency of a conformant array in addition to being considerably easier to use.

The preceding examples have all dealt with one-dimensional arrays. Consider the following C prototype:

```
void g(short **arg1);
```

This prototype can mean any number of things in C. Perhaps the function is expecting a pointer to a pointer to a single short:

```
void g(short **arg1) { // return ptr to static
  static short s;
  *arg1 = &s;
}
```

Or perhaps the function is expecting an array of 100 short pointers:

```
void g(short **arg1) { // square 100 shorts byref
  for (int n = 0; n < 100; n++)
    *(arg1[n]) *= *(arg1[n]);
```

Or perhaps the function is expecting a pointer to a pointer to an array of shorts:

```
void g(short **arg1) { // square 100 shorts
  for (int n = 0; n < 100; n++)
    (*arg1)[n] *= (*arg1)[n];
```

This syntactic nightmare is addressed in IDL by using a syntax that often sends novice IDL users running to the documentation for solace.

The IDL [size_is] and [length_is] attributes accept a variable number of comma-delimited arguments, one per level of indirection. If a parameter is missing, the current level of indirection is assumed to be a pointer to an instance and not an array. To indicate that a parameter is a pointer to a pointer to a single instance, no additional attributes are needed:

```
HRESULT Method19([in] short **pps);
```

which implies the following layout in memory:

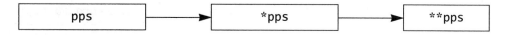

To indicate that a parameter is a pointer to an array of pointers to instances, the following IDL is correct:

```
HRESULT Method20([in, size_is(3)] short **rgps);
```

which would look like this in memory:

To indicate that a parameter is a pointer to a pointer to an array of instances, the following IDL is correct:

```
HRESULT Method21([in, size_is(,4)] short **pprgs);
```

which would look like this in memory:

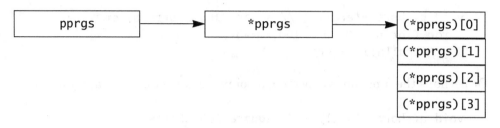

To indicate that a parameter is an array of pointers to arrays of instances, the following IDL is correct:

```
HRESULT Method22([in, size_is(3,4)] short **rgrgs);
```

which would look like this in memory:

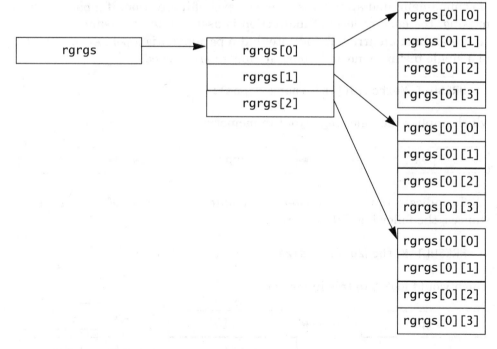

Although this syntax may leave something to be desired, it is nonetheless more flexible and less ambiguous than C.

It is important to note that the foregoing IDL method does specify a multidimensional array; it is technically an array of pointers to arrays of pointers to instances. This is *not* the same as a C language multidimensional array, which can be specified in IDL using standard C syntax:

```
HRESULT Method23([in] short rgrgs[3][4]);
```

This syntax assumes that all elements of the array will be allocated in memory contiguously, which is definitely *not* the assumption of the previous example.

It is legal to specify the first dimension of a multidimensional array using the [size_is] attribute:

```
HRESULT Method24([in, size_is(3)] short rgrgs[][4]);
```

but it is not possible to specify any dimension other than the leftmost dimension.

The expressions used by [size_is], [length_is], and other array dimensioning attributes cannot be based on function calls. This would make using strings, whose conformance and/or variance is based on calls to wcslen or strlen, difficult to marshal. This means that the following is illegal IDL:

```
HRESULT Method24([in, size_is(wcslen(wsz) + 1)]
                const OLECHAR *wsz);
```

Because this limitation would make using strings extremely inconvenient for client programs, IDL supports the string attribute, which tells the marshaling layer to call the appropriate xxxlen function to calculate the conformance of an array. The following is the correct way to specify a string as an input parameter:

```
HRESULT Method25([in, string] const OLECHAR *wsz);
```

or

```
HRESULT Method26([in, string] const OLECHAR wsz[]);
```

When using strings as output or input/output parameters, it is almost always a good idea to specify the capacity of the caller's buffer explicitly to ensure that the server-side buffer is large enough. Consider the following buggy IDL:

```
HRESULT Method27([in, out, string] OLECHAR *pwsz);
```

If the caller invokes this method with some fairly short string:

```
void f(IFoo *pFoo) {
  OLECHAR wsz[1024];
  wcscpy(wsz, OLESTR("Hello"));
  pFoo->Method27(wsz);
 // .. process updated string
}
```

then the capacity of the array allocated on the server side will be calculated
based on the length of the input string (which is six including the terminating
null character). Consider the following server-side method implementation:

```
HRESULT CFoo::Method27(OLECHAR *wsz) {
   DisplayString(wsz);
// wsz only can hold 6 characters!
   wcscpy(wsz, OLESTR("Goodbye"));
   return S_OK;
}
```

Because the conformance of the array was based on wcslen(OLESTR("Hello")
+ 1), when the method implementation overwrites the string with something
longer, the tail end of the string will overwrite random bytes of memory, hope-
fully causing fatal errors before the software is released. This means that even
though the caller had ample storage preallocated to hold the resultant string,
the marshaling layer on the server side was unaware of this seemingly extra-
neous memory and allocated only enough space to hold six characters worth of
Unicode string. The IDL should have been:

```
HRESULT Method28([in] long cchMax,
           [in, out, string, size_is(cchMax)] OLECHAR *wsz);
```

which the caller could have used as follows:

```
void f(IFoo *pFoo) {
  OLECHAR wsz[1024];
  wcscpy(wsz, OLESTR("Hello"));
  pFoo->Method28(1024, wsz);
 // .. process updated string
}
```

The most unfortunate aspect of the [in, out, string] example is that it
works fine when the input string is at least as long as the output string. The

errors related to this method will be intermittent and may never occur in the testing phase of a project.

In most conventional APIs, when a function returns a variable length data structure to a caller, the caller preallocates a buffer to contain the results of the function, and the function implementation fills the buffer provided by the caller. It is up to the caller to determine the correct buffer size. The problem with using caller-sized buffers for returning variable length data structures such as strings is that it is possible that the method implementation may want to return more data than the caller has anticipated. Consider the following Windows SDK code that displays the text of an edit control:

```
void Show(HWND hwndEdit) {
    TCHAR sz[1024];
    GetWindowText(hwndEdit, sz, 1024);
    MessageBox(0, sz, __TEXT("Hi!"), MB_OK);
}
```

Notice that the implementor of Show guessed that the edit control would never contain more than 1,024 characters. How did he or she know? Exactly. One might think that this implementation would be safer:

```
void Show(HWND hwndEdit) {
    int cch = GetWindowTextLength(hwndEdit);
    TCHAR *psz = new TCHAR[cch + 1];
    GetWindowText(hwndEdit, psz, cch);
    MessageBox(0, sz, __TEXT("Hi!"), MB_OK);
    delete[] psz;
}
```

but in this example, how can the caller be certain that the user will not type in a character after the call to GetWindowTextLength but before the call to GetWindowText? The fact that the allocation is based on potentially stale information makes this idiom susceptible to race conditions.

The programming idiom preceding may be acceptable for HWNDs, but it is intolerable for COM objects. Unlike HWNDs, COM objects are very likely to be accessed by multiple parties concurrently. In addition, the cost of making two method calls to perform one operation as just shown would cause performance to degrade very quickly, especially in a distributed environment where the latency introduced by packet transmission and reception imposes a tremendous penalty on caller-method round-trips. Because of these two factors, when variable length data types are passed from the method implementation to the caller as an [out] parameter, a properly designed COM interface forces the method implementation to allocate space for the result using the COM task allocator. This is necessary because the actual size of the result can be known only inside the method implementation. This dynamically allocated buffer is returned to the caller of the method, and when it is no longer needed, it is the caller's responsibility to free the buffer from the COM task allocator in the calling process. To express this idiom for a string parameter, the following IDL will work correctly:

```
HRESULT Method29([out, string] OLECHAR **ppwsz);
```

which implies the following server-side implementation:

```
HRESULT CFoo::Method29(OLECHAR **ppwsz) {
  const OLECHAR wsz[] = OLESTR("Goodbye");
  int cb = (wcslen(wsz) + 1) * sizeof(OLECHAR);
  *ppwsz = (OLECHAR*)CoTaskMemAlloc(cb);
  if (*ppwsz == 0) return E_OUTOFMEMORY;
  wcscpy(*ppwsz, wsz);
  return S_OK;
}
```

To use this method properly, the following client-side code is required:

```
void f(IFoo *pFoo) {
  OLECHAR *pwsz = 0;
  if SUCCEEDED(pFoo->Method29(&pwsz)) {
    DisplayString(pwsz);
    CoTaskMemFree(pwsz);
  }
}
```

Although this usage may result in additional memory copying overhead, this must be weighed against the reduction in round-trip cost and the guarantee that strings of any length can be returned without requiring the caller to tie up additional buffer space in anticipation of arbitrarily large strings.

The array syntax shown in this section is perfectly reasonable for C or C++ programmers. Unfortunately, at the time of this writing, Visual Basic is incapable of dealing with any variable size arrays and can recognize only fixed arrays. To allow Visual Basic to send and receive variable sized arrays, the COM IDL files define a composite type called a SAFEARRAY. The

SAFEARRAY is a fairly unusual data structure that allows multidimensional arrays of VARIANT-compatible types to be passed as parameters. To express the dimensions of a SAFEARRAY, COM provides the SAFEARRAYBOUND data type:

```
typedef struct tagSAFEARRAYBOUND {
    ULONG cElements;  // size_is for dimension
    LONG  lLbound;    // min index for dimension (usually 0)
} SAFEARRAYBOUND;
```

The SAFEARRAY data type internally uses a conformant array of SAFEARRAYBOUNDs to put some shape around the array's contents:

```
typedef struct tagSAFEARRAY {
  USHORT cDims;       // # of dimensions
  USHORT fFeatures;   // flags describing contents
  ULONG  cbElements;  // # of bytes per element
  ULONG  cLocks;      // used to track memory usage
  void*  pvData;      // actual elements
  [size_is(cDims)] SAFEARRAYBOUND rgsabound[];
} SAFEARRAY;
```

The preceding IDL is not actually used to describe the wire format of SAFEARRAYs, but it is used to describe them programmatically.

To allow the user maximum flexibility with respect to memory management, COM defines the following flags that can be used with the fFeatures field:

```
FADF_AUTO         /* array is allocated on the stack */
FADF_STATIC       /* array is statically allocated */
FADF_EMBEDDED     /* array is embedded in a structure */
FADF_FIXEDSIZE    /* may not be resized or reallocated */
FADF_BSTR         /* an array of BSTRs */
FADF_UNKNOWN      /* an array of IUnknown* */
FADF_DISPATCH     /* an array of IDispatch* */
FADF_VARIANT      /* an array of VARIANTs */
```

To allow the data type of the SAFEARRAY's elements to be specifed, the IDL compiler recognizes a special SAFEARRAY-specific syntax.

```
HRESULT Method([in] SAFEARRAY(type) *ppsa);
```

where *type* is the type of element in the SAFEARRAY. The corresponding C++ method prototype would look like this:

```
HRESULT Method(SAFEARRAY **psa);
```

Note that only one level of indirection is used in the IDL definition; however, two levels of indirection are used in the corresponding C++ definition. Assuming the following IDL definition that specifies a SAFEARRAY of short integers:

```
HRESULT Method([in] SAFEARRAY(short) *psa);
```

the corresponding Visual Basic definition would look like this:

```
Sub Method(ByVal psa As Integer())
```

Note that there are no explicit array dimensions in the Visual Basic prototype. Recall, however, that Visual Basic does support fixed arrays.

The SAFEARRAY data type is supported by a fairly rich API set that allows arrays to be redimensioned and traversed portably. For accessing the elements of a SAFEARRAY, COM provides the following API calls:

```
// get a pointer to the actual array elements
HRESULT SafeArrayAccessData([in] SAFEARRAY *psa,
                                  [out] void ** ppv);
// release pointer returned by SafeArrayAccessData
HRESULT SafeArrayUnaccessData([in] SAFEARRAY *psa);
// Get number of dimensions
ULONG SafeArrayGetDim([in] SAFEARRAY *psa);
// Get upper bound of a dimension
HRESULT SafeArrayGetUBound([in] SAFEARRAY *psa,
                [in] UINT nDim, [out] long *pUBound);
// Get lower bound of a dimension
HRESULT SafeArrayGetLBound([in] SAFEARRAY *psa,
                [in] UINT nDim, [out] long *pLBound);
```

These methods provide a portable and safe method for accessing the actual contents of the array. Assuming the following IDL:

```
HRESULT Sum([in] SAFEARRAY(long) *ppsa,
            [out, retval] long *pSum);
```

the following method implementation calculates the sum of a SAFEARRAY of long integers:

```
STDMETHODIMP MyClass::Sum(SAFEARRAY **ppsa, long *pnSum) {
    assert(ppsa && *ppsa && pnSum);
    assert(SafeArrayGetDim(*ppsa) == 1);
    long iUBound, iLBound;
// note that dimension indices are one-based
    HRESULT hr = SafeArrayGetUBound(*ppsa, 1, &iUBound);
    assert(SUCCEEDED(hr));
    hr = SafeArrayGetLBound(*ppsa, 1, &iLBound);
    assert(SUCCEEDED(hr));
    long *prgn = 0;
    hr = SafeArrayAccessData(*ppsa, (void**)&prgn);
    *pnSum = 0;
    for (long i = 0; i <iUBound - iLBound; i++)
        *pnSum += prgn[i];
    SafeArrayUnaccessData(*ppsa);
    return S_OK;
}
```

Note that any API calls that deal with the dimensions of the array use one-based indices.

The preceding code fragment simply manipulated the contents of an existing SAFEARRAY. To create a one-dimensional SAFEARRAY to pass as a method parameter, COM provides the following API function that allocates the memory for the SAFEARRAY structure and its array elements in one contiguous block of memory:

```
SAFEARRAY *SafeArrayCreateVector(
        [in] VARTYPE vt,            // element type
        [in] long iLBound,          // index of lower bound
        [in] unsigned int cElems);  // # of elements
```

COM also provides a variety of functions to allocate multidimensional arrays, which are beyond the scope of this discussion. Given the following IDL method definition:

```
HRESULT GetPrimes([in] long nStart, [in] long nEnd,
            [out] SAFEARRAY(long) *ppsa);
```

the following C++ method definition returns a callee-allocated **SAFEARRAY** to the caller:

```
STDMETHODIMP MyClass::GetPrimes(long nMin, long nMax,
                                  SAFEARRAY **ppsa) {
    assert(ppsa);
    UINT cElems = GetNumberOfPrimes(nMin, nMax);
    *ppsa = SafeArrayCreateVector(VT_I4, 0, cElems);
    assert(*ppsa);
    long *prgn = 0;
    HRESULT hr = SafeArrayAccessData(*ppsa, (void**)&prgn);
    assert(SUCCEEDED(hr));
    for (UINT i = 0; i < cElems; i++)
        prgn[i] = GetNextPrime(i ? prgn[i - 1] : nMin);
    SafeArrayUnaccessData(*ppsa);
    return S_OK;
}
```

The corresponding client-side code would look like this in Visual Basic:

```
Function GetSumOfPrimes(ByVal nMin as Long,
                          ByVal nMax as Long) as Long
  Dim arr() as Long
  Dim n as Variant
  Objref.GetPrimes nMin, nMax, arr
  GetSumOfPrimes = 0
  for each n in arr
    GetSumOfPrimes = GetSumOfPrimes + n
  Next n
End Function
```

which translates to the following C++:

```
long GetSumOfPrimes(long nMin, long nMax) {
  SAFEARRAY *pArray = 0;
  HRESULT hr = g_pObjRef->GetPrimes(nMin, nMax, &pArray);
  assert(SUCCEEDED(hr) && SafeArrayGetDim(pArray) == 1);
  long *prgn = 0;
  hr = SafeArrayAccessData(pArray, (void**)&prgn);
  long iUBound, iLBound, result = 0;
  SafeArrayGetUBound(pArray, 1, &iUBound);
```

```
      SafeArrayGetLBound(pArray, 1, &iLBound);
      for (long n = iLBound; n <= iUBound; n++)
        result += prgn[n];
      SafeArrayUnaccessData(pArray);
      SafeArrayDestroy(pArray);
      return n;
    }
```

Note that the caller is responsible for freeing the resources allocated for the SAFEARRAY returned as an [out] parameter. Calling `SafeArrayDestroy` correctly releases all memory and resources held by the SAFEARRAY.

Flow Control

Note that in the previous examples using arrays and SAFEARRAYs, the sender of the data decides how much data will be transmitted in the ORPC message. Assume the following simple IDL method definition:

```
HRESULT Sum([in] long cElems,
            [in, size_is(cElems)] double *prgd,
            [out, retval] double *pResult);
```

If the caller were to invoke this method as follows:

```
double rgd[1024 * 1024 * 16];
HRESULT hr = p->Sum(sizeof(rgd)/sizeof(*rgd), rgd);
```

the resultant ORPC request message would be at least 128MB. Although the underlying RPC protocol is perfectly capable of fragmenting large messages into multiple network packets, there are several problems related to using large arrays. One obvious problem is that the caller must have an additional 128MB+ of available memory beyond the memory occupied by the presented array. This duplicate buffer is needed by the interface proxy to build the ORPC request message into which the array will ultimately be copied. A closely related problem is that the object's process must also have 128MB+ of available memory in order to reconstruct the received RPC packets into a single contiguous ORPC message. Had the array used the [length_is] attribute, budget yet another 128MB to duplicate the array into memory to pass to the method. This problem applies to both [in] and [out] parameters. In either case, the sender of the array may have ample buffer space to build the ORPC message, but the receiver of the array may not. This problem is the result of receivers not having a mechanism for flow control at an application level.

A more subtle problem with the preceding method definition has to do with latency. The semantics of an ORPC call require the RPC/ORPC layer to reconstruct the entire ORPC message prior to invoking the method on the object. This means that the object cannot begin processing the presented data until the last packet has been received. Given that the overall transmission time for a large array will be quite long, the object will remain idle for a considerable period of time, waiting for the last packet to arrive. During this idle period, it is likely that many elements have been successfully received in the object's address space; however, the semantics of COM method invocation require all elements to be present prior to the actual call. The same problem applies when arrays are passed as [out] parameters, as the client cannot begin processing the partial results of an operation that may already have been received.

To address the problems related to passing large arrays as method parameters, COM has a standard interface design idiom that allows the receiver of the data to perform flow control of the array elements explicitly. This idiom is based on passing a special COM interface pointer in lieu of actual arrays. This special interface is called an enumerator and allows the receiver to pull elements from the sender at a rate that is appropriate for the receiver. To apply this idiom to the previous method definition, the following interface definition would be required:

```
interface IEnumDouble : IUnknown {
// pull a chunk of elements from the sender
   HRESULT Next([in]  ULONG cElems,
[out, size_is(cElems), length_is(*pcFetched)]
                   double *prgElems,
            [out] ULONG *pcFetched);
// advance cursor past cElems elements
   HRESULT Skip([in] cElems);
// reset cursor to first element
   HRESULT Reset(void);
// duplicate enumerator's current cursor
   HRESULT Clone([out] IEnumDouble **pped);
}
```

It is important to note that the IEnum interface simply models the cursor, not the actual array. Given this interface definition, the original IDL method definition:

```
HRESULT Sum([in] long cElems,
            [in, size_is(cElems)] double *prgd,
            [out, retval] double *pResult);
```

becomes this:

```
HRESULT Sum([in] IEnumDouble *ped,
            [out, retval] double *pResult);
```

Note that the element count is no longer mandatory, as the receiver of the data will discover the end of the array when the IEnumDouble::Next method returns a distinguished HRESULT (S_FALSE).

Given the preceding interface definition, the following would be the correct method implementation:

```
STDMETHODIMP MyClass::Sum(IEnumDouble *ped, double *psum) {
  assert(ped && psum);
  *psum = 0;
  HRESULT hr;
  do {
// declare a buffer to receive some elements
    enum { CHUNKSIZE = 2048 };
    double rgd[CHUNKSIZE];
// ask data producer to send CHUNKSIZE elements
    ULONG cFetched;
    hr = ped->Next(CHUNKSIZE, rgd, &cFetched);
// adjust cFetched to address sloppy objects
    if (hr == S_OK) cFetched = CHUNKSIZE;
    if (SUCCEEDED(hr)) // S_OK or S_FALSE
// consume/use received elements
      for (ULONG n = 0; n < cFetched; n++)
        *psum += rgd[n];
  } while (hr == S_OK); // S_FALSE or error terminates
}
```

Note that the Next routine will return S_OK if the sender has additional elements to send and S_FALSE if the sender is done. Also note that the code is written defensively to compensate for sloppy implementations that neglect to set the cFetched variable when returning S_OK (S_OK implies that all of the requested elements were fetched).

One of the advantages of using the IEnum idiom is that it allows the sender to postpone generating the elements of the array. Consider the following IDL method definition:

```
HRESULT GetPrimes([in] long nMin, [in] long nMax,
                  [out] IEnumLong **ppe);
```

The object implementor could create a special class that generates primes on demand and implements the IEnumLong interface:

```
class PrimeGenerator : public IEnumLong {
    LONG m_cRef;               // COM reference count
    long m_nCurrentPrime;      // the cursor
    long m_nMin;               // minimum prime value
    long m_nMax;               // maximum prime value
public:
    PrimeGenerator(long nMin, long nMax, long nCurrentPrime)
      : m_cRef(0), m_nMin(nMin), m_nMax(nMax),
        m_nCurrentPrime(nCurrentPrime) {
    }
// IUnknown methods
    STDMETHODIMP QueryInterface(REFIID riid, void**ppv);
    STDMETHODIMP_(ULONG) AddRef(void);
    STDMETHODIMP_(ULONG) Release(void);
// IEnumLong methods
    STDMETHODIMP Next(ULONG, long *, ULONG *);
    STDMETHODIMP Skip(ULONG);
    STDMETHODIMP Reset(void);
    STDMETHODIMP Clone(IEnumLong **ppe);
};
```

The generator's implementation of Next would simply generate the requested number of primes:

```
STDMETHODIMP PrimeGenerator::Next(ULONG cElems,
                        long *prgElems, ULONG *pcFetched) {
// ensure that pcFetched is valid if cElems > 1
    if (cElems > 1 && pcFetched == 0)
        return E_INVALIDARG;
// fill the buffer
    ULONG cFetched = 0;
```

```
      while (cFetched < cElems && m_nCurrentPrime <= m_nMax) {
        prgElems[cFetched] = GetNextPrime(m_nCurrentPrime);
        m_nCurrentPrime = prgElems[cFetched++];
      }
      if (pcFetched) // some callers may pass NULL
        *pcFetched = cFetched;
      return cFetched == cElems ? S_OK : S_FALSE;
    }
```

Note that even if millions of possible values are possible, no more than a small number will ever be resident in memory simultaneously.

The generator's Skip method simply needs to generate and discard the requested number of elements:

```
    STDMETHODIMP PrimeGenerator::Skip(ULONG cElems) {
      ULONG cEaten = 0;
      while (cEaten < cElems && m_nCurrentPrime <= m_nMax) {
        m_nCurrentPrime = GetNextPrime(m_nCurrentPrime);
        cEaten++;
      }
      return cEaten == cElems ? S_OK : S_FALSE;
    }
```

The Reset method resets the cursor to the initial value:

```
    STDMETHODIMP PrimeGenerator::Reset(void) {
      m_nCurrentPrime = m_nMin;
      return S_OK;
    }
```

and the Clone method creates a new prime number generator based on the current generator's minimum, maximum, and current values:

```
    STDMETHODIMP PrimeGenerator::Clone(IEnumLong **ppe) {
      assert(ppe);
      *ppe = new PrimeGenerator(m_nMin, m_nMax, m_nCurrent);
      if (*ppe)
        (*ppe)->AddRef();
      return S_OK;
    }
```

Given the `PrimeGenerator` implementation, the actual object's implementation of the `GetPrimes` method becomes trivial:

```
STDMETHODIMP MyClass::GetPrimes(long nMin, long nMax,
                                IEnumLong **ppe) {
    assert(ppe);
    *ppe = new PrimeGenerator(nMin, nMax, nMin);
    if (*ppe)
       (*ppe)->AddRef();
    return S_OK;
}
```

Note that the majority of the implementation is now in the `PrimeGenerator` class, not the object's class.

Dynamic versus Static Invocation

As it has been presented so far, COM is based on client programs having a priori knowledge of an interface's definition at development time. This is accomplished either through C++ header files (for C++ clients) or through type libraries (for Java and Visual Basic clients). In general, this is not a problem, as programs written in these languages typically go through some sort of compilation phase prior to being deployed. Some languages do not go through such a compilation phase at development time and instead are deployed in source code form to be interpreted at runtime. Perhaps the most pervasive of such languages are HTML-based scripting languages (*e.g.,* Visual Basic Script, JavaScript) that execute in the context of either a Web browser or a Web server. In both of these cases, script text is stored in its raw form embedded in an HTML file, and the surrounding runtime executes the script text on the fly as the HTML is parsed. To provide a rich programming environment, these environments allow scripts to invoke methods on COM objects that may be created in the script text itself or perhaps elsewhere in the HTML stream (*e.g.,* a control that is also part of the Web page). In these environments, it is currently impossible to use type libraries or other a priori means to provide the runtime engine with a description of the interfaces being used. This means that the objects themselves must assist the interpreter in translating the raw script text into meaningful method invocations.

To allow objects to be used from interpretive environments such as Visual Basic Script and JavaScript, COM defines an interface that expresses the functionality of interpretation. This interface is called `IDispatch` and is defined as follows:

```
[ object, uuid(00020400-0000-0000-C000-000000000046) ]
interface IDispatch : IUnknown {

// structure to model a list of named parameters
   typedef struct tagDISPPARAMS {
     [size_is(cArgs)] VARIANTARG * rgvarg;
     [size_is(cNamedArgs)] DISPID * rgdispidNamedArgs;
     UINT cArgs;
     UINT cNamedArgs;
   } DISPPARAMS;

// can the object describe this interface?
   HRESULT GetTypeInfoCount([out] UINT * pctinfo);

// return a locale-specific description of this interface
   HRESULT GetTypeInfo(
        [in] UINT iTInfo, // reserved, m.b.z.
        [in] LCID lcid,   // locale ID
        [out] ITypeInfo ** ppTInfo // put it here!
   );

// resolve member/parameter names to DISPIDs
   HRESULT GetIDsOfNames(
        [in] REFIID riid,    // reserved, must be IID_NULL
    [in, size_is(cNames)] LPOLESTR * rgszNames,  // method+params
        [in] UINT cNames,    // count of names
        [in] LCID lcid,      // locale ID
    [out, size_is(cNames)] DISPID * rgid // tokens of names
   );

// access member via its DISPID
   HRESULT Invoke(
        [in] DISPID id,      // token of member
        [in] REFIID riid,    // reserved, must be IID_NULL
        [in] LCID lcid,      // locale ID
        [in] WORD wFlags,    // method, propput, or propget?
     [in,out] DISPPARAMS * pDispParams,    // logical parameters
        [out] VARIANT * pVarResult,     // logical result
        [out] EXCEPINFO * pExcepInfo,   // IErrorInfo params
        [out] UINT * puArgErr           // used for type errors
   );
```

When a scripting engine first tries to access an object, it uses QueryInterface to request the object's IDispatch interface. If the object fails the QueryInterface request, the scripting engine cannot use the object. If the object successfully returns its IDispatch interface to the scripting engine, the engine will use the object's GetIDsOfNames method to translate method and property names into tokens. These tokens are formally called DISPIDs and are simply efficiently parsed integers that uniquely identify a property or method. After tokenizing the method or property name, the engine will request that the named method/property be invoked via the object's IDispatch::Invoke method. Note that because IDispatch::Invoke accepts the operation's parameter values as an array of named VARIANTs using the DISPPARAMS structure, the range of supported parameter types is limited to what can be stored in a VARIANT.

IDispatch-based interfaces (often called *dispinterfaces*) are logically equivalent to a normal COM interface. The primary distinction is in how the logical operations of the interface are actually invoked. With a normal COM interface, methods are invoked based on static, a priori knowledge of the interface's method signatures. With a dispinterface, methods are invoked based on textual representations of the method call's anticipated signature. If the caller correctly guesses the method signature, then the call can be properly dispatched. If the caller incorrectly guesses the method signature, then it may not be possible to dispatch the call. If incorrect data types are used for method parameters, it is the object's job to convert them to what is required if possible.

The simplest way to express a dispinterface in IDL is using the dispinterface keyword:

```
[ uuid(75DA6450-DD0F-11d0-8C58-0080C73925BA) ]
dispinterface DPrimeManager {
properties:
   [id(1),readonly] long MinPrimeOnMachine;
   [id(2)] long MinPrime;
methods:
   [id(3)] long GetNextPrime([in] long n);
}
```

This syntax is very readable; however, it assumes that the caller will always access the object's properties and methods via IDispatch. History has shown that as development and runtime environments evolve, they often become capable of using normal COM interfaces. To ensure that a dispinterface can be efficiently accessed from future scripting environments, it is usually better to model the interface as a *dual* interface.

Dual interfaces are simply normal COM interfaces that derive from IDispatch. Because IDispatch is a base interface, the interface is completely compatible with fully interpretive scripting clients. However, the interface is also upwardly compatible with environments that can bind directly to a statically defined COM interface. The following is the IDL definition of the dual interface version of DPrimeManager:

```
[ object, dual, uuid(75DA6450-DD0F-11d0-8C58-0080C73925BA) ]
interface DIPrimeManager : IDispatch {
  [id(1), propget] HRESULT MinPrimeOnMachine(
                            [out, retval] long *pval);
  [id(2), propput] HRESULT MinPrime([in] long val);
  [id(2), propget] HRESULT MinPrime(
                            [out, retval] long *pval);
  [id(3)] long GetNextPrime([in] long n);
}
```

Note that the interface derives from IDispatch, not IUnknown. Also note that the interface has the [dual] attribute. This attribute causes the generated type library to contain a dispinterface version of the interface that is compatible with non-dual-interface-aware environments. The [dual] attribute subsumes the [oleautomation] attribute and also causes the type library to add the registry keys for the universal marshaler at RegisterTypeLib time.

Implementing the methods of IDispatch is trivial if the interface is defined as a dual interface. This is because the type library parser implements two of the four IDispatch methods. Assuming the dual interface defined previously, the object simply needs to load the type library at initialization time:

```
class PrimeManager : DIPrimeManager {
  LONG m_cRef;                  // COM reference count
  ITypeInfo *m_pTypeInfo;       // ptr. to type desc.
// IUnknown methods...
// IDispatch methods...
// IPrimeManager methods...
  PrimeManager(void) : m_cRef(0) {
    ITypeLib *ptl = 0;
    HRESULT hr = LoadRegTypeLib(LIBID_PrimeLib,1,0,0, &ptl);
    assert(SUCCEEDED(hr));
    hr = ptl->GetTypeInfoOfGuid(IID_DIPrimeManager,
                          &m_pTypeInfo);
```

```
      ptl->Release();
    }
    virtual ~PrimeManager(void) {
     m_pTypeInfo->Release();
    }
};
```

Given the preceding class definition, the GetTypeInfo method simply returns the description of the interface:

```
STDMETHODIMP PrimeManager::GetTypeInfo(UINT it, LCID lcid,
                                       ITypeInfo **ppti) {
  assert(it == 0 && ppti != 0);
  (*ppti = m_pTypeInfo)->AddRef();
  return S_OK;
}
```

If the object supported multiple localized type libraries, the implementation would use the LCID parameter to determine which type description to return. The corresponding implementation of GetTypeInfoCount is even simpler:

```
STDMETHODIMP PrimeManager::GetTypeInfoCount(UINT *pit) {
  assert(pit != 0);
  *pit = 1; // only 0 or 1 are allowed
  return S_OK;
}
```

The only legal counts are zero (which means the object does not provide descriptions of its interface) and one (which means the object does provide descriptions of its interface). Even if the object supports multiple localized type description, the resultant count is still one.

The GetTypeInfo and GetTypeInfoCount methods are technically optional. The real meat of the IDispatch interface is GetIDsOfNames and Invoke. The GetIDsOfNames implementation simply forwards the call to the type library parsing engine that is built into COM:

```
STDMETHODIMP PrimeManager::GetIDsOfNames(REFIID riid,
                OLECHAR **pNames, UINT cNames,
                LCID lcid, DISPID *pdispids) {
  assert(riid == IID_NULL);
```

```
            return m_pTypeInfo->GetIDsOfNames(pNames,cNames,pdispids);
    }
```

Because the type library contains all of the method names and their corresponding DISPIDs, this is trivial for the parser to implement. The Invoke method is implemented in a similar fashion:

```
STDMETHODIMP PrimeManager::Invoke(DISPID id,
        REFIID riid, LCID lcid, WORD wFlags,
        DISPPARAMS *pd, VARIANT *pVarResult,
        EXCEPINFO *pe, UINT *pu) {
    assert(riid == IID_NULL);
    void *pvThis = static_cast<DIPrimeManager*>(this);
    return m_pTypeInfo->Invoke(pvThis, id, wFlags,
                               pd, pVarResult, pe, pu);
}
```

Note that the first parameter to ITypeInfo::Invoke is a pointer to an interface. The type of this interface must be the same as the interface that is described by the type information. When the presented arguments have been correctly parsed onto the call stack, the parser will call through this interface pointer to invoke the actual methods. Figure 7.6 illustrates the call sequence for scripting environments that call through dual interfaces.

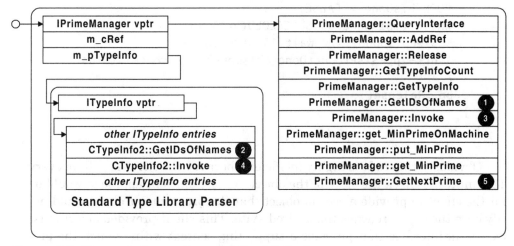

Figure 7.6 Dynamic Invocation and Dual Interfaces

Bidirectional Interface Contracts

As illustrated in Chapter 5, objects that reside in different apartments can utilize each other's services without concern for which apartment the other object resides in. Because COM remoting is based on the concept of apartments, developers need to view processes not as purely clients or servers but rather as a collection of one or more apartments that are simultaneously capable of exporting and importing interfaces.

How two objects negotiate which interfaces will be used to collaborate is largely domain specific. For example, consider the following interface that models a programmer:

```
[uuid(75DA6457-DD0F-11d0-8C58-0080C73925BA), object]
interface IProgrammer : IUnknown {
  HRESULT StartHacking(void);
  HRESULT IsProductDone([out, retval] BOOL *pbIsDone);
}
```

This interface implies the following client usage pattern:

```
HRESULT ShipSoftware(void) {
  IProgrammer *pp = 0;
  HRESULT hr = CoGetObject(OLESTR("programmer:Bob"), 0,
                           IID_IProgrammer, (void**)&pp);
  if (SUCCEEDED(hr)) {
    hr = pp->StartHacking();
    BOOL bIsDone = FALSE;
    while (!bIsDone && SUCCEEDED(hr)) {
      Sleep(15000); // wait 15 seconds
      hr = pp->IsProductDone(&bIsDone); // check status
    }
    pp->Release();
  }
}
```

Obviously, this code is highly inefficient, because the client is polling every 15 minutes to check the state of the object. A more efficient approach would be for the client to provide a second object that the programmer object could notify once the object reaches the desired state. This client-provided object must export an interface that provides a supporting context within which the programmer object can operate:

```
[uuid(75DA6458-DD0F-11d0-8C58-0080C73925BA), object]
interface ISoftwareConsumer : IUnknown {
  HRESULT OnProductIsDone(void);
  HRESULT OnProductWillBeLate([in] hyper nMonths);
}
```

With this mating interface definition in place, there needs to be a mechanism to inform the programmer object that the client has an implementation of ISoftwareConsumer that can receive the notifications of state changes from the programmer object. One common technique is to define the IProgrammer interface to have explicit methods through which clients can associate their consumer objects. The canonical form of this idiom is to provide an Advise method:

```
interface IProgrammer : IUnknown {
  HRESULT Advise([in] ISoftwareConsumer *psc,
                 [out] DWORD *pdwCookie);
    :            :              :
```

through which the client provides the mating consumer object and the programmer returns a DWORD to represent the association. This DWORD could then be used in the corresponding Unadvise method:

```
interface IProgrammer : IUnknown {
    :            :              :
  HRESULT Unadvise([in] DWORD dwCookie);
}
```

to inform the programmer object to terminate the association. By using unique DWORDs to represent programmer/consumer associations, this interface design allows an arbitrary number of consumers to connect and disconnect to the object independently of one another.

If these two methods are present in the IProgrammer interface, the programmer implementation can hold on to the consumer object in its Advise method:

```
STDMETHODIMP Programmer::Advise(ISoftwareConsumer *pcs,
                                DWORD *pdwCookie) {
  assert(pcs);
  if (m_pConsumer != 0) // is there already a consumer?
    return E_UNEXPECTED;
  (m_pConsumer = pcs)->AddRef(); // hold onto new consumer
  *pdwCookie = DWORD(pcs); // make up a reasonable cookie
```

```
    return S_OK;
  }
```

The corresponding implementation of Unadvise would look like this:

```
STDMETHODIMP Programmer::Unadvise(DWORD dwCookie) {
// does the cookie correspond to the current consumer?
  if (DWORD(m_pConsumer) != dwCookie)
    return E_UNEXPECTED;
  (m_pConsumer)->Release(); // release current consumer
  m_pConsumer = 0;
  return S_OK;
}
```

This relationship between the programmer and the consumer is shown in Figure 7.7. Although this implementation allows only one consumer at a time, it is possible that a more sophisticated programmer could handle multiple consumers simultaneously by managing a dynamic array of ISoftwareConsumer interface pointers.

Given the preceding implementation, the programmer's StartHacking method can now use the consumer to indicate when the product is complete:

```
STDMETHODIMP Programmer::StartHacking(void) {
    assert(m_pConsumer);
// preemptively notify of lateness
    HRESULT hr = m_Consumer->OnProductWillBeLate(3);
    if (FAILED(hr))
       return PROGRAMMER_E_UNREALISTICCONSUMER;
// generate some code
```

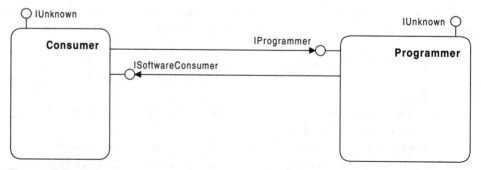

Figure 7.7 Collaborating Objects

```
    extern char *g_rgpszTopFiftyStatements[];
    for (int n = 0; n < 100000; n++)
      printf(g_rgpszTopFiftyStatements[rand() % 50]);
// inform consumer of done-ness
    hr = m_pConsumer->OnProductIsDone();
    return S_OK;
}
```

The fact that the ISoftwareConsumer implementation may or may not belong to the same apartment as the programmer object is immaterial. In fact, the StartHacking method may be invoked from the apartment that contains the consumer object, in which case the caller's apartment will be reentered to service what in effect is a synchronous callback. While this implementation makes nested calls to the consumer object, it is also possible for the programmer object to invoke methods on the consumer at any time in the future. This privilege lasts until a call to Unadvise is made, terminating the association.

Because the IProgrammer and ISoftwareConsumer interfaces were probably designed in tandem to work together, the use of an explicit method on the IProgrammer interface to establish the relationship simply becomes part of the protocol for using programmer objects and is completely reasonable. The fact that programmer implementations can utilize one or more software consumer objects can be documented as part of the protocol of the IProgrammer interface, refining the semantic contract of IProgrammer. However, there are scenarios in which collaborative or callback interfaces are designed outside the scope of any other interface. The following is an example of such an interface:

```
[ uuid(75DA645D-DD0F-11d0-8C58-0080C73925BA), object ]
interface IShutdownNotify : IUnknown {
   HRESULT OnObjectDestroyed([in] IUnknown *pUnk);
}
```

This interface assumes that the IShutdownNotify implementor is interested in receiving termination events from other objects. What is not specified in this definition is the mechanism through which these interested parties can inform objects that they would like to be notified of the object's destruction. As shown in Figure 7.8, one possible strategy would be to define a second mating interface that objects could implement:

```
[ uuid(75DA645E-DD0F-11d0-8C58-0080C73925BA), object ]
interface IShutdownSource : IUnknown {
   HRESULT Advise([in] IShutdownNotify *psn,
                 [out] DWORD *pdwCookie);
```

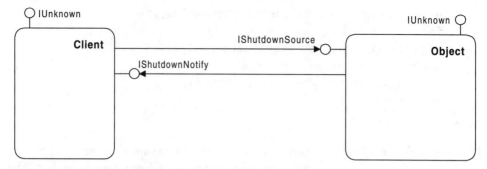

Figure 7.8 Ad Hoc Outbound Interface Management

```
        HRESULT Unadvise([in] DWORD dwCookie);
}
```

However, this interface simply exists to allow observers to connect their
IShutdownNotify interfaces to an object. If a large number of callback interface types exist, then a correspondingly large number of simple connection
management interfaces would also need to be defined. Clearly, a more generic
mechanism would be in order. Enter connection points.

Connection points are a COM idiom for registering and revoking callback interfaces with an object. Connection points are not required to build
highly connected networks of objects. Nor do connection points enable bidirectional communications. Instead, the connection point idiom expresses
the general concept of outbound interface registration as a small number of
standard infrastructure interfaces. The most fundamental of these interfaces is IConnectionPoint:

```
[ object, uuid(B196B286-BAB4-101A-B69C-00AA00341D07) ]
interface IConnectionPoint : IUnknown {

// which type of interface can be connected
   HRESULT GetConnectionInterface([out] IID * pIID);

// get a pointer to identity of "real" object
     HRESULT GetConnectionPointContainer(
             [out] IConnectionPointContainer ** ppCPC);

// hold and use pUnkSink until notified otherwise
   HRESULT Advise([in] IUnknown * pUnkSink,
             [out] DWORD * pdwCookie);
```

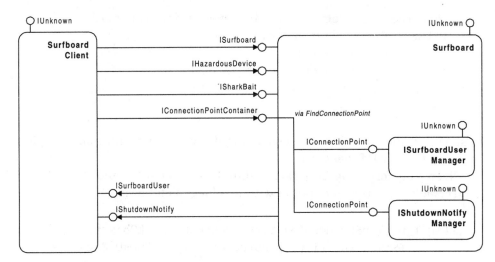

Figure 7.9 Connection Point Architecture

```
// stop holding/using the pointer associated with dwCookie
   HRESULT Unadvise([in] DWORD dwCookie);

// get information about currently held pointers
   HRESULT EnumConnections([out] IEnumConnections ** ppEnum);
}
```

As shown in Figure 7.9, objects provide a distinct implementation of this interface for each type of interface an object can use as a callback interface. Since IConnectionPoint is not exposed as part of the object's identity, it cannot be discovered via QueryInterface. Instead, COM provides a second interface that is exposed as part of the object's identity that allows clients to query for the IConnectionPoint implementation that corresponds to a particular type of callback interface:

```
[ object,uuid(B196B284-BAB4-101A-B69C-00AA00341D07) ]
interface IConnectionPointContainer : IUnknown {

// get all possible IConnectionPoint implementations
   HRESULT EnumConnectionPoints(
        [out] IEnumConnectionPoints ** ppEnum);
```

```
// get the IConnectionPoint implementation for riid
  HRESULT FindConnectionPoint(
        [in] REFIID riid,
        [out] IConnectionPoint ** ppCP
    );
}
```

As shown in Figure 7.9, each IConnectionPoint implementation is exposed from a distinct COM identity.

Given the foregoing interface definitions, a client could associate its IShutdownNotify implementation with an object as follows:

```
HRESULT HookupShutdownCallback(IUnknown *pUnkObject,
        IShutdownNotify *pShutdownNotify,  DWORD &rdwCookie)
{
   IConnectionPointContainer *pcpc = 0;
   HRESULT hr = pUnkObject->QueryInterface(
            IID_IConnectionPointContainer, (void**)&pcpc);
   if (SUCCEEDED(hr)) {
     IConnectionPoint *pcp = 0;
     hr =pcpc->FindConnectionPoint(IID_IShutdownNotify,&pcp);
     if (SUCCEEDED(hr)) {
       hr = pcp->Advise(pShutdownNotify, &rdwCookie);
       pcp->Release();
     }
     pcpc->Release();
   }
}
```

The corresponding code to tear down the association is as follows:

```
HRESULT TeardownShutdownCallback(IUnknown *pUnkObject,
                                          DWORD dwCookie) {
   IConnectionPointContainer *pcpc = 0;
   HRESULT hr = pUnkObject->QueryInterface(
            IID_IConnectionPointContainer, (void**)&pcpc);
   if (SUCCEEDED(hr)) {
     IConnectionPoint *pcp = 0;
     hr =pcpc->FindConnectionPoint(IID_IShutdownNotify,&pcp);
     if (SUCCEEDED(hr)) {
       hr = pcp->Unadvise(dwCookie);
```

```
            pcp->Release();
        }
        pcpc->Release();
    }
}
```

Note that in both examples, the client uses the IConnectionPointContainer::
FindConnectionPoint method to query the object for its IShutdownNotify-
specific implementation of IConnectionPoint. If the object fails the call to
FindConnectionPoint, it is indicating that it does not understand the semantics of the IShutdownNotify interface. This prevents users from attaching arbitrary callback interfaces to an object without the full consent of the object's
implementor.

As with IUnknown, the implementations of IConnectionPointContainer
and IConnectionPoint are largely boilerplate. The C++ object requires a distinct COM identity for each outbound interface type that it expects to support.
One technique for implementing IConnectionPoint is to use a variation on
the nested class/composition technique, taking into account the differences in
identity relationships:

```
class Surfboard : public ISurfboard,
                  public IHazardousDevice,
                  public ISharkBait,
                  public IConnectionPointContainer {
  LONG m_cRef; // COM reference count
// Surfboards don't support multiple outbound interfaces
// of a given type, so it simply declares single pointers of
// each possible type of callback interface
  IShutdownNotify *m_pShutdownNotify;
  ISurfboardUser *m_pSurfer;

// to deal with identity relationship of IConnectionPoint,
// define an IShutdownNotify-specific nested class + member
  class XCPShutdownNotify : public IConnectionPoint {
    Surfboard *This(void); // use fixed offset
  // IUnknown methods...
  // IConnectionPointMethods...
  } m_xcpShutdownNotify;

// define an ISurfboardUser-specific nested class + member
  class XCPSurfboardUser : public IConnectionPoint {
```

```
      Surfboard *This(void); // use fixed offset
    // IUnknown methods...
    // IConnectionPointMethods...
    } m_xcpSurfboardUser;
  // IUnknown methods...
  // ISurfboard methods...
  // IHazardousDevice methods...
  // ISharkBait methods...
  // IConnectionPointContainer methods...
};
```

Note that instances of the Surfboard class will have two distinct
IConnectionPoint implementations, one that is used for attaching
IShutdownNotify callback interfaces and one that is used for attaching
ISurfboardUser interfaces. These two implementations are partitioned into
distinct C++ classes to allow each IConnectionPoint implementation to have
its own unique IUnknown and IConnectionPoint implementations. In particular, there will be three distinct implementations of QueryInterface that will
have their own distinct sets of interface pointers that can be given out, creating three distinct COM identities.

The preceding class definition implies the following QueryInterface implementation for the main Surfboard class:

```
STDMETHODIMP Surfboard::QueryInterface(REFIID riid,
                                       void**ppv) {
  if (riid == IID_IUnknown || riid == IID_ISurfboard)
    *ppv = static_cast<ISurfboard*>(this);
  else if (riid == IID_IHazardousDevice)
    *ppv = static_cast< IHazardousDevice *>(this);
  else if (riid == IID_ISharkBait)
    *ppv = static_cast<ISharkBait *>(this);
  else if (riid == IID_IConnectionPointContainer)
    *ppv = static_cast<IConnectionPointContainer *>(this);
  else
    return (*ppv = 0), E_NOINTERFACE;
  ((IUnknown*)*ppv)->AddRef();
  return S_OK;
}
```

Note that the IConnectionPoint interface is not accessible via this main
QueryInterface implementation. Each of the nested class' QueryInterface
methods would look like this:

```
STDMETHODIMP
Surfboard::XCPShutdownNotify::QueryInterface(REFIID riid,
                                             void**ppv) {
  if (riid == IID_IUnknown || riid == IID_IConnectionPoint)
    *ppv = static_cast<IConnectionPoint *>(this);
  else
    return (*ppv = 0), E_NOINTERFACE;
  ((IUnknown*)*ppv)->AddRef();
  return S_OK;
}
```

This same implementation would apply to the XCPSurfboardUser class as well. Note that there is no identity relationship between the Surfboard object and the two subobjects that implement the IConnectionPoint interface.

To ensure that the surfboard object does not destroy itself prematurely, the connection manager subobjects simply forward their AddRef and Release methods to the containing surfboard object:

```
STDMETHODIMP_(ULONG)
Surfboard::XCPShutdownNotify::AddRef(void) {
{ return This()->AddRef(); /* AddRef containing object */ }

STDMETHODIMP_(ULONG)
Surfboard::XCPShutdownNotify::Release(void) {
{ return This()->Release();/* Release containing object */}
```

The foregoing methods assume that the This method returns a pointer to the containing Surfboard object using some fixed offset calculation.

Clients discover the object's IConnectionPoint interfaces by calling the object's FindConnectionPoint method, which for the Surfboard class would look like this:

```
STDMETHODIMP Surfboard::FindConnectionPoint(REFIID riid,
                                IConnectionPoint **ppcp) {
  if (riid == IID_IShutdownNotify)
    *ppcp = &m_xcpShutdownNotify;
  else if (riid == IID_ISurfboardUser)
    *ppcp = &m_xcpSurfboardUser;
  else
    return (*ppcp = 0), CONNECT_E_NOCONNECTION;
  (*ppcp)->AddRef();
```

```
        return S_OK;
    }
```

Note that the object hands out IConnectionPoint interface pointers only when asked for interfaces it knows how to call back through. Also note the striking similarity to most QueryInterface implementations. The primary distinction is that QueryInterface negotiates *inbound* interfaces, whereas FindConnectionPoint negotiates *outbound* interfaces.

Because the IConnectionPoint::Advise method accepts only a statically typed IUnknown interface as the callback interface pointer,[3] the object's implementations of Advise must use QueryInterface to coerce the callback pointer to the appropriate type of interface:

```
STDMETHODIMP
Surfboard::XCPShutdownNotify::Advise(IUnknown *pUnk,
                                     DWORD *pdwCookie){
  assert(pdwCookie && pUnk);
  *pdwCookie = 0;
  if (This()->m_pShutdownNotify) // already have one
    return CONNECT_E_ADVISELIMIT;
// QueryInterface for correct callback type
  HRESULT hr = pUnk->QueryInterface(IID_IShutdownNotify,
              (void**)&(This()->m_pShutdownNotify));
  if (hr == E_NOINTERFACE)
    hr = CONNECT_E_NOCONNECTION;
  if (SUCCEEDED(hr)) // make up a meaningful cookie
   *pdwCookie = DWORD(This()->m_pShutdownNotify);
  return hr;
}
```

Recall that QueryInterface implicitly calls AddRef, which means that the Surfboard object now holds callback reference that remains valid beyond the scope of the Advise method. Also note that the resultant HRESULT is mapped to CONNECT_E_NOCONNECTION if the callback object does not implement the

---

[3] This is one of the known flaws in the design of connection points. Another well-known flaw is that for each callback interface type, an explicit call to FindConnectionPoint is required. Both of these flaws adversely affect performance due to the increased number of round trips each flaw implies. The performance impact of using connection points acts as a reminder that interfaces should be designed with interapartment access in mind.

appropriate interface. If the QueryInterface fails for any other reason, the HRESULT from QueryInterface is propagated to the caller.[4]

Based on the preceding Advise implementation, the corresponding Unadvise method is as follows:

```
STDMETHODIMP
Surfboard::XCPShutdownNotify::Unadvise(DWORD dwCookie) {
// ensure that the cookie corresponds to a valid connection
  if (DWORD(This()->m_pShutdownNotify) != dwCookie)
    return CONNECT_E_NOCONNECTION;
// release the connection
  This()->m_pShutdownNotify->Release();
  This()->m_pShutdownNotify = 0;
  return S_OK;
}
```

The IConnectionPoint interface has three additional supporting methods, two of which are trivial to implement:

```
STDMETHODIMP
Surfboard::XCPShutdownNotify::GetConnectionInterface(
                                              IID *piid) {
  assert(piid);
// return IID of the interface managed by this subobject
  *piid = IID_IShutdownNotify;
  return S_OK;
}
STDMETHODIMP
Surfboard::XCPShutdownNotify::GetConnectionPointContainer(
                    IConnectionPointContainer **ppcpc) {
  assert(ppcpc);
  (*ppcpc = This())->AddRef(); // return containing object
  return S_OK;
}
```

The remaining method, EnumConnections, allows callers to enumerate the connected interfaces. This method is optional, and implementations can legally return E_NOTIMPL.

---

[4] One common error that can occur is an access denial when the object tries to contact the callback object's process due to the caller's access control not allowing calls from the object's security principal.

To advertise which outbound interfaces an implementation class supports, IDL provides the [source] attribute:

```
[ uuid(315BC280-DEA7-11d0-8C5E-0080C73925BA) ]
coclass Surfboard {
  [default] interface ISurfboard;
  interface IHazardousDevice;
  interface ISharkBait;
  [source] interface IShutdownNotify;
  [source, default] interface ISurfboardUser;
}
```

In addition, COM provides two interfaces that allow runtime environments to ask an object to return information introspectively about its inbound and outbound interface types:

```
[ object,uuid(B196B283-BAB4-101A-B69C-00AA00341D07) ]
interface IProvideClassInfo : IUnknown {
// return description of object's coclass
  HRESULT GetClassInfo([out] ITypeInfo ** ppTI);
}
```

```
[ object,uuid(A6BC3AC0-DBAA-11CE-9DE3-00AA004BB851) ]
interface IProvideClassInfo2 : IProvideClassInfo {
  typedef enum tagGUIDKIND {
    GUIDKIND_DEFAULT_SOURCE_DISP_IID = 1
  } GUIDKIND;
// return IID of default outbound dispinterface
  HRESULT GetGUID([in]  DWORD dwGuidKind,
                  [out] GUID * pGUID);
}
```

Both of these interfaces are trivial to implement:

```
STDMETHODIMP Surfboard::GetClassInfo(ITypeInfo **ppti){
  assert(ppti != 0);
  ITypeLib *ptl = 0;
  HRESULT hr = LoadRegTypeLib(LIBID_BeachLib, 1,0,0, &ptl);
  if (SUCCEEDED(hr)) {
    hr = ptl->GetTypeInfoOfGuid(CLSID_Surfboard, ppti);
    ptl->Release();
```

```
      }
      return hr;
   }
   STDMETHODIMP Surfboard::GetGUID(DWORD dwKind, GUID *pguid){
      if (dwKind != GUIDKIND_DEFAULT_SOURCE_DISP_IID || !pguid)
         return E_INVALIDARG;
   // ISurfboardUser must be defined as a dispinterface
      *pguid = IID_ISurfboardUser;
      return S_OK;
   }
```

Although outbound interfaces are not required to be dispatch interfaces, some scripting environments require this in order to allow a natural mapping of callbacks onto script text.

Assuming that the ISurfboardUser interface is defined as the following dispinterface:

```
[ uuid(315BC28A-DEA7-11d0-8C5E-0080C73925BA) ]
dispinterface ISurfboardUser {
methods:
   [id(1)] void OnTiltingForward([in] long nAmount);
   [id(2)] void OnTiltingSideways([in] long nAmount);
}
```

Visual Basic programmers can declare variables that understand the default callback interface type as follows:

```
Dim WithEvents sb as Surfboard
```

The presence of this variable definition allows Visual Basic programmers to write event handlers. Visual Basic event handlers are simply functions or sub-routines that use the *VariableName_EventName* convention. For example, to handle the OnTiltingForward callback on the preceding sb variable, the Visual Basic programmer would write the following code:

```
Sub sb_OnTiltingForward(ByVal nAmount as Long)
   MsgBox "The surfboard just tilted forward"
End Sub
```

The Visual Basic virtual machine will actually craft an implementation of ISurfboardUser on the fly, mapping the incoming method invocations onto the appropriate user-defined subroutines.

Aliasing in IDL

It is often necessary to integrate legacy data types and programming idioms into a COM-based system. Ideally, there is a simple and obvious mapping of legacy code onto IDL-compatible analogues. If this is the case, then the transition to COM can be fairly straightforward. However, there are times when an application's legacy data types or idioms simply cannot map reasonably onto IDL. To address this problem, IDL provides several aliasing techniques that allow the interface designer to provide conversion routines that map legacy data types and idioms onto legal, remotable IDL representations.

A great example of where this technique is useful is in the IEnum idiom. The COM enumerator idiom was designed prior to the availability of a COM-aware IDL compiler. This meant that the original designer of the IEnum interface was not able to validate the interface design against known IDL mapping rules. The enumerator's Next method does not map cleanly onto IDL.[5] Consider the ideal IDL prototype for a Next method:

```
HRESULT Next([in] ULONG cElems,
   [out, size_is(cElems), length_is(*pcFetched)] double *prg,
             [out] ULONG *pcFetched);
```

Unfortunately, the original pre-IDL interface definition for the Next method stated that callers could pass a null pointer as the third parameter, provided that the first parameter indicated that only one element was being requested. This allowed callers to conveniently fetch one element at a time:

```
double dblElem;
hr = p->Next(1, &dblElem, 0);
```

Unfortunately, this legal usage of the interface violates the preceding IDL definition, as it is illegal for top-level [out] parameters to be null (there is no place for the interface proxy to store the result). To solve this inconsistency, each Next method definition must use the [call_as] attribute to alias the callable form of the method onto the remotable form.

---

[5] One could argue that the original interface definition was reasonable and that IDL is simply not flexible enough to describe common programming idioms. Although this may be a valid defense for an interface defined in 1992 prior to the availability of COM IDL, it is definitely *not* justification for interfaces defined today. Simply put, all interfaces should follow the rules of COM IDL unless there is an extremely compelling reason to do otherwise.

The [call_as] attribute allows the interface designer to express one method in two forms. The callable form of the method must use the [local] attribute to suppress the generation of marshaling code. This version of the method matches what clients will call and what objects will implement. The remotable form of the method must use the [call_as] attribute to associate the generated marshaler with the appropriate method in the interface stub. This version of the method describes the remotable form of the interface and must use standard IDL constructs to describe the request and response messages required to remote the method. To apply the [call_as] technique to the Next method, the IDL would look like this:

```
interface IEnumDouble : IUnknown {
// this method is what the caller and object see
   [local] HRESULT Next([in] ULONG cElems,
                        [out] double *prgElems,
                        [out] ULONG *pcFetched);

// this method is how it goes out on the wire
   [call_as(Next)] HRESULT RemoteNext([in] ULONG cElems,
   [out, size_is(cElems), length_is(*pcFetched)] double *prg,
                        [out] ULONG *pcFetched);
   HRESULT Skip([in] ULONG cElems);
   HRESULT Reset(void);
   HRESULT Clone([out] IEnumDouble **ppe);
}
```

The resultant C/C++ header file will contain an interface definition that contains the Next method but not the RemoteNext method definition. As far as the client and object are concerned, there is no RemoteNext method. It exists only so that the interface marshaler can remote the method properly. Although the Next and RemoteNext methods both have identical parameter lists, this is by no means required when using this technique. In fact, it is sometimes necessary to add additional parameters to the remotable form of a method in order to express fully how the operation should be remoted.

By adding the [local]/[call_as] method pair, the generated interface marshaler source code will no longer successfully link due to unresolved external symbols. This is because the interface designer must now provide two additional routines. One of these routines will be used by the interface proxy to transform the [local] form of the method into the [call_as] form. For the preceding interface definition, the IDL compiler will expect the following function to be provided by the interface designer:

CHAPTER 7: MISCELLANEA

```
     HRESULT STDMETHODCALLTYPE IEnumDouble_Next_Proxy(
                    IEnumDouble *This, ULONG cElems,
                    double *prg, ULONG *pcFetched);
```

The second required routine is used by the interface stub to transform the [call_as] form of the method into the [local] form. For the preceding interface definition, the IDL compiler will expect the following function to be provided by the interface designer:

```
     HRESULT STDMETHODCALLTYPE IEnumDouble_Next_Stub(
                    IEnumDouble *This, ULONG cElems,
                    double *prg, ULONG *pcFetched);
```

The prototypes for these two routines will appear in the generated C/C++ header file for convenience.

As shown in Figure 7.10, the user-defined [local]-to-[call_as] routine is used to populate the interface proxy's vtable and is called by the client. This routine is expected to translate the call into a remote invocation by calling the remotable version that is generated by the IDL compiler. For the enumerator's Next routine, all that is needed is to ensure that a non-null pointer is passed as the third parameter:

```
     HRESULT STDMETHODCALLTYPE IEnumDouble_Next_Proxy(
                    IEnumDouble *This, ULONG cElems,
                    double *prg, ULONG *pcFetched) {
// enforce semantics on client-side
```

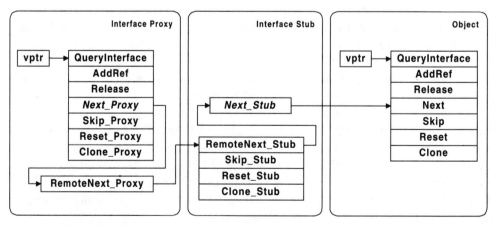

Figure 7.10 Method Aliasing

```
      if (pcFetched == 0 && cElems != 1)
         return E_INVALIDARG;
   // provide a location for last [out] param
      ULONG cFetched;
      if (pcFetched == 0) pcFetched = &cFetched;
   // call remote method with non-null pointer as last param
      return IEnumDouble_RemoteNext_Proxy(This, cElems,
                                          prg, pcFetched);
   }
```

Note that in all cases, the remotable version of the method receives a non-null pointer as its last parameter.

The user-defined [call_as]-to-[local] routine will be called by the interface stub after unmarshaling the remotable form of the method. This routine is expected to translate the remotable form of the call onto a local invocation on the actual object. Because object implementations are sometimes sloppy and neglect to indicate how many elements are being returned when returning S_OK, the object-side mapping routine ensures that this parameter is set properly:

```
HRESULT STDMETHODCALLTYPE IEnumDouble_Next_Stub(
                IEnumDouble *This, ULONG cElems,
                double *prg, ULONG *pcFetched) {
   // call method on actual object
      HRESULT hr = This->Next(cElems, prg, pcFetched);
   // enforce semantics on object-side
      if (hr == S_OK) // S_OK implies all elements sent
         *pcFetched = cElems; // [length_is] must be explicit
      return hr;
   }
```

Note that the interface stub will always call this routine with a non-null last parameter.

The [call_as] technique is useful for providing callable-to-remotable conversions on a method-by-method basis. COM also provides the capability to specify user-defined conversions for individual data types using the [transmit_as] and [wire_marshal] typedef attributes. All three of these techniques should not be considered mainstream interface design techniques and exist largely to support legacy idioms and data types. One additional hook provided by the IDL compiler is cpp_quote. The cpp_quote keyword allows *arbitrary* C or C++ statements to appear in an IDL file, even if the statement is not legal

IDL. Consider the following simple usage of `cpp_quote` to inject an inline function definition into the IDL-generated header file:

```
// surfboard.idl
cpp_quote("static void Exit(void) { ExitProcess(1); }")
```

Given this IDL, the generated C/C++ header file would simply contain the following:

```
// surfboard.h
static void Exit(void) { ExitProcess(1); }
```

The `cpp_quote` keyword can be used to play a variety of tricks on the IDL compiler. One example is the data type REFIID. The actual IDL definition for this type is

```
typedef IID *REFIID;
```

However, the C++ type is defined as

```
typedef const IID& REFIID;
```

However, C++-style references are not allowed in IDL. To address this, the system IDL file uses the following technique:

```
// from wtypes.idl (approx.)
cpp_quote("#if 0")
typedef IID *REFIID; // this is the pure IDL definition
cpp_quote("#endif")
cpp_quote("#ifdef __cplusplus")
cpp_quote("#define REFIID const IID&") // C++ definition
cpp_quote("#else")
cpp_quote("#define REFIID const IID * const")// C definition
cpp_quote("#endif")
```

The resultant C/C++ header file looks like this:

```
// from wtypes.h (approx.)
#if 0
  typedef IID *REFIID;
#endif
```

```
#ifdef __cplusplus
  #define REFIID const IID&
#else
  #define REFIID const IID * const
#endif
```

Again, this somewhat grotesque hack is required because many core COM interfaces were defined without IDL in mind.

Asynchronous Methods

COM method calls are synchronous by default. This means that the client thread is blocked until the ORPC response message is received and unmarshaled. This perfectly models how normal same-thread method invocation works and is a reasonable default. Prior to Windows NT 5.0, there was no way to issue a method request and continue processing while the method executes concurrently without explicitly spawning additional threads. The Windows NT 5.0 release of COM introduces support for asynchronous method invocation. Asynchrony is a method attribute and must be expressed in IDL using the [async_uuid] attribute.

The details of this technique were in flux at the time of this writing. Consult the current documentation for more details.

Where Are We?

This chapter discussed a variety of topics related to designing and using COM interfaces. Although this chapter by no means contains an exhaustive catalog of useful design idioms, it did attempt to address several critical topics not discussed in the previous chapters of the book. As my own personal understanding of COM has evolved over the two years it took to write this book, I have come to believe that developers need to pay less attention to the esoteric facilities of COM (*e.g.,* connection points, monikers, dispatch interfaces) and instead focus on the three basic atoms of COM: *interfaces, class objects,* and *apartments.* Armed with a thorough understanding of these three topics, I firmly believe there is no mountain that cannot be climbed using COM.

A | The Evolution of Objects

An abbreviated version of this essay will appear in the January 1998 issue of Microsoft Systems Journal. *It is included here as an appendix because it brings COM into historical perspective.*

Object-oriented software development achieved widespread commercial acceptance in the late-1980s. The central theme of circa-1980s object orientation was the use of classes, which allowed developers to model state and behavior as a single unit of abstraction. This bundling of state and behavior helped enforce modularity through the use of encapsulation. In classic object orientation, objects belonged to classes and clients manipulated objects via class-based references. This is the programming model implied by most C++ and Smalltalk environments and libraries of the era. Although it had been possible to achieve many of the benefits of class-based programming using procedural-based languages through the use of disciplined programming style, widespread acceptance of object-oriented software development did not happen until there was explicit support for object orientation from tool and language vendors. Key environments that were pivotal to the success of object orientation include Apple's MacApp framework based on Object Pascal, ParcPlace's and Digitalk's early SmallTalk environments, and Turbo C++ from Borland.

One of the key benefits of using a development environment that explicitly supported object orientation was the ability to use polymorphism to treat groups of similar objects as if they were all type compatible with one another. To support polymorphism, object orientation introduced the notion of inheritance and dynamic binding, which allowed similar classes to be explicitly grouped into collections of related abstractions. Consider the following very simple C++ class hierarchy:

```
class Dog {
  public:
    virtual void Bark(void);
};
class Pug : public Dog {
  public:
    virtual void Bark(void);
};
class Collie : public Dog {
  public:
    virtual void Bark(void);
};
```

Because the classes Collie and Pug are both type compatible with class Dog, clients can write generic code as follows:

```
void BarkLikeADog(Dog& rdog) {
  rdog.Bark();
}
```

Since the Bark method is virtual and bound dynamically, the method dispatching machinery of C++ ensures that the correct code is executed. This means that the BarkLikeADog function does not rely on the precise type of the referenced object, only that it is type compatible with Dog. This example could easily be recast in any number of programming languages that support object-oriented programming.

The preceding class hierarchy typifies the techniques that were practiced during the first wave of object-oriented development. One characteristic that dominated this first wave was the use of implementation inheritance. Implementation inheritance is a powerful programming technique when used in a disciplined fashion. However, when misused, the resultant type hierarchy can exhibit undue coupling between the base class and the derived class. One common aspect of this coupling is that it is often unclear whether or not the base class implementation of a method must be called from a derived class' version. For example, consider the Pug class' implementation of Bark:

```
void Pug::Bark(void) {
  this->BreathIn();
  this->ConstrictVocalChords();
  this->BreathOut();
}
```

What happens if the underlying Dog class' implementation of Bark is not called, as is the case in this code fragment? Perhaps the base class method records the number of times that a particular dog barks for later use? If this is the case, the Pug class has violated that part of the underlying Dog implementation class. To use implementation inheritance properly, a nontrivial amount of internal knowledge is required to maintain the integrity of the underlying base class. This amount of detailed knowledge exceeds the level needed to simply be a client of the base class. For this reason, implementation inheritance is often viewed as *white-box* reuse.

One approach to object orientation that reduces excessive type system coupling while retaining the benefits of polymorphism is to inherit only type signatures, not implementation code. This is the fundamental principle behind *interface-based* development, which can be viewed as the second wave of object orientation. Interface-based programming is a refinement of classical object orientation that assumes that inheritance is primarily a mechanism for expressing type relationships, not implementation hierarchies. Interface-based development is built on the principle of separation of *interface* from *implementation*. In interface-based development, interfaces and implementations are two distinct concepts. Interfaces model the abstract requests that can be made of an object. Implementations model concrete instantiable types that can support one or more interfaces. Although it was possible to achieve many of the benefits of interface-based development using traditional first-wave era environments through the use of disciplined programming style, widespread acceptance of interface-based development did not happen until there was explicit support from tool and language vendors. Key environments that were pivotal to the success of interface-based development include Microsoft's Component Object Model (COM), Iona's Orbix Object Request Broker environment, and Java's explicit support for interface-based development.[1]

One of the key benefits of using an environment that supported interface-based development was the ability to model the "what" and the "how" of an object as two distinct concepts. Consider the following very simple Java type hierarchy:

```
interface IDog {
  public void Bark( );
};
class Pug implements IDog {
```

---

[1] Technically, Java also supports traditional implementation inheritance, unlike COM and virtually all CORBA-style products (*e.g.,* Iona's Orbix, IBM's DSOM, BEA's Object Broker).

```
      public void Bark( ) { ... }
   };
   class Collie implements IDog {
      public void Bark( ) { ... }
   };
```

Because the classes Collie and Pug are both type compatible with interface IDog, clients can write generic code as follows:

```
   void BarkLikeADog(IDog dog) {
      dog.Bark();
   }
```

From the client's perspective, this type hierarchy is virtually identical to the previous C++-based example. However, because the IDog interface's Bark method cannot have an implementation, there is no coupling between the IDog interface definition and the Pug or Collie classes. Although this does imply that the Pug and Collie each have to fully define their own notion of what it means to bark, the Pug and Collie implementors do not need to wonder what side effects their derived classes will impose on the underlying IDog base type.

One striking similarity between the first and second waves is that each could be characterized by a simple concept (class and interface, respectively). In both cases, it was not the concept itself that acted as the catalyst for success, but instead, one or more key environments were required to spark the interest of the software development industry at large.

An interesting aspect of second-wave systems is that the implementation is viewed as a black box; that is, all implementation details are considered opaque to the clients of an object. Often, when developers begin to use interface-based technologies such as COM, the degree of freedom afforded by this opacity is ignored, causing novice developers to view the relationship between interface, implementation, and object fairly simplistically. Consider an Excel spreadsheet that exposes its functionality using COM. Excel's spreadsheet implementation class exposes roughly 25 distinct COM interfaces that allow the spreadsheet to participate in a variety of COM-based technologies (Linking, Embedding, Inplace Activation, Automation, Active Document Objects, Hyperlinking, etc.). Because each interface requires a 4-byte virtual function pointer (vptr) per object, this implies that spreadsheet objects carry roughly 100 bytes worth of overhead in addition to any spreadsheet-specific state that may be needed to keep track of user data. Since a given spreadsheet object can potentially contain a very large number of cells, this 100 bytes worth of overhead is amortized across the hundreds of kilobytes a large spreadsheet might require to manage the contents of each cell in use.

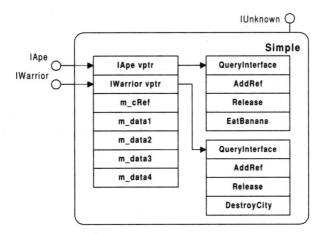

Figure A.1 A Simple COM Object

The actual implementation of an Excel spreadsheet is complicated by the fact that each individual cell in a spreadsheet is accessible via COM interfaces as well. From a COM perspective, these cell interfaces each belong to distinct COM identities and cannot be discovered via QueryInterface calls on the spreadsheet object. Instead, these cell interfaces are discovered using some alternative interface (*e.g.*, IOleItemContainer) that the spreadsheet object exposes to its clients. The fact that each cell is now exposed to clients via COM interfaces means that the implementor of Excel must take care to avoid excessive COM-related overhead. Consider a spreadsheet object that contains 1,000 cells. Assume for rough calculation that each cell requires an average of 16 bytes of memory to hold Excel's native cell state. This means that a 1,000-cell spreadsheet object consumes roughly 16,000 bytes of non-COM-related memory. For this spreadsheet, the 100 bytes of virtual function pointer overhead imposed by the spreadsheet-level interfaces have very little impact on memory consumption. However, since each individual cell may itself expose roughly eight distinct COM interfaces, this implies a potential of 32 bytes of COM-related overhead per cell to manage each cell's virtual function pointers. Assuming the naive implementation techniques implied by most COM development environments, the 1,000-cell spreadsheet will need roughly 32,100 bytes of memory for virtual function pointers, which is roughly double the amount of memory consumed by Excel's native data. Clearly, this overhead is excessive.

To understand how the Excel team solved this problem of vptr overhead, it is useful to reexamine the relationship between state and behavior as it is typically implemented in COM. Figure A.1 shows a simple COM object in memory. Note that the block of memory that the object occupies contains both

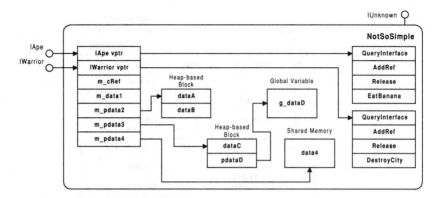

Figure A.2 Not-So-Simple COM Object.

vptrs and data members. One way to look at this figure is to consider that the data members represent the *state* of the object and that the virtual function pointers (and their corresponding virtual function tables) represent the object's *behavior*. In most object implementations, these two aspects of the object reside in a contiguous block of memory. However, COM does not require this. COM simply deals in vptrs and leaves state management up to the implementor. COM is perfectly happy if the implementor decides to allocate the object's state and vptrs in distinct blocks of memory, as shown in Figure A.2. After all, how an object's state is managed is simply another implementation detail that is hidden from the client behind the firewall of the object's interfaces.

Since COM does not require an object's state to be allocated contiguously with its vptrs, the Excel team was able to optimize memory consumption considerably. Consider a single spreadsheet cell. Although 16 bytes of memory must be allocated to hold the cell's contents, the 32 bytes of memory required for the cell's vptrs do not need to reside in a contiguous block of memory with the cell data. In addition, unless a cell is being accessed via its COM interfaces, the 32 bytes of vptr memory are not required at all. This means that Excel can simply dynamically allocate blocks of memory for vptrs as needed on a cell-by-cell basis. Since most cells will never be accessed via COM interfaces, this means that there is virtually no vptr overhead in most cases. This approach of building *flyweight* objects to provide behavior as needed is a variation on the tearoff technique originally proposed in Crispin Goswell's excellent *COM Programmer's Cookbook* (http://www.microsoft.com/oledev). Both techniques use lazy evaluation to delay allocation of vptr memory.

Flyweights and tearoffs are COM development techniques that are not mandated or explicitly supported by COM. Instead, these techniques grew out of a need to manage state efficiently. In applying COM to distributed application development, additional state management issues arise, including distributed error recovery, security, concurrency management, load balancing, and data consistency. Unfortunately, COM is ignorant of how an object manages its state, so there is little that COM can do to address these issues. Although it is possible for developers to concoct their own schemes for dealing with state management, there are clear benefits in having a common infrastructure for developing objects in a state-conscious manner. Microsoft Transaction Server (MTS) is one such infrastructure.

The COM programming model extended the traditional object-oriented programming model by forcing developers to be conscious of the relationship between interface and implementation. The MTS programming model extends the COM programming model by forcing developers to also be conscious of the relationship between state and behavior. The fundamental principle of MTS is that an object may *logically* be modeled as state and behavior, but its *physical* implementation needs to distinguish the two explicitly. By explicitly allowing MTS to manage the state of an object, the application developer can leverage the infrastructure's support for concurrency and lock management, error recovery, data consistency, and fine-grain access control. This means that the majority of an object's state may *not* be stored contiguously with its vptrs (which represent the object's behavior). Instead, MTS provided facilities for storing object state in either durable or transient storage. This storage is under the control of the MTS runtime environment and can be safely accessed from an object's methods without concern for lock management or data consistency. Object state that must remain consistent in the presence of machine failure or abnormal program termination is stored in durable storage, with MTS ensuring that all updates are atomic throughout the network. State that is transient can be stored in MTS-managed memory, with MTS ensuring that memory accesses are serialized to prevent data corruption.

As with class-based and interface-based development, the state-conscious programming model of MTS requires additional discipline and attention on the part of the developer. Fortunately, as with class-based and interface-based development, the state-conscious model of MTS can be adopted incrementally. Of course, incremental adoption means that the benefits of MTS will be realized incrementally as well. This allows developers to adopt MTS at a pace that is appropriate for the local development culture.

With the merging of the MTS and COM development teams within Microsoft, it is clear that MTS represents the next step in the evolution of COM. I highly encourage all COM developers to get involved in this third wave of object-oriented development.

B | Selected Code

The source code that accompanies this book contains a complete COM application (COM Chat) in addition to a library of utility code used by the author. The source code can be downloaded in electronic form at http://www.develop.com/essentialcom. The COM Chat application is included here in printed form for convenience.

COM Chat—A COM-based Chat Program

COM Chat is a complete COM-based program that implements a multi-topic distributed chat application. There are three binary component that comprise the application: comchat.exe is the chat server, comchatps.dll is the interface marshaler for all COM Chat interfaces, and client.exe is a console-based client application. The application is based on a single COM class (CLSID_ChatSession). As is shown in Figure B.1, the class object implements the IChatSessionManager interface, and each chat session implements the IChatSession interface. Clients that wish to receive chat notifications must supply an IChatSessionEvents interface to the chat session object.

comchat.idl

```
// comchat.idl

import "objidl.idl";
interface IChatSessionEvents;

[ uuid(5223A050-2441-11d1-AF4F-0060976AA886), object ]
interface IChatSession : IUnknown {
  [propget] HRESULT SessionName([out, string] OLECHAR **ppwsz);
  HRESULT Say([in, string] const OLECHAR *pwszStatement);
  HRESULT GetStatements([out] IEnumString **ppes);
  HRESULT Advise([in] IChatSessionEvents *pEventSink,
                 [out] DWORD *pdwReg);
```

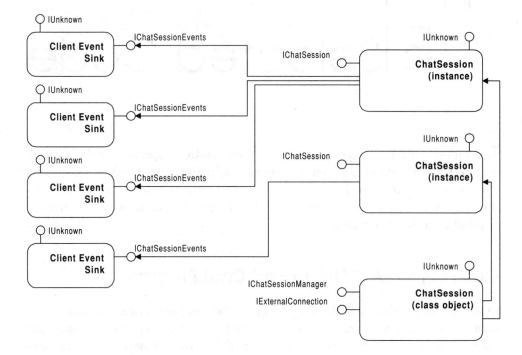

Figure B.1 COM Chat

```
  HRESULT Unadvise([in] DWORD dwReg);
}


[ uuid(5223A051-2441-11d1-AF4F-0060976AA886), object ]
interface IChatSessionEvents : IUnknown {
  HRESULT OnNewUser([in, string] const OLECHAR *pwszUser);
  HRESULT OnUserLeft([in, string] const OLECHAR *pwszUser);
  HRESULT OnNewStatement([in, string] const OLECHAR *pwszUser,
                         [in, string] const OLECHAR *pwszStmnt);
}


[ uuid(5223A052-2441-11d1-AF4F-0060976AA886), object ]
interface IChatSessionManager : IUnknown {
  HRESULT GetSessionNames([out] IEnumString **ppes);
  HRESULT FindSession([in, string] const OLECHAR *pwszName,
                      [in] BOOL bDontCreate,
                      [in] BOOL bAllowAnonymousAccess,
```

```
            [out] IChatSession **ppcs);
    HRESULT DeleteSession([in, string] const OLECHAR *pwszName);
}

cpp_quote("DEFINE_GUID(CLSID_ChatSession,0x5223a053,0x2441,")
cpp_quote("0x11d1,0xaf,0x4f,0x0,0x60,0x97,0x6a,0xa8,0x86);")
```

client.cpp

```cpp
/// client.cpp

#define _WIN32_WINNT 0x403
#include <windows.h>
#include <stdio.h>
#include <initguid.h>
#include <wchar.h>
// include IDL-generated header files
#include "COMChat.h"
#include "COMChat_i.c"

void Error(HRESULT hr, const char *psz)
{ printf("%s failed and returned 0x%x\n", psz, hr); }

// utility function to print command line syntax
int Usage(void) {
  printf("usage: client.exe <action> <user> <host>\n");
  printf("\twhere:\n\t\taction = /sessions|/chat:session|");
  printf("/delete:session\n\t\tuser = /user:domain\\user ");
  printf("/password:pw |/anonymous |<nothing>");
  printf("\n\t\thost = /host:hostname | <nothing>\n");
  return -1;
}

// utility function for printing a list of strings
void PrintAllStrings(IEnumString *pes) {
  enum { CHUNKSIZE = 64 };
  OLECHAR *rgpwsz[CHUNKSIZE];
  ULONG cFetched;
  HRESULT hr;
  do {
```

```
        hr = pes->Next(CHUNKSIZE, rgpwsz, &cFetched);
        if (SUCCEEDED(hr)) {
          for (ULONG i = 0; i < cFetched; i++)
            if (rgpwsz[i]) {
              wprintf(L"%s\n", rgpwsz[i]);
              CoTaskMemFree(rgpwsz[i]);
            }
        }
    } while (hr == S_OK);
}

// utility function to print initial state of a chat session
void PrintToDate(IChatSession *pcs) {
  IEnumString *pes = 0;
  HRESULT hr = pcs->GetStatements(&pes);
  if (SUCCEEDED(hr)) {
    PrintAllStrings(pes);
    pes->Release();
  }
}

// this class implements the callback interface that receives chat
// notifications. It simply prints the event to the console
class EventSink : public IChatSessionEvents {
// IUnknown methods
  STDMETHODIMP QueryInterface(REFIID riid, void**ppv) {
    if (riid == IID_IUnknown)
      *ppv = static_cast<IUnknown*>(this);
    else if (riid == IID_IChatSessionEvents)
      *ppv = static_cast<IChatSessionEvents*>(this);
    else
      return (*ppv = 0), E_NOINTERFACE;
    reinterpret_cast<IUnknown*>(*ppv)->AddRef();
    return S_OK;
  }
  STDMETHODIMP_(ULONG) AddRef(void)  { return 2; }
  STDMETHODIMP_(ULONG) Release(void) { return 1; }
// IChatSessionEvents methods
  STDMETHODIMP OnNewStatement(const OLECHAR *pwszUser,
                              const OLECHAR *pwszStmt) {
    wprintf(L"%-14s: %s\n", pwszUser, pwszStmt);
```

```
        return S_OK;
    }
    STDMETHODIMP OnNewUser(const OLECHAR *pwszUser) {
        wprintf(L"\n\n>>> Say Hello to %s\n\n", pwszUser);
        return S_OK;
    }
    STDMETHODIMP OnUserLeft(const OLECHAR *pwszUser) {
        wprintf(L"\n\n>>> Say Bye to %s\n\n", pwszUser);
        return S_OK;
    }
};

// type of operations this client can perform
enum ACTION {
    ACTION_NONE, ACTION_CHAT,
    ACTION_DELETE_SESSION, ACTION_LIST_SESSION_NAMES,
};

// run chat command
void Chat(const OLECHAR *pwszSession, // session
          IChatSessionManager *pcsm,  // manager
          COAUTHIDENTITY *pcai,       // user
          bool bAnonymous)            // anonymous
{
// create or get the named session
    IChatSession *pcs = 0;
    HRESULT hr = pcsm->FindSession(pwszSession,FALSE,TRUE,&pcs);
    if (SUCCEEDED(hr)) {
// adjust security blanket for session interface
        if (!bAnonymous)
            hr = CoSetProxyBlanket(pcs, RPC_C_AUTHN_WINNT,
                                   RPC_C_AUTHZ_NONE, 0,
                                   RPC_C_AUTHN_LEVEL_PKT,
                                   RPC_C_IMP_LEVEL_IDENTIFY,
                                   pcai, EOAC_NONE);
// catch up on past messages
        PrintToDate(pcs);
// hook up event sink to receive new messages
        EventSink es;
        DWORD dwReg;
        hr = pcs->Advise(&es, &dwReg);
```

```
          if (SUCCEEDED(hr)) {
// run UI loop to get statements from console and send them
          OLECHAR wszStmt[4096];
          while (_getws(wszStmt) && SUCCEEDED(hr)) {
            hr = pcs->Say(wszStmt);
            if (FAILED(hr))
              Error(hr, "Say");
          }
// tear down connection for event sink
          pcs->Unadvise(dwReg);
        }
        else
          Error(hr, "Advise");
// release chat session
      pcs->Release();
    }
    else
      Error(hr, "FindSession");
}


// run delete command
void Delete(const OLECHAR *pwszSession,
            IChatSessionManager *pcsm)
{
  HRESULT hr = pcsm->DeleteSession(pwszSession);
  if (FAILED(hr))
    Error(hr, "DeleteSession");
}


// run list command
void List(IChatSessionManager *pcsm) {
  IEnumString *pes = 0;
  HRESULT hr = pcsm->GetSessionNames(&pes);
  if (SUCCEEDED(hr)) {
    printf("Active Sessions:\n");
    PrintAllStrings(pes);
    pes->Release();
  }
}


int main(int argc, char **argv) {
```

```cpp
// declare client control state
   bool bAnonymous = false;
   OLECHAR wszSessionName[1024] = OLESTR("");
   OLECHAR wszDomainName[1024] = OLESTR("");
   OLECHAR wszUserName[1024] = OLESTR("");
   OLECHAR wszPassword[1024] = OLESTR("");
   OLECHAR wszHostName[1024] = OLESTR("");
   COSERVERINFO csi = { 0, wszHostName, 0, 0 };
   COSERVERINFO *pcsi = 0;
   COAUTHIDENTITY cai = {
     wszUserName, 0, wszDomainName, 0, wszPassword, 0,
     SEC_WINNT_AUTH_IDENTITY_UNICODE
   };
   COAUTHIDENTITY *pcai = 0;
   ACTION action = ACTION_NONE;

// parse command line
   for (int i = 1; i < argc; i++) {
     if (strcmp(argv[i], "/anonymous") == 0)
       bAnonymous = true;
     else if (strstr(argv[i], "/delete:") == argv[i]) {
       if (action != ACTION_NONE)
         return Usage();
       action = ACTION_DELETE_SESSION;
       mbstowcs(wszSessionName, argv[i] + 8, 1024);
     }
     else if (strstr(argv[i], "/chat:") == argv[i])  {
       if (action != ACTION_NONE)
         return Usage();
       action = ACTION_CHAT;
       mbstowcs(wszSessionName, argv[i] + 6, 1024);
     }
     else if (strcmp(argv[i], "/sessions") == 0) {
       if (action != ACTION_NONE)
         return Usage();
       action = ACTION_LIST_SESSION_NAMES;
     }
     else if (strstr(argv[i], "/host:") == argv[i]) {
       if (pcsi != 0)
         return Usage();
       mbstowcs(wszHostName, argv[i] + 6, 1024);
```

```
          pcsi = &csi;
        }
        else if (strstr(argv[i], "/password:") == argv[i]) {
          mbstowcs(wszPassword, argv[i] + 10, 1024);
          cai.PasswordLength = wcslen(wszPassword);
        }
        else if (strstr(argv[i], "/user:") == argv[i]) {
          if (pcai != 0 || bAnonymous)
            return Usage();
          char *pszDelim = strchr(argv[i] + 7, '\\');
          if (pszDelim == 0)
            return Usage();
          *pszDelim = 0;
          pszDelim++;
          mbstowcs(wszDomainName, argv[i] + 6, 1024);
          cai.DomainLength = wcslen(wszDomainName);
          mbstowcs(wszUserName, pszDelim, 1024);
          cai.UserLength = wcslen(wszUserName);
          pcai = &cai;
        }
      }

    if (action == ACTION_NONE)
      return Usage();
    HRESULT hr = CoInitializeEx(0, COINIT_MULTITHREADED);
    if (FAILED(hr))
      return hr;

// allow anonymous callbacks from chat server
    hr = CoInitializeSecurity(0, -1, 0, 0, RPC_C_AUTHN_LEVEL_NONE,
                RPC_C_IMP_LEVEL_ANONYMOUS, 0, EOAC_NONE, 0);

    if (SUCCEEDED(hr)) {
// grab the requested session manager
      IChatSessionManager *pcsm = 0;
      hr = CoGetClassObject(CLSID_ChatSession, CLSCTX_ALL,pcsi,
                IID_IChatSessionManager, (void**)&pcsm);
      if (SUCCEEDED(hr)) {
// apply security blanket if desired
        if (!bAnonymous)
          hr = CoSetProxyBlanket(pcsm, RPC_C_AUTHN_WINNT,
```

```
                              RPC_C_AUTHZ_NONE, 0,
                              RPC_C_AUTHN_LEVEL_PKT,
                              RPC_C_IMP_LEVEL_IDENTIFY,
                              pcai, EOAC_NONE);
// dispatch request
      switch (action) {
      case ACTION_CHAT:
        Chat(wszSessionName, pcsm, pcai, bAnonymous);
        break;
      case ACTION_DELETE_SESSION:
        Delete(wszSessionName, pcsm);
        break;
      case ACTION_LIST_SESSION_NAMES:
        List(pcsm);
        break;
      default:
        Usage();
      }
// release session manager
      pcsm->Release();
    }
  }
  CoUninitialize();
  return hr;
}
```

chatsession.h

```
// ChatSession.h

#ifndef _CHATSESSION_H
#define _CHATSESSION_H

// this pragma shuts up the compiler warnings due to
// the pre MSC11SP1 debugger choking on long template names.
#pragma warning(disable:4786)

#define _WIN32_WINNT 0x403
#include <windows.h>
#include <map>
```

```cpp
#include <vector>
#include <string>
using namespace std;

// bring in IDL-generated interface definitions
#include "COMChat.h"

// this class models a particular chat session
class ChatSession : public IChatSession {
  friend class StatementEnumerator;
  friend class ChatSessionClass;
  LONG              m_cRef;
  CRITICAL_SECTION  m_csStatementLock;
  CRITICAL_SECTION  m_csAdviseLock;
  OLECHAR           m_wszSessionName[1024];
  bool              m_bIsDeleted;
  bool              m_bAllowAnonymousAccess;
  vector<wstring>   m_statements;
// each session maintains a linked list of LISTENERs that
// represent the connected clients
  struct LISTENER {
    LISTENER            *pPrev;
    LISTENER            *pNext;
    OLECHAR             *pwszUser;
    IChatSessionEvents *pItf;
  };
  LISTENER            *m_pHeadListeners;

// concurrency management helpers
  void SLock(void);
  void SUnlock(void);
  void ALock(void);
  void AUnlock(void);

// security helpers
  bool CheckAccess(const OLECHAR *pwszUser);

// Event notification helpers
  void Fire_OnNewStatement(const OLECHAR *pwszUser,
                           const OLECHAR *pwszStatement);
  void Fire_OnNewUser(const OLECHAR *pwszUser);
```

```
      void Fire_OnUserLeft(const OLECHAR *pwszUser);
// constructor/destructor
   ChatSession(const OLECHAR *pwszSessionName,
                  bool bAllowAnonymousAccess);
   virtual ~ChatSession(void);


   void Disconnect(void);
// IUnknown methods
   STDMETHODIMP QueryInterface(REFIID riid, void **ppv);
   STDMETHODIMP_(ULONG) AddRef(void);
   STDMETHODIMP_(ULONG) Release(void);


// IChatSession methods
   STDMETHODIMP get_SessionName(OLECHAR **ppwsz);
   STDMETHODIMP Say(const OLECHAR *pwszStatement);
   STDMETHODIMP GetStatements(IEnumString **ppes);
   STDMETHODIMP Advise(IChatSessionEvents *pEventSink,
                     DWORD *pdw);
   STDMETHODIMP Unadvise(DWORD dwReg);
};


// this class enumerates the statements of a session
class StatementEnumerator : public IEnumString {
   friend class ChatSession;
   LONG                     m_cRef;
   ChatSession              *m_pThis;
   vector<wstring>::iterator  m_cursor;
   CRITICAL_SECTION         m_csLock;
// concurrency helpers
   void Lock(void);
   void Unlock(void);


// constructor/destructor
   StatementEnumerator(ChatSession *pThis);
   virtual ~StatementEnumerator(void);


// IUnknown methods
   STDMETHODIMP QueryInterface(REFIID riid, void **ppv);
   STDMETHODIMP_(ULONG) AddRef(void);
```

```
    STDMETHODIMP_(ULONG) Release(void);
    // IEnumString methods
    STDMETHODIMP Next(ULONG cElems, OLECHAR **rgElems, ULONG
*pce);
    STDMETHODIMP Skip(ULONG cElems);
    STDMETHODIMP Reset(void);
    STDMETHODIMP Clone(IEnumString **ppes);
};

// this class models the management of chat sessions
// and acts as the class object for CLSID_ChatSession
class ChatSessionClass : public IChatSessionManager,
                         public IExternalConnection {
    friend class SessionNamesEnumerator;
    typedef map<wstring, ChatSession *> SESSIONMAP;
    LONG                m_cStrongLocks;
    SESSIONMAP          m_sessions;
    CRITICAL_SECTION    m_csSessionLock;
// concurrency helpers
    void Lock(void);
    void Unlock(void);

// security helpers
    bool CheckAccess(const OLECHAR *pwszUser);

// constructor/destructor
public:
    ChatSessionClass(void);
    virtual ~ChatSessionClass(void);

// IUnknown methods
    STDMETHODIMP QueryInterface(REFIID riid, void **ppv);
    STDMETHODIMP_(ULONG) AddRef(void);
    STDMETHODIMP_(ULONG) Release(void);

// IExternalConnection methods
    STDMETHODIMP_(DWORD) AddConnection(DWORD extconn, DWORD);
    STDMETHODIMP_(DWORD) ReleaseConnection(DWORD,DWORD,BOOL);

// IChatSessionManager methods
    STDMETHODIMP GetSessionNames(IEnumString **ppes);
    STDMETHODIMP FindSession(const OLECHAR *pwszSessionName,
```

```
                        BOOL bDontCreate,
                        BOOL bAllowAnonymousAccess,
                        IChatSession **ppcs);
    STDMETHODIMP DeleteSession(const OLECHAR *pwszSessionName);
};


// this class enumerates the session names of a server
class SessionNamesEnumerator : public IEnumString
{
    friend class ChatSessionClass;
    LONG                     m_cRef;
    vector<wstring>          *m_pStrings;
    SessionNamesEnumerator   *m_pCloneSource;
    vector<wstring>::iterator m_cursor;
    CRITICAL_SECTION         m_csLock;

// accessor function to get string vector
    vector<wstring>& Strings(void);

// concurrency helpers
    void Lock(void);
    void Unlock(void);

// constructor/destructor
    SessionNamesEnumerator(ChatSessionClass *pSessionClass);
    SessionNamesEnumerator(SessionNamesEnumerator *pCloneSource);
    virtual ~SessionNamesEnumerator(void);

// IUnknown methods
    STDMETHODIMP QueryInterface(REFIID riid, void **ppv);
    STDMETHODIMP_(ULONG) AddRef(void);
    STDMETHODIMP_(ULONG) Release(void);

// IEnumString methods
    STDMETHODIMP Next(ULONG cElems, OLECHAR **rgElems, ULONG *pce);
    STDMETHODIMP Skip(ULONG cElems);
    STDMETHODIMP Reset(void);
    STDMETHODIMP Clone(IEnumString **ppes);
};

#endif
```

chatsession.cpp

```cpp
// chatsession.cpp

#include "ChatSession.h"
#include <iaccess.h>

// these server lifetime control routines are defined in svc.cpp
extern void ModuleLock(void);
extern void ModuleUnlock(void);

// these access control objects are created in svc.cpp to control
// various privileged operations. Most operations in this class
// are non-privileged, so anyone can get in.
extern IAccessControl *g_pacUsers;
extern IAccessControl *g_pacAdmins;

// utility functions //////////////////////////

// duplicate an OLECHAR * using CoTaskMemAlloc
OLECHAR *OLESTRDUP(const OLECHAR *pwsz) {
  DWORD cb = sizeof(OLECHAR)*(wcslen(pwsz) + 1);
  OLECHAR *pwszResult = (OLECHAR*)CoTaskMemAlloc(cb);
  if (pwszResult)
    wcscpy(pwszResult, pwsz);
  return pwszResult;
}

// get the caller's username (or "anonymous" if
// no authentication was specified by the caller).
OLECHAR *GetCaller(void) {
  OLECHAR *pwsz = 0;
  HRESULT hr =
            CoQueryClientBlanket(0,0,0,0,0,(void**)&pwsz,0);
  if (SUCCEEDED(hr))
    return OLESTRDUP(pwsz);
  else
    return OLESTRDUP(OLESTR("anonymous"));
}
```

```
// class ChatSession ///////////////////////////////

ChatSession::ChatSession(const OLECHAR *pwszSessionName,
                         bool bAllowAnonymousAccess)
: m_cRef(0),
  m_bAllowAnonymousAccess(bAllowAnonymousAccess),
  m_pHeadListeners(0)
{
  wcscpy(m_wszSessionName, pwszSessionName);
  InitializeCriticalSection(&m_csStatementLock);
  InitializeCriticalSection(&m_csAdviseLock);
}


ChatSession::~ChatSession(void) {
  DeleteCriticalSection(&m_csStatementLock);
  DeleteCriticalSection(&m_csAdviseLock);
  // tear down connected listeners
  while (m_pHeadListeners) {
    LISTENER *pThisNode = m_pHeadListeners;
    if (pThisNode->pItf)
      pThisNode->pItf->Release();
    if (pThisNode->pwszUser)
      CoTaskMemFree(pThisNode->pwszUser);
    m_pHeadListeners = pThisNode->pNext;
    delete pThisNode;
  }
}


// helper methods //////////

void ChatSession::Disconnect(void) {
  CoDisconnectObject(this, 0);
  // tear down connected listeners
  ALock();
  while (m_pHeadListeners) {
    LISTENER *pThisNode = m_pHeadListeners;
    if (pThisNode->pItf)
      pThisNode->pItf->Release();
    if (pThisNode->pwszUser)
      CoTaskMemFree(pThisNode->pwszUser);
```

```
      m_pHeadListeners = pThisNode->pNext;
      delete pThisNode;
    }
    AUnlock();
}


// send the OnNewStatement event to all listeners
void ChatSession::Fire_OnNewStatement(const OLECHAR *pwszUser,
                      const OLECHAR *pwszStatement) {
    ALock();
    for (LISTENER *pNode = m_pHeadListeners;
          pNode != 0; pNode = pNode->pNext)
      if (pNode->pItf)
        pNode->pItf->OnNewStatement(pwszUser, pwszStatement);
    AUnlock();
}


// send the OnNewUser event to all listeners
void ChatSession::Fire_OnNewUser(const OLECHAR *pwszUser) {
    ALock();
    for (LISTENER *pNode = m_pHeadListeners;
          pNode != 0; pNode = pNode->pNext)
      if (pNode->pItf)
        pNode->pItf->OnNewUser(pwszUser);
    AUnlock();
}


// send the OnUserLeft event to all listeners
void ChatSession::Fire_OnUserLeft(const OLECHAR *pwszUser) {
    ALock();
    for (LISTENER *pNode = m_pHeadListeners;
          pNode != 0; pNode = pNode->pNext)
      if (pNode->pItf)
        pNode->pItf->OnUserLeft(pwszUser);
    AUnlock();
}


// lock wrappers
void ChatSession::SLock(void)
{ EnterCriticalSection(&m_csStatementLock); }
```

```cpp
void ChatSession::SUnlock(void)
{ LeaveCriticalSection(&m_csStatementLock); }

void ChatSession::ALock(void)
{ EnterCriticalSection(&m_csAdviseLock); }

void ChatSession::AUnlock(void)
{ LeaveCriticalSection(&m_csAdviseLock); }

// helper method to check access to Say method
bool ChatSession::CheckAccess(const OLECHAR *pwszUser) {
  if (wcscmp(pwszUser, L"anonymous") == 0)
    return m_bAllowAnonymousAccess;
  // form trustee from caller and use Access Control
  // object hardwired to COMChat Users group
  TRUSTEEW trustee = {
    0, NO_MULTIPLE_TRUSTEE, TRUSTEE_IS_NAME,
    TRUSTEE_IS_USER, const_cast<OLECHAR*>(pwszUser)
  };
  BOOL bIsAllowed;
  HRESULT hr = g_pacUsers->IsAccessAllowed(&trustee,0,
                  COM_RIGHTS_EXECUTE, &bIsAllowed);
  return SUCCEEDED(hr) && bIsAllowed != FALSE;
}


// IUnknown methods
STDMETHODIMP
ChatSession::QueryInterface(REFIID riid, void **ppv) {
  if (riid == IID_IUnknown)
    *ppv = static_cast<IUnknown*>(this);
  else if (riid == IID_IChatSession)
    *ppv = static_cast<IChatSession*>(this);
  else
    return (*ppv = 0), E_NOINTERFACE;
  reinterpret_cast<IUnknown*>(*ppv)->AddRef();
  return S_OK;
}


STDMETHODIMP_(ULONG) ChatSession::AddRef(void) {
  ModuleLock();
```

```
      return InterlockedIncrement(&m_cRef);
   }


STDMETHODIMP_(ULONG) ChatSession::Release(void) {
   LONG res = InterlockedDecrement(&m_cRef);
   if (res == 0)
      delete this;
   ModuleUnlock();
   return res;
}


// IChatSession methods
STDMETHODIMP ChatSession::get_SessionName(OLECHAR **ppwsz) {
   if (!ppwsz)
      return E_INVALIDARG;
   else if ((*ppwsz = OLESTRDUP(m_wszSessionName)) == 0)
      return E_OUTOFMEMORY;
   return S_OK;
}


STDMETHODIMP ChatSession::Say(const OLECHAR *pwszStatement) {
   HRESULT hr = S_OK;
// protect access to method
   OLECHAR *pwszUser = GetCaller();
   if (pwszUser && CheckAccess(pwszUser)) {
      SLock();
      try {
         wstring s = pwszUser;
         s += L":";
         s += pwszStatement;
         m_statements.push_back(s);
      }
      catch(...) {
         hr = E_OUTOFMEMORY;
      }
      SUnlock();
      if (SUCCEEDED(hr))
         Fire_OnNewStatement(pwszUser, pwszStatement);
   }
   else
      hr = E_ACCESSDENIED;
```

```cpp
      CoTaskMemFree(pwszUser);
      return hr;
}


STDMETHODIMP ChatSession::GetStatements(IEnumString **ppes) {
   if (ppes == 0)
      return E_INVALIDARG;
   if ((*ppes = new StatementEnumerator(this)) == 0)
      return E_OUTOFMEMORY;
   (*ppes)->AddRef();
   return S_OK;
}


STDMETHODIMP
ChatSession::Advise(IChatSessionEvents *pEventSink, DWORD *pdwReg)
{
   HRESULT hr = S_OK;
   if (pEventSink == 0 || pdwReg == 0)
      return E_INVALIDARG;
// create a new LISTENER node
   LISTENER *pNew = new LISTENER;
   if (pNew == 0)
      return E_OUTOFMEMORY;
   OLECHAR *pwszUser = GetCaller();
   if (pwszUser)
   {
// notify other clients of new user
      Fire_OnNewUser(pwszUser);
      ALock();
// insert listener node in list
      pNew->pwszUser = pwszUser;
      if (pNew->pItf = pEventSink)
         pEventSink->AddRef();
      pNew->pNext = m_pHeadListeners;
      if (m_pHeadListeners)
         m_pHeadListeners->pPrev = pNew;
      pNew->pPrev = 0;
      m_pHeadListeners = pNew;
      AUnlock();
   }
   else
```

```
      {
        delete pNew;
        return E_OUTOFMEMORY;
      }
  // return node pointer as cookie
      *pdwReg = reinterpret_cast<DWORD>(pNew);
      return hr;
  }

  STDMETHODIMP ChatSession::Unadvise(DWORD dwReg) {
      if (dwReg == 0)
        return E_INVALIDARG;
      HRESULT hr = S_OK;
  // get node ptr from cookie
      LISTENER *pThisNode = reinterpret_cast<LISTENER *>(dwReg);
      ALock();
  // remove node
      if (pThisNode->pPrev)
        pThisNode->pPrev->pNext = pThisNode->pNext;
      else
        m_pHeadListeners = pThisNode->pNext;
      if (pThisNode->pNext)
        pThisNode->pNext->pPrev = pThisNode->pPrev;
      if (pThisNode->pItf)
        pThisNode->pItf->Release();
      OLECHAR *pwszUser = pThisNode->pwszUser;
      delete pThisNode;
      AUnlock();
  // notify other users this caller has left
      Fire_OnUserLeft(pwszUser);
      CoTaskMemFree(pwszUser);
      return hr;
  }


  // class StatementEnumerator //////////////////

  StatementEnumerator::StatementEnumerator(ChatSession *pThis)
  : m_cRef(0),
    m_pThis(pThis), m_cursor(pThis->m_statements.begin())
  {
      m_pThis->AddRef();
```

```
    InitializeCriticalSection(&m_csLock);
}

StatementEnumerator::~StatementEnumerator(void) {
  m_pThis->Release();
  DeleteCriticalSection(&m_csLock);
}

// lock helpers (note that ChatSession is locked simultaneously)
void StatementEnumerator::Lock(void) {
  EnterCriticalSection(&m_csLock);
  m_pThis->SLock();
}

void StatementEnumerator::Unlock(void) {
  LeaveCriticalSection(&m_csLock);
  m_pThis->SUnlock();
}

// IUnknown methods
STDMETHODIMP
StatementEnumerator::QueryInterface(REFIID riid, void **ppv) {
  if (riid == IID_IUnknown)
    *ppv = static_cast<IUnknown*>(this);
  else if (riid == IID_IEnumString)
    *ppv = static_cast<IEnumString*>(this);
  else
    return (*ppv = 0), E_NOINTERFACE;
  reinterpret_cast<IUnknown*>(*ppv)->AddRef();
  return S_OK;

}

STDMETHODIMP_(ULONG) StatementEnumerator::AddRef(void) {
  return InterlockedIncrement(&m_cRef);
}

STDMETHODIMP_(ULONG) StatementEnumerator::Release(void) {
  LONG res = InterlockedDecrement(&m_cRef);
  if (res == 0)
    delete this;
```

```
      return res;
  }


  // IEnumString methods
  STDMETHODIMP StatementEnumerator::Next(ULONG cElems,
              OLECHAR **rgElems, ULONG *pcFetched) {
    if (pcFetched == 0 && cElems > 1)
      return E_INVALIDARG;
    ZeroMemory(rgElems, sizeof(OLECHAR*) * cElems);
    Lock();
    ULONG cActual = 0;
    while (cActual < cElems
          && m_cursor != m_pThis->m_statements.end())  {
      if (rgElems[cActual] = OLESTRDUP((*m_cursor).c_str())) {
        m_cursor++;
        cActual++;
      }
      else { // allocation error, unwind
        while (cActual > 0) {
          cActual--;
          CoTaskMemFree(rgElems[cActual]);
          rgElems[cActual] = 0;
        }
        break;
      }
    }
    Unlock();
    if (pcFetched)
      *pcFetched = cActual;
    return cElems == cActual ? S_OK : S_FALSE;
  }


  STDMETHODIMP StatementEnumerator::Skip(ULONG cElems) {
    Lock();
    ULONG cActual = 0;
    while (cActual < cElems
          && m_cursor != m_pThis->m_statements.end()) {
      m_cursor++;
      cActual++;
    }
    Unlock();
```

```
    return cElems == cActual ? S_OK : S_FALSE;
}

STDMETHODIMP StatementEnumerator::Reset(void) {
  Lock();
  m_cursor = m_pThis->m_statements.begin();
  Unlock();
  return S_OK;
}

STDMETHODIMP StatementEnumerator::Clone(IEnumString **ppes) {
  if (ppes == 0)
    return E_INVALIDARG;
  if ((*ppes = new StatementEnumerator(m_pThis)) == 0)
    return E_OUTOFMEMORY;
  (*ppes)->AddRef();
  return S_OK;
}

// class ChatSessionClass //////////////////

ChatSessionClass::ChatSessionClass(void)
: m_cStrongLocks(0)
{
  InitializeCriticalSection(&m_csSessionLock);
}

ChatSessionClass::~ChatSessionClass(void) {
  DeleteCriticalSection(&m_csSessionLock);
}

void ChatSessionClass::Lock(void)
{ EnterCriticalSection(&m_csSessionLock); }

void ChatSessionClass::Unlock(void)
{ LeaveCriticalSection(&m_csSessionLock); }

// helper method to protect access to DeleteSession
// to only allow COMChat Admins to delete groups
bool ChatSessionClass::CheckAccess(const OLECHAR *pwszUser) {
  if (wcscmp(pwszUser, L"anonymous") == 0)
    return false;
```

```
    TRUSTEEW trustee = {
      0, NO_MULTIPLE_TRUSTEE, TRUSTEE_IS_NAME,
      TRUSTEE_IS_USER, const_cast<OLECHAR*>(pwszUser)
    };
    BOOL bIsAllowed;
    HRESULT hr = g_pacAdmins->IsAccessAllowed(&trustee,0,
                        COM_RIGHTS_EXECUTE, &bIsAllowed);
    return SUCCEEDED(hr) && bIsAllowed != FALSE;
}


// IUnknown methods
STDMETHODIMP
ChatSessionClass::QueryInterface(REFIID riid, void **ppv) {
  if (riid == IID_IUnknown)
    *ppv = static_cast<IChatSessionManager*>(this);
  else if (riid == IID_IChatSessionManager)
    *ppv = static_cast<IChatSessionManager*>(this);
  else if (riid == IID_IExternalConnection)
    *ppv = static_cast<IExternalConnection*>(this);
  else
    return (*ppv = 0), E_NOINTERFACE;
  reinterpret_cast<IUnknown*>(*ppv)->AddRef();
  return S_OK;
}


STDMETHODIMP_(ULONG) ChatSessionClass::AddRef(void) {
  return 2;
}


STDMETHODIMP_(ULONG) ChatSessionClass::Release(void) {
  return 1;
}

// IExternalConnection methods
STDMETHODIMP_(DWORD)
ChatSessionClass::AddConnection(DWORD extconn, DWORD) {
  if (extconn & EXTCONN_STRONG) {
    ModuleLock();
    return InterlockedIncrement(&m_cStrongLocks);
  }
```

```
      return 0;
    }

    STDMETHODIMP_(DWORD)
    ChatSessionClass::ReleaseConnection(DWORD extconn, DWORD,
                                BOOL bLastReleaseKillsStub) {
      if (extconn & EXTCONN_STRONG) {
        LONG res = InterlockedDecrement(&m_cStrongLocks);
        if (res == 0 && bLastReleaseKillsStub)
          CoDisconnectObject(static_cast<IExternalConnection*>(this),
                      0);
        ModuleUnlock();
        return res;
      }
      return 0;
    }


    // IChatSessionManager methods
    STDMETHODIMP
    ChatSessionClass::GetSessionNames(IEnumString **ppes) {
      if (ppes == 0)
        return E_INVALIDARG;
      if ((*ppes = new SessionNamesEnumerator(this)) == 0)
        return E_OUTOFMEMORY;
      (*ppes)->AddRef();
      return S_OK;
    }


    STDMETHODIMP
    ChatSessionClass::FindSession(const OLECHAR *pwszSessionName,
                                BOOL bDontCreate,
                                BOOL bAllowAnonymousAccess,
                                IChatSession **ppcs) {
      if (ppcs == 0)
        return E_INVALIDARG;
      HRESULT hr = E_FAIL;
      *ppcs = 0;
      OLECHAR *pwszUser = GetCaller();
      Lock();
      SESSIONMAP::iterator it = m_sessions.find(pwszSessionName);
      if (it == m_sessions.end()) {
```

```
      if (bDontCreate)
        hr = E_FAIL;
      else if (!bAllowAnonymousAccess
              && wcscmp(pwszUser, L"anonymous") == 0)
        hr = E_ACCESSDENIED;
      else {
        ChatSession *pNew =
                new ChatSession(pwszSessionName,
                              bAllowAnonymousAccess != FALSE);
        if (pNew) {
          pNew->AddRef();
          m_sessions.insert(
            pair<wstring,ChatSession*>(pwszSessionName, pNew));
          (*ppcs = pNew)->AddRef();
          hr = S_OK;
        }
        else
          hr = E_OUTOFMEMORY;
      }
    }
    else {
      (*ppcs = (*it).second)->AddRef();
      hr = S_OK;
    }
    Unlock();
    CoTaskMemFree(pwszUser);
    return hr;
}


STDMETHODIMP
ChatSessionClass::DeleteSession(const OLECHAR *pwszSessionName) {
  if (pwszSessionName == 0)
    return E_INVALIDARG;
  HRESULT hr = E_FAIL;
  OLECHAR *pwszUser = GetCaller();
  if (pwszUser && CheckAccess(pwszUser)) {
    Lock();
    SESSIONMAP::iterator it = m_sessions.find(pwszSessionName);
    if (it == m_sessions.end()) {
      hr = E_FAIL;
    }
```

```
      else {
        (*it).second->Disconnect();
        (*it).second->Release();
        m_sessions.erase(it);
        hr = S_OK;
      }
      Unlock();
    }
    else
      hr = E_ACCESSDENIED;
    CoTaskMemFree(pwszUser);
    return hr;
}


// class SessionNamesEnumerator

SessionNamesEnumerator::SessionNamesEnumerator(
                        ChatSessionClass *pSessionClass)
: m_cRef(0), m_pStrings(new vector<wstring>), m_pCloneSource(0)
{
    typedef ChatSessionClass::SESSIONMAP SESSIONMAP;
    typedef ChatSessionClass::SESSIONMAP::iterator iterator;
    SESSIONMAP &sessions = pSessionClass->m_sessions;
// take snapshot of strings from session class
    pSessionClass->Lock();
    for (iterator it = sessions.begin(); it != sessions.end(); it++)
      m_pStrings->push_back((*it).first);
    pSessionClass->Unlock();
    m_cursor = Strings().begin();
    InitializeCriticalSection(&m_csLock);
}


SessionNamesEnumerator::SessionNamesEnumerator(
                        SessionNamesEnumerator *pCloneSource)
: m_cRef(0),m_pStrings(0),m_pCloneSource(pCloneSource)
{
    m_pCloneSource->AddRef();
    m_cursor = Strings().begin();
      InitializeCriticalSection(&m_csLock);
  }
```

```cpp
SessionNamesEnumerator::~SessionNamesEnumerator(void) {
  if (m_pCloneSource)
    m_pCloneSource->Release();
  else if (m_pStrings)
    delete m_pStrings;
  DeleteCriticalSection(&m_csLock);
}


vector<wstring>& SessionNamesEnumerator::Strings(void) {
  if (m_pStrings)
    return *m_pStrings;
  else
    return *(m_pCloneSource->m_pStrings);
}


void SessionNamesEnumerator::Lock(void)
{ EnterCriticalSection(&m_csLock); }


void SessionNamesEnumerator::Unlock(void)
{ LeaveCriticalSection(&m_csLock); }


// IUnknown methods

STDMETHODIMP
SessionNamesEnumerator::QueryInterface(REFIID riid, void **ppv) {
  if (riid == IID_IUnknown)
    *ppv = static_cast<IUnknown*>(this);
  else if (riid == IID_IEnumString)
    *ppv = static_cast<IEnumString*>(this);
  else
    return (*ppv = 0), E_NOINTERFACE;
  reinterpret_cast<IUnknown*>(*ppv)->AddRef();
  return S_OK;
}


STDMETHODIMP_(ULONG) SessionNamesEnumerator::AddRef(void) {
  ModuleLock();
  return InterlockedIncrement(&m_cRef);
}
```

```cpp
STDMETHODIMP_(ULONG) SessionNamesEnumerator::Release(void) {
  LONG res = InterlockedDecrement(&m_cRef);
  if (res == 0)
    delete this;
  ModuleUnlock();
  return res;
}


// IEnumString methods
STDMETHODIMP
SessionNamesEnumerator::Next(ULONG cElems, OLECHAR **rgElems,
                             ULONG *pcFetched) {
  if (cElems > 1 && pcFetched == 0)
    return E_INVALIDARG;
  ULONG cActual = 0;
  Lock();
  while (cActual < cElems && m_cursor != Strings().end()) {
    if (rgElems[cActual] = OLESTRDUP((*m_cursor).c_str())) {
      m_cursor++;
      cActual++;
    }
    else { // allocation error, unwind
      while (cActual > 0) {
        cActual--;
        CoTaskMemFree(rgElems[cActual]);
        rgElems[cActual] = 0;
      }
      break;
    }
  }
  Unlock();
  if (pcFetched)
    *pcFetched = cActual;
  return cActual == cElems ? S_OK : S_FALSE;
}


STDMETHODIMP SessionNamesEnumerator::Skip(ULONG cElems) {
  ULONG cActual = 0;
  Lock();
  while (cActual < cElems && m_cursor != Strings().end()) {
    m_cursor++;
```

```cpp
      cActual++;
  }
  Unlock();
  return cActual == cElems ? S_OK : S_FALSE;
}

STDMETHODIMP SessionNamesEnumerator::Reset(void) {
  Lock();
  m_cursor = Strings().begin();
  Unlock();
  return S_OK;
}

STDMETHODIMP SessionNamesEnumerator::Clone(IEnumString **ppes) {
  if (ppes == 0)
    return E_INVALIDARG;
  SessionNamesEnumerator *pCloneSource = m_pCloneSource;
  if (pCloneSource == 0) // we are the source
    m_pCloneSource = this;
  if ((*ppes = new SessionNamesEnumerator(pCloneSource)) == 0)
    return E_OUTOFMEMORY;
  (*ppes)->AddRef();
  return S_OK;
}
```

svc.cpp

```cpp
// svc.cpp

#define _WIN32_WINNT 0x403
#include <windows.h>
#include <olectl.h>
#include <initguid.h>
#include <iaccess.h>

#include "ChatSession.h"
#include "COMChat_i.c"

#if !defined(HAVE_IID_IACCESSCONTROL)
// there is a common bug is the SDK headers and libs that
```

```
// causes IID_IAccessControl to be undefined. We define it here
// to give the GUID linkage.
DEFINE_GUID(IID_IAccessControl,0xEEDD23E0, 0x8410, 0x11CE,
            0xA1, 0xC3, 0x08, 0x00, 0x2B, 0x2B, 0x8D, 0x8F);
#endif

// standard MTA lifetime management helpers
HANDLE g_heventDone = CreateEvent(0, TRUE, FALSE, 0);

void ModuleLock(void) {
  CoAddRefServerProcess();
}

void ModuleUnlock(void) {
  if (CoReleaseServerProcess() == 0)
    SetEvent(g_heventDone);
}

// standard self-registration table
const char *g_RegTable[][3] = {
  { "CLSID\\{5223A053-2441-11d1-AF4F-0060976AA886}",
    0, "ChatSession" },
  { "CLSID\\{5223A053-2441-11d1-AF4F-0060976AA886}",
  "AppId", "{5223A054-2441-11d1-AF4F-0060976AA886}"
  },
 { "CLSID\\{5223A053-2441-11d1-AF4F-
  0060976AA886}\\LocalServer32",
  0, (const char*)-1 // rogue value indicating file name
  },
  { "AppID\\{5223A054-2441-11d1-AF4F-0060976AA886}",
  0, "ChatSession Server" },
  { "AppID\\{5223A054-2441-11d1-AF4F-0060976AA886}",
  "RunAs", "Domain\\ReplaceMe"
  },
  { "AppID\\{5223A054-2441-11d1-AF4F-0060976AA886}",
  "Chat Admins Group", "Domain\\ReplaceMe"
  },
  { "AppID\\{5223A054-2441-11d1-AF4F-0060976AA886}",
  "Chat Users Group", "Domain\\ReplaceMe"
  },
  { "AppID\\COMChat.exe",
```

```cpp
        "AppId", "{5223A054-2441-11d1-AF4F-0060976AA886}"
      },
    };

// self-unregistration routine
STDAPI UnregisterServer(void) {
  HRESULT hr = S_OK;
  int nEntries = sizeof(g_RegTable)/sizeof(*g_RegTable);
  for (int i = nEntries - 1; i >= 0; i--){
    long err = RegDeleteKeyA(HKEY_CLASSES_ROOT, g_RegTable[i][0]);
    if (err != ERROR_SUCCESS)
      hr = S_FALSE;
  }
  return hr;
}


// self-registration routine
STDAPI RegisterServer(HINSTANCE hInstance = 0) {
  HRESULT hr = S_OK;
// look up server's file name
  char szFileName[MAX_PATH];
  GetModuleFileNameA(hInstance, szFileName, MAX_PATH);
// register entries from table
  int nEntries = sizeof(g_RegTable)/sizeof(*g_RegTable);
  for (int i = 0; SUCCEEDED(hr) && i < nEntries; i++) {
    const char *pszKeyName   = g_RegTable[i][0];
    const char *pszValueName = g_RegTable[i][1];
    const char *pszValue     = g_RegTable[i][2];
// map rogue value to module file name
    if (pszValue == (const char*)-1)
      pszValue = szFileName;
    HKEY hkey;
// create the key
    long err = RegCreateKeyA(HKEY_CLASSES_ROOT,
      pszKeyName, &hkey);
    if (err == ERROR_SUCCESS) {
// set the value
      err = RegSetValueExA(hkey, pszValueName, 0,
                          REG_SZ, (const BYTE*)pszValue,
                          (strlen(pszValue) + 1));
      RegCloseKey(hkey);
```

```
        }
      if (err != ERROR_SUCCESS) {
// if cannot add key or value, back out and fail
        UnregisterServer();
        hr = SELFREG_E_CLASS;
      }
   }
   return hr;
}


// these point to standard access control objects
// used to protect particular methods
IAccessControl *g_pacUsers = 0;
IAccessControl *g_pacAdmins = 0;


// this routine is called at process init time
// to build access control objects and to allow
// anonymous access to server by default
HRESULT InitializeApplicationSecurity(void) {
// load groupnames from registry
   static OLECHAR wszAdminsGroup[1024];
   static OLECHAR wszUsersGroup[1024];
   HKEY hkey;
   long err = RegOpenKeyEx(HKEY_CLASSES_ROOT,
      __TEXT("AppID\\{5223A054-2441-11d1-AF4F-0060976AA886}"),
            0, KEY_QUERY_VALUE,&hkey);

   if (err == ERROR_SUCCESS) {
     DWORD cb = sizeof(wszAdminsGroup);
     err = RegQueryValueExW(hkey, L"Chat Admins Group",
                            0, 0, (BYTE*)wszAdminsGroup,&cb);
     cb = sizeof(wszAdminsGroup);
     if (err == ERROR_SUCCESS)
       err = RegQueryValueExW(hkey, L"Chat Users Group", 0, 0,
                              (BYTE*)wszUsersGroup, &cb);
     RegCloseKey(hkey);
   }
   if (err != ERROR_SUCCESS)
     return MAKE_HRESULT(SEVERITY_ERROR, FACILITY_WIN32,
     GetLastError());
```

```
// declare vectors of user/groups for 2 access
// control objects

ACTRL_ACCESS_ENTRYW rgaaeUsers[] = {
  { {0, NO_MULTIPLE_TRUSTEE, TRUSTEE_IS_NAME,
    TRUSTEE_IS_GROUP, wszUsersGroup  },
    ACTRL_ACCESS_ALLOWED, COM_RIGHTS_EXECUTE, 0,
    NO_INHERITANCE, 0 },
};
ACTRL_ACCESS_ENTRY_LISTW aaelUsers = {
  sizeof(rgaaeUsers)/sizeof(*rgaaeUsers),
    rgaaeUsers
};
ACTRL_PROPERTY_ENTRYW apeUsers = { 0, &aaelUsers, 0 };
ACTRL_ACCESSW aaUsers = { 1, &apeUsers };

ACTRL_ACCESS_ENTRYW rgaaeAdmins[] = {
  { {0, NO_MULTIPLE_TRUSTEE, TRUSTEE_IS_NAME,
    TRUSTEE_IS_GROUP, wszAdminsGroup },
    ACTRL_ACCESS_ALLOWED, COM_RIGHTS_EXECUTE, 0,
    NO_INHERITANCE, 0 },
};
ACTRL_ACCESS_ENTRY_LISTW aaelAdmins = {
  sizeof(rgaaeAdmins)/sizeof(*rgaaeAdmins),
    rgaaeAdmins
};
ACTRL_PROPERTY_ENTRYW apeAdmins = { 0, &aaelAdmins, 0 };
ACTRL_ACCESSW aaAdmins = { 1, &apeAdmins };

// initialize process-wide security
  HRESULT hr = CoInitializeSecurity(0, -1, 0, 0,
                                    RPC_C_AUTHN_LEVEL_NONE,
                                    RPC_C_IMP_LEVEL_ANONYMOUS,
                                    0, EOAC_NONE, 0);
  if (SUCCEEDED(hr))  {
// create access control objects
    hr = CoCreateInstance(CLSID_DCOMAccessControl, 0, CLSCTX_ALL,
            IID_IAccessControl, (void**)&g_pacUsers);
    if (SUCCEEDED(hr))
      hr = g_pacUsers->SetAccessRights(&aaUsers);
```

```
        if (SUCCEEDED(hr)) {
          hr = CoCreateInstance(CLSID_DCOMAccessControl,0, CLSCTX_ALL,
                     IID_IAccessControl,(void**)&g_pacAdmins);
          if (SUCCEEDED(hr))
            hr = g_pacAdmins->SetAccessRights(&aaAdmins);
        }
        if (FAILED(hr)) {
          if (g_pacAdmins) {
            g_pacAdmins->Release();
            g_pacAdmins = 0;
          }
          if (g_pacUsers) {
            g_pacUsers->Release();
            g_pacUsers = 0;
          }
        }
    }
    return hr;
}

// the main thread routine that simply registers the class
// object and waits to die
int WINAPI WinMain(HINSTANCE, HINSTANCE, LPSTR szCmdParam, int) {
    const TCHAR *pszPrompt =
      __TEXT("Ensure that you have properly configured the ")
      __TEXT("application to run as a particular user and that ")
      __TEXT("you have manually changed the Users and Admins ")
      __TEXT("Group registry settings under this server's AppID.");

    HRESULT hr = CoInitializeEx(0, COINIT_MULTITHREADED);
    if (FAILED(hr))
      return hr;

    // look for self-registration flags
    if (strstr(szCmdParam, "/UnregServer") != 0
       || strstr(szCmdParam, "-UnregServer") != 0)  {
      hr = UnregisterServer();
      CoUninitialize();
      return hr;
    }
    else if (strstr(szCmdParam, "/RegServer") != 0
```

```
                  || strstr(szCmdParam, "-RegServer") != 0) {
        hr = RegisterServer();
        MessageBox(0, pszPrompt, __TEXT("COMChat"), MB_SETFOREGROUND);
        CoUninitialize();
        return hr;
    }

// set up process security
    hr = InitializeApplicationSecurity();
    if (SUCCEEDED(hr)) {
// register class object and wait to die
        DWORD   dwReg;
        static ChatSessionClass cmc;
        hr = CoRegisterClassObject(CLSID_ChatSession,
                    static_cast<IExternalConnection*>(&cmc),
                        CLSCTX_LOCAL_SERVER,
                        REGCLS_SUSPENDED|REGCLS_MULTIPLEUSE,
                        &dwReg);
        if (SUCCEEDED(hr)) {
          hr = CoResumeClassObjects();
          if (SUCCEEDED(hr))
            WaitForSingleObject(g_heventDone, INFINITE);
          CoRevokeClassObject(dwReg);
        }
        g_pacUsers->Release();
        g_pacAdmins->Release();
    }
    if (FAILED(hr))
        MessageBox(0, pszPrompt, __TEXT("Error"), MB_SETFOREGROUND);

    CoUninitialize();
    return 0;
}
```

Index